Southern Brigadier Generals
in the Revolutionary War

ALSO BY DOUGLAS M. BRANSON
AND FROM McFARLAND

*Major League Turbulence: Baseball in the Era of Drug Use,
Labor Strife and Black Power, 1968–1988* (2021)

Southern Brigadier Generals in the Revolutionary War

Eighteen Commanders Instrumental in American Victory

Douglas M. Branson

McFarland & Company, Inc., Publishers
Jefferson, North Carolina

LIBRARY OF CONGRESS CATALOGING-IN-PUBLICATION DATA

Names: Branson, Douglas M., author.
Title: Southern brigadier generals in the Revolutionary War : eighteen commanders instrumental in American victory / Douglas M. Branson.
Other titles: Eighteen commanders instrumental in American victory
Description: Jefferson, North Carolina : McFarland & Company, Inc., Publishers, 2024 | Includes bibliographical references and index.
Identifiers: LCCN 2024017242 | ISBN 9781476692920 (paperback : acid free paper) ∞
ISBN 9781476651347 (ebook)
Subjects: LCSH: United States—History—Revolution, 1775-1783—Biography. | United States. Continental Army—Biography. | Generals—United States—Biography. | Southern States—History—Revolution, 1775-1783. | Generals—Southern States—Biography. | Southern States—Biography. | BISAC: HISTORY / Military / United States | HISTORY / United States / Revolutionary Period (1775-1800)
Classification: LCC E206 .B73 2024 | DDC 973.3092/2—dc23/eng/20240418
LC record available at https://lccn.loc.gov/2024017242

BRITISH LIBRARY CATALOGUING DATA ARE AVAILABLE

ISBN (print) 978-1-4766-9292-0
ISBN (ebook) 978-1-4766-5134-7

© 2024 Douglas M. Branson. All rights reserved

No part of this book may be reproduced or transmitted in any form or by any means, electronic or mechanical, including photocopying or recording, or by any information storage and retrieval system, without permission in writing from the publisher.

Front cover image: "The Death of General Mercer at the Battle of Princeton, January 3, 1777." Artist: John Trumbull (American, 1756–1843), Oil on canvas, 21 × 30¾ inch (53.3 × 78.1 cm) (Trumbull Collection/Yale University Art Gallery)

Printed in the United States of America

McFarland & Company, Inc., Publishers
Box 611, Jefferson, North Carolina 28640
www.mcfarlandpub.com

Acknowledgments

In researching this book, I toured many Revolutionary War sites and battlefields. In the north, I visited Concord, Lexington, Bunker Hill, Bennington, Saratoga, Fort Ticonderoga, and sites of the Battle of Brooklyn (also known as the Battle of Long Island). In the Middle Department, I visited Trenton, Princeton, Brandywine, Germantown, Valley Forge, Washington's Headquarters at Morristown, and Monmouth Courthouse. Most apropos here, in the Southern Department, I visited Savannah, Charleston, Camden, Ninety-Six, Kings Mountain, Cowpens, Davidson and Lake Norman, Hillsborough, Richmond, and Yorktown. On the western frontier, I visited Forts McIntosh, Defiance, and Patrick Henry (aka the British Fort Sackville in Vincennes, Indiana) as well as Point Pleasant on the Ohio River. In those sites that are administered by the National Park Service, I benefited greatly from presentations by and conversations with park rangers, in addition to viewing the displays, reading the historical markers, and taking notes. I wish to thank the many well-informed park personnel with whom I spoke.

Certain sites are very evocative: Concord Bridge, Saratoga, Valley Forge, Monmouth Courthouse, and Yorktown, for example. Others, such as Kings Mountain and Cowpens, are greatly overgrown from what they must have been 250 years ago. Nonetheless, by visiting all these places, I gained a better understanding of spatial relationships, the distances involved, and the length of marches troops had to undertake.

I also undertook library and other research at the Virginia Historical Society in Richmond, the University of Virginia Alderman Library in Charlottesville, and the Historical Libraries of the Carolinas, at Raleigh and at Charleston, respectively, and the Historical Society of Georgia at Savannah. Librarians and staff at each institution aided me in my searches for relevant material.

I also wish to thank Helen Jarosz, our interlibrary loan librarian here at the University of Pittsburgh School of Law. She procured hard-to-find sources of authority for points made in the text. Our reference librarian, Linda Tashbook, was helpful in tracking down hard-to-obtain portraits of the brigadiers. She has been a great and gracious resource for me over the years.

Paulette Green of Ambridge, Pennsylvania, is the graphic artist who drew the maps contained in this book. She worked economically and efficiently.

Table of Contents

Acknowledgments — v
Introduction — 1

PART I—VARYING PRECURSORS TO WAR — 5
1. Pre-Revolution Call to Arms — 6
2. George Weedon's Tavern in Virginia — 13
3. Backcountry Patriots? The Regulators in North Carolina — 24
4. Earliest Military Exploits: North Carolina's James Moore and Richard Caswell — 28
5. Threats on the Southern Border: Defending Coastal Georgia — 37
6. Character Attacks, Misfortune, and Survival: Brigadier Lachlan McIntosh of Georgia — 39

PART II—SOUTHERNERS AND THE EARLIEST BEGINNINGS OF WAR — 51
7. Battle of Point Pleasant (1774) — 52
8. Largely Forgotten: Brigadier Andrew Lewis of Virginia — 54
9. The Failed Assault on Charles Town (1776) — 62
10. Brigadier William Moultrie of South Carolina — 66

PART III—DIFFICULTIES OF REVOLUTIONARY COMMAND — 77
11. Service and Travel in Colonial Times — 78
12. Intoxicating Beverages and Inebriation — 83
13. Militia Units versus the Continental Line — 89

PART IV—ALSO MENTIONED IN THE DISPATCHES: 1775 — 97
14. War Within the War: Lord Dunmore's Second War — 98
15. Virginia Planter William Woodford — 103

PART V—MENTIONED IN THE DISPATCHES — 113
16. "Give Me Liberty or Give Me Death": Virginia's Brigadier Hugh Mercer at Princeton — 114

17. Scout and Woodsman: Charles Scott — 124

18. Fighting Parson: Lutheran Minister Peter Muhlenberg at Brandywine — 134

19. Brigadier Francis Nash of North Carolina at Germantown — 147

PART VI—PUNCTILIOS OF HONOR BEYOND SENSITIVE — 155

20. Rivalries and Resignations — 156

21. Pretenders, Parvenus, and Armchair Generals — 162

PART VII—THE SOUTHERN CAMPAIGN: 1779–1781 — 167

22. Civil War Commences in the South: Patriot versus Loyalist at Kings Mountain and Cowpens — 168

23. Waggoner Daniel Morgan of Virginia — 176

24. The Piedmont Partisan: William Lee Davidson of North Carolina — 189

25. Route to Yorktown: The Battle of Guilford Courthouse — 198

PART VIII—BRITISH FOMENT AMONG AND ALLIANCES WITH NATIVE AMERICANS — 203

26. Attempts to Neutralize the Northwest Territory: George Rogers Clark of Virginia — 204

27. Postscript: Post War Biographies — 209

28. Society of the Cincinnati — 217

Chapter Notes — 223
Bibliography — 261
Index — 269

Introduction

"Unhappy is the land that needs a hero," wrote Bertolt Brecht in *Life of Galileo*.[1] The South had no shortage of heroes in the Revolution. This book, then, is about the Revolutionary War's Continental Line brigadier generals from four southern colonies. It is not about the conflict's tactics, strategies, or battles, except as engagements shed light on officers' character and exploits. Biographical facts aside, the study's most intriguing aspects are the comparative ones and revelations that emerge for the first time.

General George Washington commanded fifty-eight brigadiers in the Revolution. Eighteen of those were from four southern colonies: Virginia, North Carolina, South Carolina, and Georgia. Some, for instance—Hugh Mercer, Daniel Morgan, William Davidson, and Peter Muhlenberg—were remarkable in their own right. Others' service, such as that of William Woodford, Lachlan McIntosh, and James Moore, does not rise to the remarkable level.[2] But as a collective group, they were remarkable, extraordinarily so. Ten spent periods of time as prisoners of war. Thirteen were wounded in combat. Overall, thirteen Revolutionary War brigadier generals died in combat or from combat-related causes; seven of those, more than half the total, were from the South. Remarkable, indeed.

Acclaimed recent books promise but do not deliver regarding significant "wars within the War."[3] Wars within the war were particularly poignant in the South. This book discusses them: Anglican versus Presbyterian; wealthy coastal planters opposed to hardscrabble settlers in the backcountry; ersatz English dandies in Charles Town and Savannah as opposed to upcountry hunters in deerskin leggings and linen hunting shirts; and coastal planters' extensive slaveholdings versus the backcountry's near complete absence of enslaved people. Extreme differences lay beneath obvious labels: Patriot or Loyalist, Whig or Tory. How did they affect these brigadiers of the Revolutionary War?

Why brigadiers? Why not the major generals who commanded departments of the Continental Army and ranked above the brigadier generals? At least in the South, the four higher-ranked generals were ineffectual. They—Adam Stephen, Horatio Gates, Charles Lee, and Robert Howe—ended their careers long before the war concluded, directly or indirectly for drunkenness, insubordination, or cowardice.[4] It was the brigadiers, and the officers and men beneath them, who served for the war's duration, carrying the war to a successful conclusion.

Of necessity, the book's scope does not extend to militia generals (*see also*

Chapter 13), for they were a varied lot, most of whom served short to medium terms. By contrast, Continental Line generals signed on for three or more year-long terms, including many who served for the war's duration. Second, militia generals' activities by and large were local in character. For example, as militia brigadiers, Andrew Pickens and Francis Marion, "the Swamp Fox," engaged in daring, courageous skirmishes and raids, but mostly all in South Carolina and late in the war.[5] Third, politicians and wealthy coastal planters, some of whom performed valuable service but saw little in the way of hardship or combat, peopled militia generals' ranks. Thomas Nelson of Virginia, a wealthy coastal merchant, signed the Declaration of Independence; acted as a Virginia delegate to Continental Congresses in 1775, 1776, 1777, and 1779; and several times served as a brigadier in the Virginia Militia. While the war was ongoing, in 1781, Nelson also became Virginia's third governor, succeeding Thomas Jefferson. Valuable though his services were, Nelson never saw combat in the Revolutionary War.[6]

Sources indicate that George Washington's generals had little military experience. For example, Professor Emory G. Evans, in his biography *Thomas Nelson and the Revolution in Virginia*, unequivocally states, "Most [Virginians] had little or no military experience."[7] That is simply not true. In fact, the evidence is otherwise. Seven of eight brigadiers from Virginia, Peter Muhlenberg aside, fought in the French and Indian War (1755–1763). From his leadership of the Virginia regiment in that war, Washington knew them well. In North Carolina, John Ashe and James Moore had served in the French and Indian War as well. In the Carolinas, too, nine militia or Continental Line brigadiers fought in the Cherokee Wars of 1761–1763 in western Carolina's foothills and mountains.[8]

Seldom stated but implied was that prior military service generated experience with tactics, strategy, and armaments and that such experience was the most important attribute emerging from prior service. Again, that assumption was questionable. Prior service enhanced these men's ability to lead columns of troops through wilderness, crossing rivers and penetrating dense forests, over long distances. With their service, the generals had gained knowledge about feeding their men; keeping supply lines open; providing forage for animals; leading marches and countermarches for hundreds of miles; ensuring rudimentary sanitation in camps; communicating up and down the chain of command; keeping morale high, as best they could; and, overall, being leaders whose men respected them as such. George Washington wrote to his brother John, "[My] troops have been more harassed by marching and countermarching than by anything that has happened to them in the course of the campaign."[9] Conditions and events away from the battlefield had as much importance as what happened in combat.

One esoteric fact is that, as younger men, many of these brigadiers had been surveyors, a fact that while seemingly serendipitous makes sense. From Virginia, George Washington, Andrew Lewis, George Rogers Clark, and Charles Scott; from the Carolinas, Richard Caswell, William Davidson, and William Moultrie (briefly); from Georgia, Lachlan McIntosh; and to the north, in Pennsylvania, Anthony Wayne and Daniel Brodhead; all had been land surveyors in their youths. Surveying dovetailed with the era's fascination with acquisition of land, especially raw land, in the backcountry and over the mountains, in the Ohio Country and Fincastle County, Virginia (Kentucky). As surveyors foraging into the interior, these men knew about living rough, going without provisions, living off the land, being alone, journeying long distances through forests and over mountains, taking precautions against and dealing with hostile Native Americans, and overcoming fear of the unknown.

As has been stated, General Washington had fifty-eight brigadiers during the war.[10] Again, a striking aspect of this book's story is that of the eighteen brigadiers from the southern colonies, thirteen, or seventy-two percent, were wounded in combat. That is an extraordinary statistic, even for an era when generals led from the front rather than the rear. The British captured ten of the eighteen, over fifty percent, of the southern brigadiers.[11] Several later gained freedom by means of parole or exchange ("swaps"), but they had been captured nonetheless.[12] By contrast, a few (William Woodford, James Hogun) died because of British prisons' harsh treatment. Last of all, and most striking, seven of the eighteen southern brigadier generals, or thirty-nine percent, died from combat-related causes. No other colony or group of colonies rivaled those numbers. No other American war—neither the Civil War nor World War I ("The war to end all wars")—rivaled those proportions.

In her recent book *The Virginia Dynasty*, historian and former Second Lady Lynne Cheney chronicles "four presidents," Washington, Jefferson, Madison, and Monroe, "who led a revolution and created a nation."[13] As with many historians, Mrs. Cheney makes no mention of the military leaders who fought, historical figures who also can lay claim to have "led a revolution and created a nation."[14] The late Winston Groom's historical work, *The Patriots*, is the same, naming Alexander Hamilton, Thomas Jefferson, and John Adams as the "founding brothers."[15] Pulitzer Finalist H.W. Brands, in *Our First Civil War*, mainly writes about Ben Franklin, reprising his book *The First American: The Life and Times of Benjamin Franklin*, sprinkled with quotations from George Washington and John Adams.[16] Professor Brands omits any mention of the men who actually fought the war. Recent historical books call for recognition of pamphleteer Thomas Paine, physician Benjamin Rush, and Boston revolutionary Samuel Adams as further founding fathers.[17]

In the United States, place names surround us. Cities, towns, and counties have English names: Suffolk, Essex, Cleveland, Manchester, Boston, Richmond, Winchester, New London, and Norfolk. Others have Native American names: Oneida, Pontiac, Shawnee, Ottawa, Chicago, Miami, Sauk, Potawatomie, Waukesha, and Cheyenne. Educated guesses reveal the names' sources. That is not true of a third set of place names: Wadsworth, Lewis, Nash, Moultrie, Muhlenberg, Warren, Wooster, Montgomery, Caswell, and Davidson. They are American Revolutionary War brigadier generals' names. Few know from whence those names came, let alone biographical details concerning those "founding brothers."[18] Obscurity had even begun, according to one biographer, in 1818:

> It is a pious duty to rescue the memory of great and good men who achieved our independence, from that oblivion into which it is fast falling. ... [T]he memory of their acts, their fame, and their very names are fast fading among the people for whom they sacrificed so much....[19]

Historical works, biographies, and television have detailed two southern brigadiers. Authors have written ten biographies of Virginia's Daniel Morgan.[20] Movies, television, and books have romanticized the exploits of South Carolina's Francis Marion, the "Swamp Fox."[21] I have included General Morgan in this book as not only was he a Continental Line officer but also was far and away the war's greatest military tactician.

Southern Brigadiers
Master List

	Wounded	Captured	Died
VIRGINIA			
Weedon			
Muhlenberg			
Scott		X	
Stevens	X		
Woodford	X	X	X
Lewis	X	X	
Mercer	X		X
Morgan	X	X	
NORTH CAROLINA			
Ashe		X	X
Moore			X
Nash	X		X
Davidson	X	X	X
Hogun		X	X
Rutherford	X	X	
SOUTH CAROLINA			
Moultrie	X	X	
Huger	X		
Sumter	X		
GEORGIA			
McIntosh	X	X	

Part I
Varying Precursors to War

1

Pre-Revolution Call to Arms

Historians cite either the 1773 Boston Tea Party or the April 1775 Concord-Lexington actions as first acts of rebellion.[1] After the British Parliament had decreed Massachusetts in rebellion and occupied Boston with 4,500 troops, patriot leaders called for enlistment of a 13,600-man force.[2] Quickly, though, 20,000 men, mostly from New Hampshire, Massachusetts, and Connecticut, amassed in May and June 1775 to lay siege to Boston, America's third largest city. Sons of Liberty chapters, Committees of Correspondence, and Committees of Safety sprung up throughout New England.[3] Commentary has continued asserting that Boston was the epicenter of pre–Revolutionary War agitation. The South receives little mention.[4] "Boston remained the hotbed of resistance to British authority," wrote H.W. Brands in *Our First Civil War.*[5]

Other Hotbeds

Situated 500 miles southwest of Boston, Fredericksburg, Virginia, sat midway between Richmond and the site where the present-day Washington, D.C., stands. The thriving city of 3,000 occupied a shelf on the Rappahannock River's south bank.[6] Sixteen thousand colonists were resident in Boston, 25,000 in New York, and 43,000 in Philadelphia, America's largest city.[7] For those times, then, Fredericksburg was a medium-sized city. Fredericksburg had a dozen taverns (including Indian Queen, Whitley's, Rising Sun, and Todd's), several of which dominated the trade in liquor, food, and lodging.[8] Called "Ordinaries" in Virginia, many taverns served as post offices as well. This was true of brigadier-to-be George Weedon's Fredericksburg tavern that he had acquired from his in-laws, Margaret and John Gordon.[9]

Weedon's tavern became a center of revolutionary fervor: "Among the taverns which served as meeting places for groups whose ideas made a permanent imprint on the American republic was the…. Tavern kept by George Weedon on Caroline Street."[10] In *Bag of Nails*, John Goolrick wrote, "[H]ere … the Lees, George Mason, [Edmund] Pendleton, [George] Wythe, George Washington, and his brother-in-law, Fielding Lewis, Charles Dick, and other leading men met where Weedon was [fanning] the flames of revolution."[11] Another list of frequent attendees included "George Washington, Thomas Jefferson, Patrick Henry, Hugh Mercer, George Mason, John Marshall, Richard Henry Lee, Gustavus Browne, William Woodford, and other noted men who met to protest the mother country's unjust treatment toward its colonies and to discuss the proper steps to rid America of tyranny."[12] A new level of revolutionary fervor had begun in 1774: "Discontent in Virginia had almost reached its acme, when the news of the Boston Port Bill in 1774 blew its smoldering embers into a bright flame, and the spirit of resistance stalked openly about the land," including in Virginia.[13] On November 4, 1775, Virginia had its own tea party when revolutionaries dumped "two half-chests of Hyson [East India Company] tea" into the York River.[14] By then, the only principal matter left for debate was whether the war that was erupting "should be waged for independence or merely for the assertion of American rights within a British empire" still loyal to the king but no longer subservient to Parliament.[15]

Another attendee at the Fredericksburg tavern was future war hero, Hugh Mercer, whose wife Isabella's sister was George Weedon's wife Catherine. While resident at Weedon's establishment, Thomas Jefferson wrote the Virginia Statute of Religious Freedom.[16] The Committee to Revise the Laws of Virginia (Thomas Jefferson, George Mason, George Wythe, Edmund Pendleton, and Thomas Ludwell Lee) crafted its product at the tavern.[17]

Weedon's Hospitality

Why the attraction of George Weedon's tavern? Attracting callers was Weedon himself, a cheerful, sociable host. He had a barely concealed air of mischief, along with a resolute cheerfulness that endeared him to colleagues and subordinates alike. Joseph Waterman, Mercer's biographer, deviates from Mercer to give us a portrait of Weedon: "Weedon was a good mixer, a fluent and interesting talker, and very heated at times in his discussions."[18] Second, and further, "[a]t Weedon's ... attraction was to be found a kitchen which served distinctly unordinary food. Weedon himself [was] a well-known *bon vivant* ... noted for the fine food he prepared and served."[19] Third, tavern keeper Weedon was an avid sportsman: "He had large stables at the rear of his tavern, and it was here that gentlemen boarded their pure breeds during the Fredericksburg Fair and the races sponsored by the jockey club."[20] A fourth attraction was Weedon's reputation as a raconteur and humorist: "His sense of humor—albeit often risqué—[was] unsurpassed by any that is found in the writings of his contemporaries."[21] Fifth, and perhaps most of all, Weedon was "an ardent revolutionary."

So, in addition to Boston, Fredericksburg and George Weedon's tavern served as crucibles for forging a willingness to throw off English tyranny.[22] "[D]iscussion" at the tavern blew revolution's "smoldering embers into bright flame."[23] Coincidentally, and emblematic of pre–Revolution agitation, a principal meeting place in Boston was a tavern, The Green Dragon, where John Hancock, John Adams, and cohorts met "to drink, talk business [and] plot their next moves."[24] In Virginia, influential men patronized other taverns as well, including The Swan in Yorktown and The Raleigh in Williamsburg. There the gentry discussed politics, the discussion maturing into thoughts of intrigue against British oppression.[25]

TIDEWATER VIRGINIA

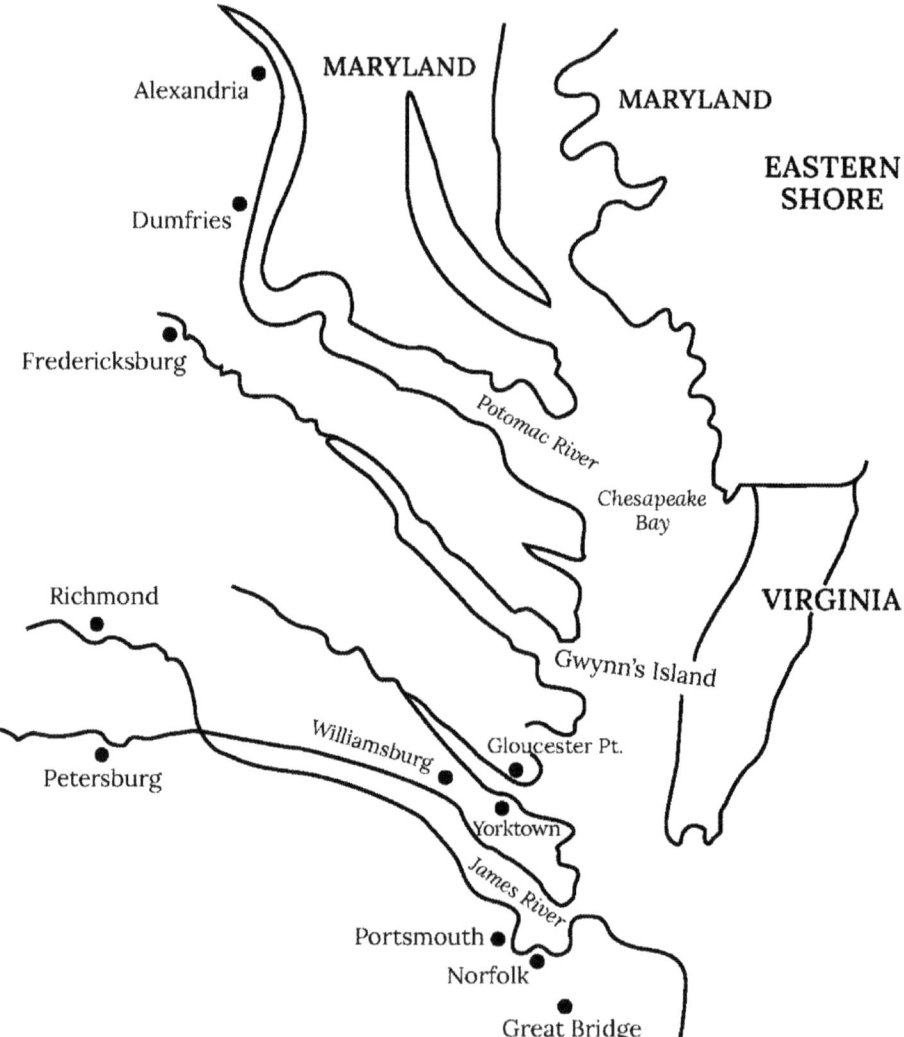

Colonies Other Than Massachusetts and Virginia

To be sure, revolutionary fever existed elsewhere but appears to have been muted. In Pennsylvania, for example, with their pacifist beliefs, Quakers dominated the colony's politics. Through the 1740s and 1750s, the Pennsylvania Assembly refused either to fund a military force or underwrite the purchase of arms for volunteers. So, the depredation of Indian raids, with the murder of women and children and burning of settlements, continued unchecked. Indian forays extended well into eastern Pennsylvania, far out from the Alleghenies, becoming not only a distraction but Pennsylvania colonists' principal focus (*see, e.g.*, Chapter 3).[26] Faced with the terrors that Indian raids foretold, Quaker attitudes softened. In 1756, the Pennsylvania Assembly authorized 50,000£ for provincial defense.[27]

In southern colonies, particularly in Virginia, other impediments remained. Tory populations matched or exceeded Sons of Liberty patrons: "Loyalism grew stronger the farther south one traveled in America. Loyalists were few and weak in New England ... most numerous and stronger in the southern colonies."[28] In 1766, North Carolinians changed the name of a principal town from Corbin's to Hillsborough. In England, Lord Hillsborough had become secretary of state for the Colonies. His harsh attitudes toward the notion of independence, elsewhere credited as a cause for revolution, appeared popular in North Carolina: "Hillsborough brooked nothing that hinted of sedition ... [ordering] the Massachusetts House of Representatives to rescind its appeal to other colonies for common action."[29] He had a great deal of popularity among North Carolina's citizens.[30] But all that creates a misleading impression. Unlike Pennsylvania, North Carolina, and to a lesser extent, South Carolina, had protracted episodes of widespread armed insurrection, the Regulator Movement most specifically, against the colonial government that may well have foretold a proclivity toward belligerence (*see* Chapter 3).

The New York Times *1619 Project: An Alternative Explanation for Revolution*

Nikole Hannah-Jones's 2019 *New York Times* article noted that the year 2019 marked the 400th anniversary of the importation and enslavement of Africans into Britain's American colonies.[31] Ms. Hannah-Jones aimed "to reframe the country's history by placing the consequences of slavery and the contributions of Black Americans at the center of the United States national narrative." Relevant here, a principal corollary of the basic theory was that the motivation to undertake a revolution to achieve independence was to preserve slavery in the colonies. A need arose because Britain could soon outlaw the practice, having signaled movement in that direction. Ms. Hannah-Jones wrote, "Conveniently left out of our founding mythology is the fact that one of the primary reasons ... the colonists decided to declare their independence from Britain was because they wanted to protect the institution of slavery."[32] In 2020, the Pulitzer Committee awarded Ms. Hannah-Jones the Pulitzer Prize for commentary. Subsequently, her reporting earned her a MacArthur "Genius" Fellowship, a Peabody Award, and two George Polk Awards.

Contentions as to the war's cause center on the argument that revolutionaries' motivations, and particularly Virginia's participation in them, magnified beliefs that continued British rule threatened an end to slavery. Echoing contentions akin to Ms. Jones's arise elsewhere.[33] For example, Alexis Coe in her 2020 book, *You Never Forget Your First: A Biography of George Washington*, argued that southern colonists were concerned with preserving slavery much more than with gaining liberty and independence.[34] Espousal of the theory was the lead piece in *The 1619 Project*, a best-selling book containing a series of articles and essays on the 400th anniversary of Africans' importation to America and slavery. The series' lead essay, by Nikole

Hannah-Jones, bore the title "America Wasn't a Democracy Until Black Americans Made It One."[35]

Critics flag the theory as elevating ideology over historical fact.[36] The theory, though, continues gathering adherents. In 2021, Random House published a volume of essays, *A New Origin Story*, in support of the theory.[37] In 2021, Simon & Schuster published University of South Carolina history professor Woody Holton's *Liberty Is Sweet: The Hidden History of the Revolution*, which advanced the thesis.[38] A very recent *New York Times* retrospective elevated the theory several notches higher, calling for "legislation that *requires* us to study basic concepts, beginning with … [a]ll men are created equal."[39]

Adam Kirsch published his essay, "What's Really at Stake in America's History Wars" in the *Wall Street Journal*, with the caveat, "Our most charged historical debates boil down to the same…. Is America 'exemplary' and 'honorable,' or the reverse?"[40] That caveat has to be borne in mind as the theory and its offshoots are examined.

Objections to the 1619 Conception of the War

Some proponents such as Professor Holton seem prone to exaggeration. For example, threatened by revolutionary agitators, colonial governor John Murray, 4th Earl of Dunmore, in May 1775 retreated to Tidewater Virginia and British warships moored there. In the process, Governor Dunmore issued a proclamation promising freedom to any enslaved person who joined him (Dunmore's "Emancipation Proclamation") and his Ethiopian Brigade (*see* Chapter 14). A small number of enslaved people, approximately 800 out of more than 220,000 in Virginia, responded. Professor Holton asserts "that the [Dunmore] proclamation did more, than any other document, including Thomas Payne's 'Common Sense' and the Declaration of Independence, to convert Virginians to the cause of independence." Adam Kirsch, the reviewer, finds such "interpretive claims … exaggerated or downright fanciful."[41]

Perhaps half of American brigadiers were slave owners. The other half (for example, Peter Muhlenberg of Virginia or William Davidson of North Carolina) were not. Against the 1619 theory are several contentions. One, a principal motive and motto for independence, "No taxation without representation," has a long, well-known tradition that predates slavery.[42] When in 1215 the English nobles assembled at Bury St. Edmonds, "No taxation without representation" was their rallying cry as commenced their ride to Runnymede. England incorporated the freedom in the Magna Carta, "The Great Charter of Freedoms," which became foundational to the Anglo-American legal system long before agitation for independence.

Two, in the historical accounts of debate in public fora, most particularly the taverns—the Rising Sun, the Raleigh, the Green Dragon—no mention of slaves or preservation of slavery exists. Virginia planters must have had a healthy regard for their pocketbooks that would have led to some discussion of slavery, but it seems to have been peripheral at best.

Three, slavery was common in only three colonies, and scant or practically non-existent in the others.[43] In the northern and mid–Atlantic colonies, enslaved people account for less than three percent of the population. In Massachusetts, enslaved people accounted for 1.6 percent of the population, in Pennsylvania 2 percent, and in New Hampshire, eight-tenths of one percent.[44] In only three of thirteen colonies was slave-holding extensive: South Carolina (60.5 percent of the population), Virginia (42 percent), and North Carolina (35 percent). Adam Kirsch again: "Today's wars over history [and] fights over the past aren't so much about what happened as much as what we should feel about it."[45] In this instance, however, a strong argument may be made that 1619 Project proponents have their facts ("what happened") mis-aligned.

Four, heavy-handed, repressive British rule dated from before the Stamp Act (1765), showing little or no letup for the American colonies. This fueled ever-increasing resentment of British rule.

Extension of the 1619 Theory

As high school history students, certain of us learned that the Monroe Doctrine (1823) had as its intent deterrence of European nations' attempts to re-colonize the western hemisphere's newly emerging states, many of which had been colonies. Not so, according to Professor Ada Ferrer in *An American History—Cuba*.[46] To Ms. Ferrer, the Monroe Doctrine of 1823 had as its primary purpose erection of "a bulwark against European and especially British abolitionist efforts."[47] The revisionist Ferrer thesis, while speaking of events long after the war, points to gathering support behind the *1619 Project*'s view of the Revolutionary War's origins, especially among younger scholars.

A theory for interpretation of historical facts or of sociological data is only as good as it enables one accurately to summarize the facts or data and to extrapolate or to predict from it. Overall, then, the *1619 Project*'s thesis provides some valuable insights. African American citizens bear extreme disadvantages bought on by institutionalized racism that, in turn, dates from the 1619 importation of slavery and Jim Crow laws and regulations that succeeded slavery's abolition. African Americans continue to suffer disadvantages in education, health care, housing, employment, salaries, benefits, and every other aspect of modern life. But as for making a case for preservation of slavery as a cause of the American Revolution? I am skeptical. To me, that corollary of the *1619 Project* has scant evidentiary or predictive worth. Yet, I leave discussion of the subject to other works and other commentators.

Western Lands

Another theory about which historians argue is that Virginia's and other colonies' revolutionary fervor was a product of colonial leaders' desire for western lands. Claims to lands in the "Ohio Territory" could become forfeit by a treaty the British had threatened, and then enacted, as one of the "Intolerable Acts," the 1774 Quebec Act ceding the territory north of the Ohio River to Canada.[48] In 1763, Virginians had received from the Crown large land grants in the Ohio territory for having served with the British in the 1750s' French and Indian War. Virginia veterans could not obtain title to those lands, however, until such time as those veterans had the tracts surveyed. Surveys had been delayed by expense, danger of Indian raids, and a paucity of willing surveyors.

None of these explanations seems persuasive enough to relegate Weedon's tavern in Virginia, or the Green Dragon in Massachusetts, the personages that met there, and the discussions that took place, to secondary roles or, indeed, knock them from ascendancy. Little evidence exists that those claims to western lands entered debates there. In 1775, throughout the Commonwealths of Virginia and Massachusetts, and in their churches, the salutation "God Save the King" gave way to "God Preserve the Just Rights and Liberties of America."[49]

2

George Weedon's Tavern in Virginia

George Weedon was well-padded though not corpulent, loquacious, a connoisseur of drink and good foods, and the welcoming operator of Fredericksburg's popular tavern. He went from table to table, group to group in his tavern, bemoaning the depredations of British rule over the colonies, setting forth the case for independence. Weedon was "an ardent revolutionary." As an English traveler, John F.D. Smyth, later recorded, "I put up at the tavern of one [George] Weedon who was then very active and ever zealous in blowing the flames of revolution."[1]

Virginia's Northern Neck is a broad flat peninsula running from northwest to southeast, bound on the north by the Potomac River and on the south by the Rappahannock. The peninsula terminates at the shores of Chesapeake Bay. By the early eighteenth-century, settlers had cleared the Northern Neck. George Washington was born and raised on the Northern Neck, a short distance outside Fredericksburg. George Weedon, too, was born on the Northern Neck in 1734, baptized by the Rev. Roderick McCullough, who had also baptized George Washington.

Using slave labor, Washington's and Weedon's ancestors farmed tobacco, some on large plantations. Shipment of tobacco to Europe with the importation of goods in return made Fredericksburg a prosperous hub.

Weedon as a Young Soldier

As the introduction pointed out, some historians hazard the opinion that George Washington's higher-ranking officers lacked military experience.[2] That guesstimate is wide of the mark. As noted, many officers (Charles Scott, Adam Stephen, Andrew Lewis, Hugh Mercer, William Woodford, George Rogers Clark) had served with Washington in the Virginia Regiment under the British in the French and Indian War. Virginia's Major Generals Charles Lee and Horatio Gates served in the French and Indian, or Seven Years, War as officers in the British Army. George Weedon was one of the Americans who served.[3]

Several hundred Virginians, in a regiment led by a young George Washington, joined first the disastrous 1755 Braddock expedition and then the successful 1758 Forbes expedition to oust the French from Fort Duquesne, located at the forks of the Ohio River. The confluence controlled the path westward, deemed the Gateway to the West, which in those years was by the Ohio River.[4]

Any man who could recruit and arm twelve was eligible for a commission in Washington's Virginia Regiment. Weedon reached the goal, receiving a commission as an ensign in 1755.[5] A contingent including Weedon marched northwest to Fort Cumberland, 45 miles northwest of Winchester, where Weedon and his men stayed. Later, though, they marched 29 miles northward to Bedford, Pennsylvania, in 1758 joining Scots General John Forbes, the 535-man Virginia force boosting Forbes's command to 1,484 men.[6] Marching on to the site of modern-day Pittsburgh, the Forbes force found that the French had abandoned Fort Duquesne.

Lt. George Weedon was recorded as being at the re-named Fort Pitt in 1760. He joined the Bouquet expedition that marched ten days north to Presque Isle (now Erie, Pennsylvania), and then eastward by boat to Fort Niagara to obtain supplies for the Fort Pitt garrison.

Return to Fredericksburg

Next, as a captain, Weedon served under Adam Stephen in the Cherokee Wars, Stephen's Regiment being disbanded in 1762. In 1763, by virtue of the King's Proclamation, Weedon received 3,000 acres in bounty lands in Ohio (then western Virginia) for his French and Indian War service (although the land was not deeded to him until 1780).[7] By 1763, Weedon had hung his military uniform in a cupboard and, in Fredericksburg, was well into his vocation as a tavern keeper.

Revolutionary War Sold

In September 1775, a notice in the *Virginia Gazette* advertised Weedon's tavern for rent: "The subscriber intending to quit publick business after the first day of January next, would rent his house and lot in this town upon reasonable terms."[8] The previous summer, the Virginia Convention (June 17 to August 26) formed two military regiments, one under Patrick Henry and the other under William Woodford. In late 1775 and early 1776, the Virginia forces expanded by six regiments. Colonel Hugh Mercer commanded the Virginia Third Regiment, composed of Fredericksburg and Northern Neck men, with Lt. Colonel George Weedon second-in-command.[9] Accordingly, "It was his involvement in the Revolution which bought an end, on December 31, 1775, to his career as a Tavern-keeper."[10]

There then began a series of marches and counter marches by the regiment. The Third went north to Dumfries, ten miles south of Alexandria, as a worry existed that the British would cross the Potomac and descend on Virginia. On June 5, 1776, the Continental Congress elevated Hugh Mercer to Brigadier General, sending him north to New York to take charge of troops preparing to defend Long Island. The British had landed 27,000 men on Staten Island. Weedon became the Third Regiment's commanding officer.

Belatedly then, Washington and his staff called Weedon and his regiment (603 men) to Long Island's defense, but Weedon and the Third Regiment, arriving on

September 11, were too late. The battle, a disaster for the Americans, had taken place on August 27, 1776.

After the Battle of Long Island, or Battle of Brooklyn as it is also known, the colonials crossed the East River, retreating to Manhattan and establishing there a position at Kip's Bay on the East River shore, a third of the way up the island.[11] British General Sir William Howe, with 4,000 men, attacked the American position. The shell-shocked colonials folded like cardboard, despite George Washington's effort to rally them, as Weedon recorded in a letter to this friend John Page:

> [The troops] ware not to be raly'd till they had gone several miles. The General [Washington] struck several officers in their flight, [and] three times dashed his hatt on the Ground, and at last exclaimed "Good God, have I got such Troops as These." It was with difficulty that his friends got him to quit the field....[12]

It was "extraordinary to think of Washington flogging his officers amid a battle," according to Weedon, "a measure of his ... frustration and shattered nerves."[13]

For a time, Weedon and his troops defended a swale near present-day Morningside Heights. In a skirmish with advancing British, Weedon had "a narrow escape. A spent musket ball strung the guard of his sword, knocking away part of the hilt."[14] Casualties included nine British redcoats, with four of Weedon's colonials killed.

North of Manhattan Island

A British end run at Throng's Neck, where the East River flows into Long Island Sound (spanned by a suspension bridge today), was turned back by Connecticut's General Joseph Spence leading Pennsylvania and Connecticut riflemen. The British thus were unable to move to the rear of the slowly retreating American forces, a mere four miles away to the west. The Americans had, though, left 2,800 of their 11,000 effectives to garrison Fort Washington, situated on a point of high ground.

The Americans retreated northward, beyond the Croton River, leaving Fort Washington behind. There, beyond the Croton, was fought the Battle of White Plains against British and Hessian forces. It was a desultory engagement with advantage to the British. Not pressing their advantage, on November 4–5, 1776, Howe and his troops headed southwest, back toward Manhattan.[15] Weedon then advised Washington to evacuate Fort Washington, advice that Washington ignored, listening instead to a subordinate, General Nathanael Greene, giving Greene discretionary orders either to defend or to evacuate the fort. Greene later confessed the decision not to order an evacuation his greatest blunder of the war. As Weedon later recalled,

> I observed to his Lordship [Washington] we had it now in our power to end it most gloriously on the part of America by evacuating Fort Washington before the enemy could sit down before it and leave them [the British] an Empty Shell.... My old friend gave me a stern look, and pushing up the cock of his hatt with his right hand, said, "Colo. Weedon, when I was a Field Officer I never took the liberty of addressing my superiors...."[16]

There followed the American surrender of Fort Washington with a loss of 2,800 men.

Lowest Points of the Revolution

The defeated colonials, including Weedon and his men, crossed the Hudson to Fort Lee on the Jersey shore. A cloud of dejection hovering over it, the decimated army began the long trek southwest across New Jersey, dogged by Major General Charles Lord Cornwallis and his force. With cold weather coming on, enlistments expiring, desertions increasing, with defeats at Long Island, Kip's Bay, White Plains, and Fort Washington's surrender in the rearview mirror, and supplies and clothing in short supply, the colonial force had dwindled to 3,400. The small American force had its tail tucked between its legs. In 1776, "George Weedon had seen long marches, dreary encampments, and action himself in one battle … that of Harlem Heights."[17]

The Upsurge That Saved the Revolution

Washington posted Weedon and his force along with Lord Stirling's brigade to fight, if necessary, a delaying action against Lord Cornwallis should Cornwallis harass the retreating Americans. On December 8, 1776, Washington and his men crossed the Delaware River, above Trenton and below Princeton, landing on the river's Pennsylvania shore.

More bad news ensued. Word came that the British had captured the eccentric American Major General Charles Lee, who had overnighted apart from his troops at an inn in central New Jersey. Salvaging the day, New Hampshire's General John Sullivan led Lee's 2,000 troops into camp, soon to be followed by General Horatio Gates with 500 troops, Arthur St. Clair with a similar number, and Pennsylvania's Colonel John Cadwalader with 1,000 militia. General Washington could now count on 6,000 effectives.

Washington Crossing the Delaware

Holding a council of war, Washington decided that the Americans needed a bold move. He decreed that on Christmas night, the Americans would cross the Delaware River, marching eight miles southward in two columns to attack Trenton the following day. In the Battle of Trenton, on Boxing Day, December 26, 1776, Weedon's Third Virginia Regiment "had the honor of being the first to charge down King's and Queen's Streets," Trenton's main thoroughfares.[18] As Weedon wrote to his frequent correspondent, "[t]he behavior of Our People … far exceeded anything I saw. [N]ot one Officer or privt was known that day to turn his back."[19] General Washington then detailed Weedon and his men to conduct the 919 Hessian prisoners captured at Trenton to Philadelphia, 35 miles south.

Sadness and Satisfaction

After Trenton, Washington eyed Princeton, ten or twelve miles to the north, where the British quartered a substantial force. He detailed General Hugh Mercer

(Chapter 16) to lead reconnaissance in force on a diagonal from the main American body. On January 3, 1777, a British force surprised Mercer. When Mercer resisted, the British bayoneted him, continuing to club him where he lay. Mercer died January 12: "To George Weedon Mercer's death was a stunning blow."[20] Mercer and Weedon regarded themselves as brothers (they were married to sisters), dear and close friends. Both had been leading citizens of Fredericksburg.[21] Overall, however, Trenton and Princeton marked a resurgence of the Continental Army that was to sustain it through the spring and summer until fall of 1777, with defeat at Brandywine followed by defeat at Germantown. A question that arises is whether the victories in early 1777 resulted in over-confidence, in Professor Robert Schiller's terms "irrational exuberance."[22]

Despite his sadness over Mercer's death, Weedon experienced a measure of satisfaction in January. George Washington appointed Weedon his interim adjutant general (executive assistant), in which capacity Weedon served six weeks before returning to the field. On February 21, 1777, Congress promoted Weedon to Brigadier General, along with nine other colonial officers.[23] Weedon himself remained over-the-top in his praise of George Washington: "[N]o other man but our present General, who is the greatest that ever did or will adorn the Earth, could have supported himself under the many disappointments and disgraces he has been subjected to from the Irregular System of carrying on this war...."[24]

Campaigns of 1777

Planning his summer strategy, Washington divided his troops into five divisions to be led by generals Israel Putnam, Nathanael Greene, Lord Stirling (William Alexander), Adam Stephen, and Benjamin Lincoln. Weedon and his regiment were in Nathanael Greene's division.[25] Washington sent Putnam's division northward to garrison the New Jersey Highlands, across the Hudson from Manhattan Island. He led the remainder northward to Middlebrook, in the Watchung Mountains, twelve miles northwest of British-occupied New Brunswick, New Jersey. There followed several skirmishes against British parties sortieing out of Perth Amboy, in several of which Weedon and his men were involved. There were moves and countermoves by both sides, but late spring and early summer 1777 were desultory seasons.

Finally, though, on August 22, a British fleet of 260 ships was sighted in upper Chesapeake Bay.[26] There now could be little doubt where Lord William Howe intended to attack. His 17,000 troops would land at Head of Elk, where Pennsylvania's Susquehanna River empties into Chesapeake Bay.[27] The British forces would march on Philadelphia, fifty miles northeast.

Earlier George Washington had pulled his troops back from central New Jersey to a point twenty miles north of Philadelphia, where Washington and his generals played a guessing game as to where the British were headed. Hearing of the possible landing by the British, Washington marched his troops south and through Philadelphia's streets, "down Front Street and then up Chestnut to the Common, to the sounds of drums and fifes.... The Virginia brigades of Muhlenberg, Weedon, Scott, and Woodford, at one hundred-yard intervals, marched near the front of the parade."[28]

Indeed, the parade was Washington's 1777 campaign's high point. Once again, as he had at Long Island, Washington deployed his troops with little thought southwest of Philadelphia, evincing his penchant for aggressiveness rather than in anticipation of what the British might do. Washington fortified Chadds Ford, east and west, along Brandywine Creek, flowing from north to south, into the Christiana River. The ford was twenty-five miles southwest of Philadelphia on the route to the city. The British made a feint at Washington's forces but did not attack, leaving a large Hessian force to menace the Americans. Meanwhile, Lord Cornwallis led a 6,000-man British contingent upstream to cross the creek on the American right, flanking the American defensive line.[29] As a result, "Once again, as in the Battle of Long Island, Washington, committed a fatal error in not protecting his flank." In the two largest battles of the war, Brooklyn and Brandywine, the colonials lost, and lost badly, by being out flanked.[30]

Belatedly, realizing what was happening, Washington ordered Lord Stirling's and Adam Stephen's divisions northward to defend the secondary road toward Philadelphia. Washington then sent out General John Sullivan, who took field command of Stirling's and Stephens's divisions in addition to his own.

Sullivan ordered Weedon and his brigade to defend the right flank of the Sullivan-Stephen-Stirling line the colonials had thrown up to defend against Cornwallis and the flanking move: "Weedon, in the thick of the fighting himself, had to make quick decisions. As Sullivan's troops ... fell back, Weedon opened his ranks to let them pass through, and then tightly closed them once more. For twenty minutes or more, Weedon and his men held off the enemy by hand-to-hand bayonet combat." *See, e.g.*, Map, "Battle of Brandywine," Chapter 19.

A Boston newspaper reported, "[Weedon and his men] sustained a close and heavy fire for a long time without moving an inch."[31] Sullivan later reported that Weedon and his men "did themselves honor." "Especially Weedon's brigade made a heroic stand in a plowed field, covering the American retreat. ... [t]he Virginia troops distinguished themselves. The Third Regiment, Colonel Thomas Marshall commanding, with Weedon's brigade were the last to leave the field, and most of [the 3rd Virginia's] officers were killed"[32] General "Light Horse Harry" Lee wrote in his memoirs that Weedon's Third Virginia "[b]ravely sustained itself against superior numbers, never yielding one inch of ground and expending thirty rounds a man in forty-five minutes."[33] Seldom one to single out this or that of his general officers, after Brandywine, Washington asked his generals why his other troops could not have matched Weedon and his brigade in courage and bravery.[34]

At Brandywine, with twilight setting in, Cornwallis called off the attack. Washington and his troops made a general retreat to Chester, twelve miles east. The following day the colonials marched northward, crossing the Schuykill River, camping at the Falls of the Schuykill and at Germantown.

Massacre and Further Defeat

On September 19, Howe's troops engaged in atrocity. General Anthony Wayne had his division bivouacked at Paoli, eighteen miles northwest of Philadelphia, near the present-day site of Malvern, Pennsylvania. Without shots fired, British Major General Charles Grey had his men attack the sleeping colonials in the dark with bayonets. Wayne lost 272 men, sixty or so brutally murdered. The even became known as the Paoli Massacre; nothing resembling a "battle" took place.

More disaster followed. On October 4, the colonials were to advance on those of Howe's forces who had advanced outward from Philadelphia to Germantown: "At nightfall, Weedon's brigade ... along with the rest of the army, leaving packs behind, began the fourteen-mile march to Germantown." In columns, the Americans were to attack the 10,000 British: Greene and Stephen on the left, Wayne and Sullivan in the center and right, and Conway's brigade in advance of the right wing. Then tragedy struck. General Stephen ordered his troops to go right instead of left. They butted up against Wayne's troops in the center. In the early morning fog, mistaking the friendlies for British troops, Stephen's men opened fire, killing numbers of their comrades. The American attack crumbled; a miles long retreat ensued.

Weedon later wrote, "[T]he misfortunes of the day were owing to the more horrid Fogg I ever saw. That with the Smoak rendered it impossible to Distinguish our men from the enemy.... Advantage were lost, from not being certain who ware friends & who foes."[35] The more accurate version was that General Adam Stephen, in charge of the left wing, was thoroughly drunk. His inebriated state caused him to wheel his column to the right, rather than staying to the left, and in the center, they opened fire upon Wayne's soldiers ahead of them in the fog. After the confusion and retreat, "General Stephen was [found] stretched out beside a fence drunk. Stephen [also] supposedly gave the order to retreat prematurely, which may have contributed to the panic of the American troops."[36] Ever the optimist, General Weedon wrote his correspondent that the Americans could have achieved victory "had we continued the Attack fifteen minutes longer."[37]

The saving grace came with the news of American victories in upstate New York at Freeman's Farm on September 9 and at Bemis Heights on October 7, collectively known as Saratoga. Horatio Gates and his forces had stopped British General Gentleman Johnny Burgoyne's attempt to split the colonies in two. Burgoyne and his force surrendered on October 17, 1777.

Despite the good news from Saratoga, after a council of war, Washington and generals decided to take the colonial army into winter quarters at Valley Forge, eight miles to the west.

Weedon's Umbrage and Resignation

The winter encampment began on a sour note.[38] Rampant intoxication, gambling, and assault affected everyone's morale, including Weedon's, at Valley Forge. Mass desertions ensued, including 300 Pennsylvania volunteers assigned to Weedon. In contrast to his sometimes "haughty display" of temper, overall Weedon was popular with his troops, They called him "Joe Gourd," based upon Weedon's practice of distributing alcoholic punch to his troops using gourds.[39]

What affected Weedon most, and other general officers as well, was the

Continental Congress's near constant intervention in the matter of promotions and seniority. Congress elevated foreign volunteers, many parvenus, to officer and general ranks over the heads of battle-tested and deserving American officers (Chapter 20). For instance, on December 13, 1777, Congress promoted the Irishman "Thomas Conway to Major General over twenty-three brigadier generals.... Several major generals and nine brigadier generals—including Weedon—protested to Congress and threatened to resign."[40]

Previously, in August 1776, General William Woodford resigned his commission after Congress had appointed first Hugh Mercer and then Adam Stephen over him. Woodford returned to the service in February 1777.[41] In March 1778, Congress re-ranked the Virginia generals, now placing the unretired Woodford at the head, ahead of Generals Charles Scott, Peter Muhlenberg, and George Weedon. Taking into account Woodford's split service, Woodford should have ranked inferior to Muhlenberg and Weedon. Taking umbrage at the re-ranking, the latter two left Valley Forge in a huff, eventually reaching homes in Woodstock and Fredericksburg. Weedon stopped in York, Pennsylvania, where, having fled Philadelphia, the Continental Congress was sitting. He pled his case, to no avail. He attempted to resign his commission.[42]

Such sensitivity about rank and seniority abounded among Continental officers.[43] One who did resign, John Stark, did return to the fray, leading an independent army to victory at Bennington.[44]

Commander-in-chief Washington begged Weedon to rescind his resignation:

> The situation of the Army ... and fast approach of the period for opening the [1778] campaign urge me to request that you return to Camp as soon as possible. [Y]our presence here is exceedingly material. ... I am heartily sorry that there should have been grounds for a dispute of this nature and should be happy if the parties would cheerfully acquiesce. I have been told, if precedence is settled in Genl. Woodford, that Genl. Muhlenberg as well as Genl. Scott will submit to it without hesitation.[45]

Even though Weedon regarded General Washington as "the nation's Christ,"[46] Weedon renewed his resolve, replying to Washington on March 29, 1778. "What must the world think when they see me banded about like a football," Weedon wrote to Henry Lee that April.[47] Sometime thereafter, Weedon returned to Fredericksburg, where he invested in real estate and oversaw the education of the late Hugh Mercer's children.[48]

Reincarnation and Redemption

As governor of Virginia, in 1780 Thomas Jefferson called up 5,000 militia for protection of the colony, appointing Daniel Morgan (recovering from health problems) and George Weedon as commanding officers of the militia. Later, General Muhlenberg, assisted by militia Generals Thomas Nelson and Edward Stevens (Chapter 26), joined Weedon in the effort to raise troops to defend Virginia against 1779–1781 British raids up its rivers.

Weedon faced daunting logistical difficulties. On May 10, 1779, a British force under British General Edward Mathew, landed a 2,000-man force at Hampton Roads. The British destroyed supplies of coal and tobacco, raided the towns of Norfolk and Portsmouth, destroyed the American Gosport shipyard, and sailed away on May 24. The raid alarmed Virginia's politicians, giving impetus to Weedon's mission.

Generals Weedon and Muhlenberg set about frantically raising a force from various Virginia counties to oppose British Generals Alexander Leslie in 1780 and later Benedict Arnold in late December and early January 1781. Plaguing Weedon and Muhlenberg, forces' enlistments expired, and the militia dwindled to little more than nothing.[49] As Nell Moore Lee summarized, "[F]renzied activity to find men and funds filled [Virginia] that summer. All across Virginia recruiting officers were trying to swell the ranks."[50]

In late October 1780, British General Alexander Leslie landed with 2,500 at Hampton Roads. By late November, the British force had not moved up the river and soon withdrew. Historians have later identified the raids as distractions the British designed to hold colonial forces in place so that they would not march into the Carolinas and aid Nathanael Greene and his defense against Cornwallis there. The Virginians of the time, however, did not know that. "What the devil these fellows can be waiting for I cannot conceive. They have had two or three fair winds and still remain at Hampton Roads," General Nelson wrote of Leslie's feint.[51] Soon thereafter, the British packed up, sailing out to sea. The Leslie raid added to the Virginians' sense of alarm.[52]

Combined, the efforts of Generals Weedon and Peter Muhlenberg never produced more than 3,500 troops, even that being a fluctuating number as troops deserted, enlistments expired, and militia commanders sent home troops that lacked armaments. On November 3, 1780, militia General Nelson, also charged with recruiting, wrote to George Weedon, "The militia have appear'd in such small detachments, that it is impossible to make any proper arrangements."[53] Virginia's citizenry had lapsed into indifference and "talk about inflation" rather than defense. "The first warm fervor for liberty was cooling and had been replaced by a spirit of inaction and indifference."[54]

Between December 31, 1780, and January 4, 1781, British brigadier Benedict Arnold landed with 1600 troops. Under sail, Arnold's force proceeded up the James River, landing at Westover Plantation, southeast of Richmond. The British marched on by land, raiding Richmond (where the capital had been relocated from Williamsburg), destroying buildings and supplies, and causing the Virginia Assembly and governor to flee.

An Important Supporting Role at Yorktown

Weedon's next challenge, after the British raids and the frustrating attempts to enlist militia, requires background. The British had changed strategy once again, sending Lord Cornwallis and 7,000 men from New York south to lay siege to Savannah, Georgia, and then Charles Town, South Carolina, the latter beginning March

29, 1780. After 44 days, the colonials under General Benjamin Lincoln surrendered. The British force then marched inland from Charles Town, defeating the Americans at Camden, South Carolina, 110 miles distant. Crown forces then continued on a northwest tangent, lengthening their communication and supply lines. At Kings Mountain on October 7, 1780, and then at Cowpens, northeast of present-day Spartanburg, South Carolina, on January 17, 1781, the British suffered defeats, the latter at the hands of Daniel Morgan's Virginia riflemen.

Cornwallis was now two hundred northwest of Charles Town, in hostile country, far away from the coast and supplies. Eventually, he wheeled toward the northeast, with Nathanael Greene, now in command of the southern sector, falling back before him. On March 15, 1781, another major battle was fought at Guilford Courthouse, site of present-day Greensboro, North Carolina. The invading British force crossed Carolina, curving into Virginia, occupying Richmond, Virginia, for a day or two. Cornwallis and his men finally wound up on the north side of the York Peninsula, southeast of Richmond and south of the York River. The British general expected that a Royal Navy fleet could land there at Yorktown's small port, board Cornwallis's battle-weary columns onto British transports, and sail back to New York.

Major General Marquis de Lafayette and Commander-in-Chief Washington, leading the troops of the Middle Department south, boxed in Cornwallis, the Americans surrounding the redcoats on three sides. French ships in the lower Chesapeake Bay prevented the British transports from nearing Yorktown. The arrival of French Admiral De Grasse's fleet thus thwarted the British evacuation plan.

Weedon's Role: Sealing Cornwallis's Fate

One potential avenue for escape remained. Cornwallis and his troops could ferry across the York River, half a mile wide at that point, land on Gloucester Point and retreat up the Gloucester Peninsula, thus slipping the noose the Americans had fixed around the British neck.

Here, once again, Washington called upon George Weedon. Close in by the York River, British Lieutenant Colonel John Simcoe, with 1,000 men, garrisoned Gloucester Point. Washington gave Weedon and his 1,500 militia the job of installing a line at the base of the Gloucester Peninsula to box in Simcoe and Banastre Tarleton and close as best they could the line of retreat open to the main British force.

From his post ten or so miles distant, Weedon sent out reconnaissance in force parties numbering 400 each, as the British foraging parties were ranging farther north in search of food for men and horses. French General Jean-Baptiste Rochambeau dispatched 600 troops under Brigadier Duc de Lauzun to reinforce the Gloucester Point Virginia militia, manning the right wing of the American line.[55] Lauzun was no armchair general. Shortly after arrival, he led his troops out against a foraging party escorted by Banastre Tarleton's cavalry, with fifty British soldiers killed or wounded. In a letter to George Washington, Weedon "praised the conduct of the distinguished Officer [Lauzun]."[56]

Lauzun did not reciprocate. In letters to his superiors, he wrote, "[Weedon] was more than fifteen miles from the enemy posts, frightened to death, and he did not dare to send a patrol half a mile from his army. He was the best [highest ranking] man alive and all that he desired was not to take responsibility."[57] Lauzun's charges were unfounded. Weedon had been in the thick of combat, at Brandywine, Harlem Heights, Kip's Bay, Trenton, and elsewhere. In identifying "the pantheon of the best combat commanders in the Continental Army," author Andrew Zambone lists Peter Muhlenberg and George Weedon.[58] Along with his commanding officers, too, at Gloucester Point, Weedon had adopted the cautious approach that was winning a war of attrition. Earlier that year, in fact, Weedon had written his good friend Nathanael Greene, retreating before Cornwallis, "[t]hat it was better to yield ground to the enemy that to risk defeat," lessons Weedon derived from having observed Washington.[59] Moreover, Weedon had logistical difficulties of his own. "Citizens think about strategy; generals think about logistics," the saying goes. Weedon faced desertions and expiring enlistments along with a shortage of weapons, forage, and food.

The War's Conclusion

On October 19, 1781, the British at Gloucester Point surrendered, one hour before the force on the opposite shore surrendered. Skirmishes aside, the combat phase of the war had ended. The preliminary peace treaty was published November 30, 1782. The warring nations signed the final version, the Treaty of Paris, in September 1783. The victory celebration, with Washington in attendance, was held at Smith's tavern (formerly Weedon's), in Fredericksburg.

After the Military

George Weedon resigned his commission on July 11, 1783. Thereafter, he served as president of the Virginia Chapter, Society of the Cincinnati, an organization of Revolutionary War officers (*see* Chapter 27). Weedon built a comfortable house, the Sentry Box, east of central Fredericksburg. In 1791, George Weedon served as the executor of Isabella Gordon Mercer's will.

General George Weedon died in 1793.

George Weedon. A Fredericksburg tavern keeper and ardent revolutionary, Weedon was a jovial raconteur (Artist Unknown, Yale University Art Gallery).

3

Backcountry Patriots?

The Regulators in North Carolina

In some ways, the 1760s Regulator movement resembles the "Don't Tread on Me" advocacy of today. Colonial officials' corruption (sheriffs, tax collectors, registrars, clerks of court, judges, land agents) in 1750s and 1760s colonial governments and indifference or neglect by eastern Carolina interests of central and western North Carolina, including neglect by the government at New Bern, were motivating factors for the North Carolina Regulator movement.[1] More galling, the corruption then was open and prominent, to the distinct disadvantage of that era's settlers on the piedmont (known as the backcountry) and on the frontier.[2]

David Wilson, in *Southern Strategy*, defines the Regulator movement through description of its causes: "[C]itizens felt neglected by the tidewater-dominated legislatures. Lawlessness was rampant in the backcountry, and yet the problem was ignored by those in power on the coast." In addition, "[t]he backcountry settlements bore the brunt of keeping the Indian nations in check—something the backcountry settlers felt the tidewater elites failed to appreciate."[3] Perhaps more succinct is David Lee Russell's definition of the "Regulator Movement" as a "term for the attempts of western people to take control of their affairs," against the background of their grievances, such as severe under-representation and significant corruption by local officials, including "misappropriation of collected taxes, fraudulent handling of foreclosure activities, and excessive [filing fees] and penalties."[4]

How did the Regulator movement represent a precursor to revolution? The movement awakened a streak of militarism, a willingness to bear arms, as well as manifestation of a "Don't Tread on Me" spirit prevalent among segments of the North Carolina populace.[5] In the 1760s and 1770s, as stated, the animus was aimed at the coastal elites and the royal government in the capital of New Bern.[6] As the 1770s progressed, however, that animus, fueled by feelings of alienation, shifted and increased toward a thirst for liberty. Hostility shifted from the local government in North Carolina to the royal government in Great Britain.[7] Regulators and their supporters, as well as coastal regions' aristocratic wealthy merchants, resented the taxes, lack of any effective voice in London, actual and threatened British colonial military presences, and the heavy hands of King George III, his ministers, and Parliament. Backcountry and coastal elites coalesced as more and more both chafed under the mother country's thumb.

The Movement's Early Beginnings

On May 22, 1767, several hundred Orange County (Hillsborough) North Carolinians passed a five-point resolution regarding unjust taxation, collection of unauthorized fees, crown officials' deficient record-keeping, and officials' withholding of funds from the public treasury.[8] Thereafter, the movement gained momentum for several reasons. One was royal Governor William Tryon's (governor 1765–1771) appropriation of 15,000 pounds for construction of a governor's palace at New Bern, a magnificent structure that, rebuilt, stands today. When settlers compared the governor's profligacy to the hardscrabble existences they eked out, the comparison hardened feelings of alienation.

Two was the continued collection of excessive filing and other fees, despite predecessor Royal Governor Arthur Dobbs' proclamation forbidding the taking of illegal fees: "One regulator swore that he paid [the Orange County Court Clerk] two pounds, seventeen shillings and five pence for a letter of Administration and he got none."[9] That court clerk happened to have been Francis Nash (Chapter 20), who was to become one of North Carolina's Revolutionary War heroes.

Three, Governor Tryon refused to negotiate with the Regulators or acknowledge their existence. Indeed, he placed troops on the streets of Hillsborough, guarding the courts, the jail that housed certain of the Regulators' leaders, and the judge's home and plantation: "Fifty men guarded the market house ... [t]wenty more guarded the prison ... [S]oldiers patrolled the streets ... intimidating anyone known to be associated with the Regulators."[10]

Governor Tryon's Ire

Tryon attempted a settlement, albeit on harsh terms. If the Regulators agreed "to lay down and deliver up their Arms," agree to pay back taxes, and surrendered their leaders to Governor Tryon, he would pardon the insurgents. Unwilling to accept the Governor's terms, the Regulators did not answer, "simply disappearing into the night."[11]

The final straw came in late–1770 to early–1771. A Regulator mob announced a plan to march on New Bern in time for the General Assembly scheduled for December 5, 1770.[12] Governor Tryon had had enough. In April 1771, he sent North Carolina Militia General Hugh Waddell and 236 men of the Cape Fear militia straight west toward Salisbury with a mission to intimidate the region's Regulators. With a force of 1,068 men, the governor journeyed northwest to Hillsborough, arriving there on May 9. General Waddell then wheeled, journeying straight north, joining Tryon and his force at Alamance Courthouse, twenty or so miles west and a bit south of Hillsborough.

On May 16, the royal colonial battle group of 1,300 men met a force of 2,000 Regulators near Alamance Creek. Governor Tryon fired the first shot, killing the man at whom he had aimed the borrowed musket. Two hours of fighting followed, with the first hour more-or-less a draw, with action "equal and well-sustained."

In the second hour of battle, Regulator groups' partial and then total retreat from the field induced panic among the rebel mob. As a result, "The ill-prepared Regulators were routed."[13] Fatalities were minimal, as they often were in those days of highly inaccurate musket fire: "Estimates of the dead and wounded vary, possibly as many as 20 Regulators killed, 9 [government] militiamen. Altogether, more than 150 men (on both sides) were wounded, many seriously."[14] The Governor's troops captured fifteen enemy troops. Tryon ordered six or seven of those be executed. One, James Few, was twice offered a pardon if he would repent. Few refused. Governor Tryon ordered him hanged immediately on the battlefield, as an example to other would-be rebels.[15]

Today little is remembered of royal governors except for William Tryon, often regarded in favorable light. One historian, David Russell, peered more deeply, coming to regard Tryon as a tyrant:

> North Carolina's political landscape had been damaged by the tyrannical administration of Governor Tryon. His oppressive regime had created an atmosphere that ... fostered the Regulator Movement throughout the western counties of the Carolinas.... [But] hatred of the English tyrant had the effect of nurturing the seeds of discontent in the colony and served the idea of independence well.[16]

Regulators' Penultimate Hurrah: The Battle of Moore's Creek Bridge

Josiah Martin succeeded Tryon as royal governor of the North Carolina colony. In November 1775, Lord George Germain, royal secretary for North America, informed Martin that a force of over 2,000 troops, seven regiments of regulars, would embark at the Cork, Ireland, port then known as Queenstown (Cobh today) in transports destined for North Carolina. There they would join 2,000 British regulars sent south from Boston under Henry Clinton. Previously, Martin had informed Germain that he could call upon a Scots Highlander group that had settled around Cross Creek (now Fayetteville) in Cumberland County. Many of the Scots had fought in the Jacobean Revolution, after which, for the restoration of their citizenship, they had sworn an oath pledging fealty to the king, an oath to which they remained faithful. Last of all, from the north, General William Howe had promised to send experienced Scots officers. He sent Colonel Donald McDonald and Captain Donald McLeod. Totaling the various elements, Martin estimated that he would have a loyalist force of 3,000 or more men to supplement the 2,000 British regulars.

The Scots Highlanders were the first to reduce the size of their expected contribution. Leaders told Governor Martin that they could only promise 600 or so men. From the backcountry, though, the Regulator movement leaders, or what remained of them, stepped in, bragging that they could bring 5,000 more men to the field. Based upon the Regulator promises, Colonel Alex McClean, another officer sent south by General Howe, sent word to Governor Martin that they would soon have as many as 6,000 men. When the Regulator forces were not forthcoming, in February

1776, Colonel McClean travelled to Cross Hill, in the backcountry, the assembly point for the promised Regulators. Instead of the promised 5,000, Colonel McClean found only 500.[17] To his chagrin, "Ultimately, the large number of Regulators and backcountry Loyalists of whom [Governor] Martin had high hopes of support failed to participate ... [m]any remained at home."[18]

Seemingly, the stage was set for a major British campaign in the American south. What ensued was altogether different. At Moore's Creek, a minor battle—more than a skirmish, not a major conflict—took place, marking the first (Moore's Creek on February 27, 1776) and last battle on North Carolina soil until Guilford Courthouse on March 15, 1781.

Regulators as Patriots

Leaving the Battle of Moore's Creek Bridge aside, indications are that the Regulator movement and the stirrings were underpinnings of the revolutionary fervor that later arose. Recent research demonstrates that many regulators did indeed become patriots, while some remained neutral.[19] On the other side, in August 1775, the Third Provincial Congress, the legislative group replaced the British-sponsored Assemblies General, formed a special committee "to talk with the Regulator faction for support against the British."[20] The Regulator movement is an important adjunct to any description of the American Revolution in North Carolina.

4

Earliest Military Exploits

North Carolina's James Moore and Richard Caswell

In conflicts, there are fighting generals. Virginia's George Washington and Daniel Morgan, or North Carolina's Francis Nash and William Lee Davidson are examples. At the other extreme are politicians turned generals, mostly so they can sport the uniform. Outfitted, they fly a false flag of personal bravery and military prowess, impressing their colleagues as well as the ladies. In between are politicians who serve, and serve well, but who flit back and forth between the military and political worlds.[1] North Carolina's Richard Caswell falls into that latter camp.

Beginning in 1774, Caswell served as one of North Carolina's three delegates to the First and Second Continental Congresses, elected by North Carolina's First Provincial Congress.[2] Previously, he served in a number of minor government positions such as deputy clerk, tax collector, and representative in the Colonial Assemblies and then their successors, the Provincial Congresses.[3] Then, in 1776, Caswell emerged as a successful military leader, the ranking officer at Moore's Creek Bridge Battle, an impressive victory. Based upon accolades garnered after Moore's Creek, Caswell returned to politics once more. He became North Carolina's first governor, serving a stub and three one-year terms, from January 1777 to April 1780. Another generalship beckoned. In 1780, Caswell took a brigadier's commission, leading the North Carolina Militia, not always well or with bravery. Resigning in a huff over Congress's appointment of Marylander William Smallwood as commander over all North Carolina's forces instead of Richard Caswell, Caswell returned once again to politics, serving twice (1783 and 1784) as Speaker of the North Carolina Senate and governor once again (1784–1787).[4]

Portraits of the time depict Caswell as unsmiling, indeed sternly staring outward into space. He has the long, aquiline, British, upper-class nose. In contrast, he has the coiffure of a settler, a Dutch farm boy's bowl-cut.

English Versus Scots or Irish

One assumption made is that the Revolution's military leaders were of English descent.[5] That holds partially true at the major general level at which, for instance, Horatio Gates and Charles Lee were refugees from the British army. But doubt may be cast over even that.⁶ Major generals Arthur St. Clair and Adam Stephen were Scottish physicians who became high-ranking officers in the Continental Line.⁷

On the southern brigadier level, though, the heritage most frequently encountered was Scottish. To name a few, brigadiers William Rodgers Clark, Lachlan McIntosh, William Alexander, Alexander McDougal, William Moultrie, Hugh Mercer, William Smallwood, Andrew Pickens, and Charles Scott were Scottish, not English. The Highlanders supporting Charles Stuart (Bonnie Prince Charlie) fled after the British Duke of Cumberland smashed the rebel Scots forces at the Battle of Culloden (1746). Many defeated rebels emigrated to North America, either then or later.

Among other brigadiers, outliers were German (Peter Muhlenberg) and French (Francis Marion). Second to Scottish was Irish ancestry; William Davidson, Francis Nash, James Hogun, Griffin Rutherford, Edward Hand, John Sullivan, and Andrew Lewis all had Irish roots. A general who traced his roots to England rather than Scotland or Ireland was Richard Caswell.

Caswell Family History

The family patriarch, Richard Senior, emigrated to America early, in 1712, settling in Maryland. Richard Junior was born in 1729. At what today would be regarded as a tender age, 16, Richard Junior and his younger brother William left the family, migrating to New Bern, North Carolina.⁸ There Richard first trained and pursued a career as a land surveyor, an occupation, as has been seen, frequently found among Revolutionary War generals (Washington, Brodhead, Wayne, Lewis, Scott, McIntosh, and others). Caswell utilized that training for the remainder of his life as a valuable adjunct to another lifelong avocation, acquisition of land. Using George Washington as an example of a real estate speculator, historian Ron Chernow wrote, "[l]and speculation was the ideal vehicle for amassing riches, a way to invest in [one's] future and that of the country, mingling idealism and profit."⁹ Caswell acquired thousands of acres in fee as well as participating as a shareholder in land companies formed to acquire large tracts of land over the Appalachians in what became Tennessee and Kentucky: "Caswell's early career as a surveyor ... gave him the opportunity to investigate and evaluate new land for profitability."¹⁰

Following the stint at land surveying, Caswell embarked upon reading law under an established practitioner's tutelage. North Carolina's colonial courts admitted Caswell, at the seasoned age of 30, to the practice of law. Caswell, his wives (first wife Mary Mackilwean died in 1757; second wife [1758] Sarah Heritage), and his children were Anglicans, worshipping at St. Matthew's and Christ Church, respectively in Kington and in New Bern.¹¹

Military Outing and Lasting Fame

Richard Caswell did not return to Philadelphia and the Third Continental Congress as one of North Carolina's three delegates. In October 1775, the Committee on Safety at New Bern elected Caswell leader of the New Bern Militia.¹² On February

15, intelligence reported 3,500 loyalists, the core being the "Highlander Emigrant Regiment," had assembled at Cross Creek. High levels of desertion, though, quickly winnowed that force. By the time British Colonel Donald McDonald, assisted by Captains McLeod and Captain Alex McClean (Chapter 3), and the force commenced their march, "They had only 1300 Highlanders and 300 Regulator loyalists in company."[13]

McDonald's planned march was 80 miles in a straight line on the west side (right bank) of the Cape Fear River, bypassing Wilmington on the river's east shore. Reaching the Cape Fear estuary beyond Wilmington, McDonald's force would rendezvous with a British regular contingent still aboard 53 transport ships anchored in the estuary. The Cape Fear River flows on a diagonal, from northwest to southeast. On the American side from Wilmington, Patriot Colonel (later General) James Moore set out in a northwest direction with a force of Wilmington Militia and Continental regulars to block McDonald and the Highlanders.[14] Having gone only seven miles, upon learning of the impending opposition, the pro–British Highlanders retreated toward Cross Creek, crossed the river, and proceeded along the river's left bank.[15]

Meanwhile, Caswell and an 800-man militia left New Bern, marching in a west by southwest direction.[16] Eventually, Caswell and his men would intercept the Cape Fear River twenty or so miles above Wilmington.[17] Arriving in the vicinity of where the battle would take place, and after one false start, Caswell and his men camped with their backs to Moore's Creek, a tributary of the Black River, in turn a tributary of the Cape Fear River. Military tacticians regarded such a deployment as disadvantageous. With a fifty-foot wide and five-to-ten-foot-deep stream behind them, defending troops would have their backs to the wall, having eliminated ready means for a retreat, strategic or otherwise.[18] Colonel Caswell, though, was a novice who evidently had made a beginner's mistake: "[T]o the delight of the advancing Scots, it seemed that the inexperienced Whig commander had blundered."[19]

During the night before the battle, Caswell's troops left the campfires burning. They retreated across the bridge, removing the bridge's planks after them, greasing or soaping the stringers (trusses) that spanned the creek and supported the planking. The same tactic had been used at the Battle of Great Bridge in southeastern Virginia the previous December, a conflict in which North Carolina's Robert Howe led a North Carolina regiment and Virginia troops.

Beyond the bridge and the creek's bank, the North Carolinians threw up a semicircular defensive earthwork. The Highlander force, down to 1,000 due to desertions, approached.[20] Thinking that the Patriot force had fled, *en masse,* the Highlanders and Regulators began to cross the partly dismantled bridge. As they were in the process of the difficult crossing, they met shot from a thousand or more American muskets.[21] Thirty British bodies lay on the bridge. An equal or greater number, mortally wounded or killed, fell into the deep creek, with the bodies never recovered. It was "a terrible slaughter ... the Patriot militia released volley after volley."[22] The Patriots lost one man.

The Americans quickly replaced the bridge's planking, giving chase to the fleeing loyalists: "[O]ver 850 Highlanders and Regulators were apprehended."[23] Waiting aboard ship in the Cape Fear estuary, the British regulars never came ashore. British officers terminated invasion plans.[24] The British force sailed to New York; British forces did not set foot in North Carolina again until 1780. In a bit of seeming overstatement, Colonel Moore remarked, "[This], I trust, put an effectual to Toryism in this country."[25] Thereafter, the Battle of Moore's Creek Bridge was referred to as "the Lexington and Concord of the South."[26]

Lasting Fame for Richard Caswell

Historians point out that by their leadership and bravery, Colonels Alexander Lillington and John Ashe deserved credit for the American victory at Moore's Creek.[27] Other historians credit Colonel James Moore with devising the scheme.[28] The credit and the fame, however, went largely to Richard Caswell. For example, David Wilson in *Southern Strategy* identifies Caswell as "Richard Caswell of Moore's Creek fame" and as "the hero of Moore's Creek."[29] In his Caswell biography, author Joe A. Mobley says much the same, adding, "Caswell's role in the Battle of Moore's Creek Bridge did much to bolster his reputation."[30] Though small in relation to better known Revolutionary War conflicts, the Battle of Moore's Creek Bridge "established the permanent ascendancy of Patriot military and political power in North Carolina," as David Wilson concludes his discussion in *Southern Strategy*.[31] Undoubtedly, that was true. Whether deserving or not, Richard Caswell received credit for the achievement.

In December 1776, Caswell captured enough General Assembly votes to become the first governor of North Carolina, albeit on an interim basis. He swore an oath, taking office on January 16, 1777.[32] Seemingly, his military career had ended. Beginning in April 1777, Caswell served three one-year terms as governor, serving until April 1780.[33]

Facing Threats from All Directions

From without, Governor Richard Caswell faced threats on the state's western frontier (Indian raids, often induced by settler land grabs) as well as on the state's eastern, or coastal, flank (British raids, principally to rustle cattle and sheep). From the north, the Continental army asked for more—Caswell was constantly beset with recruiting necessities—and was given little or nothing in the way of uniforms, weapons, ammunition, food, or pay. From within, he faced two significant issues. One was the inadequacy of responses by the legislature to Caswell's incessant requests for more: pay, clothing, ammunition, blankets, and so on. Second was the constant, "considerable trouble dealing with Loyalists, or Tories, who lived throughout North Carolina."[34]

The British replicated French efforts of 20 years before as the British riled up Indians, settling upon them weapons, ammunition, and supplies if they would raid the American communities and farms on the western flanks of Georgia, the

Carolinas, Virginia, and Pennsylvania. Early on, the Carolinas sent invading expeditions that destroyed many of the 80 Cherokee villages (*see* Chapter 10). North Carolina Militia General Griffith Rutherford of Salisbury led one such expedition into the western North Carolina foothills and mountains. The military effort bore fruit as the Cherokees signed a peace treaty in 1777, ceding to the state all lands east of the Blue Ridge. Settlers, though, disregarded the treaty's provisions, carving out homesteads west of the treaty line. In turn, the Cherokees reacted by raids on the offending settlements. For the length of his governorship, Caswell had to police the relations between the two groups.[35]

North Carolina supplied ten regiments to the Continental army with a head count that varied from 6,086 to 7,663. As early as 1777, George Washington wrote to Caswell about soldiers and officers leaving the army. The high proportion of Tory and Tory sympathizers in the state posed a problem for recruiting efforts: "A large part of the [North Carolina's] population were Loyalists unwilling to fight against the crown."[36] Within the state, "[t]he governor also had trouble keeping the state militia up to strength."[37]

An empty state treasury and weak constitutional grants of power to the governor rendered futile attempts at support for the military. From within the state as well, armed Loyalists groups engaged in raids on powder magazines and armories, also assisting the British war effort by overt joinder with British troops in skirmishes and raids.

Exhausted and unwell, Richard Caswell left the governorship in April 1781: "For years [Caswell] had suffered from ill health, which included severe headaches, dizziness, and other symptoms, probably caused by hypertension."[38] He was succeeded in office by Abner Nash, brother of Francis Nash who had been killed at Germantown in 1777 while leading North Carolina's regiments (Chapter 20).

Not So Ill After All?

A short time after leaving the governor's mansion, Caswell recovered his health, seemingly miraculously. The North Carolina General Assembly and Governor Nash appointed Caswell a major general, in command of all North Carolina Militia.[39] Caswell set about his command immediately. He ordered militia muster at Cross Creek, in southeastern North Carolina. By late June, two thousand or more men gathered in response.[40]

In 1780, the commander of the Continental Army's Southern Department was Massachusetts Major General Benjamin Lincoln. The British, however, had imprisoned Lincoln after he and 5,000 Americans had surrendered Charles Town to the British in May 1780. So, the Congress appointed as the new Southern Department Commander the hero of Saratoga, General Horatio Gates. Gates had been a career British army officer who, facing scant chances for further promotion, had retired at half-pay. He emigrated to America, settling in Virginia and assiduously courting the favor of the new overall American commandant, George Washington.

At the time of Saratoga (September 1777), where he commanded the Northern

Army, Horatio Gates was forty-nine years old, "but at a distance looked and acted a senior. He had thinning gray hair, wore spectacles perched low on his nose, and even stooped when he walked." Those who encountered him "appeared to think of Gates as an old man," Dean Snow writes.[41] The troops Gates commanded nicknamed him "Granny Gates."[42] Hoffman Nickerson rated Gates "a snob of the first water [who had] an unctuously pious way with him." Perhaps ascending a notch, Nickerson opined, "Gates had such a repellent personality that," as of 1928, "he still lacks a biographer." By the time of Saratoga, "Gates was so empty of fighting spirit … as to lay him open to suspicion of cowardice."[43] There were few contrary views.[44]

Three years later, the views of Gates were similar. According to David Russell in *The American Revolution in the Southern Colonies*, Gates was "a flabby, bespectacled, grandfatherly looking gentleman who gave the appearance of a man without military bearing."[45] He had "slanted eyes which gave him a hangdog appearance, a large, hooked nose, and a long skinny face."[46]

Generals Gates and Caswell at the Battle of Camden

Whatever accolades and credit Horatio Gates had garnered at Saratoga, and Richard Caswell at Moore's Creek, both detracted from praise for past accomplishments and did so significantly at the August 1780 Battle of Camden, in South Carolina. It was the second greatest loss by the Americans in their War of Independence. Gates's and Caswell's actions guaranteed a harmful outcome. Gates's megalomania infused his actions as Southern Army Commander. His previous machinations included an underground effort to have Congress replace Washington with himself: "Washington felt badly used. He was being blamed for having won no victories comparable to that of General Gates, who indeed was being spoken of as Washington's replacement at the head of the Continental Army."[47] Congress answered Gates by appointing him to a high post, that of Southern Department Commander.

On July 25, 1780, Gates arrived in Hillsborough, North Carolina, where the Southern Army's remnants had sheltered, 230 miles north of Charles Town. Two days after arriving, Gates marched his army toward Camden, South Carolina, 152 miles southwest of Hillsborough. The march was no easy one, as the route of the march crossed miles of harsh countryside. In the words of Colonel Ortho Holland Williams, the land "was by nature barren, abounding with sandy plains, intersected by swamps and thinly populated, the people there mostly hostile to the American cause," many being dyed-in-the-wool Loyalists.[48] With little to eat, the American troops nourished themselves by picking and eating green apples and unripe peaches. On August 7, having marched southeast into South Carolina, General Caswell and 2,100 militia troops joined Gates and his "grand army."[49]

To complicate matters, Gates and Caswell operated with bad intelligence. First, General Gates thought he had an army of 7,000, reinforced by Caswell's 2,100 North Carolina and General Edward Stevens's 700 Virginia militia. In truth, the head count was no more than 3,200 effectives.[50] Second, Gates thought he would oppose only a 700-person British force under Lieutenant Colonel Lord Francis Rawdon, left in central South Carolina after a raid upon the Camden supply depot. In truth, General Lord Charles Cornwallis was about to reinforce Rawdon with 2,239 men, "all of them a tough, tenacious breed." John Buchanan summarized the approaching British force: "[Cornwallis] had a good army. It was small but very professional."[51]

Fifteen miles short of Camden, Gates called his procession to a halt along Waxhaw's Road. The British troops, too, were a bit north of Camden itself, along the same Waxhaw Road. On August 15, Gates ordered a night march straight south by his emaciated forces, including the untrained militia. The orders filled Gates's officers "with consternation": "[H]ow could an army of untrained militia who had never before done it do a night march?" John Buchanan asked.[52]

By coincidence, Cornwallis also ordered a night march north. The American and British forces met on August 16, at two o'clock in the morning. Limited skirmishing and pickets' exchanges of gunfire filled the time until sunrise, which occurred at 4:20 a.m. that August 16 morning. Informed that the British were nearby, sometime before the 4:20 a.m. sunrise, General Gates called a Council of War, exclaiming, "Gentlemen, what is to be done?" Only Virginia's Edward Stevens answered, "[I]t is not too late now to do anything but fight!"[53] So, once again, as at Saratoga, there was no battle plan for Gates's army: "There was no indication that Gates had a plan or had put his mind seriously to work."[54] In addition, the order of battle Gates

Governor Tryon and the Regulators. The British colonial governor confronts an early 1770s backcountry mob (Artist Unknown, Library of Congress).

handed down was seriously flawed, lopsided with Caswell and North Carolina Militia, joined by the Virginia volunteers on the left and the battle-tested Delaware and Maryland troops all on the right, under General Baron De Kalb, assisted by Maryland General Mordecai Gist. Gates stationed himself over 200 yards in the rear, too far to observe events or intervene as the battle unfolded. He was even to the rear of the American reserve force, Maryland's General William Smallwood's 400 regulars.

In a report to Congress then, Gates greatly exaggerated, or completely fabricated: "I ordered the left [all militia] to advance and attack the enemy ... [North Carolina] General Caswell and myself did all in our power to rally the broken troops."[55] Eyewitnesses impeached Gates's version of events. Garret Watts of the North Carolina Militia recalled, "There was no effort to rally, no encouragement to fight."[56]

Caswell's biographers attribute to Caswell one or two attempts to rally his fleeing troops. "[T]he North Carolina militia broke and ran, throwing away arms and equipment ... [m]any never fired a shot," Caswell biographer Joe Mobley recorded.[57] Gates broke and ran shortly after the battle began. Caswell rode with him, stopping only when he and Gates were five miles in the rear. They then continued together to Charlotte, seventy miles away. Those actions contradicted any attempts to rally fleeing troops.

As the militia at Camden dropped their weapons and sprinted rearward, on the American army's right wing at Camden, Johann De Kalb suffered more than eight wounds. Again, it took General Gates "three days to reach Hillsborough. It took DeKalb three days to die."[58]

A Fit of Pique and Resignation

In September following the Battle of Camden, the North Carolina Assembly replaced Caswell as commanding general of the North Carolina home guard. Undoubtedly, Caswell's and the North Carolina Militia's actions at Camden influenced the legislators. Caswell, though, took great umbrage at not only his replacement but replacement by a Marylander rather than a North Carolinian. The North Carolina Assembly chose the one American general who had distinguished himself at Camden, William Smallwood of Maryland. In a huff, Caswell resigned his commission. Five months later, in February 1781, the North Carolina Assembly restored Caswell's general rank, re-installing him in a command. The legislature placed him in charge of North Carolina Militia but only in the state's eastern region.[59]

Richard Caswell's military career ended on neither a high nor low note. It just ended. Caswell returned to politics. He became Governor of North Carolina once more, serving from 1784 to 1787.[60]

Historian John Buchanan's epitaph for Horatio Gates could, in part at least, apply to Richard Caswell too:

> One hesitates to call any man a coward.... But we are entitled to expect of officers that they never shirk, never run. In an age when generals commonly exposed themselves to inspire their men and often paid with their lives, Major General Horatio Gates ... rode far and fast from Camden's terrible field.[61]

True, Richard Caswell's situation differed. At Camden, General Gates fled from his troops while with General Caswell, his troops fled from him. That imbroglio seems not to have scared Caswell. In historical accounts, he has gone down as North Carolina's "Versatile Leader of the Revolution."[62] Caswell's biographer, Joe Mobley, concludes, "Richard Caswell's contribution to the cause of American independence was substantial."[63] Hugh Rankin and William Powell hail Caswell as "the hero of Moore's Creek," enshrined in the state's pantheon.[64] Caswell did indeed play pivotal roles in both the state's political and military histories.

5

Threats on the Southern Border

Defending Coastal Georgia

In 1775, Georgia was a thinly populated colony with approximately 10,000 citizens. By contrast, neighboring colonies to the north had greater populations: North Carolina with 150,000, and Virginia with 305,000 (the most populated of thirteen colonies).[1] Further, of the colonies, Georgia was the most physically remote from the Massachusetts-based agitation over the Crown's heavy handedness in dealing with its American colonies. With 930 miles between Boston and Savannah, Georgia was far removed from New England. Georgians thus looked more at provincial concerns rather than possible joinder with sister colonies. Georgia looked south rather than north. British, Loyalist, and British-inspired Indian raids came into the colony from the south, the site of British East Florida.

In the 1770s, the Florida Rangers, led by the "notorious and capable" Thomas Brown and consisting of Loyalist irregulars, began raiding Georgia settlements and plantations south of the Altamaha River and north of the Florida border. Pursuant to the 1763 Treaty of Paris, the Spanish had ceded the Florida peninsula to Britain, who then garrisoned St. Augustine with British troops.[2] They christened a portion of the peninsula British East Florida. As unease with its American colonies increased, the British inspired Indian attacks. Britain also inspired raids by Loyalists, later involving British troops, invading north from Florida into southern Georgia.

The commanding general of the Georgia Militia, such as it was, was Lachlan McIntosh, later to become a brigadier of the Continental line (Chapter 6). As one of his first actions, McIntosh had a unit of 60 horsemen commanded by his older brother William attempt protection of the sparsely populated villages and plantations of southern Georgia. McIntosh also ordered a fort, Fort Barrington (later renamed Fort Howe after North Carolina's General Robert Howe), built on the Altamaha River, halfway between Savannah and the Georgia-Florida border.

Effects of Georgia Politics

Even at that early point, Georgia politics intervened in military matters. The Georgia Council of Safety, Archibald Bulloch presiding, "pleaded with Lachlan McIntosh to stop the [British and Tory] invaders at the Satilla River [in Georgia's coastal south between the St. Mary's and the Altamaha] if possible and to fall back to the Altamaha only if absolutely necessary."[3] Again and again, political sentiment and its adherents urged the military to look south and only south. The so-called Georgia radicals pushed for an invasion of Florida.[4] Despite misgivings, McIntosh undertook to do their bidding: "The attempt to take St. Augustine was doomed to fail. [C]ontinental troops sickened in coastal Georgia's semi-tropical climate.... Georgians did not provide medical supplies ... the death rate was fourteen or fifteen a day. The main body of American troops advanced no farther than Sunbury," little more than a dozen miles south of Savannah.[5] McIntosh then ordered defensive stations on the Sapelo River and at additional locations on the Altamaha.

On February 17–18, 1777, Florida Rangers, Indian allies, 150 British infantry, and 120 horsemen laid siege to Fort McIntosh on the Satilla River. The seventy Americans garrisoning the fort surrendered when their ammunition ran low. The British then proceeded northward to the Altamaha River, where Lachlan McIntosh and his men succeeded in preventing a British river crossing. McIntosh took a musket ball to the foot, suffering a wound that took two months to heal.

McIntosh and the Entry of Button Gwinnett

With the last accounts, the book's development gets ahead of itself. This short chapter's purpose was to illustrate how concerns in Georgia differed. In fact, in each of the southern colonies, concerns inducing military action and joinder with the independence movement differed from one southern colony to another. That was particularly true in Georgia. The entry of Button Gwinnett, Georgia's sole signatory on the Declaration of Independence, into the picture magnified the difference, much to Lachlan McIntosh's lasting misfortune.

6

Character Attacks, Misfortune, and Survival

Brigadier Lachlan McIntosh of Georgia

A planter in coastal Georgia, "[L]achlan McIntosh was a cautious, conservative man, noted for his 'superior sense & understanding' in public matters, serious, conscious of status and procedure ... often striking contemporaries as cold and abrupt. Yet, in private, to the small circle he drew around him, he was a hospitable, loyal friend.... He was, in the classic eighteenth-century sense, an American country gentleman, a bit rough around the edges, but a man with whom others had to reckon."[1] Contemporary portraits showed a long narrow English face, flushed pink cheeks, and a very long, aquiline nose, portraits such as those hanging in the drawing rooms of English country manor houses.[2]

Throughout the Revolutionary War, backbiting, backstabbing, and political intrigue deeply affected Lachlan McIntosh's military career. As has been seen, a source was the fixation many influential Georgians had with the South and British East Florida rather than with developments in the North. Moreover, it came from not from within but from without the army, namely, from local and state politicians and their supporters. McIntosh's adversaries feigned concern for Georgia's defense (not the colonies'). They expressed constant assertion of the need for civilian ascendancy over the military and continuously and falsely propagated the ill-conceived idea that McIntosh had "murdered" Button Gwinnett, despite the two men having shaken hands before and declaring a truce after their duel. In the duel, both men were wounded, each shot in the thigh.

The Duel

Gwinnett died four days after his duel with McIntosh, from seemingly mild wounds, ostensibly from inadequate medical care rather than the severity of his injury. Defamation of McIntosh as one who had "murdered Gwinnett" followed McIntosh through the war and to the end of his days. As late as 1780, a disgusted Southern Department Commander, Major General Benjamin Lincoln, himself a New Englander, hearing of the false McIntosh-Gwinnett narrative, remarked of Georgians, "Good God, will the Malice of these people never be at an end?"[3] Describing McIntosh's string of travails, biographer Harvey Jackson titles a chapter

"Implacable Mallice [sic] of Implacable Enemies."[4] Lachlan McIntosh's travails were like any other in the Continental Army.[5]

As with the Carolinas, Georgia contained many ardent Loyalists, bordering on a majority of its inhabitants. In 1774, for instance, Georgia did not join the other twelve colonies in sending delegates to the initial Continental Congresses. In *Our First Civil* War, Professor H.W. Brands hazards a partial excuse. The colony was "in a war with the Indians and loath to lose the help of the British Army."[6]

McIntosh the Planter

Georgia's only leading military figure in the Revolutionary War was born in 1725 in Scotland. McIntosh emigrated in 1736. A group of Scots, including the McIntosh family, settled in coastal Georgia and founded the town of Darien.

Lachlan McIntosh. McIntosh was a Scottish immigrant coastal planter who faced not only military but also constant political adversity over his entire career (Artist Unknown, Georgia Historical Society).

In 1748, when he was in his early twenties, Lachlan and his eleven-year-old brother George were ordered by their parents to move from coastal Darien northward to Charles Town, South Carolina. They lived in lodgings for the next eight years. Lachlan began office work for trader Henry Laurens, later president of the Second Continental Congress. Lachlan and Laurens later had many business dealings and became fast friends.[7] Upon returning to Georgia, in the late 1750s, Lachlan gradually acquired fourteen thousand acres of agricultural land in mid-coastal Georgia, primarily in St. Andrew's Parish surrounding Darien, and became a rice farmer. His earlier association with Laurens gave McIntosh a window on the markets. McIntosh barged the rice to Charles Town where Laurens sold and shipped the product along the East Coast, in the Caribbean, and in South America.[8] Lachlan McIntosh had become a successful, prosperous planter. Six feet tall, athletic and muscular, Lachlan was described by a friend "as the handsomest man he had ever seen."[9] McIntosh became a highly visible figure in the "planter aristocracy" of coastal Georgia. He was a member of "Georgia's small but powerful planter elite."[10]

In the other southern colonies, sometimes inchoate, sometimes express rivalries existed between the coastal aristocracy and the back country, today really the center of those states.[11] Georgia was different. The rivalry constantly in the forefront existed north to south rather than east to west. Savannah and surroundings were in Christ Parish, parishes being the forerunners of counties. Down the coast were St. John's and St. Andrew's Parishes, extending from Darien northward to Sunbury on the Medway, a dozen or more miles below Savannah.[12] Persons with political interests in the more established Christ Parish were known as conservatives because they favored limited action and not an all-out campaign against East Florida.[13] By contrast, political interests in rural coastal parishes became known as "the radicals," who among other things favored invasion in force that would not stop until St. Augustine and East Florida had been annihilated.[14] *See generally*, Map, ""Revolutionary War in the South," Chapter 22.

Conservatives nominated Savannah's Samuel Elbert, one of the few Georgians with military experience, to command Georgia's continental troops. Radicals nominated Button Gwinnett of St. John's Parish, and "The compromise candidate turned out to be Lachlan McIntosh who was not affiliated with either faction.... Lachlan took command of the Georgia battalion [regiment] in January of 1776."[15] Again, McIntosh "did not openly ally himself with either group," conservative or radical, leading to his choice by the Georgia Counsel of Safety and the colony's Second Provincial Assembly.[16]

Button Gwinnett

Button Gwinnett, the son of a Gloucester vicar, emigrated in 1765 at age 30 to America and to Savannah. Two months later, he purchased St. Catherine's Island in St. John's Parish. He became Button Gwinnett, Georgia planter.[17] In two or so years, in contrast to the success of neighboring McIntosh's plantation, Gwinnett's plantation failed. He was forced to put his land upon the auction block: "His once promising future seemed dismal indeed."[18]

Gwinnett quickly righted himself, becoming a leader of the radicals in St. John's Parish. "Colonel Gwinnett" vied with Samuel Elbert for command of the single Georgia regiment the Continental Congress had authorized. Gwinnett, however, "withdrew from consideration, as did Elbert, and a compromise candidate was sought ... [a]fter some deliberation, the radical leaders reached a decision, and the man they selected, for better or worse, was Lachlan McIntosh of Darien."[19] Meanwhile, though, the Georgia Assembly selected Button Gwinnett delegate to the Second Continental Congress in Philadelphia. It was a first plank in the platform from which sprung the incessant Gwinnett political interference and calumny that Lachlan McIntosh faced.

Military Action

The first action for McIntosh and his men, in March 1776, was the Battle of the Rice Boats, a small, small engagement that kicked off the Revolutionary War in Georgia: "In all, the Americans counted two white men and an Indian wounded while the British acknowledged six casualties."[20] Physically, just below the border with South Carolina, Hutchinson's Island splits the Savannah River below the bluffs at the northern edge of the city of Savannah. Rice boats were moored on the far side of Hutchinson's Island, for the most part laden with cargo. On March 2, 1776, two

British warships, the *Hinchinbrook* and the *St. John*, sailed into the river's estuary and then upriver to the island's backside. McIntosh and his troops attempting to foil the British effort, engaged in a scorched earth defense by aiming fire boats at the moored rice boats. Partly or wholly destroyed, the rice boats would lose their attraction to the British raiders. Nonetheless, on March 3, the British made off with ten of the vessels. Two days later, with the defrocked Royal Governor Sir James Wright aboard, the British warships sailed out to sea.

The next episode of the war in Georgia took place far to the south. In mid–1776, political interests in Georgia urged McIntosh and his men to undertake an expedition to protect the colony's southern flank. The so-called radicals pushed incessantly for an invasion of Florida. Despite misgivings, McIntosh undertook to do their bidding. "The attempt to take St. Augustine was doomed to fail," which it did (*see* Chapter 5).[21]

Political Interference, Slander, and False Insinuation Escalate

Shortly thereafter, Lachlan McIntosh's troubles, political rather than military, increased dramatically. The contest—the military leader versus the politician—escalated. Archibald Bulloch, president of the Georgia Council of Safety, died. Button Gwinnett succeeded to the position, in the process gaining control of the Georgia State Militia. Thereafter, "Gwinnett tried to restrict and delay plans of McIntosh … whenever possible."[22] Gwinnett desired control of the Continental Regiment as well as of the militia. Admittedly biased, McIntosh's biographer Harvey Jackson, in *The Politics of Revolutionary Georgia*, strongly states, "[f]rom the beginning of the war, Gwinnett had wanted military command and had envied Lachlan McIntosh's position." Gwinnett began his quest for absolute command indirectly, "by smearing the honor of Lachlan's brothers William and George."[23]

Politician versus Patriot

Gwinnett's assault commenced with the saga of George McIntosh, Lachlan's closest sibling, ten years his junior. In June 1776, George discovered that a cargo of rice from his plantation, destined for Surinam, had been diverted to Jamaica, a British possession, without George's permission or knowledge: "The incident would come back to haunt the McIntosh family."[24] Second, Lachlan McIntosh's older brother William had commanded a detachment in southeast Georgia. For a full year, William conducted raids into British East Florida as well as fended off British and Loyalist counterraids, arduous duty in tangled forests and treacherous swamps.

Then the rivalry between Button Gwinnett and Lachlan McIntosh engulfed William as it had young George: "[Gwinnett's supporters] claimed that William's soldiers had failed to protect Georgians who had ventured into East Florida to raid loyalist settlements. They charged William with abandoning the area south of the Altamaha." William McIntosh resigned; "Many of his officers resigned in protest."[25] Next, as president of the Georgia Council of Safety, Gwinnett had George McIntosh, Lachlan's youngest brother and roommate from Charles Town days, not only jailed but also kept in irons, accused of being a Tory, having furnished rice to a British possession. "Simultaneously.... Gwinnett made plans for [a second] invasion of Florida without consulting Lachlan McIntosh despite Lachlan's position as commander of Georgia's Continental troops." Gwinnett beseeched North Carolina's Major General Robert Howe, commander of the Southern Army, to remove McIntosh, but Howe refused to do so: "Howe did not follow Gwinnett's recommendation." Gwinnett's "Don Quixote expedition to St. Augustine," as with the previous expedition, got no farther than Sunbury, below Savannah.[26]

Later, General McIntosh wrote to his friend Henry Laurens:

> Ever since Mr. Gwinnett was disappointed in the Brigadier General's commission ... himself and his party seemed to lose sight of everything else, except to render the army obnoxious and create the utmost confusion and disorder ... [finding] themselves every way disappointed by my circumspection and caution, they [have fallen] to personal abuse, slanderous and false insinuations, and assertions of prejudice.[27]

Button Gwinnett: "St. Augustine Must Fall."

To mount any credible assault on Florida, Gwinnett needed Continental line forces. A force of militia only would not do. Nevertheless, believing that toppling McIntosh would produce a more pliant continental command, Gwinnett and his allies—The Liberty Society—began "to spread it abroad that, had it not been for the Georgia Tories and the supplies they had provided [to the British], St. Augustine would have fallen long before. ... As Gwinnett saw it, Lachlan McIntosh was included in his definition [of Georgia Tories and 'traitors within the state']."

Simultaneously, Gwinnett "wasted no time.... He decided to proceed" with an attack on St. Augustine "without McIntosh and the Georgia Continentals."[28]

But when Gwinnett called out the militia, the only county that responded was Gwinnett's home parish, St. John's. "[O]nce preparations" for the invasion "were underway, Gwinnett began to experience the difficulties that had plagued previous endeavors ... [f]ood, clothing, and ammunition were scarce [and transportation facilities were inadequate....]"[29] Gwinnett used what authority he had to renew a call-out of the Continental force. To his credit, McIntosh and the main force responded, arriving near Savannah in early April.[30] "McIntosh was still in pain from the wound he had received earlier" in action on the Altamaha.[31] "[H]e also was disturbed by charges," trumped up by rival politicians, "that he too had traded with the enemy." Nonetheless, he sublimated his personal feelings to assist the ill-conceived Gwinnett plan. "[T]he St. Augustine invasion [led by Colonel Samuel Elbert] was a disaster. Inability to coordinate the land and sea force, lack of provisions, and oppressive heat combined to bring the operation to a halt. Finally, the expedition was forced to retreat with little accomplished," summarized Harvey Jackson in *The Politics of Revolutionary Georgia*.[32]

The Duel

In May 1777, the new Georgia Assembly met, as a first order of business examining the St. Augustine debacle. Along with his mentor Lyman Hall, Gwinnett argued that "the salvation of the State [of Georgia] depended on the Removl of Brigadr G. McIntosh." The Liberty Society, Hall's and Gwinnett's front, published a pamphlet, "The Case of George McIntosh."[33] McIntosh, too, was in attendance at the Assembly hearing into Gwinnett's behavior. During a recess, McIntosh told Button, "You, sir, are a scoundrel and a lying rascal." As was the custom of the times, in reply Gwinnett challenged McIntosh to a duel.[34] The two met on the morning of Friday, May 16 in James Wright's pasture at Savannah. They fired pistols, shooting over a twenty-something-foot separation: "Gwinnett fell to the ground with a wound to the knee and said his thigh was broken. McIntosh remained standing despite a wound through the thick of his thigh. ... McIntosh walked across the dueling ground to Gwinnett and shook his hand."[35]

Returned to his home, Gwinnett declined over the weekend, expiring the following Monday, May 19. The General Assembly, populated with Gwinnett disciples, had General McIntosh arrested for murder. McIntosh was quickly acquitted, "but that did not quell a political firestorm raging around him."[36] Due to the allegations of McIntosh supporters and others, the cause of Gwinnett's death was "the unskillfulness of the doctors." For a short while, Georgians accepted the duel's outcome. "Then, as if by a signal, the truce ended. By the end of May, party jealousies reemerged." Lyman Hall, his colleague James Wood, and their supporters "attempted to bring criminal charges against the general ... and continued to press the case against McIntosh's brother, George." To the radicals, "Gwinnett had lost his life in endeavoring to maintain the Civil power in opposition to the cunning & subterfuges of a designing man, Lachlan McIntosh." Hall and Wood "left no stone unturned in their attempt to discredit McIntosh."[37]

Thereafter, giving up on the idea of invading Florida, Georgia adopted a defensive strategy, eschewing calls for an invasion. The Second Georgia Regiment, led by Samuel Elbert, stationed itself on the Savannah River. The Third Georgia Regiment was stationed to the south, on the Ogeechee River.[38] Still, the indirect attacks on Lachlan McIntosh continued. On June 5, 1777, Gwinnett's allies in the Georgia Assembly resolved to send Lachlan's younger brother George north to the Continental Congress for trial. They further decreed that a twenty-person armed guard transport young McIntosh to Philadelphia in chains. Young MacIntosh, however, evaded the posse, journeying north to Philadelphia on his own. During that time, supposedly on Governor John Adam Treulen's orders, a St. John's Parish raiding party ransacked George's home and plantation.

Leaving Georgia Behind

Stung by repeated attacks on his patriotism, his character, his brothers, and his plantation, McIntosh was disgusted with Georgia politics. From North Carolina, though, the general commanding the Southern Department, Robert Howe, never lost faith in McIntosh. On November 3, 1777, General Howe wrote to John Hancock, president of the Continental Congress: "I think it but justice to [General McIntosh] to say that he ever appeared to me to have the warmest attachment to the cause of America, to have ever endeavored by every effort to promote its service, and that I have not the least doubt that his zeal and spirit will be of benefit to our common cause."[39] Responding, in 1778, Congress sent McIntosh north to join General Washington at Valley Forge.[40]

General Washington held a firm belief in McIntosh. Throughout the war, McIntosh had maintained a correspondence with Washington that included more than an element of friendship. They both were planters; in their youths, both had been surveyors. Washington "consistently supported McIntosh and always spoke highly of him ... describ[ing] McIntosh as 'an officer of great merit.'"[41] Professor Stephen Taaffe, in *Washington's Revolutionary War Generals,* writes that, at Valley Forge, "[McIntosh] had impressed Washington with his good conduct, common sense, devotion to duty, and efforts to maintain camp discipline."[42]

Washington put McIntosh in command of the North Carolina Brigade, devoid of leadership since General Francis Nash's death at Germantown the past October (1777). The brigade consisted of nine regiments and a total of 2,700 men, only 928 of whom were in camp.[43] Then, in April 1778, Washington dispatched McIntosh on a two-month tour and inspection of Continental military hospitals.

Commanding the Country's Western Border

On May 26, General Washington wrote to Lachlan McIntosh, "The Congress having been pleased to direct me to appoint an officer to command at Fort Pitt and on the western frontiers.... I am indeed, but not without reluctance, from the sense I entertain of your merit, to nominate you, as an officer well qualified from a variety of considerations to answer the object" Congress has in view.[44] Thus, McIntosh came to succeed Pennsylvania's General Edward Hand in command of the Continental Army's Western Department.

Nagging Western Department concerns were British-sponsored Indian-British attacks on the new nation's western flank. The British were copying from the playbook the French had employed twenty-five years previously. Back then, "The Indian tribes understood the competition between the two European empires [Britain and France] and played one against the other."[45] Later, on the western frontier, the Indians' shifting loyalties replaced France with Britain in opposition to the fledging United States.[46] Treaty Commissioners from Virginia and Pennsylvania decided that the "surest way" to quell the attacks was to send an expedition aimed at the British headquarters at Detroit. Congress then ordered the foray, authorizing two new regiments, one from Virginia and one from Pennsylvania, for the incursion.[47]

The grand plan involved assembly of the force east of the Alleghenies, a journey over the mountains, rendezvous with further troops at Fort Pitt, crossing the Pennsylvania boundary, transiting the hostile Ohio country, and turning north into what today is the state of Michigan with an attack on the British headquarters. In August 1778, however, a wishy-washy Congress ordered that the grand plan be abandoned. Taking the plan's place was a design to establish a series of forts a day's ride apart across northern Ohio, along the route to Detroit, from which Continental forces could subdue Indian villages and raiding parties. Augmented by Colonel Daniel Brodhead (also by trade a surveyor) and his Eighth Pennsylvania Regiment, Brigadier McIntosh eventually had a 1,300-man army.[48]

His force assembled, McIntosh's men left Fort Pitt on October 8, 1778, halfway through autumn, with winter in sight. While still in Pennsylvania, the force established their first fort, Fort McIntosh, near the junction of the Beaver with the Ohio River. The party set out again on November 4, 1778, quickly encountering resistance. On November 7, two soldiers who had left the formation to hunt were killed, scalped by Indians. McIntosh then entered strict orders that no one was to leave the formation. Soldiers who had been frontiersmen wished to hunt to augment sparse food supplies, and they resented the restrictive order.

On November 13 and continuing through the following day, heavy snow fell. On November 18, the expedition reached the banks of the Muskingum River bisecting central Ohio, flowing southward to the Ohio River. There, on the upper Muskingum, McIntosh's men constructed a second fort, which McIntosh named in honor of his friend, Henry Laurens of South Carolina.[49] Soldiers re-named Fort Laurens "Fort Nonsense."

But it was far from nonsense: "British officials at Detroit directed attacks against American outposts and settlements.... Loyalists and Indian allies sporadically besieged Fort Laurens.... A party of sixteen who left the fort to retrieve [stolen] horses [was] ambushed; only one of the men survived."[50] On February 26, 1779, an Indian scalping party carried off 18 persons who were on the road from Fort Laurens to Pennsylvania.[51]

With enlistments soon to expire and the weather cold and formidable. McIntosh called off the expedition. "A frontiersman escorting supplies from Fort McIntosh to Fort Laurens remembered meeting the army coming the opposite way." They arrived back at Fort Pitt in mid–December 1778.[52]

Critics emerged, focusing their attacks upon General McIntosh. Colonel George Morgan, who had been an Indian agent counseling neutrality toward the Indians, referred to "the ignorant, absurd, and contradictory conduct and orders of General McIntosh throughout the campaign."[53] An unnamed settler joined in: "[t]he General has got the ill will of all his officers, the militia in particular."[54]

The most stinging criticism came from Pennsylvania's Daniel Brodhead, a colonel who served under McIntosh and subsequently a brigadier general himself, who claimed, "General McIntosh ... [is] universally hated by every man in this department."[55]

Belying the Brodhead criticism, in 1779 McIntosh led a 500-person relief column to re-supply Fort Laurens. For that and other reasons, discrediting McIntosh proved no easy matter. Washington dismissed Brodhead's repeated accusations as insufficient for action on his part, continuing to support the embattled Georgian: "[B]ut Brodhead, unsatisfied, continued his attacks."[56]

The Failed Siege of Savannah

In July 1779, McIntosh journeyed south, returning to the provisional Georgia capital, Augusta, 110 miles northwest of Savannah, although now he had to watch his back (Brodhead) as well as his front (Georgia politics). In the south, the British had occupied coastal Georgia, including Savannah. "In the summer of 1779, there were few places where American prospects were more dismal than in Georgia. [M]ost populous and productive areas were in enemy hands. [G]overnment had fled inland and set up makeshift operations in Augusta." Continental rosters listed only 158 men, of whom only 42 were present: "[T]he Georgia military establishment was pitiful to behold."[57]

Upon arrival in Augusta, McIntosh's first order of business was to lead the Georgia Continentals down the Savannah River to assist in a planned siege of Savannah. In August, French Admiral Count D'Estaing with his fleet of thirty-three vessels had laid to off the coast, with four thousand French troops on board.[58] On September 6, General Benjamin Lincoln arrived with 1,500 American troops from Charles Town, 107 miles to the north. Lincoln assigned command of the First and Fifth South Carolina Continentals to General McIntosh.

On September 16, growing impatient, Admiral D'Estaing demanded that the occupying force of 7,165, led by British General Augustine Prevost, surrender. Prevost received twenty-four hours to evaluate the proposal, using the time to add finishing touches to his fortifications. On September 22, the French disembarked 3,000 troops, who commenced an attack. The siege of a fortified position such as Savannah by 4,800 (3,000 French augmented by American forces) against a defending force of 7,165 was a dubious proposition. Rains complicated any siege effort as muddy ground made it impossible to move up American artillery, an important component of siege warfare.[59] The siege failed miserably, with Admiral d'Estaing having not only lost his patience and many soldiers but also having suffered a wound. The French admiral and his troops re-boarded their transports, sailing away.

"The results were devastating;" the French lost 521 men, the Americans 231. British losses were only 18 men killed, 39 wounded. "MacIntosh, leading the Georgia troops and the First and Fifth Carolina regiments, arrived at the 'Scene of Confusion' just in time to witness the final retreat." American General Lincoln led his men back to Charles Town. Georgia remained saddled with "dismal prospects."[60]

Politics Surface Once More:
Seemingly It Never Ends

Late in 1779, McIntosh learned that his brother George, his closest sibling, had died at age 40. Political opponents of Lachlan McIntosh had utilized attacks on George as indirect means to tarnish the older brother general.[61] While McIntosh had been in the north, however, a shift in Georgia politics had occurred. With the removal of the political center to Augusta, backcountry Georgians assumed control of the radical movement and the radicals' Popular Party. "[W]hat greeted McIntosh when he arrived ... was a coalition bent on stripping power from the low country elite," including McIntosh, "once and for all. [M]cIntosh failed to realize how 'revolutionary' this new movement was."[62]

To the backcountry leaders, General McIntosh had several strikes against him. First were lingering, albeit false, accusations of Toryism, based upon his younger brother George's shipment to Jamaica years earlier. Second were McIntosh's origins and plantation in the coastal lands, his wealth, and accusations of snobbery. Third was the failure of the siege at Savannah even though McIntosh had commanded under 300 men in a 4,000 troop force attacking an ensconced British army of 7,165.

As a result, McIntosh had not only to grieve his brother's death but confront again politically motivated treachery. George Walton, Georgia's governor, wrote a cover letter that forwarded to the Continental Congress a document supposedly enacted by the Georgia General Assembly, purportedly signed by William Glascock, speaker of the Assembly. The letter alleged "common dissatisfaction ... grounded on weighty reasons," and requested that Congress "direct McIntosh to some distant field." Following that purported request, on March 17, 1780, McIntosh received a return letter from the Continental Congress noting that "[h]e be informed Congress deem it inexpedient to employ him at present in the southern army, and therefore that his services in that department be dispensed with, until the further order of Congress."[63]

While in South Carolina, at Camden, settling his family in accommodations away from the coast and the war, McIntosh received a letter from Samuel Huntington, president of the Continental Congress, that on the recommendation of Georgia Governor George Walton and the General Assembly, the Congress was relieving McIntosh of command.[64] General McIntosh shared the letter with General Benjamin Lincoln and Governor John Rutledge. General Lincoln and South Carolina's Rutledge were dubious. Whatever the letter's provenance, the missive was of no force or effect if they had placed McIntosh in command of South Carolina Militia units, under state rather than continental control.[65] Rutledge made the appointment.

The Final Military Engagement

General Lincoln ordered Brigadier McIntosh to report to Charles Town, then under siege. As McIntosh attempted to participate in the city's defense, the situation in Charles Town deteriorated. The British tightened their noose around the city, cutting off routes of escape. "[British] artillery fire ... struck a church steeple and damaged a statue of English political leader William Pitt in the main square.... [A] barrage killed a Charleston resident and wounded a woman in bed with him. A cannon ball killed an aide to General William Moultrie, small arms fire killed two men, artillery shells wounded three men," wrote Carl Borick in his description of the siege. The British kept up fire with small arms and small-bore artillery, more to chip away at American morale than to destroy the city.[66]

Charles Town surrendered on May 12, 1780. On May 18, the British transported the American officers to prison barracks at Haddrell's Point, across the Cooper River from the city. Some officers left the disgusting barracks, moving to neighboring houses, while others built huts in nearby woods.[67] Fourteen months later, the British paroled General McIntosh. Under a flag of truce, McIntosh journeyed north to Philadelphia.

Lachlan McIntosh was fifty-five years old when, in 1782, he returned to Georgia. There, he found his Darien plantation in ruins, his finances in shambles, and his Savannah house severely damaged, having been cannonaded in the siege.

The rice harvests of 1786, 1787, and 1788 proved to be disasters from which he never recovered: "They exhausted his capital and forced him to curtail his operations."[68] He and his family removed to a permanent residence in Savannah. There "McIntosh resumed his role as a member of the land-owning coastal aristocracy." When the Georgia officers who had fought in the Revolution formed a chapter of the Society of the Cincinnati, they "showed their respect for him by choosing him as their president."[69] McIntosh died in Savannah on February 20, 1806, shortly before his seventy-ninth birthday.

Evaluations

In 1954, Georgia historian Alexander A, Lawrence referred to McIntosh as "the soldier who stood up to misfortune so stoutly." McIntosh "was a man of larger mold than has been supposed. The trials and tribulations he underwent in the American Revolution would have broken a less indominable spirit."[70]

Perhaps even more impartial, in 1960, Pennsylvania historian Edward G. Williams concluded: "Long range appraisal of all the evidence available has vindicated McIntosh's military acumen and the wisdom of his policy. He [also] has been vindicated in other ways from a stigma that attached to him and seemed never to have been dispelled during his lifetime."[71]

McIntosh endured not only criticism but overt actions to destroy him and members of his family. In Georgia, politics interceded, and in an extraordinarily harmful way, in military matters and the life of the colony's leading military figure in a manner and extent unrivaled in any other colony. One irony of it all is that Button Gwinnett, a parvenu, manipulator, backstabber, and principal detractor not only of McIntosh but also of his siblings, lives on as Georgia's principal revolutionary figure.[72] The principal county adjacent to Atlanta is Gwinnett County with nearly a million inhabitants (943,000 in 2020). Meanwhile, Lachlan McIntosh, Georgia's foremost revolutionary figure, languishes in obscurity.[73] A principal memorial to him is a smallish rural southeastern county on the coast with 14,000 inhabitants, approximating that of all of 1775 revolutionary-era Georgia.[74]

PART II

Southerners and the Earliest Beginnings of War

7

Battle of Point Pleasant (1774)

Historians recite and school children learn that the Revolutionary War began with Lexington and Concord on April 19, 1775. Certain Revolutionary War cognoscenti would argue that the Battle of Point Pleasant on October 10, 1774, was the first military engagement of the war. The battle took place below the confluence of the Kanahwa and Ohio rivers in what today is West Virginia. A British royal governor, Lord Dunmore of Virginia, rather than American patriots, conceived of an expedition, a two-pronged affair, originating at Fort Pitt in western Pennsylvania and Augusta County in western Virginia. The proposed action's objective was neither British soldiers nor soldiers of any kind, say, Hessians or Brunswickers. Rather, the opposition consisted of a confederation of 500–600 Indians from various tribes under the leadership of Shawnee Chief Cornstalk.

In 1774, Lord Dunmore chose Virginian Andrew Lewis to lead the southern contingent of volunteers in what was the first of two "Dunmore's Wars." Colonel Lewis assembled his force, leading then up through country with which he was familiar, the Greenbrier region, from his days as a surveyor. A hundred miles northwest of Augusta, in the lower Shenandoah Valley, Lewis and his party picked up a trail along the Kanawha River southeast of present-day Charleston, West Virginia, following the river forty-five miles northwest to just below the Kanawha-Ohio confluence.

Andrew Lewis's 1,000-man force was only one portion of a planned two-pronged offensive. As to the second prong, from northern Virginia, "Colonel Adam Stephen would accompany Governor Dunmore with militia from Frederick, Berkeley, and Hampshire Counties and proceed to Fort Dunmore (Fort Pitt) and from there down the Ohio" from western Pennsylvania. Under Andrew Lewis, "men collected from Augusta and Botecourt [sic] counties would journey overland to the mouth of the Kanawha River," there to join forces with Dunmore.[1] The purpose was to quell the Indians, who had loosely united, threatening settlements on the western flank of Virginia as well as western Pennsylvania. Lord Dunmore's and Adam Stephen's (to be a major general in the Revolutionary War) contingent was to journey down the Ohio River on flatboats for a score of miles, then proceed overland, westward through the Ohio territory. Eventually, the Dunmore-Stephen contingent was to rendezvous with the Lewis contingent at Point Pleasant. Dunmore and Stephen never showed. Instead, they continued to proceed inland, raiding several Indian villages and engaging in minor skirmishes.

7. Battle of Point Pleasant

With a 500–600 warrior band, in the main Shawnee and Mingo, Chief Cornstalk led an attack on the Lewis camp on October 10, 1774.[2] A full day of fighting, furious at times and degenerating into hand-to-hand combat, followed. That night the defeated Indians, as was their custom, recovered their dead and escaped back across the Ohio River.[3] "The spirit of the Indians had been broken, and Cornstalk was ready to sue for peace."[4] The Lewis force that day on the Kanawha included Andrew's brother Charles; his brother William's son, John Lewis; and three of Andrew's six sons, one of whom was wounded in the battle.[5] Overall, the Virginia Militia suffered 75 killed and 100 wounded. The victory forced the Indians to sign the Treaty of Charlotte, ceding all lands south of the Ohio River to the colony of Virginia.

Today the Point Pleasant Battle site boasts little more than a historical marker. In comparison, Lexington and Concord rate a national park, preservation of the bridge from which the minuteman "fired the shot heard round the world," statues and memorials to the patriot militia, and more. The paucity of memorials at Point Pleasant should not relegate the engagement to the low point it has merited in most historical works about American progress to independence and freedom.[6]

8

Largely Forgotten

Brigadier Andrew Lewis of Virginia

"He looks like a genius of the forest, and the very ground seems to tremble as he walks along," a Colonel Stewart who served under Brigadier Lewis said of him. Continuing, Stewart reported Lewis "as of upwards of six feet tall, of uncommon strength and agility ... stern [of] countenance and of reserved and distant deportment."[1] To Alexander Reed of Rockbridge County, Virginia, who served under him at Point Pleasant (Chapter 7), Lewis "was a man of reserved manners, and great dignity of character somewhat on the order of George Washington."[2] A third account states, "He was at least six feet tall, and had a shock of unruly red hair.... He was so respected and feared by those who served under him that it was said by them that 'the ground quaked beneath his feet when he walked.'"[3] Lewis was of Celtic stock. Like many of Irish descent, Lewis maintained his red hair through middle age and beyond.

Despite those accolades, memories of and memorials to General Lewis are few. A truly forgotten general of the Revolution, then, has been Andrew Lewis. A Revolutionary War historical article bore the title, "The Neglected Andrew Lewis."[4] A Richmond newspaper piece's caption read, "Andrew Who? The Famous Virginian You Might Not Know."[5] Lewis, though, has not been forgotten altogether. Lewisburg, West Virginia, the seat of Greenbrier County, West Virginia, lies within a region Andrew Lewis first surveyed, in 1745–1750, and the county seat, Lewisburg, bears his name.[6] A few other memorabilia exist.[7]

Outside of West Virginia's panhandle, the only memorial stands, paradoxically, on the Virginia Capitol Grounds in Richmond. A likeness of Lewis stands as one of five figures on the plinth for a George Washington equestrian statue. The other supporting figures are political rather than military leaders, although John Marshall, later fourth Chief Justice of the United States, fought in the Revolution as a young man.[8] How Lewis's likeness, rather than, say, General Mercer's or General Muhlenberg's, appeared there is not indicated.

Apparent Facts

One salient fact is how many American Revolutionary War generals were immigrants themselves or direct descendants of immigrants from countries that

Andrew Lewis statue, Salem, Virginia. Of Irish stock, Lewis is largely unknown outside of Virginia's southern Shenandoah Valley (author photo).

suffered under English rule, namely, Ireland and Scotland (*see* Chapter 4). Andrew Lewis was born in 1720 in County Donegal, Ireland, and emigrated with his parents in 1732.[9] Fleeing Ireland because John Lewis, Andrew's father, had struck, or killed, his landlord (stories differ), the Lewis family settled in the far western region of central Virginia, over the Blue Ridge and under the shadow of the Alleghenies. Andrew's parents, John "The Pioneer" and Margaret, were the first residents of that area, around which a town, Staunton, grew. Local history records Lewis Senior as the city's founder.

In their youth, Andrew and brother Thomas trained as land surveyors. For fifteen years, beginning about 1740, the two brothers mapped an area about 100 miles southwest of Staunton, now Botetourt, Goodpasture, and Greenbrier Counties, then sprawling Augusta County. Beginning a decade after they had commenced, the brothers surveyed "for the Greenbrier Land Company, a consortium of speculators ... [who had] been granted 100,000 acres on condition that they survey and eventually settle the land."[10]

One story is that, indirectly at least, Andrew Lewis named the region. While surveying, he was caught up in one of the numerous bramble patches, which he called "Green Briars."[11] The appellation lived on in Greenbrier River, Greenbrier County, and the Greenbrier Resort.[12]

Andrew Lewis never lived in the Greenbrier region. Instead, in the early 1740s, he purchased 640 acres of land seventy-five miles south of Staunton. There, Andrew and wife Elizabeth built a home they christened Richfield, where they parented seven children: six sons and one daughter (Ann). The Lewises were the first settlers. Thus, like father, like son. Andrew Lewis became for Salem, Virginia, as his father, John, had become for Staunton: founders of the cities. Although smaller (25,000 residents) and a satellite town of sorts, Salem rather than the larger city of Roanoke (population 100,000) became the seat of Roanoke County, Virginia, and is important in its own right.[13]

French and Indian War Service

In terms of military exploits, Andrew Lewis is known for three principal endeavors. The second is the Battle of Point Pleasant against the Shawnee and Chief Cornstalk, said to be the first battle of the Revolutionary War (Chapter 7). Third was Lewis's command of the Virginia and Continental forces at the 1776 Battle of Gwynn's Island that forced the Scottish colonial governor, Lord Dunmore, and his small Tory army, from Virginia for good, after the second "Dunmore's War."

First was Lewis's extensive French and Indian War experience. Andrew Lewis served as George Washington's and later Adam Stephen's second-in-command of Virginia contingents supporting the British forays to Western Pennsylvania and the "Forks of the Ohio."[14] In 1755, the 300-man Virginia Regiment, under George Washington, accompanied British General Edward Braddock northwest from Winchester and Cumberland on the 144-mile diagonal trek toward the French Fort Duquesne. The expedition involved a long march over the Alleghenies, to what today is the site of Pittsburgh, where the Allegheny and Monongahela Rivers join to form the Ohio, gateway to the west.

Andrew Lewis was not present at the Battle of Monongahela, at which a French and Indian force decisively defeated the British force, fatally wounding General Edward Braddock. Braddock had held George Washington, Andrew Lewis, and the Virginia force in reserve, ready to support British Major Horatio Gates (wounded in the battle). Of Braddock's 1,459 troops, 914 men and 63 officers were killed or wounded, a disastrous defeat for the British.

On the retreat, Lewis was present when General Braddock died several score miles southwest of the battle. At Great Meadows, amidst the mountains, the defeated army re-formed. Washington and Lewis found their troops disorganized, useless for battle should the enemy pursue them: "What was still worse [than the defeat], it was no sooner dark than one-half our Men got drunk."[15]

After the Braddock Expedition

Lewis was active in the interlude that followed the Braddock expedition. As with settlements in Eastern Pennsylvania, settlers in Virginia's Shenandoah Valley and the Alleghenies' first range were subject to Indian war parties sortieing eastward out of the mountains to rape, murder, burn, and pillage. To protect the southern settlements, Colonel George Washington selected Andrew Lewis, who lived in a southern Virginia region particularly susceptible to Indian depredations. For the

Sandy Creek expedition, Lewis assembled a 340-man force. Beginning in February 1756, Lewis led a search and destroy mission that "encountered an acute shortage of provisions, unfordable rivers, and desertions. After several weeks," Professor Harry Ward recorded, "Lewis had to abandon the mission."[16] Other interactions with raiding Indians, including with the renegade Killabuck, followed.[17]

July 1758 began Andrew Lewis's most significant military experience yet. He led a contingent of 200 Virginians north toward Bedford, Pennsylvania, where they joined 400 other Virginians under Adam Stephen. The 600-man force was to support General John Forbes's expedition. The Scottish Forbes had chosen a straight east-west route over the Alleghenies rather than the diagonal route Braddock had chosen three years earlier.

The east-west Forbes Road reached a site fifty miles east of Fort Duquesne. There the 1,850 British (two regiments) and the 600 Americans built Fort Loyalhanna, née Ligonier, on the banks of Loyalhanna Creek.[18] From the fort, the Swiss-born Forbes' second-in-command, Colonel Henry Bouquet, sent an 800-man reconnaissance party toward Fort Duquesne. Scottish Colonel James Grant led the 800-troop of 600 Highlanders and 200 Virginians under Andrew Lewis. On September 14, 1758, Grant bought the force to within a quarter mile of the French Fort Duquesne. Thinking the fort garrisoned by only 200 French and Indians, rather than waiting and observing, the reckless Grant had Captain William McDonald and 100 Highlanders march "up to the fort with drums beating." A French and Indian force many times larger than 200 emerged, defeating Grant and his force. The French wounded Andrew Lewis, taking him prisoner, transporting him to Montreal or Quebec City (accounts differ).[19] The French held Colonel Lewis there for nearly a year, finally releasing him for return to Virginia.

The Next Principal Episodes

Returning to Virginia, Andrew Lewis became a leader of the south Augusta County Militia. During the 1760s and early 1770s, he served in the House of Burgesses and later in the Virginia Conventions that came into existence after British Governor Lord Dunmore dissolved the House of Burgesses. Lewis demonstrated inspired leadership on many fronts. In 1774, Lord Dunmore chose Lewis to lead the southwestern contingent of volunteers in what was the first of two "Dunmore's Wars" (Chapter 7).

The "Second" Lord Dunmore's War

In the 1760s, Lewis assisted George Washington in the construction of several of the fifteen small forts along the Alleghenies' front range to protect settlers from Native American raids. In those and other endeavors, "Lewis and Washington became both friends and close business associates."[20] In 1775, Congress created the Continental Army. George Washington asked that Lewis be made a brigadier general. At the time, Washington wrote to his brother that he, Washington, had "always look'd upon [Lewis] as a man of spirit and a good Officer—his experience is equal to any we have."[21] Despite Washington's regard, "[t]he Continental Congress had decided that there should only be one general from each state [later increased to three], and Virginia's position had already gone to Charles Lee."[22]

Nonetheless, a short time later, on March 1, 1776, Congress created Lewis a brigadier. Andrew Lewis, then, not Charles Lee, commanded Virginia forces in the Revolutionary War's first chapters. In his 776-page treatise, *The British Are Coming*, Rich Atkinson mentions Andrew Lewis but once, highlighting Lewis's obscurity. Nonetheless, Atkinson's description of the final engagement in Lord Dunmore's [Second] War, the battle of Gwynn's Island, framed the issue nicely: "At eight A.M. on Tuesday, July 9 [1776], ten rebel militia companies from Williamsburg massed along the shoreline with half a dozen guns. Their commander, General Andrew Lewis, personally touched the first match to an 18 pounder."[23] In this war within the war, Dunmore's pocket army had lost at the battle of Great Bridge, burned the city of Norfolk, and raided coastal Virginia towns.

Then, in July 1776, prior to the small war's final installment, Dunmore's small flotilla anchored seaward of a narrow barrier island, Gwynn's Island, on the Chesapeake Bay's western shore. From the mainland, General Lewis and his artillery arched shots over the island, striking in and around Dunmore's fleet anchored on the other side. One militia cannon shot scored a direct hit on Dunmore's flagship. Splinters flew, striking Dunmore, who suffered moderate wounds. Showing himself to be a paper tiger, and sensing his army's vulnerability, Dunmore ordered the ships to weigh anchor, leaving the lee of Gwynn's Island. In a feint, the Dunmore fleet sailed up Chesapeake Bay, then turned, and finally sailed out to sea, bound for New York. This departure from the Chesapeake ended Lord Dunmore's second "Dunmore's War."

Gainsayers

Critics at the time faulted Andrews Lewis for Gwynn's Island. For instance, Lieutenant Thomas Townes, present at the bombardment, wrote, "Lewis who after the enemy (Lord Dunmore) were vanquished proved a traitor and suffered them to escape." Critics in Virginia "perceived Lewis as letting Dunmore flee Gwynn's Island, an act they considered insufferable."[24] That criticism was wide of the mark, failing to appreciate the situation Lewis faced. Gwynn's Island, over which Lewis's force would have charged in assaulting Dunmore's fleet, was littered with freed slaves infected with smallpox, a deadly and highly infectious disease that was humans' greatest fear at the time: "A grisly sight awaited the American troops ... at Gwynn's Island, dead and dying blacks strewn along a path for two miles. Smallpox had taken a heavy toll among Dunmore's 'Ethiopians,' the slaves who had answered the governor's emancipation proclamation."[25] Smallpox worried Benjamin Rush of the Continental Congress most of all. Dr. Rush warned, "Smallpox was the 'King of Terrors,' the enemy to be feared more than any other" by the American Army.[26] Eighteenth Century smallpox rivaled Fourteenth Century's black death as a killer, highly communicable, resulting in high fevers, pustules, and sores oozing pus over much of the body, with blindness and death quickly eventuating for fifty percent of those who contracted the disease. As the Revolutionary War progressed, the disease decimated whole armies, both British and American.[27]

Troops began to practice crude self-inoculation by taking pus from infected acquaintances and forcing the pus under their fingernails, thus causing a mild case of smallpox but creating antibodies. Among the civilian populace, the technique "was to make a small incision, then with a quill scoop the 'pus from the ripe pustules' of a smallpox victim into the open cut."[28] Self-inoculation was not safe but did offer some protection.[29]

Owing to the proximity of officers and men in the Revolution, smallpox often struck and travelled among the military with ferocity. Troops retreating from the failed Quebec assault saw their leader, Major General John Thomas, a Massachusetts physician, die June 2, 1776, "[b]lind and disfigured beyond recognition" from smallpox.[30] The army quarantined several thousand smallpox victims on the Ile aux Noix on the Richelieu River flowing between the Saint Lawrence and Lake Champlain. Returning from the failed Canadian expedition, half the American force died of smallpox, known as "the pestilence that walketh in darkness." In *The British Are Coming*, Rick Atkinson summarizes: "Day by day, twenty to fifty men fell ill in each regiment," of fifteen regiments.[31] "[S]o ended a botched campaign,"[32] fueling the universal terror the dreaded smallpox inspired.

No doubt the prospect of mass infection from passing near the dead and dying animated General Lewis's decision not to send troops pell-mell across the narrow barrier island after Lord Dunmore and his small flotilla.

Early Resignation and Withdrawal from the Military

Virginia Generals Edward Stevens and George Weedon withdrew from the Continental Army and returned to their homes. Neither, however, withdrew from matters military, becoming militia leaders. Andrew Lewis was different. His military careers, both Continental Line and Virginia Militia, came to a halt when he resigned on April 15, 1777. A difference between Lewis, on one hand, and Stevens or Weedon, on the other, was age. At the time he left the service, Lewis was 57 years of age, equivalent to mid-seventies today. Lewis pleaded ill health as a reason for resignation and return to Richfield.

To others, though, the last straw to Lewis was Congress's promotion, in February 1777, of five brigadier generals, all junior to Lewis, to the rank of major general.[33] Undoubtedly, remembering that Congress ignored George Washington's high praise and chose the ex–Britisher Charles Lee over him in 1775, Andrew Lewis felt hurt, alienated by the 1777 major general promotions list.

In 1777, Lewis corresponded with the commander-in-chief. George Washington answered, begging Lewis not to resign:

> I was much disappointed at not perceiving your name in the list of major generals lately made by Congress. [I] most sincerely wish that the neglect may not induce you to abandon the

service. Let me beseech You to reflect That the period is now arrived ... when it is highly and indispensably for Gentlemen of Abilities in any Line, but more especially in the Military one, to Withhold themselves from public employment.... The Cause requires your Aid—No one wishes it more than I do.[34]

Further pleas failed to sway the dissatisfied brigadier, who resigned from the army.[35] He wrote again to his friend Washington, expressing bitterness at what he believed had happened. Lewis found some solace at what had happened to Charles Lee, whom Congress vaulted to major general over the battle-hardened Andrew Lewis: "I hope Congress are happy in the proofs they have given of their fallibility in giving promotion out of the line of Seniority."[36] Lewis went on to remind Washington of the inglorious ends of two newly minted major generals, Adam Stephen and General Arthur St. Clair.[37]

In fact, of the five generals Congress promoted over Lewis's head, at least four came to unfortunate and blameworthy ends:

- The Continental Army court martialed Adam Stephen, with his punishment being cashiered from the army.
- Arthur St. Clair faced a court martial for the abandonment of Fort Ticonderoga. Although, exonerated, nonetheless, he never again commanded troops in the Revolutionary War.[38]
- Lord Stirling descended deeper into the alcoholism that rendered him useless as military leader.[39]
- Thomas Mifflin was a central figure in the Conway Cabal to oust George Washington, performed poorly as Quartermaster General, and argued with and criticized George Washington.[40]
- Only Benjamin Lincoln remained free of blots on his record. He ended the war as commander of the Southern Army, surrendering his command to the British at Charles Town, South Carolina, in May 1780. He became a prisoner of war, seeing no further action.[41]

Richfield

Belying any lasting case of ill health, General Lewis continued political positions and appointments. In 1778, the United States appointed him commissioner to parlay with and enter treaties with the Native Americans of Western Pennsylvania and the Ohio Territory. In that connection, Lewis traveled from Virginia to Fort Pitt in Pennsylvania. In a contemporaneous letter to Washington, Lewis complained, "I arrived at this place [Fort Pitt] on the 1st instant but found neither Indians, agent, or Commissioner from the State of Pennsylvania nor the instructions which I was told would be found on my Arrival." In common with many other high-ranking Continental Army officers and ex-officers, Lewis further lamented the "Disappointments and Embarrassments that seem to attend" all, or most all, of what Congress did.[42]

In 1780, Governor Thomas Jefferson appointed Andrew Lewis to the Governor's Council, which at that time functioned as the legislature's upper house.[43] The term Council was often used.[44] Traveling home from Richmond, where he had attended a Council meeting, Lewis fell ill. He died in Bedford County, Virginia, midway between Lynchburg and Roanoke and less than 30 miles from home. He passed away on September 28, 1781, several days before the British surrender at Yorktown. His widow and six surviving children buried him in Salem, Virginia, next to his youngest son, Charles. Andrew Lewis was 60 years old. Historians have dubbed him "Virginia's most unsung Revolutionary War hero."[45]

9

The Failed Assault on Charles Town (1776)

Coastal South Carolina produced, sold, and exported rice, indigo, and other crops. The city of Charles Town, with 10,000 residents, was the colonies' wealthiest city, the pearl of America's south. The great success of Charles Town's exports bought large stores of foreign goods that wealthier inhabitants used to purchase English imports (carriages, jewelry, dresses, suits, and other accoutrements) to mimic English manners. The town's wealthier citizens were dandies, Anglophiles of the first order. On the dark side, however, plantations' economic success derived from the labors of enslaved African Americans, who constituted over sixty percent of the colony's population, the highest proportion in the slaveholding colonies (principally Virginia, North Carolina, and South Carolina).

Aftermath of the North Carolina Battle of Moore's Creek Bridge

In February 1776, 2,000 or more British soldiers waited aboard transports anchored in North Carolina' Cape Fear estuary. The British grand plan called for the troops to disembark and link up with Scottish Loyalists marching southeast. British General Henry Clinton would lead the Loyalist-regular combined force on an incursion into the southern colonies, attacking the patriots' soft underbelly.

Richard Caswell and his men visited a devastating defeat to the Highland Loyalists at the Battle of Moore's Creek Bridge, February 27, 1776 (Chapter 4). The remnants of the Highland force fled; the British troops never disembarked. Hearing of the colonialists' unequivocal victory, General Clinton directed that the invasion be aborted, with the troops staying aboard.

Charles Town Prepares

About the same time as the failed British incursion into North Carolina, in February 1776, Congress created the Army's Southern Department. On February 29, Congress put the British soldier of fortune, Major General Charles Lee, "its star general," in command of the Southern Department, charging him with setting up defenses along the mid–Atlantic and southern state coastlines, with their many bays, inlets, and estuaries.[1] Soon thereafter, Lee wrote to General Washington, "I feel like a dog in a dancing school. I know not where to turn myself, where to fix myself…. The uncertainty of the enemy's designs and motives, who can fly in an instant to any spot they choose…."[2] Rick Atkinson, in *The British Are Coming*, records that Lee first spent six weeks along the Virginia coast, "with his dogs, his gaudy sherryvallies [Spanish chaps], and his draconian military philosophy."[3] Already over-the-top and vainglorious, Lee was arrogant and bizarre. Then word came to Lee and the Southern Department that the combined British General Henry Clinton's naval-land force was sailing toward Charles Town, South Carolina, presaging the 1776 first siege of Charles Town. General Lee "hustled southward with 2,000 troops," Virginia and North Carolina Continentals marching south to Charles Town, augmenting the 4,000 troops already in or arriving at the city. Lee set about improving the city's defenses, riding to and fro with his most beloved dog accompanying him.

Inspecting the city's defensive preparations, "[N]othing worried Lee more than the vulnerability of Fort Sullivan," on the three-mile-long barrier island north of the Charles Town harbor entrance. On the island, Lee "considered a flimsy palmetto fort [to be] a 'slaughter pen' for its defenders."[4] A thousand men manned the fort, a square sided fortress with diamond-shaped bastions at its corners.

To South Carolina Militia Colonel William Moultrie, after whom the fort was later named, Lee voiced doomsday sentiments. "Sir, when those [British] ships come to lay alongside your fort, they will knock it down in half an hour," Lee preached.[5] Incessantly, Lee advocated that the locals abandon the fort. "When Lee came to Sullivan's Island, he did not like the post at all … the garrison would be sacrificed … and [Lee] wished to withdraw the garrison and give up the post," William Moultrie remembered.[6]

The opposite occurred. Rather than absorbing enemy fire, the fort's spongy palmetto logs absorbed British cannon balls or caused them to rebound: "To everyone's surprise, the soft palmetto logs (backed by sixteen feet of earth) easily absorbed or deflected the heavy [British] heavy cannonballs."[7] The fort held.

In addition, the British landed ground troops on the next barrier island to the northeast, Long Island (the present-day Isle of Palms). Intelligence, based as it was without any reconnaissance ordered by British General Clinton, informed the British that the troops could splash through the several inches of water that separated Long and Sullivan's islands at low tide. Instead, the channel between the islands was "not eighteen inches deep at low tide, but rather a swampy morass up to seven or more feet deep in places." Across the channel, a force of 780 Americans under Colonel William Thompson stood to impede any British advance down Sullivan's Island toward Fort Moultrie. The British ground troops were marooned, unable to leave Long Island to attack Sullivan's Island.

Faced with these and other missteps, the British re-boarded their ground troops onto transport ships, sailed seaward, turned north, and set sail for New York. Charleston had defeated the British attack.

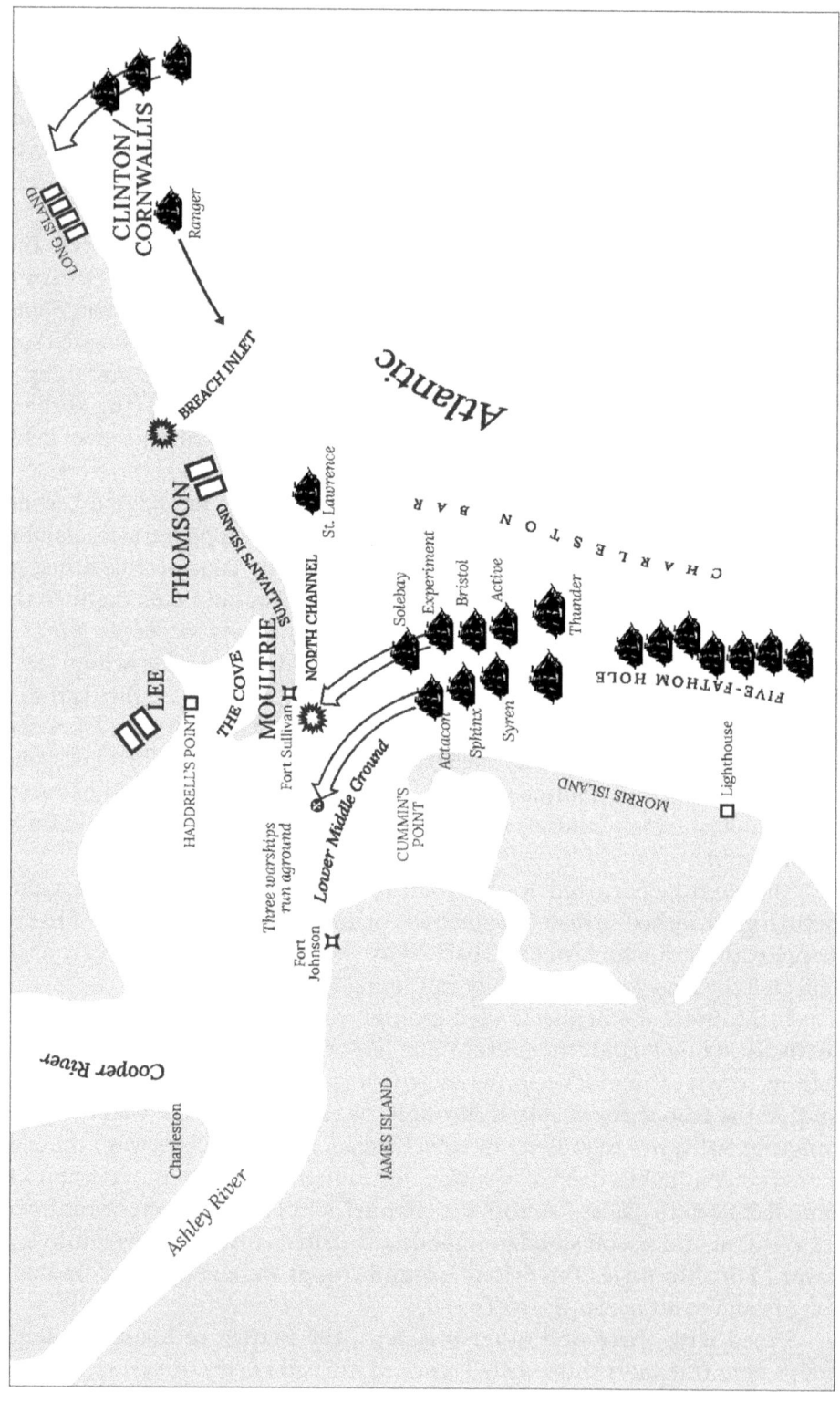

Credit Where Credit Is Due

Again, though, history is much like cement.[8] Quickly a mythical account replaces reality. Thereafter, "[n]o amount of archeology can shake the fairly dust from [the myth's] heels."[9] The cement—the mythical account—was that Charles Lee's efforts, not those of South Carolinians such as William Moultrie, South Carolina President John Rutledge, and militia forces, saved Charleston.[10]

The evening before the British bombardment of Fort Sullivan, Major General Lee, continuing as "rigid, harshly critical, and dictatorial," had resolved to replace the easy-going Moultrie with North Carolina's Colonel, later brigadier, Francis Nash.[11] Colonel Moultrie had disregarded Lee's opinion that the fort was a death trap, a slaughterhouse for Moultrie's men.[12] Lee, however, had some solid evidence. Because there had been no time in which to build a sufficient bridge from the mainland to Sullivan's Island, "an improvised one of planks floated on empty hogsheads ... across the cove was constructed."[13] This bridge proved to be of no value: "[When] 200 North Carolina troops tried to cross it ... [t]he bridge sank before the men were even halfway across."[14] Defenses were sadly lacking, or so it seemed to Lee.

There were other naysayers. American Navy Captain Lempriere had told Colonel Moultrie, "Sir, when those ships come to lay alongside of your fort, they will knock it done a half an hour." The British would have 270 guns firing at the fort, while the patriots had only 25 firing back.[15] Previously, Governor John Rutledge had written to Moultrie, "General Lee ... wishes you to evacuate the fort," to which Rutledge added, "You will not, without an order from me; I would sooner cut off my right arm than write one."[16]

On June 26, Moultrie's steady, cool, and confident personality led to the fort's survival of a ten-hour bombardment and victory over a superior British force. Moultrie lost only twelve men. The British had expended 34,000 pounds of gunpowder, the Americans only 4,766 pounds. Sending three ships—*Sphynx, Acteon,* and *Syren*—toward the cove rear of the fort to bombard the Americans from there, the British ships ran aground. The British abandoned the *Acteon*, the ship permanently lost.[17]

On the American side, the British shot away the South Carolina flag. Sergeant William Jasper retrieved the flag, attached it to a gun sponger, and raised it once more on the fort's rampart.[18] David Russell calls the 1776 Battle of Charles Town "one of the most decisive and pure victories in the South and in the entire American Revolution ... [T]he Southern colonies would remain invasion free for another three years as a result."[19]

One other result was that, on September 16, 1776, the Continental Congress promoted William Moultrie to brigadier general. Another was that South Carolina soon adopted Moultrie's blue ensign with a white star in the upper left corner as the state's flag—with one addition. At the center of the blue field, the state added a stylized rendering of a palmetto palm tree. In memory of what happened that day at Sullivan's Island, South Carolina became the "Palmetto State."[20]

10

Brigadier William Moultrie of South Carolina

A contemporary, William Hollinshead, described Moultrie as "cheerful, manly … unassuming and unostentatious … easy, affable and [an] agreeable companion."[1] He was later described as always "genial."[2] Physically, Moultrie was not quite obese, though well-padded, understandable as he was 46 years old by the time the war commenced. "Moultrie's character and disposition made him … kind and benevolent." In military matters, he was criticized "by superior officers for being too easy and goodhearted to maintain proper discipline. [But] these qualities endeared him to his men."[3] That regard, too, was understandable. A life-long resident of Charles Town, Moultrie personally knew his 19–20-year-old soldiers, as well as their parents and family members. He routinely fraternized with his men, "many of whom he had known for a long time."[4] Younger officers looked up to Moultrie as, for example, did Francis Marion of motion picture fame, who regarded Moultrie as his "mentor."[5]

Andrew Lewis of Virginia (Chapter 8) is not the only southern brigadier to have "won his spurs" early in the war. William Moultrie belongs in that group, having led the defense of Charles Town in June 1776 against an overwhelming British land and sea assault. The then Colonel "Moultrie's gallant leadership … and intrepid determination of his officers and men were the keys to the battle on June 28, 1776."[6] In his book, *Anecdotes of the American Revolution*, Andrew Garden compared the stand of "Moultrie and his South Carolinians on Sullivan's Island," foreclosing British entry into Charles Town's harbor "to Leonidas and the Spartans at Thermopylae."[7] Author C.L. Bragg's biography adds, "Hyperbole aside, the battle now known as the Battle of Fort Moultrie was the first absolute American victory, and ranks with the three most decisive victories of the Revolutionary War."[8] Based upon that one event, public remembrance and reverence for Moultrie were sharp creases pressed across his life even though he served with distinction all the days of the war.

Action Aside from the 1776 Defense of Charles Town

Moultrie's greatness at the 1776 siege shades from view William Moultrie's continuous leadership of South Carolina's Continentals and Militia. Before the siege, in November 1775, Moultrie led the troops that retook Fort Johnson on James Island, looking east over the Ashley River and Charles Town beyond. He also supervised the sinking of hulks in the Cooper River on the east, or opposite side, of the city.[9] After 1776, he was heavily involved defending the "Palmetto State."

Culture Wars Within the War

A characteristic prominent in the South was the influence that conflicting regions, religions, and cultures had on the war's prosecution (*see e.g.*, Chapter 23). Moultrie was a paradigmatic example of the phenomenon. Coastal aristocrat upbringing versus backcountry hard scabble origins; Episcopalian versus Presbyterian belief systems, English versus Scottish or Irish loyalties—in the South, these varying attributes played larger roles in terms of assignments and promotions than they did elsewhere.[10] Over time, differing treatments ameliorated, but they had an immeasurable effect. Andrew Pickens' biographer, Rod Andrew, makes the point:

> [South Carolina's] Provincial Assembly had appointed men of property, prestige, and usually aristocratic origins to the command or regiments and brigades—men with names like Moultrie, Pinckney, and Gadsden. By the time the war ended, the leading warrior chieftains on the state—Sumter, Marion, and Pickens—were all men from humbler backgrounds..... [These men] owed their military rank not to the Charleston elites ... but rather to the simple fact that other men had chosen to follow them in the darkest days of the war.[11]

Andrew's observation does not ring true for William Moultrie, who remained a hands-on leader for the war's duration.

Further adding to the mix was that the primary sources of the colony's wealth, elevating it to status as the richest, were the growth and sale of rice and indigo grown in the low country, the fifty or so miles closest the sea. From the coast, plantation owners sold their products via English factors, shipped to Britain or its possessions in the Caribbean. Prosperity had its source in great numbers of enslaved people to work plantations' fields, on the one hand, and Britain, on the other. As a result of the latter, in South Carolina at least, Tories outnumbered Whigs two-to-one:[12] "Many low country inhabitants were by no means ready to take measures that might permanently sever ties with England." The hero of Charles Town was an exception: "[W]hen the tocsin of war finally sounded Moultrie stood ready to unsheathe his sword."[13] Coastal aristocrats had wealth and influence; backcountry partisans had little of either.[14]

Military Apprenticeship in Colonial Days

As has been seen, most all southern brigadiers had prior military experience.[15] In the Carolinas, prior military experience involved the 1758–1763 excursions against the Cherokee villages of western North and South Carolina.[16] For instance, General William Lee Davidson (Chapter 23) of North Carolina served under militia general Griffin Rutherford in the 1759 Lyttelton expedition (William Lyttelton, Royal Governor of North Carolina, 1756–1760). In 1761, Andrew Pickens "served under several young officers who, like him, would later become leaders in South Carolina's Revolutionary War: Henry Laurens, William Moultrie, Frances Marion, and

Isaac Huger."[17] In 1760–1761, William Moultrie commanded a company in the newly created South Carolina Provisional Army: "Francis Marion became his lieutenant. Isaac Huger and Andrew Pickens were also company-grade field officers."[18]

These early military exploits provided experience of "living rough"—sleeping on the ground, braving the elements, trekking through thick forest, and crossing rivers and streams—while leading men.[19] From the standpoint of generalship, in the Cherokee excursions as others in the French and Indian War, future high-ranking officers learned lessons: maintenance of morale; regard for supply lines; transportation of men, artillery, food and forage; keeping units together on the march; observance of camp sanitation standards, imperfect as they were; and much more.

The Young William Moultrie

Born in 1730, Moultrie was the second son of a Scottish surgeon who emigrated directly to Charles Town in 1728, practicing medicine until his death in 1771. William's older brother John and younger brother James emigrated to the British colony of East Florida, where they occupied various governmental posts (attorney general, chief justice, governor). Moultrie's brothers spent the war and postwar as dyed-in-the-wool Loyalists.[20]

Moultrie, unlike his brothers, was a patriot revolutionary. He married Damaris de Julien in 1749, one wealthy family marrying into another wealthy family. "The Moultrie-de Julien union secured," once and for all, "William's wealth and social standing in Carolina low country society." In 1752, William obtained title to 1,020-acre plantation (rice and indigo) thirty-five miles north of Charles Town (Northampton Plantation, "North Hampton"). Later Moultrie acquired additional hundreds of acres as well as lots in the city. Moultrie had ascended to the upper reaches of low country aristocracy. Again, "[l]ow country Carolinians," including Moultrie, became "excessively fond of British manners, trying to emulate them in every way—clothes, architecture, furniture, carriages."[21]

Mixed Views of His Character

At times, superiors perceived Moultrie's attributes, good natured and laid-back, as detrimental to the accomplishment of military

William Moultrie, by Charles Willson Peale. This wealthy South Carolinian was the guardian of Charles Town not only at Sullivan's Island but for the duration of Charles Town's independence (National Portrait Gallery).

objectives, such as the construction on Sullivan's Island. David Russell in *The American Revolution in the Southern Colonies* summarizes widely held views: Moultrie "was known to be careless in the performance of his duties, a poor disciplinarian at times, and [lacking in] the punctuality expected of a military officer. ... Regardless of the total character of the officer, Colonel Moultrie was a gallant officer in battle."[22] Said Thomas Ferguson of the South Carolina Committee of Safety, "Col. Moultrie is a good man, but indolent and easy, so things go very slowly."[23] Recall that the evening before the British bombardment of Fort Sullivan, Major General Lee, Southern Department Commander, had resolved to replace the easy-going Moultrie with North Carolina's Colonel, later brigadier, Francis Nash.[24]

British Threats from Florida and the Backcountry

Following on Colonel Moultrie's and his men's successful defense of Charles Town, in late summer 1776, "the waspish and nit-picking General Lee" conceived of an advance on St. Augustine, capital of British East Florida.[25] Lee persuaded a doubting, reluctant Moultrie to join Lee and the expedition, which Moultrie did with 240 South Carolina troops. Then the Continental Congress ordered Lee northward. Lee took with him North Carolina and Virginia troops, leaving South Carolina's Moultrie in command of the expeditionary force. Needing to traverse the lengthy Georgia coast, "Moultrie's men—in hot and humid weather, transiting buggy, swampy terrain, and clothed in heavy woolen uniforms, were decimated by disease and death." Having crossed the Savannah River into Georgia, Moultrie halted the march at Sunbury, a score or so miles below Savannah. The force returned to South Carolina, in abandonment of Lee's proposal.[26]

Buildup to Charles Town's Fall

In 1777, Lord Germain succeeded Lord Dartmouth as American secretary to King George III. Germain became convinced "that the large number of Loyalists in the southern colonies, would facilitate restoration of British control."[27] Accordingly, London authorities directed North American commanders once more to redirect the British effort south. The Continental Congress responded by appointing Major General Benjamin Lincoln of Massachusetts new commander of the Southern Department, replacing the discredited North Carolina Brigadier Robert Howe, who remained commanding the Savannah garrison.[28] Further, Congress directed 1,000 Virginia and 3,000 North Carolina troops to assist Lincoln in the defense of South Carolina and Georgia.

When a 4,000-man British force under General Henry Clinton left Sandy Hook in New York's outer harbor aboard a flotilla of transports on November 26, 1778, new phase of the war had begun. Lord Cornwallis sailed from Ireland with 1,500 additional British regulars.[29] At Christmas 1778, the British force arrived at the mouth of the Savannah River, eighty-five miles below Charles Town. On December 29, a 3,000-man British force attacked Savannah. Finding an undefended pathway through swamps, the British light infantry overwhelmed the garrison of 700 Americans. The American force, summed Robert Howe's biographers Charles Bennett and Donald Lennon, "collapsed almost at once and degenerated into a desperate mob."[30]

Observing from South Carolina, Moultrie termed Howe's choice to defend Savannah "the most ill-advised, rash opinion that possibly could be given; it was absurd to suppose that 700 men, some of them raw troops, could stand up against 2 or 3,000 as good [a force of] troops as any the British had."[31] The commander could have evacuated the city, freeing the troops to fight another day.

Moultrie's Second and Third Defenses of Charles Town

Historians tend to treat the 1780 second defense of Charles Town as a one-off event, four years after the Battle of Sullivan's Island. In truth, between the two sieges, the British threatened Charles Town repeatedly after their investiture in Savannah late in 1778. In those subsequent threats to Charles Town, William Moultrie pulled the laboring oar for the Americans, just as he had in 1775.

For example, at Port Royal, south near the coast, Moultrie and his men defended Charles Town, albeit in less dramatic fashion. In early February 1779, General Lincoln sent Moultrie with 350 troops to Port Royal, 70 road miles below Charles Town. Port Royal was the island upon which Beaufort and Fort Lyttelton were located. From Savannah, the British had landed a small-to-medium size force, appearing to be exploring an initial stepping stone enroute to another British attempt to take Charles Town. Moultrie and his men entered Beaufort on February 3, 1779, finding the place practically deserted. Pulling a short way back, Moultrie and his fellow patriots defended the Beaufort Road against an advancing British force. After an hour, the patriot force ran low on ammunition. Moultrie "ordered a slow withdrawal, but before the Americans began to pull back, the redcoats started retreating." The affair was small but "South Carolina militia had vanquished British regulars who were forced to take to their boats and return to Savannah." The British left fourteen dead and wounded.[32] "The American dragoons made chase but only a few [retreating] British were taken."[33]

After the engagement, the forty-eight-year-old Moultrie reminisced, "I find my old bones yield much to fatigue; I hope, however, they will carry me through the war." Reporting upon Port Royal, a Charles Town newspaper quoted a patriot officer, "He [Moultrie] acted like himself, and his countenance inspired everyone."[34]

Continuing Defense of Charles Town

With reinforcements from the north, General Lincoln's southern army had grown to 7,000 men, spread over a hundred miles, from Augusta, Georgia, to Purrysburg, above Savannah. Moultrie captained 2,000 troops at Purrysburg. A council of war—Lincoln, Moultrie, and Brigadiers Isaac Huger and Jethro Sumner—approved Lincoln's plan to shift troops 80–90 miles upriver to meet a Loyalist threat around

Augusta. On April 20, Lincoln set off with 2,000 troops, arriving there two days later. The council of war had also instructed Moultrie that, should the British advance into South Carolina, he should fall back from Black Swamp where he and his men were then located, covering roads, bridges, and fords on South Carolina byways leading toward Charles Town.

The next threat to Charles Town came in April 1777. On April 28, British Lieutenant Colonel Mark Provost led 2,000 redcoats out of Savannah toward Charles Town. Back at Purrysburg, several miles from Savannah, as instructed, General Lachlan McIntosh of Georgia pulled the garrison back to Coosahatchie, where General Moultrie joined them. The American force continued backing toward Charles Town, messaging Lincoln, who was upriver menacing Augusta, to return downriver. The Americans also were destroying bridges to slow the British advance. On May 6, the American force reached Dorchester, 24 miles northwest of Charles Town, and on May 9, McIntosh, Moultrie, and 600 men marched into the city.[35]

In *The Southern Strategy*, David Wilson notes, "[T]he danger posed by backcountry Tories [around Augusta] was not enough to warrant Lincoln taking the better part of the southern army upriver.... Lincoln held Moultrie at Black Swamp as a precaution, but the void created by [Lincoln's] absence would place Charlestown in serious jeopardy." The fault lay in Lincoln and the other generals "interpreting British stirrings as a feint when instead British activity," a major sortie out of Savannah, "represented an advance that ultimately would lead to Charles Town."[36]

Further Threats to the South's "Holy City"

In May 1779, British General Prevost, with a force of twenty-five hundred, threatened Charles Town from James and Johns Islands to the south, for a brief time reaching the Ashley Riverbank, across from the city itself. James and Johns are sizeable, although at 84 square miles James is much larger. They lie inland from the thin barrier islands fronting onto the Atlantic, James and Johns being separated from each other and from the mainland by what was known as the Stono River.[37] An island route offered General Prevost a good route of retreat should a return to British-held Savannah prove necessary. Further, the islands' swamps, bays, and inlets lent security to an invading force. From their vantage point on James Island, the British withdrew to Johns Island, south of James.

Finally, General Lincoln, with his force of nearly 2,000, returned from Augusta in late May 1779. Having augmented his force with other men, Lincoln devised a plan to meet the British threat. With 3,000 Continental regulars and North Carolina and Virginia militia, he would attack the British force guarding the Stono Ferry that crossed from the mainland to Johns Island. In support, General Moultrie would cross the Ashley River, James Island, and by water cross to Johns Island, attacking the enemy from the rear.

Two impediments sprung up, namely, a shortage of boats for Moultrie's force to cross the Ashley and a very stiff resistance by 800 British defending the ferry crossing, stopping Lincoln, who had anticipated light resistance. As a result of the first factor, Moultrie and his men were still twelve miles away when Lincoln's group attacked at the ferry crossing. Meeting fierce opposition, the Americans withdrew, giving the British a tactical victory in the June 1779 battle: "Historians who have criticized Moultrie for his tardy arrival on James Island failed to take into account that the boats he needed were upriver at Ashley Ferry instead of docked at Charlestown."[38] In late summer 1779, the British again stationed an occupying force at Port Royal. From Charles Town, General Moultrie sent out a wait and watch force of 800, who encamped fourteen miles northwest of Beaufort.

Siege and Surrender of Charles Town

The British victory and resulting occupation of Savannah had "persuaded [British General Henry] Clinton to proceed with his plan to invade South Carolina. [F]ourteen warships and ninety transports commanded by Vice Admiral Mariot Arbuthnot sailed from New York on December 26, 1779." Aboard were eighty-seven hundred redcoats and Hessian mercenaries.[39] The Revolutionary War's most controversial episode, one of a wall-of-shame magnitude, was about to unfold.

In Spring 1779, quaking in its collective boots, Governor John Rutledge's Privy Counsel did the unthinkable, voting 5–3 in favor of Charles Town's surrender in return for British recognition of neutrality. Initially, General Moultrie, the acting military commander on site, left the decision unchallenged. He permitted civil authority to trump military control in what was a military setting. Moultrie's "giving over to civil authorities the right to negotiate with the British" was, in the eyes of author C.L. Bragg, "at best misguided."[40]

Charles Town's civil government's pandering to the British was of no effect, as the British commander stated, "peremptorily and empathically," that "he had nothing to do with the Governor and that his business was with General Moultrie." A byproduct, though, was that an equivocating civil government, "on the brink of abandoning its revolutionary ideals," wearied Moultrie "beyond measure." Moultrie, however, rallied, announcing "WE WILL FIGHT IT OUT."[41] Young John Laurens reported, "Moultrie's stand gave the garrison great satisfaction."[42]

"The decision to seek neutrality was considered a disgrace by many South Carolinians," as David Russell summarized in *The American Revolution in the Southern Colonies.*[43] Russell concluded, "The damaging revelation that the leaders of Charles Town had considered neutrality was an incredible embarrassment to all Southern patriots. ... [a] new low point in patriot morale had been reached."[44]

South of Charles Town, the British again took possession of Johns and James Islands as well as re-populating defensive works at Stono Ferry. They captured the American Fort Johnson on James Island's Ashley River shore, across from Charles Town itself. Initially, Major General Lincoln had 4,200 men under his command. Late reinforcements from Virginia (Brigadiers Scott and Woodford) swelled defenders' ranks over 5,000. At that point, Lincoln's best judgment was to abandon the city, staying alive to fight another day. Yet, "[h]e was afraid that if he abandoned the post that he was sent southward to defend, his reputation would suffer as a result," concluded David Wilson in *Southern Strategy*. "Lincoln therefore resolved to remain in Charles Town instead of withdrawing the American army into the countryside."⁴⁵

The American defenders continued to construct defenses on the "neck" of the Charles Town peninsula, including an eighteen-foot-wide canal, another defensive ditch, redoubts along the defensive line, rows of abatis, and a double fraise in front of their river-to-river ramparts. For their part, British forces began daily bombardments of the American works. Advancing down the neck, the British began digging parallels, zig-zag trenches used to approach the defender's fortified position.

Then, the Charles Town civilian authority again raised its head. At last, "General Lincoln was [again] prepared to abandon the position. [Georgia Brigadier Lachlan McIntosh] did not want to waste even an hour getting the Continentals across the Cooper River while an escape route remained open."⁴⁶ Lobbied by local government officials, Lincoln postponed any decision, giving the appearance that he had decided to defend the city. In fact, Lincoln committed worse: "Lincoln committed a fatal error. ... [H]e allowed the civil authorities a voice in proceedings that were solely the aegis of the military. [L]incoln agreed not to act without the consent of the civil authorities."⁴⁷ Meanwhile, Henry Clinton had received twenty-six hundred reinforcements from New York, bringing the attacking force's head count over eleven thousand. British Lieutenant Banastre Tarleton and his cavalry closed off the one remaining escape route, northwest of the city across the Cooper River, the backdoor out of Charles Town. It was now only a matter of time before the city fell, as the British tightened the noose around the city.

As one southern historian, Carl Borick, wondered, "Had Moultrie been in charge...."⁴⁸ The surrender devastated Moultrie, defender of Charles Town from 1776 to May 1781. He could not contain his emotions. At the formal surrender to the British on May 12, 1780, an onlooker reported that he saw "tears coursing down the cheeks of General Moultrie."⁴⁹ Ten regiments and seven general officers surrendered. The "end to the siege of the great Southern city of Charles Town ... was the greatest victory in the war for the British and there was great celebration in England."⁵⁰ On the opposite side, historians such as Stephan Taaffe term "Clinton's conquest ... the biggest American defeat of the war."⁵¹

The Final Round

American forces were not completely quiescent as the British laid siege to Charles Town. On April 24, Americans had launched a surprise attack on the British. The Americans killed fifteen redcoats and captured twelve more. The British counterattacked, but Moultrie, in tactical command, had ordered artillerists to fire grapeshot, stopping the charging British in their tracks.⁵²

Yet, by May, due to continuous naval bombardment, Charles Town lay in ruin. Provisions were scarce or non-existent. For the third time, on May 8, General Clinton called for the Charles Town garrison to surrender.⁵³ "[O]n the eleventh of May, we capitulated," Moultrie penned in his memoirs. "The Americans had had enough. Their spirits were broken, their stomachs were empty, and many parts of the town lay in ruin."[54] The following day, May 12, the surrender ceremony took place: "With a stroke of a quill, Lincoln effectively removed fifty-six hundred soldiers and sailors from the conflict [as well as] two hundred cannon and fifty thousand pounds of gunpowder."[55] The Continental Regiments of North and South Carolina ceased to exist.

Iron Bars Do Not a Prison Make

The British sent 274 American officers across the Cooper River to Haddrell's Point, housing them in three desolate, abandoned barracks. The capture included six of Washington's then active twenty-five brigadier generals, one quarter of the senior officer rank's headcount: Louis Duportail, William Moultrie, Lachlan McIntosh, James Hogun, Charles Scott, and William Woodford.[56] Owing to the dry, barren landscape and a paucity of provisions, conditions were not what they seemed. Many officers constructed shelters in the woods, in great part living off the land rather than in the barracks.

In June 1780, the British granted General Lincoln parole, making Moultrie the senior American officer. Moultrie lived in relative comfort at Charles Cotesworth Pinckney's uncle's plantation, five miles inland from Haddrell's Point. By contrast, as commandant of the prisoners, Moultrie endured disrespectful, indeed harsh, daily mistreatment by British Colonel Nisbet Balfour, who commanded the occupying force. Balfour moved many American prisoners from the city to rotting hulks of de-masted British ships anchored in Charles Town harbor.[57] In *Relieve Us of this Burden*, Carl Borick marshalls evidence that over 800 Americans died on those prison ships, succumbing to starvation, malaria, smallpox, yellow fever, or chronic dysentery.[58] Moultrie repeatedly protested conditions on the ships, along with British attempts to recruit soldiers from among the captured Americans. They did so by holding threats over the American heads to transfer patriot soldiers to the prison ships if they declined to serve the British cause. Back at Haddrell's Point, food was scarce as the British accused the American officers of inflating the head count. Accordingly, the British short rationed the officers by a significant margin. Moultrie carped loudly to Balfour about British practices every day and every week.

Friction between Moultrie and Balfour was constant. Among other things, to quash Moultrie's persistent advocacy on American prisoners' behalf, Balfour threatened to revoke Moultrie's limited parole. Then, on the other side of the coin, the British attempted to bribe Moultrie if he would agree to serve British efforts against the French and the Spanish in the Caribbean. Moultrie refused, leading to Robert Thompson's twentieth-century epitaph, "[W]hile in [Benedict] Arnold the British found a traitor, in General Moultrie they met a true patriot who rejected with scorn the offers to abandon the struggle for liberty and independence."[59]

Exchange, Repatriation, and Celebration

The British paroled Moultrie in July 1781. Joined by his family, he sailed aboard the brig *Burton* to Philadelphia. He commenced lobbying for back pay and other benefits for South Carolina's veterans. In April 1782, Moultrie and his family returned to Charles Town. On 15 October 1782, Congress promoted Moultrie "its last major general of the war."[60] Upon the British taking their leave of the city, on December 14, 1782, "Nathanael Greene, William Moultrie, Governor Matthews, and their wives," paraded in open carriages "down King Street to the sound of fifes and drums ... ahead of a column of the Continental army," acting as an honor guard for the occupying American force.[61]

Part III
Difficulties of Revolutionary Command

11

Service and Travel in Colonial Times

A modern tendency is to imagine that revolutionary era roads are similar to today's streets and roads. To the contrary, colonial roads at best were single lane, packed earth. At worst, roads were widened game trails or Indian paths. In the Revolutionary era, "[t]he condition of the Virginia roads," for example, "made any movement at all one of great difficulty."[1]

Existent Highways

The roads that did exist were filled with wagon wheel tracks, ruts, bumps, rock-strewn stream beds, and corduroyed mudholes. Corduroying laid eight or ten-foot log bolts side-by-side over a road's low, perennially muddy spots. A tree stump may have survived forty, fifty, or sixty years in the ground after loggers had cut down the tree. Pulling stumps ("grubbing stumps"), horse or human powered as it was, was difficult and for the most part left undone. Instead, up to a certain size, road builders sawed off stumps low enough so that wagons' axles could pass over them. It was therefore hazardous for a rider on horseback to navigate a road at night.[2] A coach driver could be laid low or knocked off his perch by a low hanging branch.[3] In those days, the roads were either "very bad" or "excessively bad." Bridges were "small, narrow, and badly built."[4] In summer months, clouds of dust arose, choking travelers. In winter months, deep, hard-frozen ruts could break a horse or human leg.

There were well-developed ways, such as a post road from Boston to New York, the turnpike from Philadelphia to Lancaster, Pennsylvania, and the Great Wagon Road from Philadelphia to Winchester, Virginia, and on down the Shenandoah Valley.[5] The King's Highway went from Philadelphia to Alexandria, Fredericksburg, and eventually on to Charles Town.[6] By 1763, the post road from Philadelphia to New York was developed enough to enable nighttime travel. A letter from Philadelphia could be delivered in New York the following day.[7]

In the French and Indian War, a thousand men "cut a wagon road" from Carlisle, Pennsylvania, to Fort Duquesne (the Forbes Road). Even on wagon roads such as the Forbes Road, teamsters had to utilize pack horses instead of wagons and teams when traversing stretches.[8] Today, U.S. Route 30 (the Lincoln Highway) roughly parallels the Forbes Road to "the forks of the Ohio."[9]

In those days no VDOT, PennDot, or the like existed, either to cut new roads or to maintain those that in some form existed. Road graders in whatever form, horse-drawn or human powered, did not exist. Disused roads vanished under weeds and brambles. In some instances, colonial legislation required county courts or a legislative body to appoint "three or more able and fit persons" to see that "said roads as proposed are cleared" and for a road overseer thereafter to see to maintenance of the byway.[10] That was an exception. For the most part, no group or agency had responsibility for filling holes, pruning back bushes, or trimming tree limbs.

The Pace of Travel

As any experienced hiker will tell you, an eight or ten-mile hike is an arduous undertaking. At a pace of 25 minutes per mile, with rest breaks here and there and longer breaks for meals, a ten-mile hike might involve seven or eight hours on the trail. On average, colonial soldiers on the move outdid modern hikers; soldiers marched 14 miles per day, upwards of 20 miles in a forced march.[11] Soldiers did so burdened by a four-and-half foot long, ten pound musket and a knapsack or haversack of between 20 and 30 pounds. These distances and the pace of martial marches had not much changed since medieval times.[12] Unless, of course, looting and pillaging along the route slowed a force on the march, as in the Revolutionary War for Hessian or Brunswick contingents serving the British: "Covering [only] eight or nine miles a day in the usual three lines of march, the better to live off the country and gather loot, the [English army, moving through France] inflicted wanton damage."[13]

Colonial soldiers also often marched day after day as they covered long distances, such as General Muhlenberg's 8th Virginia Regiment's trek from Winchester to Suffolk in southeast Virginia,[14] or George Weedon and his regiment's 1776 march north from Winchester to New York City.[15] Guessing what British General William Howe might do, in 1777, George Washington had his army of the Middle Department march to and fro, and back again, covering much of the terrain in New Jersey and parts of New York. Patrick O'Donnell's book, *Washington's Immortals*, "recounts the pain of long marches by hungry, barefoot skeletons; limbs blackened by the cold; and [ill due to] the typhus, scurvy, pneumonia, and dysentery that swept patriot ranks in summer and winter."[16] North Carolina Governor Richard Caswell gave directions to recruiters to enlist "able bodied men, fit for service, capable of marching well."[17] The distance from Boston to Brooklyn was 190 miles, from Brooklyn to Head of Elk, southwest of Philadelphia, was 125.

The Wear and Tear of Long Marches

Historical accounts recount the level of hardship colonial soldiers faced in marching, noting that many soldiers had little clothing and no shoes.[18] One explanation was that common shoes did not have hard soles as shoes have today. Instead, a cobbler made an entire article of footwear from a single piece of leather or deer skin,

EASTERN THEATRE

wrapped round the shoemaker's last. Thus, bottoms, or soles, were of the same material as the uppers, much like moccasins. Called "shoepacks," the footwear did not hold up well.[19]

As to the pace of marches, the other side of the coin was that when encumbered with numbers of supply wagons as well as civilian camp followers, an army's pace could be maddeningly slow. The British retreat after the Battle of Princeton, from Princeton to New Brunswick, New Jersey, averaged one mile per day, "slowed by disheartened men, knackered horses, and the wrecked bridge at Kingston."[20] In 1778, retreating across New Jersey after abandoning Philadelphia, the British force averaged two miles per day, with a train of infantry units, horse-drawn artillery, supply wagons, the baggage train, mounted riders and cavalry, spouses, families, and hangers-on stretching out for seven miles. In the French and Indian War, British

General Braddock's group traveled at a pace of two miles per day from Carlisle to Fort Duquesne.[21]

Travel by Horseback

A mounted person could travel, more or less, at twice a walker's speed. For example, it took 29 days for the Rev. Manasseh Cutler to travel from Ipswich, Massachusetts, the 751 miles to Marietta, Ohio, the first town in the Northwest Territories, a pace of 25.9 miles per day.[22] A horse and carriage could, on a decent road, move at a better pace. The Reverend Cutler, with a horse and buggy, "[c]overed ninety-five miles in just two days" but the Reverend "found himself 'a little fatigued' by the time he arrived" in Philadelphia, having traveled from New York City.[23] Ryan Cole, Light Horse Harry Lee's biographer, described Lee and his cavalry's seventy-mile ride in three days as "a breakneck pace."[24] Leaving behind the Battle of Camden, then in progress, Horatio Gates rode 180 miles from Camden, South Carolina, to Hillsborough, North Carolina, in there and a half days.[25]

Weaponry

The war began with soldiers attacking or defending with muskets such as the Brown Bess: long barreled, smooth bored, single shot weapons that fired a lead ball. Muskets were muzzle loading; the soldier inserted wadding and the ball, then used a ramrod to tamp the combination the length of the long barrel. The maximum range was 70 yards. The effective range was less, say, 50 or 60 yards, with muskets still wildly inaccurate even at those ranges.[26] The weapons' minimum effectiveness in part explains why, after hours of furious combat, Revolutionary War casualty rates were low, at least to the modern eye.

Then the rifle—also known as the musket rifle, the Kentucky rifle, or the Pennsylvania rifle—arrived on the scene. It was the weapon of choice for Daniel Morgan's Virginia rangers, "riflemen" from the frontier. "Rifle" conjures up ideas of bolt action rifles, loaded at the breech rather than at the muzzle, firing multiple rounds. "Rifle" could also conjure up the notion of semi-automatic weapons with high-capacity magazines holding twelve, fourteen, or more rounds.[27] Those are wide-of-the-mark descriptions.

The principal difference between the musket and the rifle was the graduation, in the barrel, from smooth to rifled bore, imparting a spin to the projectile that more than tripled the range as well as vastly increasing the weapon's accuracy. In most other respects, however, the musket and the rifle were similar: single shot weapons, all of which were muzzle loaders. Both required insertion of powder, wadding, and projectile. Both required that the soldier tamp down with a ramrod. A difference was that instead of a round ball, the rifle fired an early form of the miné-ball, elongated in shape, rounded only on the front end.[28]

Nonetheless, seeming counterintuitively, many colonial soldiers preferred the musket, for at least two reasons. One was that the rifle was more difficult to maintain, rendered unusable by rain and dirt and dust in the barrel that could foul the groves. Two was that the rifle was not configured to add a bayonet as was the musket.

Thus, with the rifle "there were disadvantages. The octagonal barrel [of the rifle] was not designed to take a bayonet; the rifle was designed for hunting, not military operations."[29]

The British Mode of Warfare

Bayonets were essential to warfare against the British, whose attack would begin with a long double rank marching steadily toward an opponent's position. In the colonial version of "shock and awe," the British formation would be made up of grenadiers whose minimum height was 5'10", in scarlet red coats, whose tall beaver hats made them appear even taller. The ranks would pull up short, forty or so yards from the enemy, firing one or two rounds at the opponents, with the purpose of rocking the defense onto its heels rather than accuracy *per se*. The grenadiers would then "quick step, then double quick step," advancing toward the enemy line, bayonets fixed, prepared to skewer their adversaries.[30]

From the firing point, a British formation could cover the distance in less time than it took colonial troops to reload, although a very capable American soldier could reload in fifteen or twenty seconds. Overall, an American colonial force battling with the advancing British line was in an extremely disadvantageous position if the force had only rifles. Rifles could "take a full minute to reload and fire," and were also without the bayonets needed to face off against a British bayonet charge.[31]

At Saratoga, to counter British tactics, Daniel Morgan and his riflemen climbed trees, picking off the British officers ("Boys, shoot at those who wear the epaulettes rather than the poor fellas who fight for six pence a day") and firing two or three rounds from their perches in the trees.[32] "Morgan's four hundred riflemen were ... adapted to hunting, living, and fighting on the western frontier.... Each had demonstrated his marksmanship by consistently hitting a target the size of a pie plate at two hundred yards."[33]

After firing a round or two, the riflemen would climb down from their perches in the trees, withdrawing to the rear of a conventionally equipped regiment on the ground below who carryied muskets with bayonets fixed. After forestalling the British advance, the conventional force would step back. The re-positioned riflemen could fire additional rounds at the British. The rotation would then repeat. The combination of riflemen and conventional forces worked exceedingly well.[34] The Battle of Saratoga marked a turning point in the war, not only saving a fledging nation from being split in two, but finally persuading the French to enter the war on the American side.[35]

In sum, the patriot soldier marched hundreds and hundreds of miles, with inadequate clothing and footwear, shouldering a ten-pound musket of dubious accuracy and mentally prepared to face an awe-inspiring British bayonet charge, often having gone several days with scant food and little in the way of potable water or other beverages. Indeed, the road to independence and liberty was more arduous and demanding than we today could imagine.

12

Intoxicating Beverages and Inebriation

Imbibing, often to excess, has a long association with the military for several reasons. One, in revolutionary times, a reason to partake was warmth, especially comforting on autumn and winter evenings spent in out-of-doors encampments after a long day's march.

Two was availability. The custom, indeed, a term of many enlistments, was the provision each day to each soldier of a gill: five fluid ounces of rum, whiskey, or sometimes apple brandy ("applejack," or distilled hard cider).[1] In addition, at the Battle of Saratoga, Commanding General Horatio Gates issued "a standing order for a half gill of rum for every man first thing in the morning … [as] another remedy for their stiff joints."[2] Returning midwinter from hostile Indian country in Ohio, Georgia General Lachlan McIntosh, "[a]s a mark of satisfaction with the behavior of [the men], ordered a pint of whiskey each man."[3] Whether or not enlistments required dispensation of alcohol, distribution of it was a longstanding command practice. When Ben Franklin commanded the Pennsylvania Militia in the early 1750s, he instructed the chaplain to dole out a daily ration of rum right after services: "Never were prayers more generally and punctually attended."[4] On occasion, battlefield commanders shorted soldiers on the daily rum ration, with disastrous results.[5] In addition, sutlers, purveyors of various goods, followed army units of size, standing ready to augment the military's daily whiskey or rum allowance upon payment of several pence.[6]

Three, the waters from springs, streams, and shallow wells in bivouac areas often were foul to the taste as well as polluted, a health hazard causing sickness. A widely held belief was that alcohol was both a substitute for water and a palliative for ingestion of bad water. Indeed, the rationale and equivalent rates of consumption prevailed in much of eighteenth-century American society. Describing the late eighteenth and early nineteenth Centuries, Gordon Wood observed, "Alcohol flowed freely, and Americans were drinking more per capita than nearly all other nations."[7] Harvard College fed John Adams, when he was but fifteen, a gill of hard cider at breakfast each morning: "[F]or the rest of his life, a morning 'gill' of hard cider was to be John Adams's preferred drink before breakfast."[8] The Revolutionary War military appears to have matched and at times greatly exceeded the general population's rate of consumption.

Warmth and Living Rough

In her award-winning book, *A Distant Mirror*, historian Barbara Tuchman describes life in fourteenth-century northern France.[9] A lord's court would gather evenings in the castle keep's smoky confines, smoky because no ventilation existed above the wood fire. On cold nights in Picardy, standing close to the roaring fire, a lord, knight, or lady would feel warm facing the fire and cold on the opposite flank, the side pointing away from the heat.[10] The same was true for Revolutionary War soldiers; at Valley Forge, for instance, "roaring fires served at least to roast the belly while the buttocks froze."[11]

To fight cold, the castle's inhabitants would drink themselves just short of oblivion, with wine, mead, or other alcoholic drink. At one or two in the morning, they jumped, fully clothed, under a pile of furs, sleeping until late the following morning, remaining abed until air temperatures had risen: "[T]ea, coffee, and tobacco were unknown ... [w]ine was the favorite drink of those who could afford it; the common people drank beer, ale, and cider." In that age, people "depended on wine and beer as an essential part of diet."[12]

These practices carried over into much of colonial America, especially for those living outdoors. That existence applied to many Revolutionary War officers. Major General Adam Stephen served 24 years in the military, from the French and Indian War beginning in 1753 until 1777. He headed up the task force that built the Forbes Road through the wilderness. He led Virginia forces in the Cherokee Wars as well as in Pontiac's War.[13] General Andrew Lewis, later to command all Virginia regiments in the Revolution, was as a young man a surveyor who laid out much of the territory in southwest Virginia, including what today is West Virginia (hence, Lewisburg in Greenbrier County, West Virginia). Generals Moultrie, Pickens, Davidson, Caswell, and Marion served in the Cherokee Wars in the western Carolinas. Farther north, again as a young man, George Washington surveyed and mapped the flat lands of Allegheny mountain valleys west of the Shenandoah, such as the Lost River Valley in what today is West Virginia.[14] George Rogers Clark, the "Hannibal of the West," who headed up militia forces in far western Virginia (today Kentucky) and the Illinois Territory, was a surveyor from age 19. He surveyed lands in far western Virginia and continued his profession for decades.[15] As surveyors or soldiers in the wilderness, one of the few creature comforts these men enjoyed was a drink or two in the evenings.

Provision of Alcohol to Officers and Soldiers

In commanding his New Hampshire force, General John Stark consistently put at the head of his requisition list alcoholic beverages for his troops. The lore relating to the American victory at the Battle of Bennington (1777) has it that before the battle, many of Colonel Stark's troops had fortified themselves with whiskey.[16] Part of the reason for young Colonel George Washington's 1754 surrender at Fort Necessity to the French and Indian forces was that, according to Washington, "What was worse [than a persistent downpour and being surrounded], it was no sooner dark, than one-half of our Men got drunk."[17] Twenty five years later, in January to March 1778's winter encampment at Valley Forge, and undoubtedly at other long winter encampments, "gambling, intoxication, and assault" permeated the army's ranks.[18] During the siege of Charles Town (April-May 1780), militia Captain Earle Hughston "had a fondness for rum and a seemingly endless supply from his tin canteen bottle. Every day at mid-morning and again at sunset he shared the rum" with fellow officers.[19] Early in the war, the spread of drunkenness among Charles Scott's troops at Suffolk, Virginia, caused him to order "all tippling houses ... not to sell spiritous liquors to Soldiers under pain of confinement."[20] After news of the "stupendous" October 1777 victory at Saratoga reached Virginia, "[f]or the special occasion each soldier was to receive an [extra] gill of rum."[21]

Reports of alcohol abuse could fill pages. In the French and Indian War, "[w]aggoner Joseph Coombs was regarded as an angel from heaven when he arrived at Fort Ashby in December with a wagonload of rum.... Ashby's garrison was, as a result, rendered drunk and helpless."[22] As a younger man, Revolutionary War hero Daniel Morgan was a hard drinker. Morgan "bought rum, by the pint, the quart, the half-gallon, or the gallon—and '[one] pint mugs' to drink it in."[23]

Even among New England forces, who numbered among themselves a significant conservative population, mostly of Puritan stock, ingestion of alcohol was not taboo. Historian David McCullough, in *The Pioneers*, explained why many religious conservatives' views have not been well-taken: "[S]tiff-necked and somber [a Puritan minister] was not, any more than were most Puritans, contrary to latter-day conceptions." Author McCullough explained, "Puritans were as capable as any mortals of exuding an affable enjoyment of life.... [M]any a Puritan loved good food, good wine, good stories, and good cheer."[24] Often, groups were labeled Puritan not because of any strict moral code but because of group members' desire to rid the Church of England ("purify it") of vestiges left from the Church of Rome.[25] The heavy drinking that dates from the earliest periods of organized militaries included soldiers of Puritan stock.[26]

British forces were not immune from excessive drink's perils. Early on, at the siege of Boston, "Lieutenant Frederick MacKenzie of the 23rd Foot—the Royal Welch Fusiliers—recorded in his diary that 'many men are intoxicated daily' and that two had died of alcohol poisoning in a single night." He added, "When the soldiers are in a state of intoxication, they are frequently induced to desert."[27] Seeking to court allies, the British, and the French before them, plied Native Americans with alcohol while doing nothing to restrain private merchants: "The Indians wanted powder and lead," for hunting, "but the traders brought rum."[28]

By contrast, Francis Marion, the "Swamp Fox" who in the war led a South Carolina Militia band, allowed his men to drink only water, cut with vinegar. He was fond of pointing out that in assembling a far-reaching empire, Roman soldiers drank only a water-vinegar mix. "The Roman Legions marched and conquered the world drinking nothing else," Marion exhorted his men.[29] Marion told an officer recruit, "If you served with me, you'd be as sober as a rock, day and night, or you wouldn't serve."[30]

Water Supply

In 1781, at Gloucester Point across from Yorktown, General Lafayette "[e]specially sought from [General] Weedon spiritous liquors, 'as the water of this Country is very unhealthy.'"[31] As early as 1762, while leading Virginia troops on an expedition against the Cherokee, like Colonel Stark in New England, Adam Stephen requested additional supplies of alcoholic beverages for his men: "Stephen especially complained that rum 'in the wilderness' sold for 8 [pence] per gill."[32] In January 1777, following the Colonial victory at the Battle of Princeton, in gratitude, the Philadelphia Council of Safety sent General Washington's army "twenty hogshead of rum," amounting roughly to 1280 gallons of rum.[33] In 1778, after his men stood all of a cold and rainy night on alert, General Charles Scott thought his men in such a "Horred [sic] Condition" that he bought enough rum to give each soldier a gill: "I was obliged to pay the economic price of Twelve dollars a gallon for it, which I thought better Than letting the men Suffer."[34] Rum and whiskey were important in Revolutionary War soldiers' everyday lives.

Health Concerns

Not only was the daily liquor ration a term of many enlistments, but the belief was also that alcoholic beverages, either straight up or half diluted with water, were necessary for good health. The supplies of what would have been potable water carried E Coli and other forms of coliform bacteria. George Washington was emphatic to his generals about the need for proper sanitation, but the message did not always trickle down to the lower levels. Then, too, knowledge of public health and sanitation was imperfect in those times. "In the unwholesome atmosphere [of military camps], smallpox, typhoid, dysentery, measles, malaria, and pneumonia flourished" even eighty years later in the Civil War. Generals in that war often saw a third of their armies on the sick list, Ron Chernow recounts in this biography *Grant*.[35] Revolutionary War sick lists exceeded that figure.

Today's city and county health departments insist that there be a minimum 100 foot separation between a water source (a spring or a well) and a sanitary system (a septic system drain field, outhouse, or latrine). Otherwise, bacteria from the sewage can percolate downward, infecting the water table and in turn fouling the stream, spring, or well. Revolutionary officers had an imperfect understanding about the need for separation so that, in many cases, apparently potable water was polluted with strains of bacteria. Sickness frequently resulted among the troops, including diarrheal afflictions, escalating to chronic dysentery and other illnesses.[36] During the war, "typhus, scurvy, pneumonia, and dysentery ... swept patriot ranks in summer and winter."[37] George Weedon's Third Regiment left Virginia in 1776 with 605 men. When it reported to General Washington in Manhattan, the regiment had fewer than 300 "effectives."[38] In 1776, when General Lewis ordered Stephen's brigade (three Virginia regiments) north to reinforce the northern army, the departure was delayed because "half the men were sick." When the Virginia regiments reached

Trenton, New Jersey, "324 sick men in the brigade men had to be left behind."[39] At the Battle of Long Island, in August 1776, General Washington had 16,125 men. By November, when the American force left Manhattan for New Jersey, it has dwindled to 3,400 men. The reduction was due to deaths, combat wounds, captures, and desertions. A fifth cause was illness, due in great part to imperfectly understood sanitation practices and poor-quality drinking water. Alcoholic beverage consumption was thought to be an answer to water-borne sickness.

The Generals

Neither were higher-ranking members of the Continental army immune from drinking, possibly to excess, perhaps surpassing the lower ranks in terms of volume consumed:

- In 1777, one congressman "was already impugning the character of [several] generals as alcoholics" (Stephen, Sullivan, Maxwell, and Stirling mentioned).[40]
- Major General John Sullivan of New Hampshire (later a judge) was rumored to be a hard drinker, whose performance at Brandywine was judged by some to have been deficient, influenced by alcohol.[41]
- General Benedict Arnold, later a traitor, and according to some a hero at Saratoga, was said to have drunk a dipperful of powerful New England rum before the Battle of Bemis Heights: "He gulped half a pint of encouragement and raced off to join the fight."[42]
- Brigadier William Maxwell, the "Wee Scot" from New Jersey, was accused of excessive drinking and, along with Major General Adam Stephen of Virginia, was court martialed.[43]
- One of the war's chroniclers describes General Stephen "as so utterly drunk [at Germantown] as to impair his worth completely."[44]
- In 1779, "Lord Stirling [William Alexander of New York and Jersey] was gradually marginalized due to ill health and alcoholism."[45] His death in 1783 has been linked to alcoholism.
- After the war, in considering whom to appoint as commander of a newly created U.S. force to combat Indian marauders on the frontier, President George Washington said of Virginia's General Charles Scott, "Brave and means well; but ... by report, is addicted to drinking."[46]
- The historian Harry Ward wrote that although General Adam Stephen's enjoyment of a spiritous drink was well known, the same "*could be said of all the generals, especially from Virginia.*" He added, though, that at the time of Germantown, "Stephen, however, undoubtedly was tippling a little bit more of late, fortifying his constitution wearied by the long marches and heavy responsibilities."[47]
- During the war, General Adam Stephen operated a distillery on his plantation, employing thirty men and selling to the army.[48]

Today, Navy regulations forbid intoxicating beverages aboard U.S. men-of-war. Army regulations greatly circumscribe the availability on Army posts, relegating imbibing to officers' and NCOs' clubs after working hours. By contrast, if visiting a British ship or military facility, an American can partake of a pink gin or two at luncheon, as well as alcoholic drinks before dinner.

In today's armed forces, there is excessive drinking, to be sure, but off duty, away from ships, posts, and bases. Perhaps in part because of alcohol use in the Revolutionary War, since the early eighteenth century, regulations have forbidden drinking during working hours or on operating facilities' premises.[49] Another difference is that, for the most part, today's heavy drinking is confined to younger sailors, soldiers, and junior officers. In the Revolutionary War, heavy drinking carried over to the senior ranks and to officers of all ages.

13

Militia Units versus the Continental Line

The Continental Congress created regiments of soldiers and artillery and appointed and promoted senior officers, first, to lieutenant or full colonel, second, to brigadier and, third, to major general. In June 1775, Congress appointed George Washington the Continental Army's commanding officer. On July 15, Washington assumed command of the army, relieving Massachusetts's General Artemas Ward. Continental Line officers and men generally served three-year enlistments, although with renewals, many regulars served the duration.

Militia units were of an altogether different, often haphazard, sort. First, colonial governors and legislatures rather than Congress created the units, to be under the state governors' command. In certain colonies such as Virginia, all freeholders (landowners) numbering 36,000 were required to serve in the militia.[1] Two, for deployments, militia soldiers' enlistments were short: 60 or 90 days. The government could require no freeholder to "serve [in a deployment] but on imminent danger" to the colony.[2] A partial shortcut around that gubernatorial or legislative deployment command was that the force deployed usually amounted half or less than half of the number mustered.[3] In that way, of those mustered, mainly those with a higher risk tolerance or sense of adventure volunteered. When they were deployed, though, although freed of constraints, militia took a cavalier approach even to short term enlistments, leaving camps when they deemed missions aborted or completed. Three, militia units' training varied widely, lopsided toward minimal, although militia members were required to drill once per month.[4] These monthly musters, however, "were the gayest of occasions and became primarily social and political rallies."[5] Fourth, clothing and equipment, particularly weaponry and ammunition, varied significantly. Even in the closing days of the war, generals sometimes had to furnish militia units with wooden pikes, as the unit members had no muskets.[6] Other militia members reported with blunderbusses handed down by grandfathers, previously used against pests on the farm or as fowling pieces for pheasant hunting. Fifth, militias' organizational schematics varied widely, but the most common was colony and then county-by-county within the colony.

Militia Units

Virginia's military, for example, had three levels: Continental forces from the state at the top, then higher level militia from sixteen multi-country districts, and finally lower-level militia county-by-county. The sixteen districts were to raise 500 "minutemen" each, training them for twenty days at the outset, with four days "exercise on their own" each month thereafter. Virginia forces' third tier was the traditional county militia. In 1775, the Third Virginia Convention decreed, "All male persons, hired servants, and apprentices above the age of sixteen, and under fifty years shall be enlisted into the militia."[7]

Modes of organization varied in other colonies. New Hampshire, for example, organized a state-only force of 1,500 men, the command of which the state gave to John Stark, following his resignation from Continental service.[8] Stark, a hero of the Battle of Bunker Hill, resigned from the army when, in March 1777, Congress promoted Enoch Poor and James Reed to brigadier instead of Stark. General Washington wrote to Enoch Poor, "I am apprehensive that your promotion will cause Colo. Stark to resign," which it did.[9]

In response to Stark's resignation, the New Hampshire Council of Safety and the legislature created a state-wide New Hampshire Army.[10] "Our friend John Stark ... may safely be entrusted the honor of the enterprise," said future senator, governor, and signer of the Declaration of Independence John Langdon.[11] General Stark was to act independently, without responsibility to Continental officers or to the Congress in Philadelphia.[12] Stark enlisted 1,492 New Hampshire men.[13] He led that army to victory over the Hessians at the Battle of Bennington, where Stark exclaimed, "They are ours, or this night Molly Stark sleeps a widow."[14]

Enlistments and Desertions

When in 1780, General Weedon called out the Prince William, King George, Stafford, and Spotsylvania counties' militia in Virginia, 250 of them "went home after ten days contrary to [General Weedon's] request." That is all they had agreed to.[15] Joining General Weedon to defend Virginia with militia, General Peter Muhlenberg was astonished that "[o]ne hundred had deserted in one night."[16] In New Jersey, Hugh Mercer was to staff his mobile "flying camp" with militia, yet due to the militia's uncertain commitment, the "camp" was not so mobile after all. "The New Jersey Militia were restless and half-hearted about" the enterprise. The officers and men were willing to serve "to protect their farms and their homes from attack but many of them were unwilling to go elsewhere." In all events, "they were anxious to terminate their service and return to [their] farms for the harvest."[17] Militia "were always eager to return to their homes, quick to find any reason to do so."[18] Of North Carolina military, Professor Chalmers Davidson observed, "Continentals were prone to look down upon the state troops as an inferior order of soldiery."[19]

Complaints and Criticisms of Militia

The commentary by Continental Army officers about the militia was critical, and at times derogatory. One size did not fit all, though, contrary to Continental Line officers' assertions. Certain militia units performed well. Militia contingents, such as the Culpepper Rifles and Militia under Colonel James Barbour, were crack units, early on the scene supporting General Scott and his regulars at the Battle of Great Bridge in December 1775.[20] Alexander Hamilton, before he joined the Continental Line as an artillery officer, led the New York "Hearts of Oak" Militia, a highly regarded unit.[21] General George Weedon gave high marks to the Virginia Militia, no doubt colored by his pride in all things Virginian. He praised "the citizen soldiers" for their "ready Obedience ... in Organizing, their Alacrity in duty, their perseverance in exceeding hard Service ... and their rapid Progress in Discipline."[22]

Weedon was not so sanguine other times. At Whitemarsh, north of Philadelphia, in early December 1777, Weedon advised General Washington to "avoid too much reliance on militia ... a promiscuous body of men drawn from all Quarters of the Globe. [Y]ou would find that one half would desert on their way to Camp."[23] Connecticut's Major General Israel Putnam had little use for militia. At Saratoga, Putnam came across an officer "pleading with a reluctant militiaman." Putnam snapped at the officer, "Run him through if he won't fight."[24]

Virginia Militia General Thomas Nelson expatiated on the "inherent difficulty with militia." Summarizing Nelson's conclusionary remarks, Professor Emory Evans wrote, "To keep men with families in the field, ill-housed, ill-equipped, and ill-fed, was extremely difficult. Enlistments expired, and replacements came in slowly."[25] General Nelson wrote to Virginia Governor Thomas Jefferson that the militia "would give nearly half they possess to raise Regulars, rather than be subject to the Distresses they feel at leaving their Plantations and Families."[26] After short periods of service, militia "wanted to return to their fields and shops."[27] Overall, "Continentals were prone to look down upon state troops as an inferior order of soldiery."[28]

The Commander-in-Chief's and Others' Views

Even though he had commanded a Virginia Militia regiment in the French and Indian War, General Washington expressed contempt for "minutemen." He wrote to John Hancock, president of the Continental Congress, "The militia instead of calling forth their utmost efforts to a brave & manly opposition in order to repair our Losses, are dismayed, Intractable, and Impatient...." General Washington added, "Great numbers of them have gone off; in some instances by whole Regiments ... & by Companies at a time."[29] Several days later, he wrote to the Continental Congress, "Depending upon the militia [is] akin to resting upon a broke staff."[30] Washington wrote to Thomas Nelson, Jr. upon the latter's appointment as a brigadier of the Virginia Militia, "It is without a doubt a disagreeable task to Command Militia, but we must make the best of circumstances, and use the means we have."[31]

General Hugh Mercer was much of the same opinion: "Our armies are comprised of new Militia, perpetually fluctuating between the [Flying] camp and their farms. Poorly armed and still worse disciplined, these, sir, are not a match ... for veteran troops, well fitted, and urged on by able officers."[32] Leading the 1780 defense of Virginia, Major General Marquis du Lafayette "gauged the difficulty of getting militiamen too far from their farms during planting season." At planting time, "it would take a dozen counties to furnish a thousand men."³³ There were then two periods of particular vulnerability: planting time and the harvest season, when "you will see your force diminished every day you keep [to] the field at this season of the year."

Allegations of Venality

Light-Horse Harry Lee was more colorful in his condemnation: "They exceed the goths and the vandals in their schemes of plunder, murder, and inequity." Lee was convinced "that many of the Georgians and Carolinians wanted nothing more than to extract bloody revenge on their Tory neighbors."³⁴ Last of all, Colonel Daniel Morgan, who himself had once been a militia officer, evinced little "tolerance toward the Pennsylvania militia officers.... [Morgan] thought them narrow and petty in their determination not to take advice or instructions from Continental officers."³⁵

Militia commanders complicated these pictures, as requests for absences tugged at the commanders' heartstrings. Militia members wanted leave: "Local leaders felt that [militia members'] grievances were justified since they had been hurried from their homes leaving their families unprotected."³⁶ Lieutenant Colonel James Wilkinson, General Horatio Gates's aide at Saratoga, voiced an alternative apology after John Stark and his New Hampshire army refused to reinforce the Americans prior to the Battle of Freeman's Farm. Stark and his men had won a great victory at Bennington: "They [the New Hampshire troops] are desirous to tell the tale of feats performed and look into their private affairs, after which they will be ready again to take up arms."³⁷

Dissenters

Brigadier General Lachlan McIntosh, reviewing the 1779 siege of Savannah, found that "The militia turned out cheerfully on every occasion."³⁸ Major General Charles Lee envisioned conduct of the entire war using small groups, made up with militia. "He wanted to rely on small detachments of trained soldiers drafted from the militia who would cooperate with roving bands of guerrillas and wear down the British with hit-and-run" tactics. Thus, as author Andrew Zambone concludes, "[Generals] Charles Lee and Horatio Gates burned with an ideological enthusiasm for militia."³⁹ The drawback to such a mode of operation was that, according to Gregory Urwin, "Such a strategy would have turned the War of Independence into a much more ferocious conflict and stymied the emergence of anything resembling national unity" after the war.⁴⁰

Certain prominent individuals were stronger proponents yet of militia: "Radicals called for primary dependence on militia—theoretically the citizenry in arms—which reflected the essence of their republicanism [and their animadversion to standing armies]." In argument, "Radicals insisted free men fighting for their liberties, homes, and families were infinitely superior to any professional army."⁴¹ Of the thirty something members of the Continental Congress, up to a dozen were highly critical of Washington, based in part upon the army's 1777 defeats. James Lowell,

13. Militia Units versus the Continental Line

Jonathan Dickinson Sergeant, and several others represented a subgroup of that number. "Lowell," for instance, "was furious with Washington's determination to build a Continental Line on the European model."[42] For another, "John Adams was enthusiastic about militia and skeptical of professional soldiers."[43]

The British could not fathom American attitudes. Many British made the military a career, while others served an eight-year term. American militia signed on for terms of thirty or forty-five days. Even given a stated term, as previously noted, many militia viewed themselves as obliged only for a campaign or potential engagement. If the engagement did not materialize or the campaign shape up, minute men went home. In the eyes of European professional military, the American way was loosey-goosey, informal beyond anything British could envision: "It was an army of rabble in the eyes of the British."[44] British military derogatorily termed militia "shirt men," for if a semblance of a uniform existed, it consisted of a shirt often emblazoned with a slogan such as "Give Me Liberty or Give Death," or "Liberty."

Hidden Advantages

Militia had countervailing advantages that historians mention only in passing or omit altogether:

- Militia represented a seemingly infinite source of supply. For example, over just three days at Saratoga, General Horatio Gates's force increased by 3,000 militia on September 29, 1777, to a total of 10,000. Before Burgoyne's surrender in October, the total American force had increased to 14,000, with the addition of 4,000 more minutemen, as opposed to 5,800 British, of whom only 3,500 were "effectives."[45]
- Coming from not-too-distant homes, minutemen tended to be well-nourished, especially compared to regulars who had been in service for a year or more and engaged in weeks of hard marches and countermarches.
- Militia were enthusiastic, at least until their first exposure to battle, or when spring planting or fall harvest beckoned.

An opponent's assessment, that of British General "Gentleman Johnny" Burgoyne: "The [American] militia are inferior in method and movement, but not a jot less serviceable in the woods. Their enthusiasm is extensive and permanent."[46]

Reliance on militia was many times essential. With British forays up Virginia's rivers, in 1780 and 1781, reliance was on militia to oppose British generals because Continental Line units were deployed elsewhere, namely, to slow or stop Cornwallis as he campaigned in North Carolina. In charge of Virginia's defense and reliant on the only source available, militia, Generals Muhlenberg and Weedon set about their task. Military and political authorities had instructed 5,000 soldiers' recruitment. Given a war-weary populace, the generals never achieved that goal. The headcounts of the forces they put together barely were sufficient to shadow and menace, but not face in battle, the British invaders. It must be remembered, however, the forces were composed entirely of part-time volunteers, that is, militia.

In 1781, reliance upon militia eventuated at Gloucester Point, across the York River from Yorktown (Chapter 2). With French reinforcements, Gloucester Point militia closed Lord Cornwallis's remaining escape route, across the York. General Washington also charged George Weedon with boxing in the smaller British force at Gloucester Point. The task was a difficult, nerve-wracking one, as the size of Weedon's force ebbed. Then, serendipitously, as one militia unit's tours expired, another militia unit would arrive.

A French commander, Duc de Lauzun, had nothing but contempt for the Americans. The Duc considered "Weedon the boorish leader of a peasant army."[47] Lauzun wrote to General Rochambeau, "No reliance could be placed upon the American militia. ... They were all cowards ... in five minutes as much afraid of [me] as of the English."[48] Nonetheless, Weedon's minutemen carried out the mission.

Reliance Upon Militia at Saratoga and Cowpens

Late in the war, in western South Carolina, General Daniel Morgan made effective use of the militia. Rather than utilizing militia conventionally, in a backup role, General Morgan put militia in the front ranks at the January 1781 Battle of Cowpens. Per Morgan's orders, officers instructed the militia to fire muskets twice. After firing two volleys at the advancing British line, the militia were to migrate to the rear, threading their way through the regulars who formed the third and fourth American lines.[49] General Morgan knew that untrained militia tended to break and run when the shooting started. His thinking was to raise the expectations but not to raise them too high. In historian John Buchanan's appraisal, Daniel Morgan at Cowpens was "the only general in the American Revolution, on either side, to produce a significant, original tactical thought."[50] Militia played an indispensable part in Daniel Morgan's thinking.

Reliance Upon Militia at Saratoga

In the north, the Battle of Freeman's Farm, September 19, 1777, was the first of two battles collectively known as Saratoga. Colonel Thaddeus Cook and his Connecticut Militia "came up and joined the fight" being carried on by Daniel Morgan's Corps of Virginia riflemen and Colonel Alexander Scammell's Continental New Hampshire Regiment. Cook lost eleven men killed and thirty-six wounded. Later in the day, Latimer's Connecticut Militia joined the fray.[51]

On September 22, General Benjamin Lincoln, having recovered from wounds, reported in at the American camp: "With Lincoln were his bodyguards, the mounted dragons of the 2d Regiment of the Connecticut Light Horse ... a militia unit."[52] On September 24, additional battalions of Jonathan Wagner's Massachusetts Militia arrived. Militia units frequently came in dribs and drabs, "a piecemeal arrival" not being uncommon.[53]

On September 25, General Gates welcomed Warner's Brigade of Massachusetts Militia and Wolcott's smaller brigade of Connecticut Militia. General Enoch Poor's and Ebenezer Hand's brigades "were now supported by [New York Militia General] Ten Broeck's brigade of [1,300] Albany militiamen."[54] Half of the final American troop count of 14,000 at Saratoga consisted of militia.

On October 5, 1777, the Hampshire County Massachusetts Militia under Colonel Benjamin Woodbridge arrived with "more than five hundred men."[55] At the Battle of Bemis Heights on October 7, 1777, General Enoch Poor's Brigade consisted of five regiments of regulars and two regiments of militia. General Ebenezer Learned's Brigade consisted of three regiments of regulars and three regiments of militia. At Bemis Heights, the Army's left wing consisted of only six regiments of regulars but nineteen regiments of militia. The mix on the right wing was not so lopsided, consisting of twelve regiments of regulars and eleven regiments of militia.[56]

Historian Dean Snow described the action: "Ten Broeck's Albany militiamen were behind [the Continental regulars] for support. They could not be restrained, and many started to move up among the Continentals in the front line. The flow of militiamen forward counteracted the slow retreat and steadied the American line."[57] Author Snow describes an older militiaman in picking off the British General Simon Fraser from sixty-six yards with a musket, whose effective range was estimated at forty to fifty yards. Snow labels the shot as "the tipping point," not just of the Battle of Saratoga but of the Revolution.[58] In many ways, it is emblematic that a militia minuteman took the action that constituted the tipping point, just as it had been emblematic that minutemen fired the "shot heard around the world" at Concord Bridge in 1775.

An Anti-Climax

The story of the militia in the Revolutionary War seems more nuanced than historical accounts adopt. Historians accept, uncritically, Continental officers' near-constant militia bashing. The latter carried through even after the guns had silenced. For example, in the October 19 surrender ceremony following the Battle of Yorktown, Lord Cornwallis handed over his sword while the British troops stacked their weapons. On the opposite side, the American higher-ups, including Commanding General George Washington, invited the French to join the Continental soldiers and officers to participate in the ceremony. The militia, the "minutemen," were excluded.[59] Two years later, when Continental officers formed the Society of Cincinnati (Chapter 27), the Society rules excluded militia officers, no matter how long or how bravely they had fought. When victory celebrations following Yorktown occurred, as for instance at George Weedon's tavern, militia were not welcome.

PART IV

Also Mentioned in the Dispatches: 1775

14

War Within the War

Lord Dunmore's Second War

The Revolutionary War began with a war within the war.[1] Colonial Governor Lord Dunmore (The Right Honourable Earl of Dunmore, Viscount Fincastle, Barron Murray of Blair, Moulli, and Tillimet) had been Royal Governor of Virginia since September 25, 1771.[2] In 1775, Dunmore commenced a semi-private action. A Scot, Dunmore succeeded Governor Norbonne Berkeley, 4th Baron Botetourt, who had died in office, after whom Virginia named a new county, Berkeley County (now in West Virginia).

Botetourt had been a popular governor. Dunmore was the opposite. By the end of his tenure, Dunmore was said to be the "most despised man in Virginia."[3] He was a veteran of the British Army. Most often, portraits picture Dunmore in military garb, albeit with kilts and a tam in addition to scabbard and sword. He comes down as one who ruled by fiat, accustomed not only to his orders but to his whims and suggestions being followed.[4]

Dissolution of the House of Burgesses and the Gun Powder Affair

In revolutionary times, news did not travel fast, but it did travel. Many in Virginia therefore knew of the depredations and restrictions the British Parliament and the King's Ministers had visited upon Massachusetts. Those acts had begun in earnest with quartering British troops and the occupation of Boston in 1768, the Boston Massacre in March 1770, and the Boston Tea Party in December 1773. News of these acts of oppression reached Virginia, including its leading citizens, many of whom sat in the House of Burgesses in Williamsburg. Appalled by what was happening, the Burgesses voted that June 1, 1774, would be a day of fasting and prayer for Virginians in support of their fellow colonists in Boston and Massachusetts. That was, in Dunmore's reckoning, a blasphemous act, one that enraged him. He reacted not by a reprimand but by dissolving the House of Burgesses altogether. The colony no longer would have a legislative branch. The executive, Governor Dunmore, would rule as a lord and despot.

The Gunpowder Plot

To an English man or woman, "gunpowder plot" is shorthand for Guy Fawkes and certain Jesuits' scheme to blow up the House of Lords and assassinate James I on Parliament's opening day, November 5, 1605.[5] In Williamsburg, Virginia, the gunpowder episode was less dramatic.[6] Citizens had hidden a dozen half-barrels of gunpowder. Should an armed insurrection ensue, a likely occurrence at that point with rumblings increasing daily, the insurrectionists would have powder for their muskets and shot. Upon hearing of the gunpowder hoard, Governor Dunmore ordered a dozen Royal Marines to seize the gunpowder and transport it down the James River to be stored on the British man-of-war *Magdalena*, then at anchor in Hampton Roads.

Dunmore's actions fueled outrage among patriots. In March 1775, Patrick Henry gave his "Give Me Liberty or Give Me Death" speech at St. John's Episcopal Church in Richmond. Thereafter, Henry led a contingent of Hanover County Militia toward Williamsburg. In Fredericksburg, Hugh Mercer rallied another militia force to march the short distance across the peninsula to Williamsburg.

Lord Dunmore, by Joshua Reynolds. The feisty last colonial governor of Virginia tried to enlist slaves for the British cause to start a "war within the war" (National Portrait Gallery, Scotland).

The gunpowder episode ended with a whimper, as the Crown made a payment to the patriots for the gunpowder. Militia marching toward the capital reversed course, returning home. Governor Dunmore, though, saw both the writing on the wall and the wall itself. On June 8, 1775, Governor Dunmore abandoned the capital, fleeing with his family (Lady Charlotte, five daughters, and three sons) southward from Williamsburg. At the foot of the Yorktown Peninsula, the group boarded one of four British warships. There, they could seek the protection of British marines and sailors. There as well, Dunmore could begin to push back against the wall that patriots, brick by brick, were building against continued British rule.

To increase the stakes, Dunmore solicited slaves to join his loyalist force, promising emancipation. About a thousand answered Dunmore's call. Those who accepted the bargain outlined in "Dunmore's Proclamation" would form Dunmore's Ethiopian Corps. Alarmed at these developments, in August 1775, the Virginia Convention formed two regiments for the Continental Line; their first mission would be counteracting Dunmore. They elected Charles Scott to be second-in-command of the Second Virginia Regiment, captained by Colonel William Woodford.[7] Overall commander Andrew Lewis (Chapter 8) ordered Colonel Woodford and his regiment to bring Dunmore and his forces to account.

In early October, the Committee on Safety ordered Colonel Woodford and his regiment of 476 men toward Tidewater Virginia. Desultory skirmishes that historians label the "Battle of Hampton," took place with Woodford's men firing at the ships and the Royal Navy returning fire. Dunmore had at his command four schooners, three sloops, and three tenders armed with swivel guns. He had 340 navies, 150 soldiers from the British 14th Regiment, 150 loyalists, and a number of slaves (estimated at 800–1,000).[8]

Woodford, Scott, and their regiment marched down the James River. Dunmore's force had constructed a stockade at Great Bridge, fifteen miles southeast of Portsmouth and twelve miles directly south of Norfolk. There a series of wooden bridges spanned the Elizabeth River's south branch via two small islands in the river. Colonel Woodford dispatched his second-in-command, Charles Scott, and 200 men to cross wetlands to reach Great Bridge. For the Americans, sealing off escape routes to the south from Norfolk took precedence over an artillery duel at Hampton. North Carolina, a short distance south of Great Bridge, had a significant Tory population with whom Lord Dunmore could attempt to rendezvous.

Not content with the watch and wait mission assigned, Charles Scott showed the combination of aggression and bravery that he later exhibited at Princeton and elsewhere. Scott was "eager to confront Dunmore's small force of '*Torries and Blacks*.'" Colonel Woodford held Scott back, pleading an ammunition and arms shortage. "The best he could do to support Scott," Woodworth wrote, "was to send him two more companies of regulars under Major Alexander Spotswood."[9]

Scott's men constructed a breastwork at the causeway's southern end in advance of Great Bridge village. The Americans removed planking on the bridge, greasing the long, narrow trusses underneath. Not to be idle, Colonel Scott led a 150-man party downriver to attack a Dunmore outpost. Scott's men overwhelmed the 70 defenders, killing several and wounding others. Scott's force had no casualties.[10]

On December 2, Colonel Woodford and the remainder of the Second Regiment arrived at Great Bridge. The stage was set for the first real conflict in the south, "a second Bunker Hill, in miniature."[11] On December 9, the Dunmore force, led by 120 British grenadiers, mounted a frontal attack. British Captain, later General, Phillip Leslie's force of 350 first re-laid some planking on the bridge. The British advanced six abreast, with bayonets fixed, true to British convention of frontal assaults designed to spread shock and awe among opponents. Confined as they were to the

GREAT BRIDGE

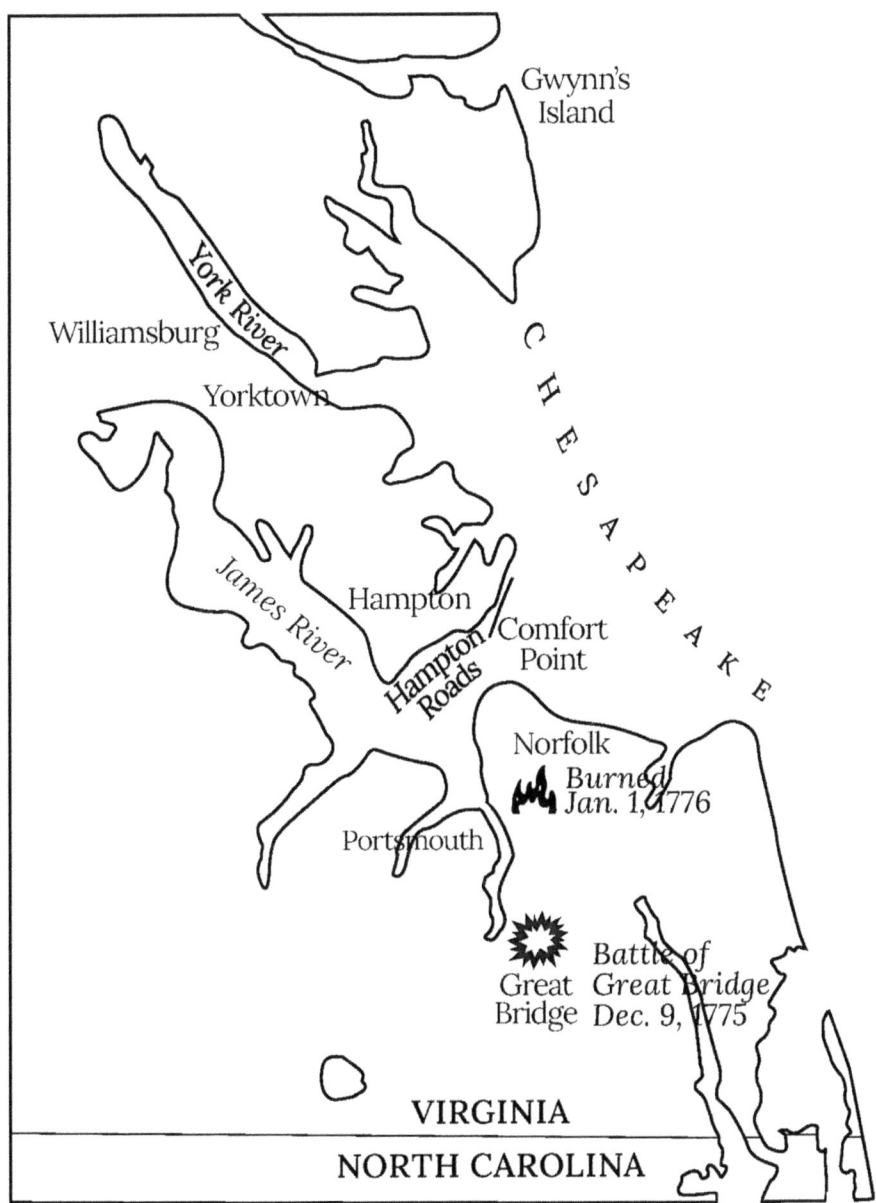

narrow bridge, though, Leslie's force had no access to cover and nowhere to scatter. The only alternatives were to continue marching ahead or retreat. The Americans decimated the advancing force, killing or wounding 50 before the British abandoned the assault. Col. Woodford's force suffered one man wounded.[12]

After the American victory, American General Lewis directed Woodford and Scott to stand, marching northwest to protect Williamsburg. Rendered ineffectual by his unpopularity with the men, and in snit over Congress's elevation of Hugh

Mercer to Brigadier, Colonel Woodford retreated farther than Williamsburg, to his Caroline County plantation, soon thereafter to resign his commission (see Chapter 15). Meanwhile, the unpolished, at times profane, brave, and aggressive Charles Scott had become "Charley Scott" to his troops.[13]

Gwynn's Island

Dunmore's War came to end at the Battle of Gwynn's Island. After Great Bridge, the British troop morale evaporated. Their leader, Captain Leslie, was dispirited. His nephew, a lieutenant in the 14th Regiment, had been killed at Great Bridge. "Captain Leslie ... declared that no more of his troops should be sacrificed to whims" of Lord Dunmore, putting them aboard ships.[14] The ships sailed north, anchoring beyond a barrier island at the foot of the Virginia's Middle Peninsula (between the York and the Rappahannock Rivers). There, as described in Chapter 8, the patriot forces under Brigadier Andrew Lewis began firing over Gwynn's Island at the ships anchored in the lee of the island. The American artillery scored a direct hit and splinters flew, several of which wounded Dunmore. He ordered ships' officers to weigh anchors, sailing first in a feint to the north, then coming about and sailing out to sea.[15]

At Gwynn's Island, the Americans suffered a single casualty, a Captain Dohickey Arundel who had invented a wooden mortar with which he intended to fire experimental shots.[16] With the first shot, the mortar exploded, killing Captain Arundel. So ended Lord Dunmore's War, the war within the war.

A short time later, though, Dunmore's War had a fleeting second life. In the American Declaration of Independence, Thomas Jefferson listed "repeated injuries and usurpations" the colonies had suffered at the hands of King George III and his ministers, those wrongs justifying independence. One such allegation was that the King and his ministers have "excited domestic insurrections against us." Historians trace the cryptic reference to British Colonial Governor Dunmore's "emancipation proclamation," a not-too-successful attempt to precipitate a slave revolt.[17]

15

Virginia Planter William Woodford

General William Woodford's wounding, capture by the British, and war-related death tell a stirring story. He appears to have ticked all the boxes for heroism. He was wounded (at Brandywine), taken prisoner (when Charles Town fell), and died a combat-related death (in New York City, where the British held him prisoner). Yet his frequent snits, incessant manipulations, shortcomings in his men's eyes, and arrogant dandyism tell another story. He had a dark, uncomfortable side in which jealousy, anger, suspicion, and envy counterbalanced his contributions to the cause.

All told, in the Revolutionary War, thirteen American generals died of wounds in combat or of combat-related causes.[1] Seven of those thirteen, more than half, were southern brigadiers. Of the South's generals who died in the Revolution, James Hogun, William Davidson, Francis Nash, and William Woodford are little-known. Woodford was one of only three southern generals of English stock. The Georges—Washington and Weedon—were the others. Woodford was a wealthy planter, a man of privilege whose sense of superiority and entitlement were strong, in part explaining his erratic behavior.

Three Beginning Tantrums

At Great Bridge, in December 1775, Colonel Robert Howe moved north with his North Carolina Regiment of 340 men. Again, Great Bridge was a short distance above the Virginia-North Carolina boundary, causing military leaders to fret that Dunmore might proceed in that direction. After the battle, Howe, senior to Woodford, assumed command. Feeling that he had pulled the laboring oar, Woodford grumbled, loudly and repeatedly. As a consolation to calm him, Howe decreed that Woodford would command all Virginia troops in the theater, which included Woodford's 2nd Virginia Regiment and the Culpeper Militia.[2]

The second tantrum followed. Having been appointed commander of the Second Virginia Regiment (Patrick Henry briefly commanded the First), Colonel Woodford was "stunned" a few months after Great Bridge to learn that in mid–June 1776, Congress appointed Hugh Mercer of the newly formed 3rd Virginia Regiment to the rank of brigadier:[3] "Woodford had assumed that when Congress had taken Virginia's regiments into continental service back in February [1776], the issue of seniority had been settled with him holding seniority over Mercer due to his earlier appointment."[4] Woodford felt that the leapfrog Mercer promotion "was an aspersion upon his character." Then came a third blow producing a third tantrum. Woodford learned that Adam Stephen, colonel of the 4th Virginia Regiment, also was to be promoted to brigadier over Woodford.

In summer 1776, Woodford penned a resignation letter to General Washington: "I feel myself much hurt by the late promotion of my very worthy friend Col. Mercer.... I conceive of the appointment and promotion of an officer at the time serving under me ... reflected dishonor upon myself." He added, "I am informed from good authority, that a similar promotion is now in contemplation in favor of Col. Adam Stephens [sic—Stephen]. For the above reasons, I request your permission to retire...."[5] Woodford, though, remained in the army until early September when he learned that Congress had finally decreed Stephen's promotion. Two promotions over Woodford had now been accomplished. "That was the final straw for Woodford; he resigned his commission in protest and returned to Caroline County," deduced biographer Michael Cecere.[6]

Storm Clouds over the Entire Revolutionary Movement

However, there were other factors that may have contributed to Woodford's resignation. In the fall 1776, it appeared that the revolution might fail completely. The American army was in disarray after losses at Brooklyn, Kip's Bay, Harlem Heights, soon to include White Plains (October 28) and Fort Washington (November 16). Woodford learned of the further defeats when in November 1776, he rode north to deliver a letter from John Augustine to General Washington. Woodford saw the "Grand Army" Washington was leading, chased out of New York, vastly diminished, and fleeing across New Jersey. "Washington worried that his army might simply melt into nothingness," Ron Chernow wrote in *George Washington: A Life*.[7] General Washington wrote to his brother Samuel, "I think that the game is pretty near up."[8]

A Better-Known Woodford Snit

Yet Woodford is perhaps best known for the umbrage he took when Congress listed Woodford junior to ten other generals in the brigadier rank.[9] In March 1777, Congress had promoted and then ranked the newly minted generals as to seniority, ranking Virginia generals George Weedon and Peter Muhlenberg senior to Woodford. Woodford protested because he had been in service longer than the two Virginians whom Congress had ranked over him: "[B]ut the majority in Congress, citing Woodford's resignation from the army, placed him at the bottom of the list."[10]

Commander-in-chief George Washington urged Woodford to accept the seniority list, writing to Woodford, "You may recollect ... that I strongly advised you against this resignation. I now as strongly recommend your acceptance of the present Appointment. You may feel somewhat hurt, in having two Officers placed before you ... but remember that this is a consequence of your own Act."[11]

Woodford listened, accepted the promotion, and was back in harness by early May 1777, after an eight to ten-month absence. General Washington gave Woodford command of a brigade consisting of the 3rd, 7th, 11th, and 15th regiments. The 11th (Col. Daniel Morgan), however, was elsewhere on special assignment, not under Woodford's command. Paper strength of Woodford's force was to be 3,000, but the brigade had only 999 men, in three regiments, fit for duty.

The snits and fits of pique of colonial officers such as Woodford (and Weedon to an extent, Muhlenberg, Sumner, Varnum—the list was lengthy) over promotions and orders of seniority, what historian Douglas Freeman pronounced "the clash of jealous and ambitious men," was astounding.[12] It was a wonder that these men were able to lead an army that ultimately prevailed. Noteworthy was George Washington's patience, demonstrated time and time again, in dealing with such matters. What an irritant it must have been for the commander-in-chief to have to deal with such personnel matters when his hands and head were, and had to be, occupied with military matters, including tactics, strategy, upcoming campaigns, logistics, constantly expiring enlistments, politics, and political interference by the armchair generals in Congress.[13]

A Virginia Elite

Woodford's father was a British army major who, after resigning his commission, emigrated to America. William Senior built up a plantation, "Windsor," in Caroline County, thirty miles northwest of Fredericksburg. Woodford Senior and his wife had their first son, also a William, in 1734. In 1755, William Senior died suddenly when young William was twenty-one, leaving William Junior free to pursue his wanderlust. William organized a volunteer company to serve under George Washington in the French & Indian War. Woodford's company spent the war at Fort Loudon (Winchester) where Washington had made his rear headquarters.[14]

In the later 1750s, Woodford returned to Caroline County. He married Mary Thornton, the daughter of George Washington's first cousin, and assumed management of his father's plantation. He became Lieutenant Colonel in the Caroline County Militia. Citizens elected him to the non-importation committee to enforce the boycott of British goods.[15] He became friends with Edmund Pendleton, first president of the Continental Congress. In fact, Woodford served as Pendleton's substitute at the Third Virginia Convention, July 17 to August 9, 1775.[16] Woodford was "one of the planter class [who] adhered to the behavior of a southern gentleman."[17] He acquired other land and political appointments.[18]

On August 5, 1775, the Third Virginia Convention formally appointed William Woodford colonel, Second Virginia Regiment.[19] Patrick Henry, the first overall commander of Virginia forces, made his stirring speech: "Is life so dear, or peace so sweet, as to be purchased at the price of chains and slavery? I know not what course others may take, but as for me, give me liberty or give me death!"[20]

Woodford and the 1777 Campaign

To recount, in May 1777, Woodford, like Lazarus, had risen from the ashes after George Washington urged Woodford to rejoin the army. The first actions of Woodford as a brigadier in command of a brigade revealed him as a martinet. His first orders were to form standing boards of inquiry and a standing court for courts martial.[21] His troops regarded their new commander's actions as a "shot across the bow." They, too, had scuttlebutt of what occurred after Great Bridge. After the victory there, "Woodford's efforts to install more discipline in his troops ... hampered his efforts [at procuring re-enlistments]. Many of his men refused to re-enlist under his command."[22] With enlistments expiring, Woodford harangued his men, a senior soldier telling him, "They say they will only serve under Lt. Col. Scott [Woodford's second-in-command]."[23]

Troops took to calling the General "Beau Woodford" and the "Damndest Partial Rascal on the earth without exception." Historian Harry Ward concluded Woodford "was not exactly a favorite with the men or the other Virginia generals."[24] In late 1779, Colonel John Neville wrote to General Daniel Morgan, "I am Sorry to inform you [General Woodford] is very Much Disliked in Particular by his Own Brigade." Neville speculated that a cause may have been Woodford's "long held belief in strict discipline."[25]

Renewed Combat: Brandywine

At Brandywine, Virginia Generals Woodford and Scott, now also a brigadier, with their brigades composed Major General Adam Stephen's division. George Washington placed Stephen's division, Woodford and Scott included, in reserve, on a hill overlooking Brandywine Creek, southwest of Philadelphia. When General Washington finally became aware that British General William Howe had split his force, thought unwise in standard military tactics and one that Washington had not anticipated, he acted. He saw that Cornwallis, several miles upstream and having forded the creek, could turn the Americans' right flank. Washington sent Stephen's division north to meet the challenge, later to be augmented by General John Sullivan with 1,100 troops. "They [Woodford's troops] doggedly pushed forward ... towards a hill overlooking the Birmingham Meeting House. General Stephen deployed the troops upon large, cleared field, just west of the Birmingham Road." They thus anchored the far-right flank of the new American line.[26]

Woodford's men performed admirably, but the day's praise went to Generals Weedon and Muhlenberg and their troops who, at great personal cost, covered the front-line troops' withdrawal from the field as twilight approached. They had prevented Brandywine from being a larger disaster than it was.

At Brandywine, British musket fire struck Woodford in the left hand. He spent several weeks at the Moravian settlement in Bethlehem, Pennsylvania, where he recuperated with a wounded Marquis de Lafayette.

Another Rank and Seniority Imbroglio

In 1778, Woodford was at Valley Forge where his brigade, now consisting of four regiments, totaled 1,287 men. He spent much time revisiting the Virginia's brigadiers' seniority ranking, becoming monomaniacal about it. He was dissatisfied with his ranking number three of four Virginia brigadiers (Weedon, Muhlenberg, Woodford, and Scott, in that order), as determined by Congress. Because he had left the army for eight months, against General Washington's advice, Woodford garnered little sympathy. Nonetheless, Woodford petitioned Congress, got a board of review appointed, got a second board of review appointed after the first board did little, and finally procured the re-ranking for which he strived. Washington called in the generals' commissions, issuing new ones with Woodford now senior to Muhlenberg and Scott, with Weedon ranked last.

Weedon was highly displeased, leaving the army in protest (Chapter 2). General Muhlenberg also left the army, journeying to Woodstock, but after several days, had second thoughts and returned to the army at Valley Forge.[27] It is easy to chalk up the other generals' reactions to ultra-sensitivity, but from their point of view, Woodford had pushed and pushed and would not be stopped until he obtained what he wished for at a time when there was a war to fight. In addition, "Beau Woodford" was popular neither with the soldiers he commanded nor his fellow officers: "Woodford had the reputation of being a dandy and [always] dressed to the hilt."[28]

British Abandonment of Philadelphia

In 1777, Lord Germain, secretary of state for America, had replaced Lord William Howe with Henry Clinton as British forces commander in North America. In spring 1778, Lord Germain ordered Clinton to send 5,000 troops to Canada and an additional 5,000 troops to the Caribbean to defend British sugar interests there. The need to transfer several regiments left Clinton with limited options. With forces so weakened, Clinton no longer felt he could continue occupation of Philadelphia.[29] In June 1778, the British abandoned the city, beginning the long trek diagonally across New Jersey, to Sandy Hook, a spit jutting out into New York's outer harbor. There the army of 10,000, its followers, and hangers-on would board transports for New York's inner harbor. Crossing New Jersey, the British army moved at two miles per day, impeded by a baggage train several miles in length. The slow-moving caravan made a tempting target.

Clinton's loss of troops, evacuation of Philadelphia, and retreat to New York may be seen as the beginnings of what was ultimately to follow: the British Southern Strategy in 1779–1781. Most immediately, though, the events set the stage for the Battle of Monmouth Courthouse.

Monmouth

In June 1778, Washington led his army out of Valley Forge, journeying straight east, crossing the Delaware River (*see also* Chapter 17). Washington then sent

General Charles Scott and his brigade of hand-picked light, mobile infantry ahead to harass the slow-moving British. Lafayette, with 1,000 additional men, joined Scott. Ultimately, the advance guard swelled to over 5,000 Americans, nipping at the British army's heels.

In a fit of petulance, brandishing his high rank, Charles Lee expressed to Washington dissatisfaction at not being in command of such a large part of the army. In reply, "General Washington appeased [Lee] by sending him forward with yet another [advance] contingent of two brigades with instructions to take overall command of the advance guard" when Lee and his force caught up with Scott and Lafayette.[30]

Just short of Tennant's Meeting House, the British turned to face the Americans and engage. On a blistering hot day, June 28, 1778, the battle commenced with a local woman, Mary Ludwig, "Molly Pitcher," standing among the American troops passing to them pitchers and buckets of drinking water.

General Lee ordered his troops to retreat. Washington, unaware of Lee's pullback, ordered a push forward on the American right flank by Nathanael Greene and William Woodford. With Lee's troops in retreat in the center, Greene's and Woodford's force on the right was exposed as a salient, its flanks unprotected.[31] "General Washington rode ahead of the main body." Upon reaching a forward position, "He discovered that his advance guard, which he believed was pushing the enemy, were actually withdrawing in disarray." Generally calm and collected, Washington flashed with anger. He "encountered General Lee on a small knoll … and demanded to know why Lee's troops were retreating. Lee, taken aback by Washington's angry tone, stammered, which Washington impatiently dismissed," ordering Lee to the rear.[32]

Unsupported on the side, Woodford's brigade nonetheless moved forward, to be met by swampy terrain. The wet ground and fading light curtailed further advance. The force retreated a short way to Comb's Hill, there unlimbering artillery pieces: "With the use of artillery, he [Woodford with his men] crushed the British army's left flank."[33] During the night, Clinton's troops turned, resuming their march to the northeast. Monmouth Courthouse was the war's last major battle in the north.[34]

For Woodford: North, Then South

After Monmouth, Washington distributed units north of New York City, ranging from White Plains north to Peekskill and across the Hudson to West Point. Woodford and his men guarded the passes in the Ramapo Mountains, the back door to West Point and a strategic point high on bluffs, thereby controlling the Hudson. In May 1779, Washington decided to send a force south to Charles Town, reinforcing the Southern Army there. General Benjamin Lincoln, who commanded the Charles Town defense, had requested reinforcement.[35] Early in 1780, British General Henry Clinton and an 8,500-man force had left New York by ship, men-of-war, and transports manned by 4,500 British sailors, who landed the force along the Savannah River, where an advance force previously had captured Savannah. From Savannah, the British marched overland eighty or so miles north to Charles Town, first crossing the Savannah River, the boundary between Georgia and South Carolina. The Clinton–led force wheeled to the right, advancing in a southeasterly direction, down the peninsula on which Charles Town sits, between the Cooper and Ashley Rivers. Two-thirds of the way down the peninsula, the British force halted to prepare "parallels" to overcome the American fortifications strung the peninsula's width, including a wide and deep ditch across the peninsula, north of the city. Meanwhile, south of the city, British men-of-war blockaded entrance to the Charles Town harbor, preparing a bombardment of the city on the peninsula's point.

Woodford's Role

In December 1779, George Washington ordered Woodford and his brigade south.[36] In March, "We arrived … to the great joy of the garrison."[37] "We" meant Woodford, 2,000 troops, and six brass cannon. A short time later, Washington sent General Charles Scott south with additional soldiers. On April 6, 1780, "The bells pealed joyously, with people celebrating as a relief column of 750 soldiers from North Carolina and Virginia arrived."[38] Washington had intended to send General Peter Muhlenberg, but Muhlenberg, reluctant to serve under Woodford, resisted the orders. Muhlenberg still disputed Woodford's advance in seniority over Weedon and himself, especially the way Woodford achieved it.[39]

In Charles Town, General Lincoln's councils of war urged Lincoln to quit the city. Citizens condemned General Lincoln, saying "His strategy will send us all to our graves" because of continuing British bombardment if American troops garrisoned the city. "General Washington is in favor of withdrawing," others said.[40] Pressured to stay by the city fathers and critics who wished his force to vacate, Lincoln dallied. Then the dreaded Banastre Tarleton and his green-coated cavalry smashed the American cavalry, cutting off the sole escape route. General Clinton reinforced the position Tarleton had cleared north of the city, along the Cooper River, with 2000 men.[41]

Serving the British, Hessian Captain Hinrichs wrote of the dire American position, "All their cavalry was annihilated. Our works come up to their ditch [a defensive moat the Americans had dug and flooded]. Fort Moultrie and the entire harbor were in our hands. They could not entertain the least hope of succor."[42] On May 11, 1781, General Benjamin Lincoln accepted British General Henry Clinton's terms of capitulation, no terms offered, formalities to be concluded the following day, May 12. Five thousand, six hundred American troops, 2,600 Continental regulars and 3,000 militia surrendered, fenced in by the British force's 12,000.[43] The pearl of the American colonies, the wealthiest American city, was in British hands.

The British put prisoners in densely packed barracks and on prison ships in Charles Town harbor. They imprisoned Woodford and other officers across the Cooper River, at Haddrell's Point (Chapter 10). The officers would remain there until the British offered them parole or the prisoner and his representative could engineer an exchange for a British officer of equal rank.[44]

The British did not act with alacrity. With the capture of both Savannah and

Charles Town, the two major coastal cities, the British felt they had the keys to the American South on their belt, so they could act at leisure. The British impression was reinforced by the Lord Cornwallis's overwhelming victory over Horatio Gates at Camden on August 16, 1780.

Woodford's Slow, Lengthy Demise

Woodford could arrange neither exchange nor parole. In stark confinement, he languished. The British refused adequate food supplies to the American officers at Haddrell's Point. Among the officers, Generals James Hogun from North Carolina and William Woodford of Virginia contracted diseases that proved fatal.[45]

> Yellow fever broke out ... there was a lack of medicine. Without hard money [the officers] found it almost impossible to make purchases. Haddrell's Point ... seemed a land of desolation—a "flat country" where the water was not fit to drink and "the soil is nothing but sand which burns the flat of the foot and binds one when the wind blows." The pine trees give no shade....[46]

In autumn 1780, the British shipped William Woodford to New York. History does not reveal what illness Woodford suffered. Probably, the British continued his imprisonment aboard a British prison ship in the East River's Wallabout Bay. While still in captivity, Woodford died there; the date of death was given as November 13, 1780. The British buried him in an unmarked grave in Trinity Churchyard on Broadway, at the foot of Wall Street. A partial epitaph read, "The fatigues of the siege, in which he bore a very active part, together with the mortification of becoming a prisoner, and the rigorous confinement he suffered, proved too much for his delicate condition. [He] fell a cheerful sacrifice to his country's glorious cause."[47]

Postscript: Barbaric Imprisonment of American Soldiers

George Washington insisted upon British prisoners' humane treatment, including by wardens who supervised captivity: "Washington seemed to believe that simply allowing German [and British] prisoners to live as Americans lived would convert them."[48] An early instance was his caution to George Weedon, tasked with escorting 919 prisoners to Philadelphia after the Battle of Trenton.[49] As he lay dying, Hessian Colonel Johannes Rall had "asked that his men be kindly treated. Washington promised that he would see that they were well cared for."[50] Later, Hessian private Ruebner admitted, "A promise was given and it was kept."[51]

In another example, at the war's end, British forces had sailed from Boston to Nova Scotia. Six hundred Scottish Highlanders arrived in Boston, late, immediately to be captured by colonial forces. The American captors parceled out the Scots to the colonies, "to become absorbed in the life and activities of the citizens." Congressional representative Richard Henry Lee hoped for a promising future for the 217 captives assigned Virginia, "distributed thro' this Colony, a few in each County, and permitted to hire themselves out to labor, thus to become Citizens of America instead of our enemies."[52]

By contrast, the British were cruel, regarding the Americans as traitors, rebels against the crown. Captured American soldiers were considered criminals rather than prisoners of war. Further, American troops were "clodhoppers" to whom the British owned not even common courtesy. At the Battle of Princeton in 1777, British cavalry bayoneted General Hugh Mercer as he lay injured on the ground. Later in 1777, British soldiers massacred General Anthony Wayne's troops as they slept at Paoli, Pennsylvania.

No greater inhumanity toward prisoners of war may be found than on the British prison ships in the East River. The East River extends north and south, between Manhattan and Brooklyn with one exception. After the Brooklyn and Manhattan Bridges, and Vinegar Hill, the river turns east for a mile, bordered by the now defunct Brooklyn Navy Yard.[53] The notch created by the irregular shoreline is Wallabout Bay.

In the Bay, the British anchored de-masted, rotting hulks of men-of-war. There they imprisoned more than 1,000 Americans per ship. The prisoners were crammed "into lower decks reeking of urine, excrement, and vomit with little ventilation owing to sealed gunports." Mortality rates approached one hundred percent "from scurvy, dysentery, and typhus." Food and water were non-existent. "Malnourishment, as a consequence of fetid water and scarce provisions, was rampant, as were rats and mosquitos."[54]

It is estimated that between 11,500 and 18,000 Americans perished at Wallabout Bay, with British warders throwing corpses overboard or burying them in mass graves on the sandy shore.[55] In contrast, 6,800 American soldiers perished in combat over the course of the entire war.[56] For decades, bones of deceased prisoners washed up on Brooklyn's shores or worked to the surface of sand landfill extending along the navy yard. Barbarous conditions such as these hastened William Woodford's death. British treatment of prisoners was one of the most shocking legacies of the Revolutionary War.[57]

PART V

Mentioned in the Dispatches

16

"Give Me Liberty or Give Me Death"

Virginia's Brigadier Hugh Mercer at Princeton

The image of Hugh Mercer that comes down to us is of a handsome, middle-aged man whom, in the biography *George Washington*, Ron Chernow describes as "the dapper, handsome Mercer."[1] "He was always valuable and dependable," wrote Colonel Robert Byrd of Mercer's militia service. "Every man was glad to know him.... [C]olonel Mercer was a conscientious officer, loyal to his superiors, undaunted by any emergency."[2] The summation of the regard for Mercer was "of universal approbation throughout his career." He was "always courteous [but] did not incur the jealousy that often crops out in any organization where ambitious men endeavor."[3] He was brave, ready to face danger and, if necessary, death, as his final actions at Princeton demonstrate. His adventurous past had color and flair.

The Jacobite Rising

In the 1740s, a movement took place to restore the Catholic Stuart monarchy to the English throne. From 1603 until 1688, Stuarts had held the English and Scottish crowns, beginning with James the 1st of England (James the 6th of Scotland). In the Glorious Revolution, William of Orange succeeded the last Stuart, James II.[4] In the 1740s, the "pretender" to the throne, Stuart descendant Prince Charles Edward Stuart, known as "Bonnie Prince Charlie," began angling for the Stuart dynasty's re-installation upon the throne. In the 1740s, he returned from exile in France to lead a 6,000-man Scottish Highlander army intent upon the Stuart restoration. Historians refer to the uprising as the "Jacobite Rebellion" or "Jacobite Rising."[5] Hugh Mercer was a veteran of the vanquished Jacobite rebel force.

Hugh Mercer came from a line of Presbyterian ministers. His father, Willian Mercer, had a church at Pitsligo, east of Inverness, Scotland.[6] Mercer was born in 1726, "in the manse of Pilsligo Kirk."[7] He pursued medicine rather than the ministry, studying at the University of Aberdeen. Led by John Augustus, the English Duke of Cumberland, the crown's forces met the Jacobite rebels on April 16, 1746, on Culloden Moor, east of Inverness. With a 12,000-man force, the English vanquished the Highlanders. Not only were the English victorious, but Augustus also declared the rebels to be outlaws. With the English pursuing them, the rebels retreated into the crags and mountains of the Highlands.[8]

16. "Give Me Liberty or Give Me Death" 115

Whether young Mercer was a warrior or a surgeon at Culloden was unclear, but, regardless, the merciless edict applied to him.[9] So, after the defeat, Mercer fled south, where he stayed on his cousins' farm west of Aberdeen, hiding for a year. He then found his way to Leith on the Firth of Forth, the seaport for Edinburgh. In May 1747, Hugh Mercer boarded a ship bound for Philadelphia.

Straight to the Frontier

Regarding himself an outlaw, Mercer did not tarry in Philadelphia. Unaware of the pardon the king had granted Scottish rebels, Mercer departed immediately for the frontier.[10] He settled into what today is Franklin County, in south central Pennsylvania, west of Gettysburg and a score of miles short of the Allegheny mountains.[11] He began practice as a frontier physician.[12] Those were perilous times on the frontier. Pennsylvania was a Quaker colony. The Quakers were pacifists and, dominated by Quakers, the colony's assembly refused to authorize a standing armed force, let alone approve public funds to buy weapons for a volunteer one.[13] Furthermore, proprietors William Penn and Thomas Penn refused to allow any tax on the vast Penn land holdings.

Hugh Mercer, sketch by John Trumbull. By all accounts most noble, Mercer was another Scottish physician whom British cavalry killed at Princeton (Metropolitan Museum, Open Access Collection).

After Mercer had been on the frontier eight years, General Edward Braddock, a Coldstream Guards veteran and former royal governor of Gibraltar arrived from England. To Benjamin Franklin, Braddock "was a brave man, and might probably made a good figure in some European war. But he had too much self-confidence; too high an opinion of the validity of regular [British] troops; too mean of one of both Americans and Indians."[14] A Virginia regiment, nine companies, 50 men each, led by a young George Washington, was to accompany Braddock to confront the French and their Indian allies. The goal was to recapture Fort Duquesne at the forks of the Ohio (present-day Pittsburgh), considered the gateway to the Ohio country and the West. The combined British-American force left Fort Cumberland, Maryland, on June 10, 1755, with 150 wagons and 2,000 horses, proceeding in a northwest direction at two miles per day.

Ten miles short of Fort Duquesne, on July 9, 1755, French and Indians ambushed Braddock's 1,400-man force with devastating effect. At the Battle of Monongahela, the British-American force lost 457 killed and 450 wounded. Braddock was severely wounded, dying two days later as his army's remnants retreated southeast.

Ranger Captain Mercer of the Pennsylvania Militia

The failure of the Braddock excursion heavily influenced frontier moods. News of the failure encouraged bolder Indian raids sweeping past the frontier into the colony's more settled eastern regions. In his Hugh Mercer biography, Joseph Waterman recounted, "A wave of terror swept across Pennsylvania."[15]

Forty-five miles northeast of present-day Pittsburgh, on the eastern shore of the Allegheny River, sat an Indian village named Kittanning.[16] "To Kittanning the [Indian] war parties returned with plunder and prisoners and here took place the orgies of triumph…. [H]ere lived the Delaware chief, Captain Jacobs, and here resided [Lenape Chief] King Shingas," also known as "Shingas the Terrible." Ranger Colonel John Armstrong, a surveyor familiar with the terrain and Mercer's friend, organized a 700-volunteer force to cross the Allegheny Mountains to subjugate Kittanning and the Indians there. Armstrong organized the militia into six companies, with Hugh Mercer as one company's captain.

The settlers' raid, "which was only was only nominally successful, given the number of casualties suffered by Armstrong," did quell hostile Indian activity for a time. The rangers killed 40 Indians and burnt down Indian structures while suffering a loss of 17. The Kittanning raid, though, "was a big success psychologically, boosting the morale of settlers throughout Pennsylvania."[17]

Hugh Mercer's Return to Civilization: The Stuff of Legends

In the Kittanning raid, the Indian defenders had shot Mercer, shattering his wrist. Mercer's men commandeered a horse, placing their wounded captain in the saddle, and retreated to the southeast. Soon, though, an Indian group ambushed the militia party. The Indians shot three or four men. Two men hopped on the horse, disappearing up the game trail they had been following. Alone, Captain Mercer hid behind a fallen tree. After a close brush with yet another warrior, Mercer stood. He was more than a hundred miles from civilization, separated from familiar surroundings by a mountain range, with neither food nor a weapon, badly wounded and bleeding: "This [was] the forest primeval. The murmuring pines and hemlocks, bearded with moss … indistinct in the twilight."[18] Thus began "an incredible ordeal."[19] Mercer survived several weeks in the wilderness, following routes indicated by moss on tree trunks and the sun's daily rise and set. He picked blackberries, ate a rattlesnake raw, and consumed freshwater clams. He finally arrived, nearly unrecognizable, at Pennsylvania's Fort Littleton.

"The story of Mercer's escape spread throughout the Colony of Pennsylvania, repeated throughout all of the colonies."[20] The New York newspaper *Mercury* reported, "We hear that Captain Mercer was fourteen days in getting to Fort Littleton. He had a miraculous escape, living … on two dried clams and a rattlesnake…."[21] He had become widely known symbol for pluck and heroism.[22]

The Forbes Expedition

Another adventure soon followed. In 1758, the colonial secretary sent General John Forbes, with 1,200 Scottish Highlanders, to America to attempt again what Braddock had failed to do. Forbes, a Scot, and like Mercer, Stephen, and St. Clair, a physician, was known to be more attuned to the Indian way of warfare. Behind his back the troops nick-named Forbes "Old Iron-Head" because of his stubbornness. Nonetheless, officers and soldiers were loyal to him.

The first order of business for the Forbes expedition was to cut a new road, more east-west in direction, from Carlisle over the mountains to Fort Duquesne, at the Forks of the Ohio. Forbes eschewed using Virginia as a starting point, as Braddock had done. In May 1758, Hugh Mercer became a colonel, commanding the Third Battalion, Pennsylvania Militia, serving in the Forbes expedition. His men's first business was six months' time expended in construction of the rough-hewn route, "the Forbes Road."

Second in command of the Scottish Highlanders accompanying Forbes was the arrogant, inflexible Colonel James Grant. Forbes's men built a stockade, Fort Loyalhanna, later re-named Ligonier, on Loyalhanna Creek, forty-five miles east of Fort Duquesne. From Ligonier, Colonel Grant persuaded General Forbes to allow Grant to take an 800-man force to probe Fort Duquesne. In an aside, Colonel Mercer confided in George Washington, whom he had known for some time, about the irony of it all. The British had sent the Highlanders from Scotland to pursue British aims in American, foreclosing the possibility that the Highlanders could serve Scots' interests in another Scottish rebellion. Now the British were sending forth Scots as "the tip of their sword."

Grant's reconnaissance was a disaster. Of 813 men, 273 were killed or severely wounded. Grant himself, in a spell of narcissism, had bagpipes played and troops pass in review in front of the fort, dissipating any element of surprise. Alerted, French and their Indian allies poured from the fort, annihilating Grant and his party.

Visions of Fredericksburg and Virginia

During the journey on the Forbes Road, Mercer came closer yet to George Washington. Mercer also met up with another Scots physician, James Craik.

Together the two men urged Mercer to open a practice in Fredericksburg, Virginia. "They pointed out to him that his old neighborhood [Franklin County, Pennsylvania] had almost been abandoned by the settlers," most of whom had migrated south, to Virginia's Shenandoah Valley, in a colony that offered protection against Indian raids.[23] Seeds had been planted in Mercer's mind.

In November, after the Grant debacle, General Forbes himself led a much larger 2,500-man force toward Fort Duquesne, upon arrival to learn that the French had abandoned the fort, settling fire to the log structures. After having defeated Colonel Grant decisively, the French nonetheless decided that the position was untenable, given the distances to Montreal and Quebec and the paucity of men and supplies.

Seeing the fort abandoned, Forbes immediately turned the expedition around, marching eastward. Forbes himself journeyed back to Philadelphia, where he died from cancer on March 11, 1759. He made the east-bound journey carried in a litter.

Because the supply lines were so long and difficult to traverse, General Forbes left only 200 Pennsylvania Militia at the fort, to be commanded by Colonel Hugh Mercer. British Brigadier General John Stanwix, who succeeded Forbes in overall command, sent Mercer additional men to help construction of a larger fort at the Forks of the Ohio.[24]

Sometime into 1760, and after more than a year at the new Fort Pitt, Mercer found himself at Fort Augusta, north of Harrisburg on the Susquehanna River. He learned there of the Pennsylvania Assembly's actions in further cutting funding for the militia. He saw the end of his five years in the military, and his thoughts turned to what he should do next. He was discharged on January 15, 1761.

Becomes a Virginian

Recollecting Colonel Washington's and Dr. Craik's entreaties, Mercer settled in Fredericksburg on the Rappahannock River. Upon arrival, Mercer went to John Gordon's Tavern, where he booked room and board. The tavernkeeper introduced Mercer to Gordon's son-in-law, a fellow French and Indian War veteran, George Weedon, soon to become the tavern's owner. Weedon was welcoming, and Mercer and Weedon become fast friends. Mercer opened an apothecary shop and a surgical practice on Caroline Street. He married Isabella Gordon, whose sister, Catherine, had married George Weedon.

Once in Fredericksburg, Mercer regularly saw George Washington. In 1767, he joined Fredericksburg Masonic Lodge No. 4. Washington, future president James Monroe, and eight persons who became generals in the Revolutionary War were also members.[25] Mercer became a colonel in the Spotsylvania County Militia. He frequented Weedon's tavern, rubbing elbows with George Mason, Fielding Lewis, Thomas Jefferson, John Dandridge, Alexander Spotswood, James Madison, and others, as well as with Washington and Weedon. He and Isabella had four children: William (born deaf and dumb), John, George, and Anna. A fifth son, Hugh Tenant

Weedon Mercer, was born during the Revolution. In 1775–1776, Mercer was a member of the Fredericksburg Committee on Safety.[26] Mercer enjoyed a thriving medical practice on top of a "quiet easy-going existence in Fredericksburg ... where even the horses dozed in the streets."[27]

And, as many other immigrants did, Mercer bought land, several thousand acres of agricultural land, lots in the town of Fredericksburg, lots purchased jointly with George Weedon, and Ferry Farm, where George Washington had been born and his mother had lived before moving to Fredericksburg proper. Mercer, immigrated from Scotland where arable land and buildable sites were precious, found Virginia expansive and the land inexpensive. Mercer gobbled up raw land, as did others of newly found means in America.

The Iron in the Fire Grows Hotter

There then came an emergency, an alarming one, namely, Governor Lord Dunmore's threats and April 1775 order to seize gunpowder stored in Williamsburg (*see* Chapter 14). The militia, including Hugh Mercer, mustered, prepared for an assault on Williamsburg. According to George Weedon:

> He faced a man [Mercer] he had never seen before. For the first time [Weedon] saw in Mercer another personality that had been hidden away. He saw Mercer's eyes become pools of fire as he strode in a military tread. The voice, usually so calm and measured, became sharp and crisp, like the crack of a whip.[28]

Weedon, Mercer, Alexander Spotswood, and John Willis organized a 700-man force to march from Fredericksburg. Meanwhile, in Hanover County, near Richmond, Patrick Henry rallied a 150-man force. A clash was averted as Dunmore settled with the incensed patriots. Nonetheless, as matters continued to escalate, the pace quickened. In September 1775, Mercer became the colonel for one of Virginia's sixteen district militias (for Spotsylvania, Caroline, Stafford, and King George Counties).[29] He became a member of the region's Committee of Safety.[30]

In January 1776, the Virginia Convention authorized the creation of six new Virginia Continental Line Regiments. Old line Virginians objected to Mercer because he was a "northerner," that is, a Scot rather than an Englishman, and a Presbyterian rather than an Anglican.[31] With those objections put aside, Hugh Mercer won election as Third Virginia Regiment commander, accompanied by George Weedon as Lieutenant Colonel and Thomas Marshall (father of future Chief Justice John Marshall) as major.[32] The regiment also included a young James Monroe and a young John Marshall.[33]

Mercer and his regiment stood by but took no active role in Dunmore's War.[34] Mercer, as ordered, then took his Third Virginia Regiment of 605 men northward to Dumfries, on the Potomac south of Mount Vernon. Fretting that the British might enter Virginia from the north, higher command assigned the Third Virginian to guard the Potomac's upper reaches. There it was that Washington reassigned General Mercer, with George Weedon taking command of the Third Regiment.

General Hugh Mercer and the Flying Camp

In 1890, Navy Captain Alfred Thayer Mahan wrote *The Influence of Sea Power Upon History: 1660–1783*, an influential military tract that has currency today.[35] Over 100 years earlier, George Washington had an intuitive feel for concepts Mahan later articulated. Based upon the Royal Navy's strength, Washington foresaw a vulnerability along the Atlantic seacoast given that the British could land, protect, and supply forces landing from sea. From Sandy Hook in the north to Cape May in the south, the New Jersey coast stretched 115 miles. Washington did not have the forces to garrison the coastal points where the Royal Navy could land an invading force. Accordingly, Washington conceived of "the flying camp," which the Continental Congress authorized in June 1776, the same month in which the Congress promoted Hugh Mercer to brigadier. Washington ordered Mercer to assume command of a force authorized for 10,000 officers and men: mobile, relatively unencumbered, able to respond upon short notice, flying to points along the eastern coast. In actuality, the force never reached its authorized goal, varying from as few as 3,000 to 8,500 men.

The reasons for the ebb and flow? One, militia units made up a good portion of the force. As Mercer wrote to Washington, "It is essential that no cause of complaint be given to the troops. This is especially true for militia, who are always eager to return to their homes and quick to find any reason to do so."[36] Two, in his defense of Long Island and Manhattan, General Washington was wont to poach troops from the flying camp.[37] Three, the threats to the coast never materialized, with the flying camp units distributed in the north around New York City's Harbor: Paulus Hook (400 Americans), Bergen Town (500), Perth Amboy (799), Woodbridge (605), Elizabeth (982), and Fort Lee (2,534).

Mercer oversaw his men building Fort Lee, an earthen redoubt, on the Hudson River's New Jersey side, opposite Fort Washington on the New York side. (The Colonials abandoned Fort Lee on November 20, 1776, four days following Fort Washington's surrender.)[38] Following defeats at Long Island, White Plains, and elsewhere, General Washington gave Nathanael Greene a discretionary order regarding Fort Washington, a fateful decision that resulted in Greene's attempt to retain the fort, leading to the capture of the entire garrison, 2,837 troops.[39] The flying camp then atomized, with General Mercer once more complaining that the "militia [acted] in a scandalous manner ... running off from their posts."[40] The war's lowest point had been reached.

The Long Retreat

No longer with a command, Mercer took control of a mongrel brigade that included the 20th Connecticut, the 27th Massachusetts, the 1st Maryland, and Rawling's Virginia and Maryland Riflemen. Tails between their legs, defeated patriots marched diagonally across New Jersey, crossing the Delaware River into Pennsylvania, with Lord Cornwallis in pursuit.[41] In the process, Mercer gathered powerful adherents. On December 21, Dr. Benjamin Rush of Philadelphia, surgeon general to the Continental Army's Middle Department, wrote to Congressman Richard Henry Lee, "Mercer must not be neglected. He has the confidence of the troops."[42]

There in Pennsylvania, desperately in need of a boost to the fledging country's morale, Washington and his men prepared for the daring re-cross of the Delaware and an assault on Trenton. General Mercer's orders to his regimental commanders for Christmas Day, 1776, read:

> You are to see that your men have three days' rations ready cooked before 12 o'clock this forenoon ... [They are] to parade precisely at four in the afternoon, with their arms, accoutrements, and ammunition in the best order.... [E]ach officer is to provide himself with a piece of white paper stuck in his hat as a field mark. You will order your men to assemble ... over the hill on the back of McConkey's Ferry, there to await further orders—a profound silence is to be observed.[43]

Christmas Day Night 1776

The weather was atrocious. Cold rain mixed with snow began to fall. Colonel John Patterson wrote, "It rained, snowed, and froze, at the same time blowing a perfect hurricane. During the Christmas day night it alternatively hailed, rained, snowed, and blew tremendously."[44] With 2,460 troops, 18 cannon, horses, and supplies, Washington led his force across the ice flow coagulated in the Delaware River. The frozen men marched nine miles south to Trenton, arriving late, at 8 a.m. the following day, nonetheless surprising the 1,400 Hessian force. Mercer's brigade, in Greene's division, approached Trenton upland, on the Pennington Road, while General John Sullivan's force attacked from the river road. They "went after them pell-mell," recorded an American soldier.[45]

Victory was complete, with 106 Hessians killed and 919 captured. The boost in colonial morale was outsized because the victory had been against feared German mercenaries. Over the course of the Revolutionary War, the petty princes of German states, particularly Hesse and Brunswick, hired 30,000 soldiers out to the British. These German mercenaries, William Stryker wrote in *The Battles of Trenton and Princeton*, "were war-hardened and well trained in European warfare ... rough in manners and low in morals. Warfare to them was a bloody business." They were looters, rapists, and savage opponents "who held in contempt the rude [American] army of yokels."[46] At Trenton, the Hessian leader Colonel Johannes Rall boasted, "Those clod-hoppers will not attack us, and if they do, we will fall upon them and rout them."[47]

As a result of the Trenton victory, the British swiftly abandoned posts south of Trenton:[48] "The effect [of our little expedition to Trenton] is amazing; the enemy have deserted Borden Town, Black Horse, Burlington, Mount Holly, and are fled to [the New Jersey capital] Perth Amboy; we are now in possession of all those places."[49] A further effect was to remove threats to Philadelphia, across the Delaware, thirty miles south.

Fearing a British counterattack from Trenton, Washington immediately marched his troops back north to McKonkey's [or McConley's?] Ferry, re-crossing the Delaware. In Pennsylvania, he permitted his fatigued men two days' rest, December 28–29. Then Washington and his troops crossed the Delaware, marching back to Trenton and camping on the town's southeast side, protected by Assunpink Creek that had but a single bridge spanning it.[50]

To an Athlete Dying Young

Hugh Mercer was to turn age 51 on January 16, 1777, not so young but still with a young man's fervor. In a session with other officers on January 1, 1777, with great eloquence, Mercer told Dr. Benjamin Rush, "My views in this contest are confined to a single object, that is, the success of the war, and God can witness how cheerful I would lay down my life to secure it."[51] The following night, as he dined with General St. Clair and Rush, Mercer said "that he would not be conquered, but that he would cross the mountains and live with the Indians rather than submit to the power of Great Britain in any of the civilized states."

There followed the Battle of Princeton, where Hugh Mercer's imaginings and prophesies became reality. To avenge the Hessian Trenton defeat, Lord Cornwallis proceeded south from Princeton with 8,000 men. In his haste, Cornwallis failed to send skirmishers and scouts ahead and on the wings of the projected route as his force-marched south toward Trenton: "During the night, heavy rains turned the roads into mud so that the movement of the British was [painfully] slow."[52] As instructed, Patriot regiments under Generals Edward Hand of Pennsylvania and Charles Scott of Virginia fought a slow, strategic retreat, slowing the British. These factors aided Washington in his plans to keep campfires burning while circling around the British left wing and marching toward Princeton unopposed in a midnight sojourn. General Hugh Mercer and his brigade, decimated by enlistments that had expired January 1 and reduced to no more than 350 men, participated in the end-run nighttime march.

Just after sunrise, Washington sent Mercer and his men to investigate a lone rider on a hill in the west, about a mile to the main American force's left. To their surprise, the patriots ran into British Lieutenant Colonel Charles Mawhood and his men, out in advance of the main British column. The lone horseman had turned, riding back over the hill to Mawhood's force that the detachment screened from view. It was much larger than the Americans anticipated, consisting of the 17th and 55th Regiments of Foot plus a hundred men of the 16th Light Dragoons. "The British deployed along a fence at the edge of William Clark's orchard and waited."[53] More of a pitched battle followed, with Mercer riding forward to rally his troops, suffering fatal bayonet wounds in the process.

Some of "Mercer's men, dreading the English bayonet, broke from their positions," retreating toward Trenton. "Mercer, raging at them, rode his horse to an orchard in front of the position. A bullet shattered his horse's leg, and it fell." A British soldier knocked Mercer to the ground by hitting his head with the muzzle of a musket.[54] Other British surrounded Mercer, lying on the ground, yelling "Surrender you rebel." Mercer made a movement toward his sword. "'I am no rebel,' cried

Mercer, while a half dozen bayonets were at his breast: instead of asking for quarter, [Mercer] determined to die fighting."⁵⁵ The surrounding British bayoneted Mercer at least five times. Mercer suffered a "merciless drubbing."⁵⁶

"[E]ven with a bayonet stuck in him," Mercer did not wish to leave his men. He ordered them to prop him up against a white oak's trunk so he could rest; his men stood guard over him. The tree became known as "the Mercer Oak."⁵⁷

Aftermath and Death

Mercer's wounds were not immediately fatal. General Washington arrived, bringing reinforcements and rallying Mercer's troops. The Americans turned the tide, driving the British back, going on to rout two British regiments at Nassau Hall, the main building of the College of New Jersey (Princeton today). Washington and Major John Armstrong found Mercer lying on the ground in the lee of the American advance, unconscious and cold but alive. Armstrong took Mercer south about a half mile to Thomas Clark's house. There Quaker inhabitants cared for General Mercer.

Mercer revived. Lord Cornwallis's surgeon and Dr. Benjamin Rush visited, examining Mercer. They both proclaimed that he would live. Mercer disagreed, pointing to the smallest of his wounds, a slit under his arm, predicting that it would prove fatal. Dr. Rush's notes were that Mercer "received seven wounds to the body and two to his head, was much bruised ... [h]is life was yesterday almost despaired of." After seeing the patient the following day, Rush was optimistic: "I found General Mercer much relieved, and some of the most dangerous complaints removed, so that I still have hopes of his recovery, and of his being again restored to the arms of his grateful country."⁵⁸

Mercer was able to explain the manner of his wounding. Lying on the ground, surrounded by armed British soldiers, "I determined to die as I had lived, an honored soldier in a just and righteous cause, without begging or making reply. I lunged with my sword at the nearest man. They then bayoneted and left me."⁵⁹

Mercer's biographer Joseph Waterman concluded, "There was no surrender in his nature. There never had been."⁶⁰ Yet his wounds were too serious: "He died the 12th of January 1777, of the Wounds He Received on the 3rd of the Same Month, near Princeton, in New Jersey, Bravely Defending the Liberties of America."⁶¹ Brigadier Hugh Mercer, in his "steadiness, sagacity, and competence, and in commanding the respect and trust of all his associates, had many of the qualities of George Washington ... that only needed a cause to call [them] forth," wrote Barbara Tuchman in extolling the qualities of another military leader.⁶²

17

Scout and Woodsman
Charles Scott

Following the Revolutionary War, Brigadier Charles Scott crossed the Alleghenies, settling in Kentucky. Kentucky was then Virginia, in its entirety Fincastle County.[1] "Various of the English colonies," including Virginia, had "[c]harters, which audaciously (and ignorantly—no one had any idea of the distances involved) granted them territory from sea to sea," Professor H.L. Brand wrote in his Ben Franklin biography.[2] Scott set down near Versailles, in the middle of the "district."[3]

After Scott had been in Kentucky for a time, he was visited by a Baptist minister, a zealot of sorts. The vignette, as well as similar interchanges throughout his career, captures Scott's persona. The minister told Scott that church members did not want "so profane & wicked a man living so near them." Scott was caught by surprise but then replied, "My friend, I had supposed your settlement … would have been much pleased to have such a barrier as mine, between you & the Savages. I have flattered myself I had gained some little reputation from the late Revolution … [and] would be some protection to the frontier settlements." Admitting this was true, the minister nonetheless renewed his request that Scott absent himself from the vicinity.[4] Scott not only did not leave, he later became the fourth governor of the fifteenth state.

Scott possessed that combination of virtue and vice, the minister aside, that frontier settlers respected. "[H]is two outstanding vices, drinking and swearing, had not diminished" from Revolutionary War days.[5] He kept a pack of dogs for bear hunting. On the other hand, Herman Bowman, Scott's adjutant in the 1790s Indian Wars, eulogized Scott: "[He] was the most agreeable companion. … Never told a vulgar lie…. Genteel, handsome, dark skin, regular neat figure, dark hair and beard, neat in person always. I never heard any man that could swear pretty, except Genl. Scott."[6]

Veterans applied the sobriquet "Old Rough and Ready" to Zachary Taylor, a hero of the Mexican War and in 1849 president of the United States.[7] Soldiers of an earlier time applied the nickname to General Scott. "Old Rough and Ready" too captured Charley Scott's essence.

True to the vision he described to the minister, Scott became a noted Indian fighter who led expeditions into Ohio to quell marauding Native American bands, culminating with service under Mad Anthony Wayne.[8] Scott was present at northern

Ohio's Battle of Fallen Timbers in 1794, which historians mark as the culmination of the 1790s' Indian Wars.[9] In the process of his service, Scott lost two sons serving under him, nevertheless continuing his military exploits well into his fifties.

Virginia Connections

Scott was born in Goochland County that today is a portion of Powhatan County, in the upper reaches of the James River, west of Richmond. Virginia law encapsulated the English concept of primogeniture, meaning that a deceased's title, estate, and other lands went to the eldest son.[10] By tradition, the second son went into the military and the third into religion as a vicar or curate. Beyond a dowry when they married, the daughters received little. The primogeniture tradition insured survival, intact, of large English estates. In America, primogeniture never took hold as it had in England, over time fading as the colonies became states. The colonies' citizens came to regard primogeniture as an attribute of the English class system from which they had fled. Georgia, in its constitution of 1777, led the thirteen original colonies in doing away with required primogeniture altogether, something England did not do until 1925.[11] In addition to primogeniture's abolition, the need to pay federal estate and state inheritance taxes further broke up larger estates in America.[12]

Charles Scott, Artist Unknown. One of George Washington's favorites, Scott was a hard-drinking, rough-hewn combat general beloved by his men (Art America).

Scott's father Samuel owned 666.66 acres. Charles Scott was born in 1739, the second of four brothers. When Samuel died in 1752, Samuel's acreage went to the eldest son, John. Charles Scott received nothing.

Little Future as a Planter

Scott trained as a carpenter and surveyor, knowing that he had little prospect of owning land. Instead of pursuing carpentry as a vocation, Scott joined a Virginia Regiment formed to assist the British in the French and Indian War. Daniel Bell's company roster, July 16, 1756, describes a seventeen-year-old Scott as "Dark and swarthy with blk hair & slim made, 5'7" tall."[13] Captain Bell brought his recruits to Winchester. From there, the regiment posted Charles Scott west to Fort Cumberland in the Maryland panhandle. Scott served as a member of scouting parties that ranged from the fort throughout the surrounding area to deter, sometimes to engage Native American warriors. Scott rose quickly to sergeant, then in 1758 to the junior officer rank ensign.

Following the French and Indian War, Scott's military career continued.[14] He volunteered for the Virginia contingent led by William Byrd, later Adam Stephen, to treat with the Cherokees in southwest Virginia and Carolina. Byrd named Scott a captain, one of five in the 750-man force.[15]

Because of the premature death of older brother John, Charles came into possession of a farm, on Muddy Creek, after all. Leaving his military exploits behind, Scott built a gristmill on Muddy Creek, raising tobacco and wheat on the farm. He was active in the local militia, one of two captains from 1766 onward. He married Eliza ("Betsy"), the union producing four sons: Merritt, Samuel, Daniel, and Charles Jr.[16]

Rumbling Toward War

Lord Dunmore, the British colonial governor, fled Williamsburg on June 8, 1775. The "war within the war" (Chapter 14) had begun. In August 1775, the Virginia Convention formed two regiments to counteract Dunmore. Charles Scott became second-in-command, Second Virginia Regiment, captained by Colonel William Woodford (Chapter 15).[17] Overall commander Andrew Lewis (Chapter 8) ordered Colonel Woodford and regiment to bring Dunmore to account.

Woodford, Scott, and the regiment marched southeast along the James River. Ultimately, below Norfolk, the Battle of Great Bridge ensued. Before the battle, not content with the watch and wait mission Woodford assigned, Scott showed a combination of aggression and bravery. Scott was "eager to confront Dunmore's small force of '*Torries and Blacks.*'"[18] Accordingly, Scott led a 150-man party downriver to attack a Dunmore outpost, overwhelming the 70 defenders.[19]

With the remainder of the Second Regiment, Colonel Woodford arrived at Great Bridge. On December 9, the Dunmore force mounted a suicidal frontal attack on the Americans. Marching across the bridge six abreast, British regulars, the heart of Dunmore's force, were slaughtered (*see* Chapter 14).

After Great Bridge

Following the American victory, Lewis directed Woodford to fall back to Williamsburg. Rendered ineffectual by his unpopularity with the men and in snit over Congress's elevation of Hugh Mercer to Brigadier, a sulking Colonel Woodford kept going past Williamsburg, retreating to his Caroline County home. Meanwhile, the unpolished, at times profane, brave, and aggressive Charles Scott had become "Charley Scott" to the troops.[20]

Regimental Command

In the summer of 1776, the Virginia Convention created new regiments, and Charles Scott, now a colonel, assumed command of the Fifth Virginia. As a component of Stephen's brigade, Scott's regiment hooked up with the retreating Patriot Army at Brunswick, New Jersey, "as it ignobly fled from the British," after losses at Brooklyn, Harlem, White Plains, and Forts Washington and Lee. Down to 121 men, Scott's regiment formed part of the rear guard as, in December 1776, Washington's army reached the Delaware River, crossing into Pennsylvania.

The army later re-crossed the Delaware, and on December 26, attacked Trenton and its Hessian garrison. It was in the Second Battle of Trenton, though, that Scott and his men merited "mention in the dispatches." On January 1, 1777, Charles Lord Cornwallis and 8,000 troops moved south from Princeton, New Jersey, to avenge the American surprise at Trenton, fifteen miles from Princeton. Mired in mud, the British moved slowly down the Trenton-Princeton Turnpike.

On January 2, after the officer in charge, General Matthias de Roche Fermoy, had mounted a horse and run away, the defense fell to a 1,000 American advance guard with overall command devolved upon Pennsylvania's Colonel (later General) Edward Hand. Hand's troops took a position at Five Mile Run, the creek that bisected the north-south turnpike, halfway between Trenton and Princeton. Scott and his men kept east, between the Princeton-Trenton Turnpike and the larger Assunpink Creek (also known as the Trenton River), then flowing from north to south, paralleling the road. At that stage, Scott and his troops began a strategic retreat, guarding the American right wing against a flanking move by the British force's left wing.

Protection of the Strategic Retreat

The American force slowly retreated toward Trenton. Scott's force waded Shabakunk Creek, folding in with other Americans, then passing through the village of Trenton. Southeast of Trenton, Scott's mission was to defend the single bridge over Assunpink Creek, that is, beyond Trenton where the Assunpink curved west to flow into the Delaware River. General Washington and his force had camped beyond the creek. The British halted before the American encampment, on the creek's opposite shore. In his memoirs, Virginian Robert Beale remembered:

> Our brigade, consisting of the Fourth, Fifth, and Sixth Virginia Regiments, was ordered to form a column at the bridge. General Washington came, and in the presence of us all, told Colonel Scott to defend the bridge to the last extremity. Colonel Scott answered with an oath, "Yes, General, as long as there is a man left alive."[21]

Scott's subordinate, Major George Johnston, publicly stated that by his actions, "Colonel Scott acquired immortal honors from his performance" at the Battle of Assunpink Creek, as the engagement became known.[22] Although greatly outnumbered, Scott and his men repulsed three British attempts to take the bridge. With darkness approaching, "General Cornwallis suspended his attack."[23] The American defense was both a delaying tactic and a diversion. That night, leaving campfires burning with a few soldiers tending them, Washington with 5,000 troops looped to the east, around the British forces' left flank, commencing a fifteen-mile march to Princeton.

Scott's Folksy Leadership

Scott's homespun manner enhanced his popularity among his men. At Assunpink Creek, George Washington addressed Scott's men, then rode away. Scott then addressed his men:

> Well, boys, you know the *old boss* put us here to defend this bridge; and by G…d it must be done. Now I want to tell you one thing. You're all in the habit of shooting too high. You waste your powder and your lead; and I have cursed you about it a hundred times. [N]othing must be wasted, every crack must count. For that reason, boys, whenever you see them fellows first begin to put their feet upon this bridge do you shin 'em.[24]

Unbeknown to Scott, Washington had halted within earshot. He let out a hearty laugh and then rode on.

Scott's regiments did not participate further in the Battle of Princeton. Instead, they diverted to the east where they guarded the slowly moving baggage train that followed the main American force toward Princeton.[25]

A few weeks later, Scott emitted another gem as he addressed another regiment: "Take care now and fire low … bring down your pieces … fire at their legs, one man Wounded in the leg is better [than] a dead one for its takes two more to carry him off and there is three gone. [L]eg them damn 'em, I say leg 'em."

A Hero Again

Spring and summer 1777 saw the American army in New Jersey, twelve miles northeast of British-occupied Brunswick. The main British force was encamped 25 miles southeast at Perth Amboy, on Arthur Kill, the waterway connecting the mouth of the Raritan River with New York's inner harbor.[26] In mid–1777, Washington had two objectives: duck British commander General Howe's attempts to lure American forces into a mid–New Jersey major battle and with light infantry, skirmish with British scouting and foraging parties that had to roam farther and farther into the countryside to obtain foodstuffs for British soldiers and forage for a thousand horses. The summer 1777 was known as the "forage war." In spring and summer, "[t]he fighting was low intensity but there was plenty of it." This was "the war Washington wanted … in fact, the only war he could risk."[27]

In one of the forage war clashes, Scott and his troops scored a victory at the Battle of Drake's Farm. Major Robert Forsyth wrote the *Virginia Gazette*, "Our hickory hearts, as usual, behaved like heroes. Ninety of them, under the command of the brave Colonel Scott, beat … 230 of their best troops."[28] Scott's light infantry vanquished the foraging party's armed guard, forcing the foragers to retreat to Perth Amboy.[29] On April 1, 1777, the Continental Congress promoted "the brave Colonel Scott" to brigadier general.

In the summer of 1777 in New Jersey, British General William Howe resigned himself that Washington would not take the bait to come out into the open for an episodic battle. General Howe and his troops left Perth Amboy, crossing Arthur Kill to Staten Island and returned to New York.

Scott versus Adam Stephen

In May 1777, General Washington re-organized his army for the coming campaign, installing a structure of five divisions. Washington placed major generals Nathanael Greene, Benjamin Lincoln, John Sullivan, William Alexander (Lord Stirling), and Adam Stephen in command of the divisions. Washington placed Scott's brigade in Adam Stephen's division. The act bought forth tests of wills and bouts of defamation between Generals Stephen and Scott.

Sniping and back-biting had already begun during the New Jersey wanderings in summer 1777. At Brandywine, the Stephen-Scott feud escalated. On the afternoon of September 11, 1777, the day of the battle, Scott and his men rushed pell-mell from a reserve position several miles northward from Chadds Ford to the countryside surrounding the Birmingham Meeting House. Leading a sizeable force, Lord Cornwallis had crossed the Brandywine six miles upstream at Jefferies Ford, flanking and hoping to roll up the American lines facing the Brandywine Creek and anticipating a British crossing at Chadds Ford. Scott's brigade, forming a new line of defense from west to east, took a beating from the advancing British, retreated, re-formed, fought again, then retreated as Cornwallis and his men ceased the attack at dusk. Historians' judgment was that "General Scott's troops fought heroically." Not only opposing that view but condemning Scott with harsh words, Stephen's "later assertion was of the ineptitude of [the brigade's] commander," namely, Scott.[30]

A rejoinder issued from Scott after another fiasco for the Americans a few weeks later at Germantown. Scott's accusation was that General Stephen, "paying no attention to his any of his officers, refused to have his troops reform and to post artillery to check the enemy's pursuit."[31] Responding to those accusations and others of his inebriation, General Stephen thought Scott the major source of discontent with his actions at Germantown. Those allegations resulted in a board of inquiry, later a court martial for Adam Stephen. More and more, Stephen had taken a dislike to Scott that now broke into the open. "Scott, eighteen years younger, had worked his way up through the enlisted ranks in the French & Indian War and was barely educated. Scott had demonstrated courage and resourcefulness," but according to Stephen, "seemed to lack the perseverance and judgment for successful command in actual battle."[32] In comparison, Adam Stephen quoted Cicero and Aristotle, was well connected to politicians, and regarded himself as one of Virginia's landed elites.

Scott survived the vilification back and forth; Stephen did not. The court martial found Stephen guilty as charged, pursuant to which General Washington discharged Adam Stephen from the army. The disgraced general returned to his plantation, gristmill, distillery, and other operations in Berkeley County, Virginia.

Charles Scott continued to serve, ending with his leadership of troops at Charles Town, South Carolina, in spring 1780.

Monmouth Courthouse

Upon the 1778 emergence from Valley Forge, Major General Charles Lee, the eccentric Englishman, led a division in Washington's army. Lee's actions at Monmouth resulted in his downfall, a fate similar to Adam Stephen's. As with Stephen, the events involved Charles Scott.

In June 1778, having abandoned Philadelphia, the British were engaged in slow crawl diagonally across New Jersey. Washington and his generals decided to give chase. General Washington ordered Scott, whom he regarded as a courageous fighter, to hand pick a light infantry contingent to go in advance, scouting and nipping at the enemy's heels.[33] Washington then ordered Marquis de Lafayette to catch up with Scott's 1500-man force with another 1,000 troops.[34] By the time General Lee rode up, the advance force contained 5,200 men, 4,000 select regulars, and 1,200 militia under Pennsylvania's Colonel John Cadwalader. "Discovering that the forward units amounted to half the army," in fit of pique Lee "asserted his right to command by virtue of the fact that he was the senior major general," that is, senior to Lafayette.[35] Washington conceded the point, compromising by stating that Lee would replace Lafayette only when Lee arrived at the front.

Various versions exist as to what occurred next. (Chapter 15 describes yet another version.) A first version is simply that Lee pulled the force up short, in the center, then ordered a retreat. A second version is more subtle. Lee, expecting the British left flank to attack Lee's right, sent messengers to Scott on the other end of the American line, where Scott had halted his force. When the messengers got there, Scott had already retreated. A third version is that Scott not only retreated but that he persuaded New Jersey's General Maxwell to retreat as well and that General Wayne, having no battle plan either and seeing Scott's and Maxwell's retreats, ordered his brigade to fall back. These falling dominos left Lee's center unsupported on his left flank. He had little choice but to retreat.

As Washington was coming up with the remainder of the army, he met General Lee riding away from the front: "Tradition has it that the commander in chief ... was so chagrined that he used intemperate language toward Lee."[36] Washington called out to Lee, "You Damned Poltroon."[37] Closing the distance between them, Washington burst out, "Damn your multiplying eyes, General Lee! Go to the front or go to hell. I care little which."[38] He then dictated what the choice was to be, relieving Lee of command on the spot and sending him to the rear. Scott, who was present, painted a picture of General Washington's vehemence: "Even the leaves shook on the trees."[39] Lafayette said it was the only time he ever heard Washington swear. The earthy Scott recalled, "I haven't enjoyed such swearing before or since."[40]

Underlying Washington's vehemence at Monmouth perhaps was the longstanding tension between Washington and Lee, first set off by Lee's foolish dereliction of duty and capture by the British in December 1776: "Major General Charles Lee, the army's second-ranking officer, was [Washington's] chief critic."[41] Around the time of his capture, Lee famously wrote to fellow British Army veteran Major General Horatio Gates, "*Entre nous*, a certain great man is most damnably deficient."[42]

All was not lost after Lee's orders to retreat. Fighting in 100-degree heat, Washington led the charges and supervised artillery duels. Washington's horse died from the activity and heat.[43] The June 28 engagement was a draw, meaning victory for the Americans. Of Washington's actions at Monmouth, Lafayette later recalled, "I thought then as now I never beheld so superb a man."[44] For Charles Scott, his actions now formed central parts of the legends surrounding two major generals' downfalls, those of Adam Stephen and Charles Lee.

New York, South Carolina, and Prisoner of War

As seen in Chapter 15, Monmouth Courthouse was the last major Revolutionary War battle in the mid–Atlantic where the major battles—save Saratoga—were fought 1776–1778.[45] After Monmouth, Washington positioned his army north of New York, with a brigade close to the city of Westchester. During this time, General Scott served as Washington's intelligence chief.

General Scott's Final Revolutionary War Months

On October 21, Scott wrote General Washington, "My long indisposition and other Obvious reasons will make it indispensable necessary for me to Retier [sic] from this Honor and Most Desirable Command. … I hope for your Excellency's Indulgence."[46] In response, Washington persuaded Scott to take a lengthy furlough rather than retirement. Scott returned to Virginia to recover from his illness, never specified, and resolve financial problems.

Supposing that Scott had sufficiently recovered, in March 1779, Washington gave Scott a new portfolio. It was "a matter of great importance" that Scott recruit 2,200 Virginians as soldiers:[47] "Our Affair in Georgia grows daily more alarming … you will exert yourself to collect them [recruits] with the utmost expedition…. There is not a Moment's Time to be lost." A British force that General Benjamin Lincoln had failed to oust had occupied Savannah. With his brigade, Lincoln had retreated north to the larger city of Charles Town, in South Carolina.

Meanwhile, there were fires to be doused closer to home. At different times under, respectively, Generals Richard Philips, Alexander Leslie, and Benedict Arnold, the British sent raiding parties up Virginia's rivers.[48] The purpose of these expeditions was not what first appeared—to invade and occupy—but to distract and divert. The British raids would occupy American troops, preventing them from journeying south to aid defense against Lord Cornwallis's campaigns in South and North Carolina. On each occasion, after raids and skirmishes including Arnold's devastation of Richmond, the British forces, rather than holding ground, retreated down the rivers, boarded transports, and sailed away.

Scott headed up the defensive efforts against the raid led by Major General Matthew Edward. Edward's force occupied Norfolk, plundered Smithfield, burned Suffolk (destroying 9,000 barrels of salt pork destined for the Patriot army), and wrecked the Americans' Gosport naval yard. In preparation for further actions by the British, Scott reinforced Williamsburg, raising up earthworks around the capital. To express citizens' gratitude to Scott, the General Assembly voted him 500 pounds and "the finest gelding that can be procured."

Charles Town

Before Lord Cornwallis's campaigns, in January 1780, British General Henry Clinton, with 8,000 troops, 90 transports, and 10 men-of-war, landed at the mouth of the Savannah River, thus separating Georgia from South Carolina. From there, the Clinton force marched north to lay siege to Charles Town. With ships of the line, British Admiral Marriott Arbuthnot sailed north to bombard Charles Town from seaward.

One American answer was to send General William Woodford and his brigade south, leaving Petersburg, Virginia, on March 11, 1780, marching 500 miles to Charles Town. General Scott also sent troops south but proceeded independently, riding inland through Salisbury, North Carolina; Camden, South Carolina; and thence to Charles Town, arriving there on March 30, 1780. Woodford arrived eight days later. Both Scott and Woodford had gotten into the city before the British tightened their noose around it.

Fort Moultrie on Sullivan's Island, adjacent the harbor's entrance, surrendered on May 7, 1780. North of the city, British parallels (siege trenches) came right up to the defensive ditch the Americans had dug across the neck of land whose tip was Charles Town. The noose tightened. Major General Lincoln and his force of 5,684 Continental Line and militia, including six brigadier generals (William Moultrie, Lachlan McIntosh, James Hogun, the engineer Louis Le Begue de Presle Duportail, Scott, and Woodford), surrendered. The British imprisoned the officers at Haddrell's Point, across the Cooper River from the city (Chapter 10).

To obtain release from British imprisonment, two pathways lay open to the officers: one, parole, signing an oath that they would fight no more, or, two, an exchange with a British prisoner held by the Americans. Exchange freed the officer to participate in the war. In January 1781, General Scott received parole.[49] Obtaining his release, Scott headed for Virginia and home. Subsequently, in February 1782, General Washington procured an exchange for Scott, enabling Scott to return to service. General Nathanael Greene, however, informed Scott that he had no position for him under his command, the Southern Army, the only theater that remained in play. In 1783, Congress breveted Scott a major general; Scott retired from the Continental Army.[50]

Blemishes on Scott's Record

Douglas MacArthur writes, "Contentions over rank among the general officers [became] increasingly acrimonious and plagued the command system throughout the war."[51] The observation rang especially true of Virginia officers. Generals Weedon, Muhlenberg, Stephen, Woodford, Hugh Mercer, Andrew Lewis, and Scott, virtually all the Virginia brigadiers, grumbled and complained about others' elevation to higher ranks and, within ranks, about the ordering of seniority (*see generally* Chapter 20). "[T]hese were accomplished, ambitious middle-aged men. [A]mong officers in the Continental Army ... successes sparked jealousy in the hearts of peers. The squabble amongst military men of ranks were a cause of no small worry to Congress" and to their commanding general George Washington.[52]

In summer 1777, Scott joined the grumblers, complaining that Congress had ranked "the portly Virginia colleague and former tavernkeeper," George Weedon, senior to Scott. Weedon had received his promotions to lieutenant colonel and full colonel before Scott's promotion, but Weedon had received command of a regiment only after Scott. Added to the mix was that Scott never cared much for Weedon personally.

Scott corresponded with a Virginia delegate to the Continental Congress: "I am Sensibly hurt. I wish to serve my Country but I cannot commit to indignity and make myself unhappy. I will sooner quit the Service altogether which would make me exceedingly unhappy." Congress should place Scott in his "Proper Rank," next to Peter Muhlenberg, senior to Weedon.[53] The controversy, stoked by William Woodford, lasted eight or more months. Scott ultimately prevailed. Weedon ranked last, below Scott.[54]

To use modern parlance, in his career overall, Scott developed a reputation as a "snitch." He had many times written to Washington complaining of various officers' acts of malfeasance. Both major generals Adam Stephen and Charles Lee complained of Scott sowing dissention, leveling charges against him. Toward the war's conclusion, Scott accused General Nathanael Greene of profiteering supply to his own army. Scott's accusations resulted in investigations continuing right up until Greene's 1786 death. Greene could never forgive Scott for initiating the libel.[55]

18

Fighting Parson

Lutheran Minister Peter Muhlenberg at Brandywine

In 1771, Woodstock's James Woods recruited Peter Muhlenberg to re-locate from Pennsylvania to Virginia. As a Lutheran minister, Muhlenberg could conduct a Lutheran service, in German: "For some years, the German inhabitants of [Pennsylvania] commenced emigrating in considerable numbers to Virginia, settling principally in the valley.... [G]erman settlements gradually became quite large."[1] Germans and others, such as the Scot Hugh Mercer, fled Pennsylvania because the Quaker-dominated legislature took no steps to protect settlements from Indian raids.[2] In turn, Virginia welcomed them. "They were precisely the lowly, hard-working, ethical Protestants that Virginia visionaries had long sought to populate Virginia ... something that generations of British settlement had not hitherto demonstrated," as Marambaud's Byrd family chronicle described them.[3]

At the outset of the Revolution, the Virginia Convention conceived of the newly created Eighth Virginia Regiment to be composed of Germans from the lower Shenandoah Valley ("the Valley"):[4] "The colonel the Convention chose to lead the Eighth was the Woodstock, Virginia, parson, Peter Muhlenberg."[5] The Convention chose Muhlenberg for the same reasons that James Woods recruited him. No sacristy-bound minister, Muhlenberg loved to fish, hunt, and be in the outdoors. He was experienced and well-traveled, having been to England and Germany. Most of all, since immigrating to Virginia, Muhlenberg had proven himself as an integral, respected part of the community, a strong leader who could garner adherents who trusted his leadership.

Northwestern Virginia

The Shenandoah is a wide, flat, long valley between the Blue Ridge Mountain to the east and the Alleghenies thirty or thirty-five miles to the west. Through the valley flow the Shenandoah River's North and South branches. Prevailing winds travel 300 miles or more, from Front Royal, Virginia in the north, where the Blue Ridge begins, south-by-southwest the length of Virginia into North Carolina. Together, the rivers and the prevailing winds ensure that the Valley is never too hot nor humid. Before white settlements, Native American tribes migrated from Pennsylvania and

New York down the long valley to winter hunting grounds in the Carolinas. As celebrated Civil War historian Bruce Catton wrote, "There may be a lovelier country somewhere ... but when the sunlight lies upon it and the wind puts white clouds to racing their shadows, the Shenandoah Valley is as good as anything America can show."[6]

In this great valley, ordained Church of England cleric Peter Muhlenberg could conduct a Woodstock service in English in accordance with the Episcopal liturgy and the *Book of Common Prayer* or in German according to the Lutheran rite. Fond of the outdoors, Muhlenberg also had a martial side in addition to his spiritual one. In 1766, a young Muhlenberg had served in a German-speaking English regiment from Lübeck, Germany, that had traveled to America.

The Famed Muhlenberg Call to Arms

In January 1776, Muhlenberg stood before his Woodstock congregation before going off to war and delivered his farewell sermon:

> 'In the language of Holy Writ there is a time for all things, a time to preach and a time to pray, but those times have all passed away. There is a time to fight, and that time has now come.' Then, after pronouncing the benediction, he opened his clerical robe and stood before his congregation in the uniform of a Virginia colonel.[7]

The congregation rose and sang "A Mighty Fortress Is Our God." "[D]escending from the pulpit, Muhlenberg ordered the drums at the church door to beat for recruits." Nearly three hundred Woodstock men joined Virginia's Eighth.[8] Few objected, and those who did soon became converts of the call to arms.[9]

The Muhlenberg Myth

In subsequent years, historians have questioned whether the farewell benediction occurred.[10] Sculptors, though, have memorialized the romantic version. Life-size bronze Muhlenberg statues exist on the town square in Woodstock; in the sculpture garden outside the Philadelphia Art Institute; and on the campus of Muhlenberg College, in Allentown, Pennsylvania.[11] In these renditions, Pastor Muhlenberg is in clerical garb, open at the front to reveal his military uniform. In Washington, D.C., on Connecticut Avenue, a bronze plaque reads, "John Peter Gabriel Muhlenberg ... 'The Fighting Parson of the American Revolution.'"[12]

A Circuitous Path to Ministry

Born in 1746, young Peter's home was Trappe, 38 miles northwest of Philadelphia, near Pottstown, Pennsylvania. Countless Indian raids took place on Pennsylvania's frontier, resulting in destruction of homesteads, kidnapping, scalping, and brutal murders.[13] The raids kept settlement from advancing westward much beyond Hanover and Lancaster. In Trappe, the Muhlenbergs sent young Peter nine miles west to live with an English woman in New Hanover. "Through this experience, Peter Muhlenberg received valuable training in English, for German was spoken at home."[14] Father Muhlenberg then sent Peter, age 17, and two younger brothers to Germany. They arrived in London, proceeded to Rotterdam, thence to Eimbeck and Halle, where a well-known Lutheran institution would school the boys. Sources reported that Muhlenberg children "studied at the University of Halle" but the eldest, Peter, attended little, if any, school.[15] On October 27, 1763, from America, Henry Muhlenberg wrote to the head of school, Dr. Ziegenhagen:

Peter Muhlenberg. Simultaneously a Lutheran and Anglican minister, Muhlenberg headed the Eighth Virginia from the northern Shenandoah Valley. Certain historians label him an unrecognized hero of Yorktown (Historic Trappe Museum).

> My son Peter['s] ... chief fault and bad inclination has been his fondness for hunting and fishing. But if our most reverend fathers at Halle observe any tendency to vice, I would humbly beg that they send him to a well-disciplined garrison town.... [T]here he may obey the drum if he will not follow the spirit of God.[16]

Young Peter was "emphatically a country boy."[17] Two salient points emerge. One, Peter had martial tendencies, not surprising given the martial milieu defense against Indians necessitated in Pennsylvania. Two, Peter's fondness for hunting and fishing fueled license for him to pursue a calling other than student.

So, Pastor Muhlenberg indentured Peter to a shopkeeper near Lübeck, in Schleswig Holstein, in Germany's far north, to learn the pharmacy trade. The arrangement was a disaster. All Peter did was measure out groceries and liquor over the counter. He worked every day, including Sunday, and every night until 10 p.m. Finally, near the end of the third year in a six-year indenture, Peter complained to his father. Shocked, the father procured Peter's release from the indenture for the following year at Easter, 1767. But several months before, Peter, age 20, went walkabout.

Young Muhlenberg "joined a regiment of troops in Lubeck—not a German regiment ...—but an English regiment" that was recruiting young Germans. "Lubeck was a 'free city,' [meaning] Great Britain had the right to recruit troops there," Edward Hocker wrote in *The Fighting Parson*.[18] The regiment's captain befriended Muhlenberg, making him the regimental secretary. After several months, the

German-speaking English regiment went to America. There Muhlenberg was released from further service and returned home to Trappe.[19]

The Ministry

There were no seminaries. Instead, Peter's father placed Peter for indoctrination at Swedish Lutheran churches along the Delaware River in lower Philadelphia. Swedish Lutherans preceded most German settlements, arriving with John Fenwick's 1675 expedition that had settled West Jersey.[20] Some Swedish migrated across the Delaware River into Delaware and Pennsylvania.[21]

Settlement in the Shenandoah Valley

As noted, many Germans settled in the Valley's northern reaches, to whence they had come via Pennsylvania.[22] They had left Pennsylvania because of the political powers' inability to protect them.[23] German names (Strasburg) and religious names (Mount Olive, Lebanon Church, Bethel) for towns revealed the region's German and Christian heritage.[24]

Should Justice of the Peace Wood convince Muhlenberg to come to Woodstock, Wood promised Muhlenberg two hundred fifty pounds salary, a parsonage, and "a Farm of at least Two hundred acres of Extremely Good Land."[25] An obstacle was that to accept the ministry in Woodstock, Muhlenberg had to be ordained in the Church of England.[26] So with two others similarly situated, Muhlenberg faced his second cross Atlantic trip: "The Bishop of Ely [north of Cambridge] conferred deacon's orders upon Muhlenberg and [William] Braidfoot, followed by private ordination to the priesthood in April 1772, by the Bishop of London in the King's Chapel at St. James [Palace]."[27] Once in Woodstock, Muhlenberg conducted services in English in Anglican-Episcopal liturgy and in German in Lutheran liturgy. Pastor Muhlenberg also rode the circuit, conducting services in Winchester, Rude's Hill, and Strasburg. On the civic side, Pastor Muhlenberg was "[c]hosen ... as chair of the six-person Committee of Safety and Correspondence for the county."[28] Thus, "[P]eter Muhlenberg was recognized not only as the spiritual but also the civic leader ... of the Woodstock region." He was a magistrate. Later, citizens chose Peter Muhlenberg as a delegate to the convention convening in Williamsburg in August 1774.[29]

The First Virginia Convention "agreed not to import goods from Great Britain.... Exports to Great Britain were to cease, and no tea was to be used so long as it was taxed." On March 25, 1775, Muhlenberg was again present for the Second Virginia Convention. Muhlenberg was in attendance when Patrick Henry delivered his "Give me liberty or give me death" oration.

As the War Begins, Colonel Muhlenberg Serves

Prior Virginia colonial governors had adopted a light touch, evincing a conciliatory attitude toward those colonists who bridled under British rule. By contrast with his predecessors, John Murray, 4th Earl of Dunmore, was not conciliatory. He took great umbrage at the Second Virginia Convention's resolutions, in March 1775 calling them "treason," commencing revolutionary conflict in Virginia.[30]

As events progressed toward war, Dunmore rallied Tory sympathizers. Along with a small force of British troops, he fled down the James River, enlisting enslaved workers in his counter-rebellion by promising them emancipation (Chapter 14). In a prequel to the Revolutionary War, namely "Dunmore's War," Lord Dunmore's force boarded *HMS Fowey*, a smaller British war ship.[31] In March 1776, Muhlenberg and the Eighth Regiment marched to Suffolk, in southeast Virginia, and stood in reserve.[32] The Eighth waited while forces under Revolutionary General Andrew Lewis bombarded Gwynn's Island, site of Dunmore's last stand.

Muhlenberg Under Fire—The First Siege of Charleston (1776)

In June 1776, with 8,500 troops and 56 Royal Navy ships, British General Henry Clinton arrived off the coast of Charles Town, the South's leading city, to lay siege to it.[33] American Major General Charles Lee, in command of the Southern Department, had 5,000 men, including Peter Muhlenberg's, who had marched south from Virginia to South Carolina after Dunmore's War. Contemporaries, including Washington, characterized Lee as "rather fickle and violent" but "the first officer in military knowledge and experience."[34]

On June 23, led by the 50-gun HMS *Bristol*, British warships began bombarding a small fort on Sullivan's Island, a narrow barrier island north of the Cooper River mouth. The ten-hour bombardment did little damage (Chapter 10). Muhlenberg's troops, 700 Virginians coming from Haddrell's Point, reinforced Colonel William Thomson's Americans defending Sullivan Island's eastern end.[35]

The British invasion attempt was a "fiasco."[36] "General Lee was astonished by the bravery of the untrained American soldiers [Muhlenberg's Regiment], about whose valor he had hitherto held no high opinion. His reports on the engagement were full of praise for the men," Edward Hocker writes in his biography, *The Fighting Parson*.[37] General Lee wrote to Congress and to the commander-in-chief, "I have the greatest reason to be pleased with Muhlenberg's Virginians ... alert, zealous, and spirited."[38]

Futility Following Action: Dunmore's War Redux

At the time, British forces in East Florida were conducting raids over the border into Georgia (Chapter 5). Fearing raids further north, Savannah's citizens agitated for protection. General Lee heeded their calls, dispatching the Virginia Eighth. Muhlenberg's regiment arrived in Savannah on August 17 and at Sunbury, south of the city, on August 22, where they camped. The weather was hot and muggy, with troops becoming ill with tropical afflictions. Washington had recalled Charles Lee to the mid–Atlantic region. In September, General William Moultrie, now in charge, canceled the expedition. Muhlenberg led his Virginia troops, hobbled by sickness and fatigue, slowly northward, reaching northern Virginia only on December 20. "Muhlenberg himself suffered all his life from the consequences of disease contracted on the futile Georgia-Florida campaign."[39] On February 21, 1777, Congress promoted Colonel Peter Muhlenberg to brigadier general.[40]

Action as a Flag Officer

As brigadier, Muhlenberg took command of one half of the Virginia regiments (the First, Fifth, Eighth and Ninth). George Weedon, now also a brigadier, took over command of the remainder. Together, the two brigades formed up as General Nathanael Greene's division.[41]

Newly arrived from the Florida expedition, Muhlenberg and his regiments missed Washington's crossing of the Delaware as well as the late 1776-early 1777 Battles of Trenton and Princeton. In spring and early summer 1777, when Muhlenberg and his charges had joined up, the American Army marched and countermarched through New Jersey and Pennsylvania as Washington and his generals conjectured as to the British's next move. Briefly, again, would British General William Howe go north from New York, linking up with Burgoyne in his effort to bisect the colonies? Or would he order a march southwest from Staten Island, across Arthur Kill, through Perth Amboy, and across New Jersey, occupying Philadelphia? Or would he sail up either the Delaware River or Chesapeake Bay, landing somewhere with his troops? That summer, intense heat and "sutlers selling liquor caused trouble" at the American army's encampments, resulting in complications. Drunkenness, gambling, and sickness rippled through the camps. Marching back and forth and back and forth again harmed morale.

British General Howe chose the latter of his three options. In September 1777, landing his force at Head of Elk, the uppermost reach of Chesapeake Bay, Howe eyed Philadelphia fifty miles away.

Brandywine

As much as any other brigade that day, Muhlenberg and his Virginians acquitted themselves with honor. His troops mirrored the late day heroics of George Weedon's regiments (Chapter 2). "Muhlenberg's brigade ... rendered service of incalculable value by holding back the British advance long enough to permit the badly battered American regiments to retire from [Birmingham Meeting House Hill]," wrote Edward Hooker. Late in the day, divisions under Generals Stirling, Stephen, and Sullivan, which had been unable to counteract Cornwallis, retreated. "[M]uhlenberg's men alone, after having marched four miles in forty minutes, faced all of Cornwallis's army. Their commander [Muhlenberg] led them in desperate hand-to-hand bayonet fighting. This fortitude of the Virginians prevented the defeat from becoming a rout...," concluded Hooker.[42] All accounts record that "Muhlenberg's brigade was the last to leave the field of battle."[43] One historian recorded, "The conduct of General Muhlenberg at this crisis was such as to win him the admiration and esteem of the whole army. Conspicuous at the head of his men, he braved every danger, leading the charges upon the enemy."[44]

The British took control of Philadelphia on September 25, 1777. The American retreated to the northwest, passing Trappe, the Muhlenberg ancestral home. The hardships of war are reflected in the September 19 journal entry of Henry Melchior Muhlenberg, Peter's father:

> The American Army, four miles from us, forded the Schuykill breast-high and came [past us] upon the Philadelphia Road.... His Excellency, General Washington, was with the troops ... who marched past here.... The procession lasted through the night [with soldiers] and officers, wet breast-high, who had to march in this condition the whole night, cold and damp as it was, and to bear hunger and thirst at the same time.[45]

Washington marched his troops to the vicinity of Pottstown. A large body of the British army remained outside Philadelphia, camping at Germantown, five miles northwest of the city. In council, Washington and his generals decided to reverse course, attacking the foe at Germantown, sixteen miles away.

Germantown

Following a long march, an assault on the British and Hessian position was to begin. The American attack was to be in four columns, two of 3,000 men each to attempt flanking movements, left and right, and two in the center under Generals Nathanael Green and John Sullivan. Muhlenberg took charge of his regiments, a portion of Nathanael Greene's division who, along with Adam Stephen's division, were to be one of the flanking detachments, moving forward on the colonials' left wing. Conway's and Sullivan's forces constituted the van of the center columns that were to proceed up the main road. In reserve, Generals Nash, Maxwell, and Stirling with their regiments followed on the main and Shippack roads. In his biography *Adam Stephen*, Professor Harry Ward described the strategy's central aspect: "For the broad pincer movement, it was of the utmost importance that the advance be synchronized to the greatest precision so that the Americans would attack at once."[46]

According to some sugar-coated accounts, an early morning fog limited visibility (Weedon's version), greatly interfering with plans for cooperation among the American army columns. A less euphemistic account was that one of the commands under Greene, that of General Adam Stephen, wandered far out of its course, moving westward until it collided with General Wayne's troops. The most credible explanation was that General Adam Stephen was drunk and ordered his force to turn right rather than to stay left. Coming up upon the American center, Stephen's troops encountered the rear of Wayne's and opened fire. Wayne's men fired back. Friendly fire killed and wounded a number of Americans.

Meanwhile, with the advantage of surprise, the other American forces had pushed the British back two miles to the center of Germantown. Unsupported on the left, the colonial advance created an unprotected salient. With the advantage to the Americans, the tide turned, with the advantage to the British. General Stephen,

BATTLE OF BRANDYWINE

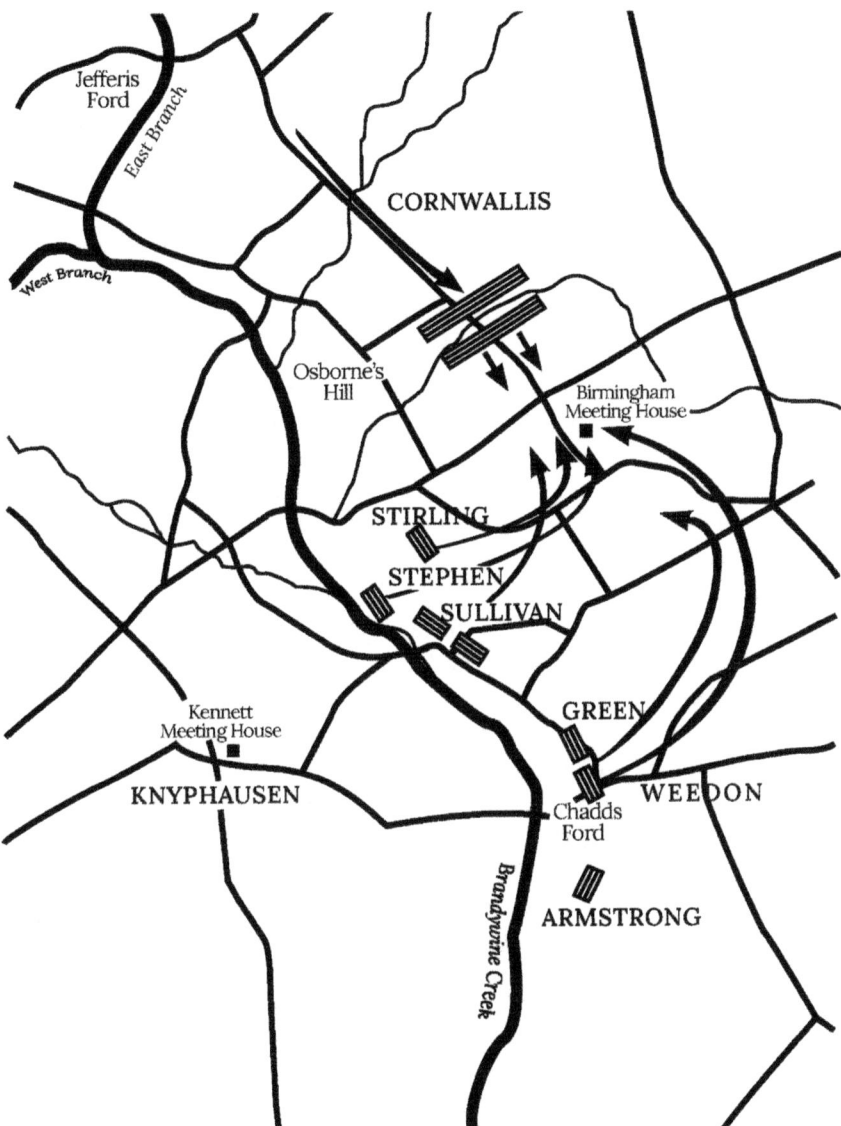

again likely intoxicated, had sounded a premature signal for a general retreat. British General Howe then was able to re-form his men, reversing direction, from retreat to attack. The American retreat turned into a rout. The Ninth Virginia Regiment, of Muhlenberg's brigade, commanded by Colonel George Matthews, found itself marooned at the head of the salient, soon surrounded by British and compelled to surrender. "Thus, after having marched all night, and fought for four hours, or longer, the tired troops retraced their steps to Worcester, and then continued the retreat some miles farther," with the British in pursuit.[47]

Washington was said to have had "the mortification to assure the troops that they had fled from Victory."⁴⁸ Quelling misgivings among his generals, "Washington did not parcel out any blame on his division commanders for the defeat at Germantown. The commander in chief thought the major problem was the fog...." Though, "As at Brandywine, [at Germantown] the Virginians had again been the heroes of the day."⁴⁹

A Lull in the Action

Eventually, the American forces camped around Whitemarsh, twelve miles north of Philadelphia. While there, during the lull in fighting, General Muhlenberg sat on two courts martial. One was of General Anthony Wayne, accused of dereliction of duty, leading to the massacre at Paoli. The court acquitted Wayne. The second tried General Adam Stephen, accused of drunkenness and premature orders to retreat at Germantown. The court found Stephen guilty. General Washington ordered that the Army dismiss General Adam Stephen from the service.

Ever aggressive, at least as he was the war's first years, Washington spoiled for another attack on the British. Successive councils of war composed of the generals, including Muhlenberg, voted against Washington's desires. In later December 1777, the army retreated westward 7–8 miles from Whitemarsh, into winter encampment at Valley Forge, 23 miles northwest of Philadelphia.⁵⁰

From Valley Forge, Muhlenberg made a Christmas visit to his parents' home in Trappe. Perhaps having learned a lesson from the 1776 British capture of Charles Lee in New Jersey, General Muhlenberg took extreme measures in Pennsylvania: "Precautions were adopted to prevent his presence from becoming known in the [Trappe] neighborhood."⁵¹ At night, "Blankets were hung over the windows and doors to prevent his being seen by lurking spies. He himself never undressed or allowed his horse to be unsaddled [which was kept] close at hand."⁵²

Ranking and Rankling Virginia's Generals

Congress and a board of officers ranked General William Woodford senior to Brigadiers George Weedon, Peter Muhlenberg, and Charles Scott. Muhlenberg and colleagues found this unfair, as they had continuous service while Woodford had resigned his commission in September 1777 and returned to the Army in February 1778. Further, cashiering General Adam Stephen for, *inter alia*, drunkenness at Germantown, had opened a major general billet that Congress bestowed upon Woodford. Both Muhlenberg and Weedon decided to resign.⁵³ Washington's April 1777 letter to Muhlenberg entreated him not to do so:

> I cannot judge the feelings of others, but my own should generally be regulated by the set of opinions of a set of gentlemen [who voted to promote Woodford] who I conceive have been actuated by the purest principles of impartiality and justice.... I would not be thought to press on you a hasty decision upon this matter but when you consider that we are upon the verge of a campaign, you will think with me that no time is to be lost....⁵⁴

Washington's frank letter placated Muhlenberg. After several days in Woodstock, Muhlenberg returned to Valley Forge.[55]

Monmouth Courthouse

On June 17, 1778, a council of war again curbed General Washington's aggressive tendencies. The generals voted, "unanimously," to recommend no attack on Philadelphia, but the issue became moot.[56] The following day, the British evacuated Philadelphia under General Henry Clinton, who had replaced William Howe. The British began a slow march across New Jersey to Sandy Hook, where they would board transports to take them into New York City. Encumbered by hundreds of wagons and thousands of camp followers who had joined the British effort in Pennsylvania, the caravan moved at a pace less than two miles per day. The American army then set out from Valley Forge toward New Jersey in pursuit.

The Americans crossed the Delaware River, catching the British at Monmouth Courthouse where, on June 28, 1778, a sweltering summer day, the two sides met (*see* Chapters 9 & 17). Monmouth Courthouse was, as it turned out, the last major northern engagement of the war. General Muhlenberg and his men fought at Monmouth, "[doing] their duty but nothing more can be claimed."[57] After the conflict, Washington marched his army north. He concentrated his forces along the Hudson, above New York City, in a watch and wait posture proximate to the main British force in Manhattan, awaiting the British force's next move.[58]

Inaction in the North and Return to Action in Virginia

The Middle Department army spent the winter at Morristown, in northern New Jersey. In December 1779, Washington detached Muhlenberg, ordering him south to lead a major portion of the Virginia's defense: "Virginia was then the richest and most populous of the thirteen states, and, so far, [the Commonwealth] had suffered comparatively little from the war."[59] Now storm clouds gathered as "The enemy deemed the breaking up of Virginia a primary object."[60] A probably more accurate view was that, by making necessary the defense of Tidewater Virginia, the British hoped to siphon off colonial troops that otherwise would go further south to aid the Continentals' Southern Army.

In October 1780, British commander-in-chief "Clinton sent 3,000 British troops from New York, under [Major] General [Alexander] Leslie to Virginia. They arrived in the James River at Portsmouth on October 15."[61] The British forces raided the countryside along the James River, pointing northwest toward Richmond. Muhlenberg and Brigadier George Weedon, whose resignation Congress had never accepted, recruited troops but stayed well back from engagement until they gathered what the generals calculated was the needed strength. Then, "Having collected 5000 men, Muhlenberg advanced with them against Leslie's army and drove in the pickets but evaded the main force."[62] In November, the British re-boarded their ships, sailing back to New York.

In January 1781, the British attempted the last of its Virginia diversions. Benedict Arnold, now a British general, sailed with 2,000 troops up the James River to Westover, twenty-five miles below Richmond.[63] General Washington had recalled Baron von Steuben from North Carolina to head up the Commonwealth's defense. Arnold and his men raided up the river, took possession of Richmond for a short time, causing damage there, and engaged in clashes with the colonials. British Generals Phillips and Arnold threw their forces into a major skirmish at City Point on April 24, 1781. Between sixty and seventy colonials, untrained and inexperienced militia, were killed, while "the British loss was trifling."[64] But Arnold and Phillips retreated down the James with their troops, boarded Royal Navy ships, and sailed out to sea.[65]

George Weedon, now back on active service, and Muhlenberg had a difficult time holding their defensive efforts intact. At one point, Muhlenberg's force had shrunk to 800. Short-term militia enlistments kept expiring: "[O]ne hundred men deserted in one night." In spring 1781, Muhlenberg and his men guarded the roads leading in and out of Portsmouth, Virginia. Near there Muhlenberg met with Major General Lafayette who, among other things, was coming south with a contingent to scout in force Benedict Arnold's positions.[66] But, by October 1781, Muhlenberg's brigade of militia expanded once more, to 1,000 men. Then, while George Weedon's militia units went north and then southeast to the Gloucester, cutting off Cornwallis's possible escape route across the York River, Muhlenberg's unit joined the siege on the York Peninsula where, eventually, 16,600 French and Americans boxed in Cornwallis.

Looking back, in 1775–1777, Virginia's leaders thought the Commonwealth would be central in the war. It was not to be; no major engagements took place in Virginia. Gwynn's Island, hardly a major engagement, took place early in 1776. So, by the time the 1780 defense became necessary as the British raided up Virginia's rivers, four years had passed, and apathy had come to prevail. Too many callouts, too many false alarms, a sense of remoteness from the war's cataclysmic conflicts, a recurrent need to plant in the spring and harvest in the fall, and the varied topography (Tidewater, Piedmont, Blue Ridge, Shenandoah Valley, Allegheny Mountains) dividing the colony into separate, distinct sections—these factors caused apathy to cast a long shadow. Brigadiers Weedon and Muhlenberg faced strong headwinds in their attempts to maintain an adequate military force until Yorktown and the arrival of Continentals in Virginia.

An Important Military Engagement in Virginia

At Yorktown, on the north side of a peninsula bound on the south by the James River and on the north by the York River, Lord Cornwallis and his men circled the wagons. They built strong defenses, including fortified redoubts, for protection while they waited for a Royal Navy fleet to board them and return to New York, safety, and comfort.

On the night of October 15, 1781, the French attacked the first of the British redoubts. The Americans, under General Muhlenberg, then attacked another. "One of his aides who survived ... was quoted as saying that General Muhlenberg led the storming party in person."[67] Current accounts credit the Marquis de Lafyette with leading the force that captured the redoubt, but it may well have been Peter Muhlenberg fronting the attack.[68]

At Yorktown, Washington divided his force onto three divisions, one of which Lafayette commanded. In command of one-half of that division, though, Washington placed Brigadier Muhlenberg in charge. Professor Stephen Taaffe writes in *Washington's Revolutionary War Generals*, "Washington had always respected Muhlenberg and took advantage of an open slot in Lafayette's outfit to give him an active position."[69]

Military Denouement

After Yorktown, with permission duly granted, Muhlenberg returned to Woodstock. "Thereafter, General Muhlenberg's headquarters were in the barracks at Winchester, at the foot of Shenandoah Valley ... thirty miles from his family in Woodstock." On September 30, 1783, Congress promoted General Muhlenberg to major general. The disbanding of the Revolutionary War army was ordered the following November. The same year, 1783, Muhlenberg became an original member of the Order of the Cincinnati.[70]

In his poem, "The Rising," Thomas Buchanan Read (1822–1872) memorializes Peter Muhlenberg:

> The pastor rose: the prayer was strong;
> The psalm was warrior David's song:
> In the text, a few short words of might—
> "The Lord of Hosts shall arm the right!"
>
> ....
>
> When suddenly his mantle wide
> His hands impatient flung aside,
> And, lo! He met their wandering eyes,
> Complete in all a warrior's guise.
> A moment there was awful pause,—
>
> When Berkeley cried, "Cease, traitor! Cease!
> God's temple is a house of peace!"
>
> The others shouted, "Nay, not so,
> When God is with our righteous cause:
> His holiest places then are ours,
> His temples are our forts and towers
> That frown upon the tyrant foe:
> In this the dawn of Freedom's day
> There is a time to fight and pray!"

Part V—Mentioned in the Dispatches

....

"Who dares"—this was the patriot's cry,
As striding from the desk he came—
"Come out with me, in Freedom's name,
For her to live, for her to die?"

A hundred hands flung up in reply,
A hundred voices answered, "I!"[71]

19

Brigadier Francis Nash of North Carolina at Germantown

Historians mention Francis Nash, if at all, as having received a fatal wound at Germantown, October 4, 1777.[1] Few accounts mention that General Nash commanded the North Carolina troops George Washington held in reserve when an errant British cannonball shattered Nash's thigh. Historians gainsay even Nash's promotion to brigadier, explaining that the Continental Congress's motivation was to enhance Nash's ability to recruit troops rather than to recognize military exploits.[2] Nash is another forgotten Revolutionary War brigadier.[3]

Nor did Nash's actions in the 1770–1771 military actions against the Regulators generate content in the dispatches. Contemporary accounts did term Francis, or Frank, Nash "the most attractive character of Revolutionary Hillsboro." One of Francis's soldiers opined "that [General Nash] was the handsomest man on horseback that he ever saw."[4] Professor Stephen Taaffe wrote, "Nash was a forty-four year old, Virginia-born, North Carolina lawyer, businessman, and legislator" described as "brave, modest, sensible, and good tempered."[5]

Virginia Roots

In his youth, Nash may have been forgotten, too, or more likely, given short shrift, as he was the seventh of John and Anna Nash's eight children, born in 1742. The Nashes emigrated from Wales in 1730, first settling in Henrico County, Virginia (Richmond). Later, probably in 1742, they migrated to Amelia County (Farmville, sixty-five miles southwest) settling what would become Prince Edward County. In those days, the gentry, including George Washington and others, saw the acquisition of land as a pathway to wealth. John Nash was no different, acquiring 13,140 acres, Prince Edward County's largest landholding.[6] The Nash's were civic minded. Over two decades, John Nash and three of his sons served in the Virginia House of Burgesses. The eldest son, John Junior, was a cofounder of Hampden-Sydney College, located seven miles south of Farmville.[7] John Sr. and John Jr. served under George Washington in the French and Indian War, so when the revolution came seventeen years later, Washington knew the Nash family.

Migration South to North Carolina

Sometime during this period, probably around 1763, Francis, the seventh child, along with Abner, the sixth, migrated to the upper reaches of North Carolina, settling in Childsburgh, in 1766 renamed Hillsborough. In those times, younger sons often left the family nest because they anticipated primogeniture's effect, that the family patriarch's interests in land and other possessions would pass to the eldest son. When John Sr. died in 1776, by will he left to his eldest son "all my horses, lands, and plantation."

By age 21, Francis had set up a law practice in Hillsborough. He and brother Abner dammed the Eno River, creating a mill stream for waterpower to operate the grist mill they built. Francis served in the Royal Governor's Colonial Assembly in 1764, 1765, and 1771, when he was 22, 23, and 29 years old, respectively, journeying to the colony's capital, New Bern.[8] He became close to William Tryon, the strong-willed, colorful Royal Governor 1764–1771. Francis also became Clerk of the Court for Orange County, serving Judge Richard Henderson. In the 1760s, the Regulators (Chapter 3) accused Nash of collecting illegal fees.[9] In Hillsborough, when Judge Richard Henderson, along with his clerk, attempted to open court, they were met by 150 or so regulators, "shouting, ballooing, and making a considerable Tumult."[10] The mob set out from the court, burning Judge Henderson's house and stables to the ground.[11] Nash thus had reason to hold the regulators in contempt for the wrongful accusations against him, arson of the judge's home, and extreme hostility. Nash, as did Governor Tryon, viewed the Regulators as nothing more than a mob.

First Military Experience

The Governor refused to negotiate with the Regulators or even to recognize their existence. Instead, the Governor led troops to Hillsborough. Two days later, militia from Rowan (Salisbury) and Mecklenburg (Charlotte) counties joined him. He had an army of 1,461 to face a mob—disorganized, many unarmed—now grown to 3,700. Tryon had soldiers patrolling Hillsborough's streets with other men guarding the market square and the jail.[12] Later, on May 16, 1771, the two sides met in the Battle of Alamance on a field twenty miles west of Hillsborough. The Governor's army included as a field officer thirty-year-old Francis Nash. The colonial army had the great advantage in arms, ammunition, and discipline. Governor Tryon not only led the force but opened the hostilities by firing the first shot. His force vanquished the Regulators; for all practical purposes, the rout at Alamance ended the saga of the Regulation movement.

Nash's brother Abner made his mark in politics rather than military exploits. Abner Nash moved to Halifax, east of Hillsborough, and later, after the death of his wife, to New Bern, where he remarried and began a successful political career. Abner Nash became North Carolina's second governor, serving 1780–1781, succeeding Richard Caswell.

North Carolina's Pathway to Revolution

In 1771 Josiah Martin succeeded William Tryon as North Carolina's Royal Governor: "He had few of the qualities possessed by Governor Tryon." In fact, he had none. As William Powell described him in *North Carolina Through Four Centuries*, "Martin was stubborn, intolerant, and completely without tact. He was a sycophant in the presence of his British superiors ... condescending towards those he considered inferior."[13]

The North Carolina revolutionary movement did not begin until three years into Martin's tenure in 1774. In contrast, in the north, the British quartering of troops in Boston occurred in 1768, the Boston Massacre in 1770, and the Boston Tea Party in 1773. What stirred the revolutionary pot in North Carolina involved neither British troops on Carolina soil nor martial acts as had occurred in the north. What riled residents was the Intolerable Act provision that English creditors could attach debtors' Carolina property in the Royal Courts, that is, in Britain, far away from the property. Governor Martin perceived as disrespectful to the King prominent North Carolinians' plotting, inspired by their revulsion at Intolerable Act provisions. To wit, Carolinians proposed to elect delegates to the initial Continental Congress, to commence September 5, 1774, at Carpenters' Hall, Philadelphia. Tit-for-tat, Governor Martin announced that the July 1774 North Carolina General Assembly, to be held in New Bern, had been canceled. Undaunted, patriot William Hooper and a group from Wilmington convened a rump group. The "First *Provincial* Congress" took place at the same time as the canceled General Assembly, at the same site, New Bern.[14] Over three days, the Provincial Congress selected three delegates—Hooper, Joseph Hewes, and Richard Caswell—to attend the First Continental Congress.

These acts further infuriated Governor Martin who, in accordance with his belief in the divine right of kings, held to the notion that appointment of delegates and the passing of legislative acts belonged to the King and his deputies rather than to the people. He wrote a long letter of grievances to Lord Dartmouth, secretary of state for the Colonies. He complained of "seditious leaders" who "talk of resorting to violence instead of submission."[15]

Governor Martin then attempted to reassert his authority over North Carolina's affairs. He noted up a meeting of the Royal Assembly to be held April 4, 1775. His adversaries preempted Martin's gesture by calling a meeting of the Second Provincial Congress commencing the day before Governor Martin's proposed meeting, on April 3.

News from the North

Meanwhile, London newspapers, making their way into North Carolina, reported Massachusetts in rebellion. The incidents at Concord—"The shot heard round the world"—and Lexington took place April 19. "When news of the fighting in the north reached North Carolina, there was great excitement," Hugh Nash penned in his biography of the Nash brothers.[16] Fearing that artillery could be turned upon himself and the governor's mansion, Governor Martin had the cannons on Tryon Palace grounds dismounted. On May 23, 1775, an angry group appeared at the palace to protest Martin's action. The protest caused Martin to abandon New Bern on May 31, taking refuge at the British Fort Johnson on the Cape River Estuary, below Wilmington. In July 1775, Martin fled further. He boarded a British warship at the Cape Fear River mouth, a day before Robert Howe and 500 patriots stormed and burned Fort Johnson.

North Carolina's Third Provincial Congress met in Hillsborough rather than New Bern to commence on August 20, 1775.[17] That Congress, with Frances Nash representing Orange County, marked the end of Nash's political career and the beginning of his military experiences. The Congress created six regiments for the six military districts into which the colony had been divided, supplementing the First and Second North Carolina regiments. The North Carolina First was to be commanded by James Moore with Lieutenant Colonel Richard Caswell second-in-command; the North Carolina Second commanded by Robert Howe with Lieutenant Colonel Francis Nash second-in-command.[18]

As Aside: The Battle of Moore's Creek

Francis Nash and men of the Second arrived hours too late to participate in the Battle of Moore's Creek, but Nash's journey to the scene was his first active role as a military leader. Instead, James Moore, Richard Caswell, and the First Carolina were the engagement's heroes (*see* Chapter 4).

Briefly, in early 1776, British from an amphibious force were to join Scottish Highlanders marching southeast from Cross Creek (present-day Fayetteville). Richard Caswell and his 1,000 North Carolinians (Chapter 4) made a stand beyond a deep stream, Moore's Creek, a tributary of the Black River.[19] The Highlanders had to cross Moore's Creek.[20] As the Americans had done at Great Bridge, the American took up the planks forming the bridge's surface.[21] The North Carolinians achieved a decisive victory, killing over thirty, capturing 35 guns, 1,500 rifles, and 13 supply wagons. Moore's Creek was a significant development in another respect.[22] North Carolina did not suffer another British unit within its borders until late 1780.[23]

Continuation of a Military Career

After Moore's Creek, Howe, Nash, and their Continental regiment moved south from North Carolina to Charles Town, arriving in the city on June 11, 1776. North Carolina regiments were to reenforce the city's garrison, preparing a defense to a British land and sea attack on the port (the "first siege," *see* Chapters 9 and 10). Due to William Moultrie's dilatory progress in building a Sullivan's Island fort, along with Southern Department Commander Major General Charles Lee's confidence in Francis Nash, Lee planned to replace the indolent Moultrie with Nash. Nash and his North Carolina men had a position further within Charleston harbor, on the Cooper River at Haddrell's Point.[24] Instead of relieving Moultrie, Nash and his North

Carolinians moved out over the flimsy walkway crossing to Sullivan's Island to assist Moultrie's men's defense of Fort Sullivan.

Colonel Moultrie assigned to the North Carolinians the difficult task of defending the fort's rear, "unfinished" and in Hugh Owen Nash's estimation (in *Patriot Sons*), "a post of great consequence."[25] Because the "rear walls of the fort were barely seven feet high, there was little protection from any British ship sailing into the cove behind the island."[26] Nash and his men defended it well, enduring a ten-hour British bombardment. As has been seen (Chapter 10), Charles Town was the first decisive American battlefield victory in the Revolutionary War, at least one against British troops, a cause for rejoicing throughout the colonies.

Here and There: Marches and Countermarches

After Charles Town, Southern Army Commander Lee ordered Nash and his men to complement an excursion southward (*see also* Chapter 18). Joining Colonel Muhlenberg and the 8th Virginia, North Carolinians were to defend Georgia from incursions by the British forces in East Florida and, if possible, advance to St. Augustine, the British capital. It was, in Hugh Rankin's words, a "fatiguing, fruitless expedition to Georgia."[27] A short way into Georgia, Charles Lee was ordered north. South Carolina's Colonel Moultrie assumed command, but with his men sickened and fatigued by the summer heat and tropical surroundings, Moultrie cancelled the expedition.

Francis Nash and his men spent the fall of 1776 in the vicinity of Wilmington, North Carolina. On February 5, 1777, the Continental Congress promoted Francis Nash to brigadier general, with the thought that Nash's notoriety and new rank would aid in recruitment. Congress had in mind for Nash to recruit in the state's west, to bring North Carolina's Continental Line headcounts up to the numbers Congress had set. Recruiting efforts pinned Nash in backcountry North Carolina for several months. In mid–April 1777, senior North Carolina General James Moore died unexpectedly from what was described as "a fit of gout in his stomach," an unexplained, ill-described malady. Suddenly, Francis Nash was in command of North Carolina's Continentals. He rendezvoused with officers and soldiers at Halifax, North Carolina, near the Virginia border.

The Journey North

Under orders from General Washington, Nash led the North Carolina Continentals "from Halifax to Petersburg [Virginia] to Richmond." By the end of May 1777, they were in Alexandria, Virginia, on the Potomac River's south shore.[28] For Nash and his men, marches and countermarches, the patriot soldier's major occupation, ensued. They ended their marches encamped at Trenton, twenty-eight miles north of Philadelphia, on the Delaware River. "Convinced that [British Commander] Howe intended to sail up the Hudson to reinforce Burgoyne near Albany, Washington had moved to Smith's Cove near West Point," positioning other troops so that they could lend the northern army support if needed. Washington, however, "received intelligence that Howe had supplied his ships for a longer voyage, indicating that his objective might be Philadelphia...."[29] With intelligence regarding Howe's provisioning for a longer voyage, Washington moved south. By August 3, 1777, Washington was at Logan's Tavern, Philadelphia, where he penned orders to Nash. John F. Reed quotes George Washington's instructions that Nash was to bring his men south from Trenton, "specifically ordered to avoid Philadelphia for fear of creating an unnecessary disturbance in the city." In small fit of picaresque behavior, Nash marched his men right through the city, August 25, 1777.[30]

At Chadds Ford, crossing Brandywine Creek, a major clash was about to occur. Little has been recorded of Nash's activities that day, September 11, at Brandywine. Washington had placed the North Carolinians in a reserve position, on the hill overlooking Chadds Ford. In his notes on the battle, George Washington wrote, "Nash's North Carolina brigade did not get into action that hot, dusty afternoon."[31]

Another Major Battle and the End

Following Brandywine, after peregrinations, the American army encamped on Skippack Creek, twenty-five miles northwest of Philadelphia. On September 26, the British occupied the American capital city. Ten thousand of the British troops bivouacked at Germantown, five miles northwest of Philadelphia.[32] Undoubtedly, with the thought of avenging the Brandywine loss, Washington and his generals conceived a complex plan to surprise the British. On the early morning of October 4, the assault to be carried out by three columns failed badly due to Major General Adam Stephen ordering his column to the right rather than onward to the left. Coming up behind General Anthony Wayne's brigade in the center, Stephen's troops fired into the fog. Friendly fire stalled the American attack, as well as neutralizing the element of surprise. Ultimately, defeat was snatched from the jaws of victory.

Again, as at Brandywine, Washington's order of battle placed Nash and his men in reserve, albeit in up-close reserve status. Nash sat upon his horse at the head of his North Carolina men, conferring with Major James Witherspoon of New Jersey.[33] An errant six-pound British cannonball, aimed at front-line attacking forces, overshot the mark. Major Witherspoon "had the side of his head shorn away and died instantly. Nash was not so lucky. The ball continued its course, striking the General in the thigh, causing a ghastly wound."[34] Thomas McGuire's book, *Surprise of Germantown*, has a slightly differing version of the event, that the cannon fire hit Nash's horse, then Nash.[35]

On the ground, Nash covered his wound to conceal its severity from his troops, "the brave General reportedly saying, 'Never mind me, I've had a devil of a tumble, rush on my boys, rush on the enemy: I'll be with you shortly.'" "One of Nash's officers, Major Hardy Murfree of the 2d North Carolina, wrapped his sash around Nash's wound as a temporary bandage."[36] Receiving news of Nash's misfortune,

BATTLE OF GERMANTOWN

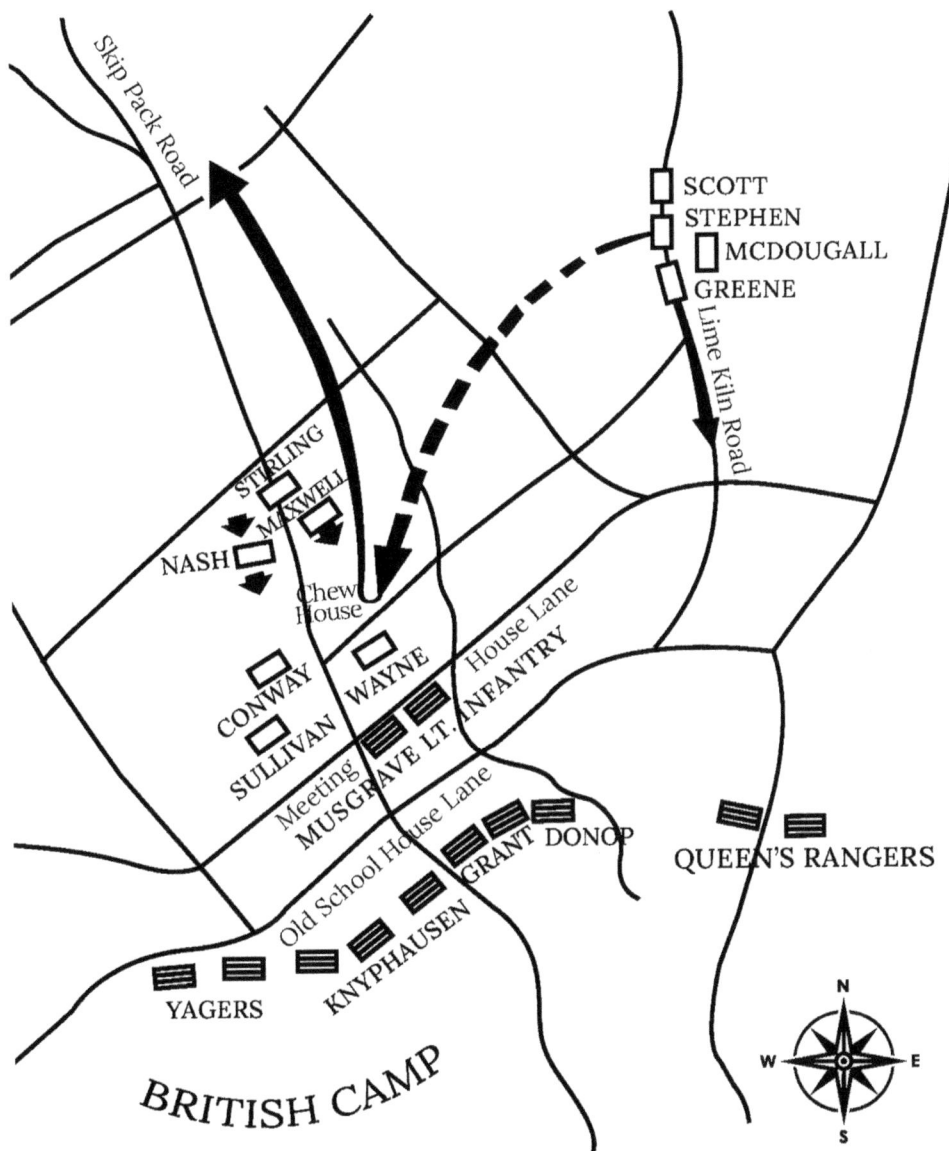

General Washington ordered surgeon James Craik to attend Nash. Location of Nash's wound, high up on the leg, precluded amputation, then the principal medical remedy for a wound to an extremity. Troops carried Nash to a nearby house. After the battle, attending physicians had General Nash transferred by empty ammunition wagon, farther to the rear. He died on October 7, 1777, "after suffering extreme agony ... bleed[ing] through two feather mattresses."[37]

The Denouement

General Washington's General Orders for October 9, 1777, read: "Brigadier General Nash will be interred, at ten o'clock this forenoon, with military honors, at the place where the troops Marched in [at] the great road.... All officers, whose circumstances will admit ... will attend to pay respect to a brave Man who died in defense of his Country." Present were Generals Greene, Sullivan, Stirling, Armstrong, Wayne, Maxwell, Smallwood, Knox, and Pulaski.[38] General Nash's remains were interred at Towamencin Mennonite Meeting Graveyard, at Forty-Foot Road and Sumneytown Pike, northwest of Philadelphia.

On May 13, 1780, citizens of Tennessee settled on the Cumberland River subscribed to the chartering of Nashborough, named after Francis Nash, now Nashville, capital city of the sixteenth state.[39]

PART VI

Punctilios of Honor Beyond Sensitive

20

Rivalries and Resignations

Of Revolutionary War generals, John Adams wrote to Abigail, "I am wearied to Death with the Wrangles between military officers, high and low. They Quarrel like Cats and Dogs. They worry one another like Mastiffs, scrambling for Rank and Pay like Apes for Nuts."[1] The Patriot army was one "staffed by officers who were exquisitely sensitive to their 'honor.'" Promotions and seniority lists set off rivalries and resignations, along with appeals to General Washington and Congress. "Political meddling," along with promotions and seniority rankings, "invited trouble," John Stark's biographers, Richard and John Polhemus, wrote.[2] Eighty-five years later, plagued by Congressional appointments, Ulysses Grant wrote that "political generals ... were the bane of his existence, a special curse on the union cause."[3] Political appointments and ranking of general officers during the Revolutionary War sent off firestorms of letter writing, lobbying, intrigue, and manipulation.[4] The southern brigadiers often were at the center of these rivalries, complaints, lobbying efforts, and resignations.

In mitigation, the honor of those times was conceptually different from today's common understanding. In the eighteenth century, honor was central "to an ethical code that profoundly influenced the behavior and self-image of Americans." Professor Rod Andrews, Jr., in his biography *The Life and Times of General Andrew Pickens*, continued, explaining, "Honor was external ... honor was public reputation," more than an internal goal or aspiration, as it tends to be today. Honor was "the status and respect that one's neighbors and peers accorded to an individual based upon perception of his or her courage, integrity, independence, patriotism, and physical and social power."[5] Honor in that sense made understanding of officers' action more palatable than more modern conceptions would.

Overall, the brigadiers were a group of men, military officers, who voluntarily endured years of hardship, separated from families and loved ones, undertaking risks of bodily harm and death. Seven southern brigadiers died in combat or from combat-related causes. They truly were patriots—but however honor is defined, patriots with a dark side.

Brigadier William Woodford

William Woodford fought from the 1775 battle of Great Bridge to the 1780 siege of Charleston.[6] Along the way he was wounded (at Brandywine in 1777), captured at

Charles Town, and died as a prisoner of war (Chapter 15). Woodford, though, at one point resigned his commission, left the army for several months, and later undertook lobbying to complain about promotions and ranking of others over him.

Earlier, in mid–June 1776, Congress appointed Hugh Mercer to Brigadier General. Woodford, also a brigadier general, "had assumed that when Congress had taken Virginia's regiments into continental service back in February [1776], the issue of seniority had been settled with him holding seniority over Mercer due to his earlier appointment," historian Michael Cerere recounts.[7] Woodford felt that the leapfrog promotion, with Mercer becoming senior to Woodford, "was an aspersion upon his character." Woodford wrote in his resignation letter to General Washington, "I feel myself much hurt by the late promotion of my very worthy friend Col. Mercer.... I conceive of the appointment and promotion of an officer at the time serving under me ... reflected dishonor upon myself." He added, "I request your permission to retire...."[8]

Brigadier George Weedon

In March 1778, as Woodford had requested, Congress re-ranked the Virginia generals, placing Woodford (who had left and then rejoined the army) ahead of generals Scott, Muhlenberg, and Weedon. Weedon left Valley Forge in a huff. Weedon pled his case, to no avail, then resigned his commission. Commander-in-chief Washington begged Weedon to reconsider, flattering him that his presence was wanted in camp. He wished Weedon would "cheerfully acquiesce" as had brigadiers Muhlenberg and Scott.[9] Even though Weedon regarded General Washington as "the nation's Christ,"[10] Weedon renewed his resolve, replying "no" to Washington. "What must the world think when they see me banded about like a football," Weedon wrote to Henry Lee.[11] While noting Weedon's attempt to resign, "Congress agreed to let Weedon stay home but insisted that he retain his rank in case he ever changed his mind and returned to duty."[12]

Brigadier Peter Muhlenberg

The same re-ranking, placing William Woodford senior to other Virginia generals, caused Muhlenberg to leave Valley Forge as well, going home to Woodstock (*see* Chapter 18). Washington petitioned Muhlenberg, too, not to resign. In contrast to Weedon, Muhlenberg listened, returning to Valley Forge, an act Stephen Taaffe denominates as "refreshingly altruistic."[13] After the episode, however, for the duration of the war, Muhlenberg refused orders to serve with William Woodford.

Brigadier Charles Scott

"Old Rough and Ready" was a popular battlefield commander. However, smarting from criticism of his actions at Monmouth Courthouse in June 1778, Scott wrote to General Washington on October 21, "My long indisposition and other Obvious reasons will make it indispensable necessary for me to Retier [sic]"[14] Washington persuaded Scott to take a lengthy furlough rather than retire. Scott returned to Virginia to recover from his illness, never specified, and his loss of face.

Brigadier Daniel Morgan

Colonel Daniel Morgan was the true hero of Saratoga, a 1777 battle after which he should have received immediate promotion to brigadier.[15] Earlier, Morgan had served well in the 1775 ill-fated assault on Quebec, imprisoned by Governor Guy Carlton and the British forces in Canada. Despite being barely able to read or write, he was the most innovative of Washington's officers. His corps of frontier riflemen was consistently the best the patriots could offer. Nonetheless, Congress never promoted Morgan. The powers-that-be even assigned leadership of his rifle corps to another senior officer.

In 1779, General Washington announced formation of a new light infantry unit. Morgan, though, was not the only high-ranking officer without portfolio. Arthur St. Clair had ousted Anthony Wayne as commander of Pennsylvania forces. General Washington gave the new light infantry's command to "Mad Anthony" Wayne. The day Morgan heard of the decision, he informed Washington of his intention to give up the service:

> As it is generally known that I commanded the light infantry of our army and that the command is now taken from me, it will naturally be judged that this [change] of officers had taken place either on account of some misconduct in me, or on account of my want of capacity. I cannot therefore but feel deeply effected [sic] with this injury done to my reputation.

Having stated the reason for the action he was about to take, Colonel Morgan continued, "I engaged in the service of my country with a full determination to continue in it as long as my services were [wanted]. I must conclude from what has happened that my country has no more occasion for me, I therefore beg leave to retire."[16] Sensing that an injustice had been done, Congress persuaded Morgan to "take an honorable furlough" rather than retirement.

In early autumn 1779, Daniel Morgan returned to Soldier's Rest, northeast of Winchester, Virginia, where, during his "time-out," he tended to his family and farm. Several times he visited with Major General Horatio Gates, whose farm, Traveler's Rest, was in Berkeley County, 20 miles from Morgan's. Morgan was a favorite of Gates, who had overall command at Saratoga. After the great victory at Saratoga, Gates embraced Morgan: "Morgan, you have done wonders." In his report to Congress, Gates wrote, "Too much praise cannot be given to the Corps commanded by Col. Morgan."[17] When Washington was forming the rifle corps, Gates wrote to Washington that Morgan "would be excellent for the service" of command.[18] In 1780, Congress appointed Horatio Gates new commander of the Southern Department, succeeding Benjamin Lincoln, whom the British had captured at Charles Town. Gates persuaded Morgan to join him in North Carolina. While in the Southern Department, Morgan received his promotion on October 13, 1780, three years after

Saratoga, when the Continental Congress finally set matters straight.[19] Another resignation had been narrowly averted.

Brigadier Andrew Lewis

Early on, Andrew Lewis commanded all Virginia forces in the revolution. Earlier still, in October 1774, he had commanded the patriot force at the Battle of Point Pleasant (Chapter 7). Later, in early 1776, Brigadier Lewis personally commanded the artillery that ended Lord Dunmore's War, at Gwynne's Island. After Patrick Henry and then others succeeded him as commander of all Virginia forces, Lewis resigned, having little further involvement in the war.[20] His was but another resignation, due to ultra-sensitivity, or unfair treatment, or both.

New Hampshire

Snits and resignations were not limited to southern colonies. In the north, New Hampshire had at least three generals of note: John Sullivan, Enoch Poor, and James Reed. The latter was infamous, an invalid who never led troops, in battle or otherwise, but had sufficient political connections to garner appointment as a brigadier.[21] The ablest of New Hampshire's officers, who had been one of Roger's Rangers in the French and Indian War, was a colonel, John Stark, hero of the Battle of Bennington and author of the New Hampshire state motto: "Live Free or Die."

In February 1777, Congress promoted New Hampshire's Colonel Enoch Poor to brigadier.[22] But Congress had left Stark off the promotion list. Disgruntled, Stark petitioned Congress with a letter outlining his contributions, including at Bunker Hill and in the Canadian campaign. However, "Stark's petition fell on deaf ears."[23] In his *Life of General John Stark*, historian Howard Parker Moore was critical: "Congress, enamored of mediocrity, ignored Stark's claim for recognition."[24]

In March 1777, Stark made his way to the New Hampshire capital, then at Exeter, to tender his recognition. "Although it might have made more sense for Stark to notify the Continental Congress ... he was sufficiently upset that he chose New Hampshire's state legislature as the venue for his decision to resign," Ben Rose, one of Stark's other biographers, wrote.[25] Stark's letter read, "I am bound on Honour to leave the service, Congress having thought to promote Junr [sic] officers over my head."[26] Stark prefaced his words of resignation with a summary of his service, saying, "Ever since Hostilities commenced, I have as far as in me Endeavored to prevent my country from bring Ravaged and Enslaved by our crude and unnatural enemies."[27]

Recognizing the error of its ways, on October 4, 1777, Congress promoted John Stark to brigadier general. On October 11, too late to reinforce the American forces at Bemis Heights, Stark swallowed his petulance, reconsidered, and led his troops across the Hudson to the north of the village of Saratoga. There, Stark and his men blocked British General John Burgoyne's escape route to the north.[28]

Massachusetts

Brigadier Ebenezer Learned commanded a brigade at Saratoga (October 1777) but resigned his commission, pleading an injured knee. He returned home to Oxford, Massachusetts.[29] Brigadier John Glover, a sea captain from Marblehead, Massachusetts, saved Washington's army by superintending the evacuation from Brooklyn to Manhattan in 1776. On resigning in 1778, he pleaded deteriorating health and the need to tend to his motherless children. He did not play any role on the war's final three years, permanently resigning his commission in 1780.[30]

Rhode Island

Historians dub Brigadier Andrew Varnum "starchy and difficult."[31] Pleading familial problems, Varnum resigned his commission on February 12, 1779. Pleading family concerns was a sham. The real cause was thought to be financial considerations, not an adequate excuse as, by virtue of protracted service, every senior officer suffered financially. Soon after the war, Varnum became a founder of Marietta, the first major settlement in the Northwest Territory. He relocated to Ohio.[32]

North Carolina

Returning to the southern brigadiers, out of five North Carolina generals, three—James Moore, Richard Caswell, and Jethro Sumner—served short periods of time, with two resigning their commissions. General Moore resigned due to illness, having commanded the North Carolina Continentals from March 1776 until April 1777.[33] The other two generals' resignations tell a familiar story, leaving the service due to loss of face, that is, loss of honor, due to civilian authorities' grants of command to other officers. In 1779, General Jethro Sumner "resigned as soon as General [William] Smallwood assumed authority over him."[34] The North Carolina Assembly appointed Continental General William Smallwood of Maryland, one of the few heroes of the Battle of Camden, over North Carolina's militia, replacing Richard Caswell, when Sumner had expected that he would receive the appointment.[35] As for Caswell, the former governor resigned after several months' service following the Battle of Camden in August 1780.[36] While Smallwood had served ably, Caswell had disgraced himself by accompanying Horatio Gates in retreat, fleeing from his retreating North Carolina forces at Camden.

Why the Rivalries and Resignations?

Idleness truly is "the devil's workshop." Eighteenth century warfare had an intermittent nature, with lengthy hiatuses between engagements and inactivity during winter encampments. During these lulls, officers spun out schemes to enhance their own status or to hamstring others in pursuit of theirs. Senses of slight and indignation festered, in many instances evolving into action. An exaggerated sense of honor combined with the intermittent nature of military action had a geometric rather than arithmetic effect on jealousies, rivalries, and resignations.

During the Civil War, magazine publisher Alexander McClure asked President Abraham Lincoln how he reacted to criticisms advocating that Lincoln remove Ulysses H. Grant. Lincoln responded, "I can't spare this man. He fights."[37] Lincoln had been exasperated by the plethora of Union generals, from George McClellan on, who put off fights, again and again, on grounds that troops were not yet properly trained or equipped. By contrast, Grant took it to his opponents every day, every week, and every month, without letup.

In the Revolutionary War era, though, legitimate reasons existed for inactivity. From November through March, snow and ice made passage difficult for horses and men. Armies went into winter encampment, postponing actions for four or five months.[38] Once patriots broke camp, they encountered spring thaw. Snowmelt rutted roads, resulting in mud over wagons' and caissons' wheel hubs. Spring rains took up where the thaw eased. Fighting was confined to four or five months, roughly June through October.[39]

Manipulation

Inordinate amounts of down time created openings for generals to attempt to pull strings. Horatio Gates was the consummate manipulator. Gates courted John Adams so much so that Gates became an Adams favorite. Adams, "usually the most sensible of men, waxed silly over Gates." Early on, Adams told Gates, "I wish you a major general," Max Mintz wrote in *The Generals of Saratoga*.[40] Gates had successfully lobbied for Congress to demote Philip Schuyler to make way for Gates's elevation to Northern Army Commander.[41] After the Saratoga victory, Gates abandoned his army, journeying to Baltimore where Congress was sitting. There he lobbied Congress to create the War Board, making Gates its first president. Then came the Conway Cabal: "Benjamin Rush, Samuel Adams, [General] Thomas Mifflin, and Richard Henry Lee were the leading Congressional instigators of the plot." According to Andrew Zambone, "Gates was their willing co-conspirator."[42]

American generals had large amounts of idle time, time in which to magnify perceived slights, map out strategies for lobbying, or conflate incipient jealousies. They had a commander-in-chief who tried, repeatedly, to pour oil upon the waters. For instance, Washington wrote to several of his generals arguing and backbiting about promotion and seniority: "Let us all be a band of brothers and rise superior to every injury real or imaginary and persevere in the arduous but glorious struggle in which we are engaged until peace and independence are secured to our country."[43] Despite Washington's near saintly entreaties, the jealousies and rivalries continued to the war's end.

Those then—an inflated sense of honor, jealousy, the intermittent nature of warfare, and instances of manipulation—account for rivalries and resignations that characterized active warfare (1775–1781) during the American Revolution.

21

Pretenders, Parvenus, and Armchair Generals

Not all snits, complaints, and resignations were internally generated. External stimuli combined with men's sense of honor to produce unsightly responses. An example of external influence was Congress's award of numerous commissions and high ranks to foreign claimants based upon claims that frequently were exaggerated or false.

The Continental Congress's constant intervention in appointments, as well as in promotion and seniority matters, affected general officers' morale. Further, Congress elevated foreign claimants, many parvenus, to general rank over battle-tested American officers. Many veteran officers viewed the war "as a hard-luck saga of talented, professional soldiers betrayed by political opportunists back in Washington."[1] At times, Congress rivaled the action of medieval clerics practicing simony, with Congress handing out commissions rather than indulgences.

Foreign Parvenus and Disappointments

Great in number were the flameouts of those to whom, based purely upon paper records, Congress awarded commissions and ranks. A spectacular flameout was General Mattias Alexis Roche de Femoy. In charge of a major contingent of troops before the Second Battle of Trenton, Fermoy mounted his horse and simply rode away before combat commenced. Called a "worthless drunkard" by his American contemporaries, Femoy resigned his American commission, returning to France in 1777.[2]

Prussian Frederick W. de Woedtke served but four months in the American Army, dying of natural causes, supposedly smallpox, but the real causes were said to be "bile and brandy." John Adams knew Woedtke, later penning next to Woedtke's signature "Good for Nothing." Those who served with him reported Woedtke as "a worthless drunkard."[3]

In May 1777, Philippe Charles Tronson du Coudray pried a general's commission from Congress. Unwilling to foist the arrogant Coudray upon troops, General Washington assigned du Coudray to inspect Forts Mifflin and Mercer guarding the Delaware River below Philadelphia. Meanwhile, Coudray sought the major general's commission that allegedly Congress had promised. Brigadiers Henry Knox,

Nathanael Greene, and John Sullivan vowed to resign if Congress promoted the Frenchman. On September 11, 1777, returning to the American camp, du Coudray's horse bolted on wooden pontoon bridge spanning the Schuylkill River. The general was thrown into the river and drowned.[4]

Another Philippe, Philippe Hubert, chevalier de Preudhomme de Borre, did command troops but considered himself a better tactician than his superiors. At Brandywine, he argued with Generals Sullivan and Washington. He publicly complained that he had been given "bad troops." Disgraced, de Borre resigned his commission, returning to France after nine months' service.[5]

The Continental Congress

Throughout the war, senior American officers received unequal and inferior treatment at Congress's hands: "After.... Princeton [early in 1777], Congress decided to strengthen its authority over the military. It prohibited Washington from appointing general officers, reserving that power to itself."[6] Instead of clarifying lines of authority, Congress muddied the waters, exacerbating jealousies, creating rivalries where none had existed, and precipitating resignations of experienced commanders, as has been seen (Chapter 20).

Congress allocated general officer positions among colonies, initially one, soon thereafter three, to each colony. Congress, though, made adjustments in the initial allotments based upon other factors. Accordingly, in February 1777, General Washington proposed that Connecticutt's Jedediah Huntington and Jeremiah Wadsworth be promoted to brigadier. He further proposed that Generals Daniel Wooster and Benedict Arnold be promoted to major general. Congress ignored Washington's recommendations, choosing to punish Connecticut for its diminishing contribution of volunteers to the Revolutionary Army.[7] Congress bypassed Arnold for promotion, "and he was furious."[8]

Foreign Officer Aspirants

Appointments of foreigners to high rank in the American army, even if premised upon genuine experience, could nonetheless constitute a blow to morale. On December 13, 1777, for example, Congress appointed the Irishman and former French officer Thomas Conway a major general. As a colonel of the French Army's Irish Brigade, Conway had led troops in combat, seeing action in several European engagements.[9] Initially, however, with no thought to potential effects on existing brigadiers, Congress appointed "Thomas Conway to Major General over twenty-three [American] brigadier[s].... Several major generals and nine brigadier generals ... protested to Congress and threatened to resign."[10] George Washington protested.[11] The protests availed them not.

In assertion of its desire to control military matters, the Continental Congress listened to scores of foreign would-be adventurers. The latter would present Congress with fabricated or exaggerated credentials:

A Swiss officer wished to become a lieutenant colonel under George Washington, despite never having risen higher than lieutenant for the Dutch. A veteran of ten years in the French army ... thought he should be a regimental quartermaster. A student from Lyon declared that the time had come for him to do something grand: he would start by killing redcoats.[12]

The flow of adventurers to America was exacerbated by the actions of Silas Deane, American envoy to the French nation, March 1776 to December 1777. Deane's portfolio was the encouragement of French aid and, hopefully, entry into the war. Deane, though, referred a stream of supplicants to Congress, which awarded them high-ranking commissions, almost "on the spot."[13]

Benjamin Franklin overlapped with Deane as American Commissioner. Franklin, too, had to cope with "European supplicants who sought commissions in the American army," Walter Isaacson recorded in his biography of Ben Franklin. In the first year alone, Franklin's letter box was "clogged ... with more than four hundred" requests: "Not a day passes in which I have not had a number of soliciting visits.... You have no conception how I was harassed."[14] These appointments over the heads of worthy Americans caused grumbling, consternation, complaint, and worse among the American officer corps.[15]

Finally, Washington put his foot down: "[D]espite the need to maintain the goodwill of influential Frenchmen ... please, no more officer candidates."[16] Nonetheless, at Paris, Professor Brands recorded, "at Franklin's end the throngs only grew, 'These applications are my perpetual torment. You have no idea how I am harassed.'" Franklin wrote that he hid away: "The noise of every coach now [in 1777] that enters my court terrifies me. I am afraid to accept an invitation to dine abroad, being most sure of meeting with some officer, or officer's friend, who ... [makes] an attack on me."[17]

Worthwhile Appointments

Several foreign appointees served with distinction, the "few diamonds amid the dross," H.W. Brands wrote.[18] In fact, their services were valuable contributions to the Revolutionary War effort. An example was Franconian-French veteran Major General Johann DeKalb, who died from multiple wounds received leading the American right at Camden in 1780. DeKalb fought bravely after Major General Gates, Brigadier Caswell, and the entire American left, composed of militia, quit the battlefield, some—Generals Gates and Caswell—curtailing their flight only after reaching Hillsborough, 180 miles away. The leaders' cowardly deed left DeKalb and his men in hell with the lid having blown off.

Polish officer Casimir Pulaski, at first arrogantly asserting that he would only take orders from George Washington, settled in and served with distinction. He died in combat at Savannah, Georgia, on October 9, 1779. Engineer Tadeus Kosciuszko, of Lithuanian-Polish extraction, supervised the building of American defenses at Saratoga and West Point. He proved his worth as a first-rate military engineer. Marquis de Lafayette became George Washington's favorite, succeeding to Adam Stephen's major general position after Germantown. Major General Frederick von Steuben, a Prussian, was a late comer, arriving at Valley Forge in February 1777. Once there he instilled discipline, order, and morale among the American ranks. In 1779–1780, he supervised the Virginia defenses against the Leslie and Benedict Arnold assaults on Tidewater Virginia.[19]

Honor and Dueling Rather than Resignation

Well-known is the 1804 duel in which Aaron Burr shot Alexander Hamilton. As a means of vindicating offenses against one's honor, duels escalated matters more than complaints or resignations. In 1777, Georgia's Brigadier Lachlan McIntosh called Button Gwinnett "a scoundrel and lying rascal." Gwinnett, who aspired to McIntosh's command of Georgia's troops, challenged Brigadier McIntosh to a duel. In the duel, both men were wounded. Gwinnett died

Johann De Kalb. A Franconian-French Army volunteer commissioned as a major general, De Kalb was killed at the 1780 Battle of Camden (Artist Unknown, Library of Congress).

a few days later (*see generally* Chapter 6). Fabricated cries of "murderer" followed and haunted not only McIntosh but family members for years.

Another example of preservation of honor involved General Enoch Poor of New Hampshire, a hero of Saratoga whom many regarded as "one of the most active and efficient officers in the Continental army."[20] "Poor was an officer who never received the recognition to which he was entitled,"[21] likely because he never returned to New Hampshire. On September 8, 1780, Poor died, 13 days after a duel with his French subordinate whom Poor had accused of lagging at Monmouth Courthouse. Poor's comrades buried him near Hackensack, New Jersey, in the First Reformed Church burying ground. George Washington, Marquis de Lafayette, Henry Knox, and other generals attended the funeral.[22] Poor's pronounced sense of honor led to premature death and, incidentally, obscurity.

Major General Robert Howe of North Carolina and militia general Christopher Gadsden of South Carolina dueled, pursuant to a challenge Howe issued after Gadsden wrote that Howe was "a low down cunning, Jockeying and sharping ... [a man] determined at any rate to wedge himself into command."[23] Militia General John Cadwalader dueled Irish-French General Thomas Conway, wounding him.

Conway's "American career was finished," soiled as it was by his participation in the cabal to replace George Washington with Horatio Gates. Shortly after the duel, Conway returned to France.[24]

Honor, Chivalry, Titles, and Nobility

In fact, in its "Foreign Emoluments Clause," the 1787 United States Constitution prohibited the United States from granting titles of nobility.[25] Although the Constitution and its Emoluments Clause had not yet been adopted and did not govern the war years, if the prohibition had been in effect, Congress came close to recidivist infringements of it.

The feature, honor above all, emanated not only from eighteenth eentury European cultures but from the twelfth and thirteenth centuries days of knights and chivalry.[26] The Revolutionary War and the culture prevalent within the officer corps is evidence that the break from Britain and European conceptions was not as complete as we believe it to have been.

PART VII

The Southern Campaign: 1779–1781

22

Civil War Commences in the South

*Patriot versus Loyalist
at Kings Mountain and Cowpens*

President Thomas Jefferson termed the Battle of Kings Mountain "the turning point in the War for Independence."[1] A later occupant of the office, President Herbert Hoover, said of Kings Mountain and the militia who achieved victory there, "It was a little army and a little battle, but it was of mighty portent."[2] Eight hundred patriot militia defeated a one thousand Loyalist militia under British Major Patrick Ferguson. What made Kings Mountain special?

One reason for the engagement's importance was that the victorious force was composed wholly of minutemen, militia who, over the course of the war, were spoken of in derogatory terms (Chapter 13). Emblematic of the militia's reputation, only two months previous, in August 1780 at Camden, Virginia, North Carolina militia had fled the field of battle without firing a shot.

Another reason for Jefferson's appraisal was that Kings Mountain signaled that the British southern strategy was not eventuating as the British had thought it would. After Kings Mountain, "Cornwallis' plan to pacify the Carolinas with the help of loyalist militia had no chance for success."[3]

Loyalist Militia

Lord Cornwallis dubbed Scottish Major Patrick Ferguson with the additional title "His Majesty's Inspector of Militia." He sent Ferguson, a handful of cadre, and a Loyalist militia brigade of 1,000 men westward from the piedmont. "The British," as well as Cornwallis, "believed that the southern colonies teemed with loyalists, and they were banking on these supporters to persuade reluctant patriots to swear allegiance to the Crown."[4] Ferguson was to capitalize on the sentiment, increasing the size of his force with western Carolina recruits. Major Ferguson and his force had a second mission as well. The force was to act as picket and skirmish lines on Cornwallis's left flank as he moved the main British force from the South Carolina Piedmont northward into North Carolina.

Ferguson's recruitment venture was an abysmal failure. Few, if any, of the settlers in the foothills and mountains to the west came to support the British cause.

REVOLUTIONARY WAR IN THE SOUTH

After victories at Savannah, Charles Town, and Camden, British and mercenary forces had become full of themselves. They plundered, raped, burned houses and crops, and generally terrorized the countryside, fueling the conservative Scots-Irish settlers' outrage toward the Crown and its representatives, the outrage increasing as Ferguson attempted to recruit them. Then Major Ferguson issued an ultimatum. If the settlers in the west did not quit opposing British arms, "he would march his army over the mountains, hang their leaders, and lay their country waste with fire and sword."[5] Ferguson's threats had effects opposite of his intent, stirring up anger and resentment among frontier settlers.

With no new recruits in hand, Ferguson gave up, marching his column east to re-join Cornwallis and the 2,500-man main British force. He reached Cowpens, a clearing southeast of Charlotte where an inspiring American victory would take place in January. Perhaps with his screening responsibilities in mind, Ferguson reversed direction, going back west thirty miles from Cowpens, where on October 6 he and his men camped on Kings Mountain.

Kings Mountain was not a mountain at all. Rather the mesa-like outcropping rose several hundred feet from the surrounding countryside. The hill was thickly forested on the sides with numerous ravines. To the American mountain men, who were used to climbing real mountains, "Kings Mountain was no mountain at all, merely a hill" wrote North Carolina's William Powell.[6] On top of the outcropping was a wide flat meadow, 600 yards long and 100–125 yards wide. There the Ferguson contingent camped.

Patriot Militia

The American groups that coalesced in late September at Sycamore Shoals, North Carolina, were no ordinary militia. From Abingdon, Virginia, Colonel William Campbell, later elected leader of the larger group, set out with 400 backwoods militia. Two hundred North Carolinians under Colonel Charles McDowell joined the group as it headed south. From Kentucky and Tennessee came 400 "Overmountain Men," who were led by Colonels Isaac Shelby and John Sevier, later to become governors of Kentucky and Tennessee, respectively.[7] These men were tough, made of sterner stuff than rank-and-file militia. British Captain George Harger wrote of them:

> This distinguished race of men are more savage than the Indians, and possess every one of their vices, but not one of their virtues. I have known ... these fellows [to] travel 200 miles through the woods, never keeping to any road or path, guided by the sun by day, and the stars by night, to kill a particular person of the opposite party.[8]

The over-the-mountain force crossed the Appalachian Mountains from Tennessee, reaching the Carolinas via the 4,700-foot Roan Mountain Pass. Coming east, they marched through early snows that were "shoe-tongue deep."[9]

The Battle of Kings Mountain

The fight lasted little more than an hour, on the afternoon of Saturday, October 7, 1780. The American militia had spent several days seeking out the Ferguson force. The patriots arrived at noon at Kings Mountain, finding their quarry bivouacked on the tabletop. The site may have been an ideal spot for the recreational camper, but it proved a killing field for the Tory force and the British cadre that accompanied them. Upon arrival, the Americans surrounded the encampment. At 3 p.m., on Colonel Campbell's command, they opened fire and commenced advancing. The patriot woodsmen took cover behind tree trunks and in the numerous ravines running down the tabletop's flanks. In return, the Loyalists mounted a bayonet charge, the favored British battlefield maneuver. The patriots simply retreated, melting into the forest for a time, only to renew their attack. Kings Mountain was not the flat terrain upon which bayonet charges had proven effective. "Punishing his horse, Major Ferguson was everywhere, a silver whistle in his mouth trilling commands." Suddenly, Ferguson fell, hit by several bullets. "He fell, one foot caught in a stirrup. His men helped him down, propping him against a tree, where he died."[10] British officers waved a white flag but, in a rage, the Americans kept firing. The Ferguson force was annihilated.

The Southern Campaign and Battle of Cowpens

Before Kings Mountain and to the north, in early autumn 1779, despairing of any promotion or command, Daniel Morgan returned to Soldier's Rest, his farm in the Shenandoah Valley (Chapter 20). Several times he visited with Major General Horatio Gates, the "Hero of Saratoga." Gates had a farm, Traveler's Rest, in Berkeley County, 20 miles north of Morgan's place, to which he had retreated after his service as American Board of War president.

In May 1780, Major General Benjamin Lincoln surrendered Charles Town, South Carolina (Chapter 7), himself becoming a prisoner of war. The British previously had captured Savannah, Georgia. The two conquests marked the beginning of the British southern campaign. In late June, the Continental Congress appointed the semi-inactive Major General Gates commander of the Southern Army, depleted as it now was and without a commanding officer. Gates had divined that he needed a battlefield command as a platform for further advancement. In turn, before he left Virginia, Gates requested Congress to call Daniel Morgan back to service. Morgan assented to serve, stipulating only that Gates lobby Congress to promote Morgan to brigadier. Gates wrote Morgan that he, Gates, would fill in Morgan as to "the particulars."[11]

The southern campaign, with its battles, marches, twists, and turns has been well-documented.[12] The Cowpens episode began with Morgan rendezvousing with Gates at Hillsborough, North Carolina. In and around Hillsboro, as it was often spelled, Morgan twiddled his thumbs while in August 1780, Gates suffered the embarrassing defeat at the Battle of Camden.[13] Gates, however, did give Morgan command of a newly created light infantry corps, consisting of three companies of Maryland and Delaware regulars, sixty Virginia riflemen, and seventy cavalry. On October 7, Morgan and his troops began a westward march, intending to harass British outposts.

On October 13, 1780, Congress removed from beneath Morgan's saddle a large burr by promoting Morgan, finally and at long last, to brigadier general.[14]

Then, in another transaction, following Gates's shameful abandonment of his army at Camden, Congress removed Gates from command, replacing him with George Washington's favorite general, Nathanael Greene, "the Fighting Quaker." Delayed, Greene did not arrive in Charlotte, North Carolina, until December 2,

1780. The group of which Greene took command, the Southern Army, was "rather a shadow than a substance," consisting of 800 inadequately clothed and equipped men.[15] Under Greene, though, the resilient army added soldiers, bit by bit, strengthened with the addition of 250 Virginia and 120 North Carolina militia under General William Lee Davidson (Chapter 23).[16]

Cowpens

Morgan and his force reached western South Carolina. Coming north, opposite Morgan, was British Colonel Banastre Tarleton, the hated British officer. Tarleton commanded an elite cavalry corps known as the "British Legion" or "Tory Legion." His mantra was aggression, swiftness, and aggression, always aggression combined with ruthlessness. "As always, speed was Tarleton's measure of imminent victory."[17] The colonials detested Tarleton, for his troops slaughtered opponents whom the Tory Legion had taken prisoner. "Tarleton's quarter" was the Americans' derogatory term for "Ban."

With a force of 1,200, Tarleton was marauding northward as advance guard for the main British force under Lord Cornwallis, who was behind Tarleton marching northward to re-enter North Carolina. Learning of the British Legion's northward thrust along the Broad River's western bank, Morgan moved his American encampment northward toward the North Carolina border (ten miles northeast of Spartanburg, South Carolina). Morgan there decided to stand and fight, at Cowpens, South Carolina. Cowpens was a rolling, grassy area with copses of "red oak, hickory, and pine" backed unto the Broad River a few miles to the east. Known as "Hannah's Cowpens," the relatively open area was where western "Carolina farmers grazed their cattle before sending them east to market."[18]

Morgan's genius, earlier demonstrated at Saratoga (Chapter 23), carried the day once more at Cowpens, called by Professor Stephen Taaffe "a tactical masterpiece."[19] First, Brigadier Morgan put a smallish group of sharpshooters in front behind a small knoll, in groups of three, huddled behind larger trees. Morgan instructed them that "only one soldier was to fire at a time, the other two keeping shots in reserve until the cavalry started to charge," then only one to fire while the other two reloaded.[20] Their shots were to give pause to the British onslaught.[21] Morgan then employed militia in the front ranks rather than, as traditionally was the case, the rear. As has been seen, the military had a low opinion of militia's usefulness. While short of an all-out endorsement, Morgan came to perceive of the militia's utility if commanders used the minutemen wisely.

So, second, after deploying his sharpshooters, Morgan positioned two ranks of militia men. He assigned to them a limited objective: firing two or three rounds, then filtering back through spaces left open in the regulars' lines. Once behind the lines, the militia were to reform. This was extraordinary, as previously "Morgan did not like or trust militia."[22] His reasoning for placing militia in the front was that "[w]hen men are forced to fight, they will sell their lives dearly ... had I [done otherwise] one half the militia would immediately have abandoned me."[23] With the collapsing

22. Patriot versus Loyalist

Banastre Tarleton, by Joshua Reynolds. "Ban," a ruthless, ever-aggressive British cavalry colonel, was despised by Americans; his orders to slaughter American captives became known as "Tarleton's quarter" (National Portrait Gallery UK).

American front line, the hard-charging British cavalry would be into the heart of the American formation before they knew it, thinking that, as before in many an engagement, they had swiftly driven in their opponent's lines. If they had known that the militia's rearward evolution was a planned maneuver, perhaps Tarleton's men would have advanced more cautiously. Perhaps not.

Third, General Morgan formed up his regulars in the crescent-shaped formation he favored rather than in the traditional straight-line deployment. At Cowpens,

Morgan's crescent formation evolved into a double envelopment, surrounding the hard charging Tarleton force. The colonials killed 120, wounded 229, and captured 702 British dragoons and grenadiers.[24] When Tarleton attempted to rally his 200-cavalry reserve, the dragoons disobeyed, turning tail and fleeing. Morgan and his men had destroyed the pride of the British military, Banastre Tarleton's Tory Legion.

A General Who Fights

By nature, Morgan was a brawler, unfazed by physical danger. William Washington, Morgan's cavalry commander, said that he had never seen a man more collected in battle than Morgan. Morgan also had supreme confidence in his own ability as a battlefield commander. Last of all, he inspired his troops. The night before Cowpens, Morgan went through the encampment, stopping by campfire after campfire, telling the troops, "Boys, get up, Banny's coming." In a lighter vein, Morgan told militia units, "Just hold your heads up, boys, three fires, and you will be free. And then, when you return ... home, how the old folks will bless you, and the girls kiss you, for your gallant conduct."[25] More seriously, he told militia, "My friends in arms, my dear boys, I request you to remember Saratoga, Monmouth, Paoli, Brandywine, and this day you must play your parts for your honor and liberty's cause."[26] The next day the result, the Battle of Cowpens, was the Revolutionary War's most decisive American victory. "I have given him [Tarleton] a devil of a whipping, a more compleat victory has never been obtained," Morgan wrote an acquaintance, giving historian Lawrence Babits the title *A Devil of a Whipping* for his work about Cowpens.[27] Author John Buchanan terms Morgan "superb, a battle captain for the ages," one whose intrepid conduct and innate military brilliance have stood the test of time.[28]

Withdrawal, Retreat, and Retirement

What followed Cowpens was a prescient retreat, Morgan anticipating his Cowpens victory's downside. Morgan knew that Lord Cornwallis, coming northward from winter encampment at Winnsboro, South Carolina, with a large force, was coming up the opposite side, that is, the eastern bank of Broad River. Morgan also surmised that Cornwallis, devastated by the British Tory Legion's complete loss at Cowpens, would be bent on seeking revenge. Reflective of his dark mood, Cornwallis told Lord Rawdon, Colonel of the Irish Regiment, that the Cowpens affair "had broken his heart."[29] Alternatively, his ox had been gored, no less in an engagement that involved a significant part for volunteer militia.

At Cowpens, the battle was over by 10:00 a.m. By noon, January 17, Morgan's men had packed, broken camp, and marched north.[30] Although slowed by the need to move 700 British prisoners, Morgan's force traveled one hundred miles, fording two major rivers, in five days. Morgan endeavored to keep fast rising and high flowing rivers between his and Cornwallis's armies. Along the way, "Morgan was indefatigable, helping his men here and there, cheering them on with praise for industry and spirit."[31]

Meanwhile, Lord Cornwallis had his 2,500-man force strip down. Cornwallis was first to throw his kit upon the bonfire. He spared only salt, ammunition, medical supplies, and four ambulance wagons. Slimmed down, the British marched on, pursuing at a heightened pace. At times, Morgan and his men saw Cornwallis's advance scouting parties on the opposite shore of rivers the Americans had crossed. Then Morgan hived off an escort force to free the American column of British prisoners captured at Cowpens, sending the force and the prisoners northeast to Salisbury, North Carolina, forty miles from Charlotte. Then, rather than heading east to join General Greene at Hillsborough, Morgan's force turned north, misleading Cornwallis once more.

Amidst his strategic retreat, Morgan doubled back to meet with North Carolina's Brigadier William Davidson and Major General Nathanael Greene. Greene tasked Davidson to employ his 800 North Carolina militia. Davidson and his men's mission was to slow—not stop—Cornwallis and the British advance by fortifying the fords of the flood-stage Catawba River north of Charlotte where, upriver, the river might be crossed. (Today this spot is under the waters of Lake Norman, formed by damning the Catawba.)

Finally reaching Hillsborough, Morgan, the "Old Waggoner" who had suffered injuries incurred as a youthful brawler, was laid low by sciatica and arthritis. Now 47 or 48 (Morgan never knew his exact age), he could no longer mount a horse. He was forced to leave the units he had commanded, spending several days lying flat in a wagon, stopping for a day's rest here and there, to return to Soldier's Rest in Virginia.

Cornwallis's pursuit of Morgan and Greene's further deployments of troops could not take away what was evident. Cowpens, "so soon after Ferguson's defeat at Kings Mountain," was in the estimation of North Carolina historian William Powell "a blow from which the British in the South never recovered."[32]

Daniel Morgan, Artist Unknown. The most brilliant tactician of the war, and the true hero of Saratoga and Cowpens, Morgan could neither read nor write until well past age 30 (Library of Congress).

23

Waggoner Daniel Morgan of Virginia

Historical society libraries lack biographies of, say, militia general Edward Stevens or Continental Line general Andrew Lewis (Chapter 8).[1] By contrast, catalogues show a dozen Morgan biographies, one appearing as recently as 2018.[2] Books also detail the Battle of Cowpens, including Daniel Morgan's tactical genius. Morgan thus is the least obscure of the southern brigadiers.[3] Biographers lavish high praise upon Morgan. For instance, author John Buchanan terms Morgan "superb, a battle captain for the ages."[4]

Why has the life of Daniel Morgan been a fertile ground for biographers? One is that Morgan's life represents a paradigmatic American success story, a Horatio Alger rising from humble beginnings. As a homeless seventeen-year-old wandering south from Pennsylvania, Morgan began "grubbing stumps" for a Winchester, Virginia, farmer. He then managed the farmer's sawmill and finally become a wagon driver taking loads from Winchester over the Blue Ridge and down to Fredericksburg on the Rappahannock, or Dumfries and Alexandria on the Potomac, returning with consumer goods. Much later, at age 45, Morgan had risen to brigadier general in the Continental army. It took twenty-eight years, but the final product achieved legendary status.

The second reason for Morgan's enduring fame were his innovations, making him "the most tactically perfect American general of the war…. Daniel Morgan was a tactical genius"[5] The tactics Morgan fashioned, for example, at Saratoga and at Cowpens (*see, e.g.,* Chapter 22), were more innovative than any his blue blooded and aristocratic peers devised.

A third condition that conflates exploration of Morgan's military career has been the aura of surprise biographers experience. As aforesaid, that an individual with such humble beginnings could advance so far, be beloved by his men, and out-general any other brigadier, whether northern or southern, seems counterintuitive. Morgan served as a Continental officer despite the fact that until age 30 he could neither read nor write and only somewhat haltingly thereafter.

"A Dandy in a Frontier Town"[6]

Errors have crept into Morgan's historical portrait. As a young man, Morgan was a drinker and a brawler. He did arduous physical labor riding the "wheel horse" of six-horse teams, frequently walking aside his loaded Conestoga wagon over hills and mountains.[7] As a military man, he led backwoods riflemen from humble and frontier backgrounds. So, the picture that his biographers deduce from the foregoing is one of a backwoods Virginian, dressed in a linen hunting shirt over fringed, deer-skin leggings.

To the contrary, Morgan was a tall, robust man who took delight in his appearance, dressing like gentleman of that age: "Morgan was quite a spendthrift ... belying his [younger days'] reputation as a drinker and a brawler." Morgan "liked socks—worsted socks, or fine English socks. He bought blue broadcloth and Irish linen, the very best kind available ... sleeve buttons in quantity; [had] a worsted cape ... fake gold shoe buckles."[8] Morgan liked to be "meticulously clothed." His tailor billed him for alterations to his red coat and to his green coat, as well as making him "a fine cloth suit." Morgan "liked to impress—with size, strength, voice, and sartorial splendor," according to Andrew Zambone's biography.[9]

Physically, Morgan was over six feet, a head taller than contemporary males. With long, ropy muscles, Morgan was strong and fast. At age 40, he could win foot races with men half his age.[10] There was "an impulsiveness to his physical actions." According to Zambone, "He [was] the first to run to something, first to push something, first to knock someone down, first to jump out of a boat." He had red-gold hair and piercing blue eyes.

The Fringe of Military Service

In 1755, British General Edward Braddock landed in America to lead a force to oust the French garrisoning Fort Duquesne, located at the Forks of the Ohio where the Allegheny and Monongahela Rivers merge, forming the Ohio. Braddock's assistant quartermaster, Major Sir John St. Clair, scouted the upper Potomac River and found it unsuitable for water transport. So, it became incumbent upon the British to enlist hundreds of civilian waggoners, their wagons, and their horse teams.[11] The British recruited waggoner Daniel Morgan.

During the 120-mile trek over the Alleghenies and beyond, a British subaltern became abusive toward Morgan. He struck Morgan with the flat of his sword. Morgan responded with one punch, knocking the subaltern to the ground. The consequences: five hundred lashes for striking an officer. For the remainder of his life, Morgan told the same tongue-in-cheek story. The soldier wielding the cat-o-nine-tails miscounted. Morgan had gotten away with 499 lashes but with countless ribbon-like scars he proudly wore all his days.[12]

Flogging, especially by the British, also made a different sort of mark. Flogging helped Morgan make something of himself. "Being flogged gained him his reputation as a man," according to early biographer James Graham.[13] It also destroyed whatever respect he had for the British military.[14]

Morgan as an Indian Fighter

In 1763, fearing Indian attacks, Virginia Governor Francis Fauquier authorized the formation of ranger companies tasked to forestall further attacks.

Morgan became a lieutenant in Ashby's Rangers. He spent several weeks guarding the Quaker Meeting House and burial ground ten miles north of Winchester.[15]

Morgan built a home three miles north of Battletown, east of Winchester, today Berryville, Virginia. The number of drinking and brawling escapades lessened. Morgan acquired land: 255 acres. He lived with a partner, Abagail Curry, with whom he had two daughters.[16] Later in 1773 Morgan and his Abagail, "[p]lain, sensible, and pious," married.[17]

In addition to the marks of flogging and bent fingers and scars from brawling, Morgan had been wounded in combat. While a ranger in the French and Indian War, in April 1756, Morgan and a companion were returning to Winchester along the Capacon River, a smaller river flowing north from near Winchester, over what is now the West Virginia panhandle, to the Potomac. A party of Indians ambushed them. The Native Americans shot both men, killing Morgan's companion. A shot entered Morgan's neck behind his left jaw, knocking out several teeth and exiting between Morgan's nose and his upper lip, but Morgan wheeled his horse about and escaped. He wore the scars, including a somewhat prominent one giving him an extra philtrum running from the upper lip to his septum, as a badge of honor.[18]

True Military Service

As a Virginia Militia captain, in June 1774, Morgan recruited a company for an expedition into the Ohio country in Governor Lord Dunmore's quest to pacify Ohio for land acquisitions (Chapter 7). Morgan's company marched to Wheeling, Virginia, on the Ohio River.[19] After a canoe trip down the Ohio, the 400-man force disembarked, journeying overland 90 miles farther west to attack the Shawnee-Mingo town of Wakatomica, on the Muskingum River. The Americans there found the village deserted. Dunmore's force burned the village before returning to Wheeling.[20]

Then, the following spring, came Concord, Lexington, and the siege of Boston. Pursuant to a Continental Congress directive that ten rifle companies be raised—six from Pennsylvania and two each from Maryland and Virginia—Morgan was assigned a company's leadership. Charged with enlisting a company of 64, Morgan raised 96 men, inspiring them to enlist in the cause of liberty. Morgan chose men "who could shoot, had the intelligence of a hunter, and had the woodcraft that allowed them in a few hours to build a camp."[21] Men from the Lower Valley and the Alleghanies beyond were "known for their amazing hardihood gained through living so long in the woods." They were "veteran hunters and Indian fighters [who] had traveled long distances without provisions and displayed remarkable dexterity with the rifle," accurate at distances of 200–250 yards, compared with the ubiquitous musket's range of a paltry 60 yards.[22]

Morgan's company began a beeline march on July 15, 1775, and arrived in Cambridge, Massachusetts, on August 6, a 484-mile march in twenty-one days. They averaged twenty-three miles per day, "a phenomenal pace" for foot soldiers. Morgan's men were the first troops from outside New England to arrive in Boston.

In Boston, though, the Virginia Militia did little. Employing the enhanced range and accuracy of their Kentucky rifles, for a time, the Virginia woodsman picked off British sentries and stragglers, until the British learned the need for cover. Otherwise, the Virginians drank, gambled, brawled, and mixed not well, or not at all, with New England patriots.

Through the Maine Wilderness to Quebec

Instead of marking time at the siege of Boston, Morgan's company formed up under Colonel Benedict Arnold, who would lead a 1,050-man force on a late autumn, early winter trek north to assault Quebec City. What followed has been described "as among the most famous marches in American military history."[23] The epic has inspired book-length works, undoubtedly spurred onward by the romance of it all.[24]

The march may have been epic, but the strategy was questionable. Early in the war, American authorities harbored a fantasy that with a small nudge, Canadian citizens would come over to the American side. Canada would become the "fourteenth state," as presumptuous colonial leaders termed it. Accordingly, Washington earlier had sent another force north, led first by General Philip Schuyler. After General Schuyler became ill, returning to Albany, General Richard Montgomery, an Irish-born British army veteran who had immigrated to the colonies, led the expedition.[25] Montgomery's force, farther to the west, followed a well-travelled route, up the Hudson River to Lake George, overland on a short portage, up Lake Champlain, into the northward bound Richelieu River, and finally into the St. Lawrence and Canada. Montgomery's force would then travel a short distance northeast along the St. Lawrence, attacking Montreal. After subjugating Montreal, Montgomery's brigade would continue upriver, assisting Arnold's force in its assault on Quebec.

The plan, the strategy, the weather, the lack of artillery—all and more added to a disaster. An element of the plan not quite a disaster was Arnold's journey toward Quebec from the southeast. At Newburyport, Massachusetts, north of Boston and north of Cape Ann, Arnold's army boarded eleven transports. The ships sailed to the northeast, past Portsmouth, New Hampshire, and past Portland, Maine, then turned north, up the Kennebec River. The soldiers disembarked near the present-day site of Augusta, Maine.

The Epic Journey

From Augusta, the American contingent including Morgan and his men began a 350-mile journey, first in bateaux and smaller craft. Almost immediately, the small army encountered waterfalls—Ticonic, Five Mile, Skowhegan, Norridgewock—necessitating back-breaking portages. Then Colonel Roger Enos of Vermont, requested permission on behalf of 300 men to return to Cambridge, which they did.

The force had started up the Kennebec on September 25. On October 7, the rains began and persisted. Far up the Kennebec, the route was to jog to the west on a portage known as the Great Carrying Place. Sent ahead, Morgan and his rifle company cleared a track over to the northward flowing Dead River. After the Great Carrying Place portage, the route toward Quebec consisted of several miles on the Dead River, turning northward through a series of ponds, and then Lake Megantic, the source of the Chaudiere River. The Chaudiere flowed into the St. Lawrence near Quebec City.

Rains, mud, rough tracks, swift currents on the rivers, early November snows, food lost and spoiled by overturning craft and invasive rain, these and more "complications" befell them. On October 23, "Arnold reviewed their critical situation ... an alarming shortage of food, an epidemic of dysentery, no warm clothing, and a week or more of hazardous travel remain[ed]."[26] Morgan, his men, and other American troops men ate dog, as well as boiled leather ammunition pouches. Miraculously, though, Arnold pulled it off, in early November arriving opposite Quebec with only minimal losses.

A Pennsylvania rifleman, Joseph Henry, declared that during the march, "an antipathy had arisen against Morgan, as too strict a disciplinarian ... [y]et Morgan was a hero to the youthful Pennsylvanian, who acknowledged that Morgan's forceful leadership did much to keep the expedition together."[27]

History records that Arnold and Morgan arrived with 600 troops.[28] Earlier on, 300 of the initial 1,050 men had returned to Boston. With minimal losses on route, the Arnold-led force should have arrived with close to 750 men. Whatever the number, the ensuing assault on Quebec was a complete defeat, for Arnold, for Richard Montgomery, for the men, and for Daniel Morgan.

The Assault on Quebec

The Americans "failed dismally."[29] From any viewpoint, "Quebec was not just a defeat but a calamity." When Morgan marched his company out of Winchester, Virginia, in July 1776, counting officers, he commanded ninety-eight. Of the ninety-eight who'd left the Shenandoah Valley, "only twenty-five returned" from Quebec.[30] The assault on Quebec, though, was noteworthy for Morgan's acts of bravery, marking the beginning of the Morgan legend.

Downriver, General Richard Montgomery has successfully captured Montreal. The Governor of Quebec Province, General Guy Carlton, escaped northwest to Quebec City, a walled town garrisoned by 1,126 British and Canadian defenders.[31] Carlton added to the garrison a small cadre of British regulars.

In November and December 1775, several incidents befell the Americans. So, the attack was delayed until the last day of the year, but it had to occur on that day as many American enlistments expired the following days. On the afternoon of December 30, the weather turned, and snow began to fall. In the evening, the storm developed into blinding snow. Beginning at 4 a.m. on the 31st, Arnold and Morgan, coming from opposite directions, northwest and southeast, would meet in the lower town on the level of the river. Arnold would lead a thirty-man advance party against the walled upper town. Morgan would follow with the remainder of the 650-man force. On the opposite side of the city, to the southwest, Montgomery would attack the city with his force coming from Montreal.

Strike one against the Americans was that the six-pounder brass cannon to support Arnold and Morgan stuck in a snow drift. Strike two was that, almost immediately, a musket ball struck Arnold in the left leg, necessitating his removal from the action. Strike three was that Arnold's battle plan had no "Plan B" that would devolve overall leadership should Arnold be disabled.[32] Nonetheless, Morgan led a charge to scale the ten-foot wall. After being blown back once by British and Canadian musket fire, Morgan scaled the wall, falling over the other side onto a cannon barrel, injuring his back. "Then," after Morgan's climb, "the redcoats hastily retreated when [American] riflemen poured over the wall," following Colonel Morgan. "Lucky to be alive and experiencing considerable pain from his fall, Morgan led an assault" on the entrenched defenders.[33]

Sometime later, Morgan arrived at the rendezvous point for Arnold, Morgan, Montgomery, and their men. Morgan wanted to "drive on," pressing the attack. "But an impromptu council of war.... [consisting] of the other American officers overruled him."[34] Visibly disheartened, Morgan waited for Montgomery to arrive.

Strike four was that Montgomery did not arrive. Meeting the very first obstacle in their path, a small blockhouse between the wall and the river path, Montgomery and six men were killed by cannon fire. Montgomery's second-in-command, Lieutenant Colonel Donald Campbell, turned coward, ordering a retreat. The prospect of a supporting pincer attack never materialized.[35]

Strike five was that perhaps a successful attack was never meant to be. Military experts opine that a force several times larger than the garrison is necessary to assault an entrenched position. Here, at best, with Montgomery's contingent, Arnold and Morgan had 1,050 men against Carlton's 1,200 inside the city. Subtracting the Montgomery force, the Americans were badly outnumbered. Battlefield experts espouse a force four times or six times greater in number than the defenders.

With "[d]awn breaking and the storm abating," Mogen rallied what Americans he could enlist, "for a second try, then a third, then a fourth, all of them repulsed."[36] Finally, Americans surrendered, on Governor Carlton's assurance of good treatment.

Surrender and Imprisonment

"Seeing the men around him throw down their arms," Morgan "burst into tears of rage." Surrounded, he dared the British to try to take his sword. "When they threatened to shoot him, he told them to go ahead." Finally, Morgan sighted a priest in the crowd of onlookers. He handed the priest his sword, angrily saying to his adversaries, "Not a scoundrel of these cowards shall take it from my hands."[37] The incident represented another addition to the Morgan legend.

Imprisonment and a Return Home

Canadian Governor Carlton proved himself humane. He imprisoned the American enlisted men in a Catholic monastery and the officers in a close-by seminary. General Carlton supplied the officers with a quantity of wine; the Bishop of Quebec supplied them with tea. British officers frequently visited Morgan and colleagues. The prisoners of war were free to walk out into the vicinities of their abodes.[38] They were not, though, completely at ease. Later, Morgan related to a British prisoner of war held in Winchester that he, Morgan, "had himself been a prisoner for five month [sic] and twelve days; six and 30 officers and servants in one room!"[39]

In late July 1776, Governor Carlton granted Morgan parole, that is, release if the prisoner pledged not to take up arms, at least until an exchange had been consummated. On August 11, the Americans sailed aboard British transports, landing on Staten Island in early September 1776, two weeks after the British had vanquished American forces at the Battle of Long Island. British ground forces turned the prisoners of war over to their American colleagues at Elizabethtown, now Elizabeth, New Jersey.

Prelude to Saratoga

In the summer of 1777, British General John Burgoyne, "Gentleman Johnny," embarked southward on the reverse of General Montgomery's northward trip to Canada. Burgoyne's objective was to split the fledging American nation roughly in half, separating New England and a slice of upstate New York from the other colonies. In his mind's eye at least, Burgoyne expected to be met by British General William Howe, leading a force northward from New York, to a point between Albany and Lake George, New York. Accompanying Burgoyne was a 9,500-troop force, exceedingly large for the day.[40] His army consisted of 4,400 British regulars, 4,700 Hessian mercenaries, 400 "assorted" (Loyalists, Canadians, and Native Americans "from the Six Nations and the tribes along the Great Lakes"), and 138 pieces of artillery.[41] Burgoyne's entourage, supported by scores of wagons, enjoyed near luxury, the accompanying wagons containing clothes, camp furnishings, fine foods, and a great quantity of wine and champagne. Thus burdened, the force's pace was agonizingly slow.

Initially, the procession achieved success. The British captured the great stone fort on Lake Champlain's western shore, Fort Ticonderoga, without a shot after its commander, General Arthur St. Clair, ordered the fort's abandonment by its 3,000-man garrison. Army Surgeon James Thacher wrote to General Philip Schuyler, "The conduct of General St. Clair ... rendered him very unpopular and subjected him to general censure and reproach; there are some, indeed, who even accused him of treachery."[42] After the abandonment, the Continental Congress decreed that Washington never again assign to St. Clair command of troops.

But, subsequently, losses more than offset Burgoyne's gains at Ticonderoga. In early August, Burgoyne sent Lieutenant Colonel Barry St. Leger and 900 troops west, to protect Burgoyne's right flank. They were to proceed up the Mohawk River, to Fort Stanwix, garrisoned by 800 Americans and 60 Oneida, commanded by General Nickolas Herkimer. Despite heavy losses, including Herkimer's death at the Battle of Oriskany, the American fort held.[43]

To protect his left flank, Burgoyne then sent 1,400 Hessian soldiers east, into Vermont, toward the Connecticut River. At the Battle of Bennington, Colonel John Stark and his 1,492 person New Hampshire army, combined with Massachusetts and

New York militia, achieved a decisive victory, slaying 200 and capturing 700 of 1,400 Hessian enemy.[44] "These two setbacks were bitter blows to Burgoyne, who now had only 6,300 effectives," concludes Don Higginbotham in *Revolutionary Rifleman*.[45]

Meanwhile, noting the feeble defense being prepared, in July, the Continental Congress replaced the patrician General Schuyler with General Horatio Gates as commander of the American Northern Department.

Horatio Gates was a former British army major who had sold his commission and emigrated to America in 1772. "Gates did not look like a soldier ... small of stature, ruddy-faced, and bespectacled, with graying hair ... [h]is enemies said he looked like an 'old granny,' and Burgoyne referred to him as an 'old midwife.'"[46]

In New Jersey, Morgan had been commanding the Seventh Virginia over several months of small skirmishes and guessing what the British might do next. In early June 1777, General Washington gave Morgan a new command: a corps of 500 hand-picked Virginia and Pennsylvania riflemen. Washington sent them north to join Gates just south of the hamlet of Saratoga, above Albany on the Hudson River.

A Morgan-Inspired Innovation

Because their barrels had spiral grooves, "Kentucky rifles" were capable of hitting objects at 200–250 yards. By contrast, balls fired from smooth-bore muskets fell harmlessly to the ground at 100 yards, were very inaccurate, and had an effective 50–60-yard range. Yet "[w]hile muskets could be fired four or five [three at most?] times a minute, riflemen were fortunate to deliver two shots in that time [a single shot?]," as their rifles' barrels and the groves' spiraling had to be absolutely clean.[47] Hence, riflemen found it impossible to stop a determined attack by concentrated firepower and, because their rifles could not take bayonets, unable to withstand a bayonet charge. The latter two were, of course, British forces' standard tactics. Riflemen's strengths were as snipers and woods-fighters.

At Saratoga, Daniel Morgan effectively married the two—infantry with muskets and his corps of riflemen—in the trees and on the flanks.

The Battles at Saratoga

Actually, "Saratoga" was two battles: the Battle of Freeman's Farm on September 19, 1777, and the Battle of Bemis Heights on October 7, 1777.[48] At both battles, Morgan combined incremental improvements with larger ones. First was positioning: he always positioned himself near the center of his troops' deployment, slightly behind his men. Second was communications: Morgan employed a turkey call that hunters used to mimic a male turkey's mating call. Morgan hung the whistle from a lanyard fastened around his neck. Using the whistle, Morgan called for his officers' and men's attention. By hand signals or gesturing with his hat, he would then signal further orders or beckon them toward the center to re-form.

Third was display, the term then used for forces' positioning. Colonel Morgan placed his riflemen on the flanks and in the trees of a flattened "U" (a crescent formation) that faced 2,200 British to the north, across the large open field of Freeman's Farm. In the American center, Colonel Henry Dearborn's infantry, later assisted by General Enoch Poor's brigade, stood to repel British bayonet charges and emit concentrated firepower as the British line attempted to advance on the American position.[49] The riflemen kept behind cover, many climbing trees for better sight lines. They shot over the heads of British infantry, using greater range to pick off British officers and then artillery men in the rear, elements the British found most difficult to replace. With Dearborn's infantry, Morgan had "a screen of bayonets [and musket fire] to guard his vulnerable, slow-loading rifles, in effect a primitive combined arms force, able to undertake multiple tasks simultaneously, staffed by men [Morgan] knew and trusted."[50]

By afternoon, all the British gunners were killed or wounded.[51] "Burgoyne [also] lost heavily in officers, most of them bought down by riflemen. As the afternoon wore on, Burgoyne's situation became critical. His artillery was silenced."[52] Gates could claim victory, with losses of 320 to Burgoyne's 600 or more. Morgan could as well; of 451 effectives in the Riflemen Corps that day, only four were killed and eight wounded. "Morgan's brilliance as a tactical commander was his ability to fuse disparate group of riflemen and musket men from different units and then use them as one weapon," summarized historian Andrew Zambone.[53]

The marriage with infantry also contributed to astonishingly low losses of Morgan's riflemen. Before the British could zero in on American snipers protected by infantry lines at the edge of the woods, the snipers could move to other locations, able not only to reposition themselves but to re-load rifles.[54]

The Battle of Bemis Heights

The engagement at Bemis Heights was much larger than that at Freeman's Farm, with 8,000 American forces, including enthusiastic 3,000 New York Militia who had arrived piecemeal in the previous days (*see, e.g.,* Chapter 13). Americans now faced an exhausted, terrorized British force of 6,000 men. In the three weeks between battles, Morgan's rifle corps wore the British down, sniping at British sentries and picking off any British soldier who failed to keep under cover. "Each night Morgan directed groups of men in scouting forays and skirmishes around the British positions."[55] During this period, Native American allies had melted away from the British as well. Marooned in unfamiliar surroundings, and intimidated by the threats snipers posed, the British were unable, or unwilling, to explore the terrain about them.

To his aide de camp, Colonel James Wilkinson, Gates's only order was a terse, "Well, then, order on Morgan to begin the game."[56] Morgan followed the formula he had introduced at Freeman's Farm, even mating his rifle corps with the same musket men, Henry Dearborn's infantry battalion. Again, in a crescent formation, the combined force moved to the left, and to the left again, flanking Burgoyne's force's right wing. "He [Morgan] would circle his rifle corps to around the British right, moving to the northwest, then appearing on some wooded heights to their right rear." If he could, following his mantra, Morgan always moved his men to the flank: "So

Morgan, as he always did, sought the enemy's flank, moving around to Burgoyne's right flank."⁵⁷

Morgan also directed one of his riflemen, Timothy Murphy, "a skilled Indian fighter and fine woodsman," to pick off the British General Simon Fraser, a brave officer who had also led the British attack at Freeman's Farm. Morgan had spotted first a large grey horse, its rider going back and forth behind British lines, shouting encouragement. Murphy climbed a tree and fired a few rounds, the last striking Fraser in the stomach. Fraser died a few hours later.⁵⁸

The Americans captured the redoubt thrown up to shelter the British camp, along with Brunswick mercenaries manning it, resulting in an opening to the British camp. Accordingly, the weary British withdrew to Saratoga village a few miles north. General John Stark arrived with his 1,500-man New Hampshire force, deploying north of Saratoga and boxing in the British. Stark's arrival bought the American headcount to over 11,000. On October 17, 1777, General Burgoyne and 5,000 British troops surrendered. Witnessing from afar that the fledging nation's military might be for real, France decided to aid the colonies' cause.

The True Hero of Saratoga Receives No Acclaim

From Saratoga, Morgan marched his rifle corps south, joining General Washington's army at Whitemarsh, north of Philadelphia, where the demoralized Middle Department Army had come to rest after Brandywine and Germantown losses. A short time later, in December 1777, Washington took his army 12 miles west into the winter encampment at Valley Forge. Twenty-first century exaggerated perceptions aside, the Valley Forge winter was a mild one.⁵⁹ Immediately, General Washington put Morgan and his men to work, patrolling around Gulph Mills and Radnor, Pennsylvania, across the Schuylkill River, midway between Valley Forge, where the Americans were, and Philadelphia, where the British were.

In the first months of 1778, Lord Dartmouth replaced General William Howe with General Sir Henry Clinton. Instructions from London also forewarned General Clinton that he would be required to dispatch 5,000 troops to the Caribbean where they would protect British sugar plantations against the French.⁶⁰ Undoubtedly in part thinking of the projected loss in manpower, Clinton decided to abandon Philadelphia in early summer following the Americans' Valley Forge winter, departing the city on June 18, 1778, for Sandy Hook, New Jersey, thence to New York. There followed a British exodus diagonally across New Jersey, with a slow moving baggage train several miles long, including loyalists, Tory sympathizers, hangers-on, camp followers, sutlers, hustlers, lady friends, prostitutes, and more.⁶¹

Ahead of other, slower-moving American units, General Washington sent Morgan's rifle corps on one British column's flank, and General Charles Scott on the other. Morgan's and Scott's tasks were to harass the British column, impeding their progress, slowing them so the main American force could catch up. The "American forward units sniped at [the British] at every opportunity and demolished bridges and felled trees in [the British] path."⁶²

As a result of his mission and accomplishment of it, Morgan and his men were out of position, three miles in advance of the scene of the Battle of Monmouth Courthouse. On the day of the battle, June 28 at 12:30, Washington wrote to Morgan, who had earlier had requested further orders: "I have just received your letter, as your Corps is out of supporting Distance, I would have you confine yourself to observing the motions of the Enemy, unless an opportunity offers for intercepting small parties."[63] Because of Washington's orders, "Morgan's corps was sidelined in the Battle of Monmouth."[64] One of the Continental Army's "crack units sat out one of the war's major contests."[65]

Disappointment

In autumn 1778, the powers-that-be not only sidelined the rifle corps, they disbanded it. Washington temporarily assigned Morgan command of General William Woodford's brigade but, when Woodford returned to the army in May 1779, Morgan was without portfolio.

Almost simultaneously, Washington announced formation of a new light infantry unit. Morgan, though, was not the only high ranking general without portfolio. General Arthur St. Clair had ousted General Anthony Wayne as commander of Pennsylvania forces. General Washington gave the light infantry's command to General "Mad Anthony" Wayne. When Morgan heard of the decision, he informed Washington of his intention to give up the service:

> As it is generally known that I commanded the light infantry of our army and that the command is now taken from me, it will naturally be judged that this [change] of officers had taken place either on account of some misconduct in me, or on account of my want of capacity. I cannot therefore but feel deeply effected [sic] with this injury done to my reputation. I engaged in the service of my country with a full determination to continue in [the war] as long as my services were [wanted]. I must conclude from what has happened that my country has no more occasion for me, I therefore beg leave to retire.[66]

Sensing an injustice had been done, the Continental Congress persuaded Morgan to "take an honorable furlough" rather than retirement from the service.

Washington truly was a great, great leader but, particularly as a commanding general, he made mistakes. One was the perfidy he demonstrated toward his loyal and most capable commander, Daniel Morgan. Morgan's soldiers had high respect for Morgan, knowing him "as a just leader." Colonel Morgan believed that "public whippings merely degraded a soldier and broke his spirit. He forbade such punishment in his corps." Morgan also made every attempt to meet his men's needs. He tried to bridge the gap between officers and enlisted. He moved freely among his men, spoke their argot, and rolled up his sleeves to give his soldiers a hand from time to time. Accordingly, "The old wagoner was known for his common touch."[67]

From above, Morgan's superiors had high praise. After Saratoga, Horatio Gates embraced Morgan, saying, "Morgan, you have done wonders." In his report to Congress, Gates wrote, "Too much praise cannot be given to the Corps commanded by Col. Morgan."[68] When Washington was forming the rifle corps, Gates wrote to Washington that Morgan "would be excellent for the service" of command.[69]

Morgan himself bordered on the sycophantic. All of his life, including in the military, Morgan "would find any reason he could to do Washington service, either militarily or personally."[70] George Washington Parke Curtis believed, "Few of his subordinates revered Washington more than Morgan." He also wrote that although Washington was "the sustaining force of the Revolution," without Morgan, the Revolution "would have collapsed in the field."[71]

Morgan's faithfulness and loyalty were unrequited. To the president of Congress, to whom Morgan had in 1779 tendered a letter of resignation, General Washington wrote, "I cannot, in justice, avoid mentioning him as a very valuable officer, who has rendered a series of important services, and distinguished himself on several occasions."[72] That was it. That was all Washington had to say. Historian Andrew Zambone could not help but observe, "It seems outrageous that [Washington] would so coldly dismiss one of his leading combat soldiers."[73] In 1780, looking back, Washington wrote that Morgan had been "a brave Officer, and a well-meaning man, but his withdrawing from the Service at the time he did it ... could not be justified on any ground; there was not ... the smallest cause for dissatisfaction."[74] Perhaps Washington, being from Virginia, bent over backwards to avoid in any way favoring officers from the Old Dominion.[75]

Washington's lukewarm attitude toward Morgan was a product of Washington's origins in Virginia's class-bound society. Most Virginia generals came from a high level of the gentry. Charles Scott (Chapter 17) may have been a partial exception, but several generations of his family had been in Goochland County, holding sizable estates there. By contrast, Morgan came, literally, from nowhere. His provenance was unknowable. He was a wagon driver who could barely read and write. Neglecting Morgan's achievements and aspirations was perhaps Washington's biggest personnel gaffe of the war.

Denouement

Following Cowpens and the strategic retreat that followed, Morgan was done in. He suffered from sciatica, hemorrhoids, and the ravages of years of brawling and drinking when he was young. He could no longer sit a horse and had to travel in a carriage, stopping several times for two days' rest before resuming his journey. He was "rheumatic from head to feet." At night as well as other times, he lay upon a bed of leaves, covered by blankets, nonetheless shivering uncontrollably. He was then 46 years old, more or less, in a time when life expectancies were much shorter than an age of 46 would portend today. Nonetheless, on February 4, 1781, Morgan marched his troops into Guilford Courthouse, having pushed his men 47 miles in 48 hours. Cornwallis stood far behind, waiting for the Yadkin River's flood tide to subside.

Morgan recovered his health, like a cat, several times over. George Washington, too, recovered his senses with regard to Daniel Morgan. He chose Morgan to lead the United States forces to Western Pennsylvania to quell the Whiskey Rebellion. After quelling the rebellion, Morgan led a large force westward, serving as a capable, understanding, and wise military governor. Later still, Morgan sought election to and served a term in the U.S. House of Representatives. In the last years of his life, Morgan moved from Soldier's Rest into Winchester, where he lived with his daughter and her husband.

Daniel Morgan died on July 6, 1802, having evolved over his lifetime from brawler to soldier to leader. The largest crowd in the history of Winchester came to the funeral. As a final tribute, "Among the men who fired a salute over his grave were seven men carrying rifles, the remaining members of the ninety men who [in 1775] had followed him out of Winchester to Boston and to Quebec."[76] Morgan's epitaph was voiced by Presbyterian Minister William Hill: "When we consider the obscurity from which he arose; the honour and power to which he ascended; and the great services which he had rendered his country—we may say that he had very few equals."[77]

24

The Piedmont Partisan

William Lee Davidson of North Carolina

William Lee Davidson's biographer, Chalmers Gaston Davidson, envisioned his ancestor as "the lodestar of backcountry patriotism," not just in North Carolina but throughout the South.[1] Davidson was at Valley Forge where, according to Ryan Cole in *The Rise and Fall of a Revolutionary Hero*, "Davidson and [the mercurial Light Horse Harry Lee] became comrades in arms."[2] Lee, the Virginia Tidewater aristocrat and College of New Jersey (Princeton) graduate, "found the backwoods Carolinian a man of popular manners, pleasing address, active and indefatigable."[3] On the opposite end of the spectrum from Lee, a rough-hewn, backcountry patriot such as Virginia's Daniel Morgan found in Davidson "a close friend ... since their days at Valley Forge."[4] Davidson, a thin wiry man like many backcountry settlers, differed from his neighbors and colleagues in another way. He was of pleasing countenance, a thin smile often on his lips, unlike the grim physiognomy so common in those parts, engendered by months and years of hard labor in near wildness.

In 1837, North Carolina Presbyterians named their college, today a well-regarded institution, Davidson College to memorialize the North Carolina brigadier who died at Cowan's Ford in the war's last principal year. Today, though, one searches in vain for mention of Davidson on the college's website or in the history books.[5] Other than the one memorial, Davidson largely is forgotten. In 1779–1779, he served directly under George Washington, first, at Valley Forge and, second, for fourteen months thereafter, returning to North Carolina only in May 1779.[6] It was only in the "guerilla war that [had] begun" after South Carolina's 1780 Battle of Camden that William Lee Davidson merited mention.[7] William Lee Davidson is a forgotten founder of our republic.

Migration South

William's father, George Davidson, immigrated from Northern Ireland in 1740 or 1741, a victim, like half the population of Ireland, of the 1740's potato famine, and settled in central Pennsylvania. Immigrants from Ulster dominated the Scots-Irish, most being Presbyterian Scots, many of whom spent a generation or two in Ireland before coming to America. In 1746, George's youngest son, William Lee Davidson, was born a few years after his parents had settled. "The hostile Indians and French traders made the Pennsylvania frontier a precarious place in which to nurture progeny, and the Quaker aristocracy of Philadelphia was not disposed to bestir itself on behalf of the westerners."[8] The Quaker-dominated assembly would not provide funds for armaments (Chapter 16). To exacerbate the problem, neither the proprietor not his successor, Thomas Penn, would permit taxation of the vast Penn landholdings, even replacing any royal governor who indicated willingness to entertain taxation proposals.[9]

Other heroes of the Revolution—Andrew Pickens, Hugh Mercer, Andrew Lewis, and Peter Muhlenberg, among others—exasperated by the colony's failure to protect them, left Pennsylvania. Many refugees from Pennsylvania, Muhlenberg included, settled in the northern Shenandoah Valley.[10] Others ventured farther afield, such as Mercer, who became a leading citizen of Fredericksburg. Pickens reached the Carolinas. The Davidsons (George, his brother John, their families, and others) ventured farther afield, making the 435-mile trip on the Great Wagon Road through Virginia's Shenandoah Valley, continuing on the old Catawba Trading Path through central North Carolina, settling west of Salisbury.

Later, in 1755, British General Edward Braddock suffered a devasting defeat in western Pennsylvania. That summer, "Word of Braddock's defeat by the French and Indians in Pennsylvania reached the Carolina Piedmont ... [Additional] refugees from Pennsylvania began to appear in Rowan County [North Carolina]" in greater numbers.[11] North Carolina, however, did not represent an escape from Indian raids that had plagued Pennsylvania settlers. "[The] Cherokees lurked in the Blue Ridge.... The Catawbas stole and the Cherokees scalped. A frontier family in an isolated [North Carolina] cabin expected no mercy when the savages took to the war path." Chalmers Davidson told of his ancestor's time: "Charred timbers and mutilated bodies alone remained to tell the tale of Cherokee marauders."[12] Settlers built a stockade near Salisbury in which they could shelter, christening it Fort Dobbs after colonial governor Arthur Dobbs.

Early Military Exploits

Davidson's first military exploit was escort duty in the spring of 1767 when, at age 21, he accompanied colonial governor William Tyron, whose palace dominated that era's North Carolina capital, New Bern. Governor Tyron ventured into southwestern Carolina, where the boundaries between Cherokee hunting grounds and land grants to white settlers remained unestablished, causing a source of friction. "His excellency [Governor Tyron] liked the plain people of the frontier." He wrote to the Earl of Shelbourne, "I found on those hilly back settlements a race of people, slightly active, and laborious, and loyal subjects of his Majesty."[13]

In December 1767, Davidson married Mary Breyard before a justice of the peace. In the colonies, dissenters' (Presbyterians, Catholics, Puritans) clergy were not permitted to officiate at the rites of matrimony, a heavy-handed restriction the British enforced.[14] In fact, pursuant to Church of England edict, "Marriages, baptisms, communions, and burial services performed by Presbyterian clergy were illegal ... clergymen could be arrested if they tried to administer those rights."[15] Britain subjected colonists to "unending burdens" directly, though enactments such as the Stamp Act and the Townshend duties, as well as indirectly, as in "delegation of power to the Anglican Church to further subjugate the Presbyterians," who predominated in the back country.[16]

The Presbyterians vs. The Government

As outlined earlier, North Carolinians came to minimize east versus west, coast versus backcountry tensions, unlike Georgia, where such a dichotomy persisted the length of the war, severely impacting military strategy.[17] Before the war, North Carolina militia met a large, armed mob of western Carolinians, aggrieved at colonial officials' alleged overcharges and arrogant behaviors (Chapter 3). At the Battle of Alamance, colonial militias defeated the regulators' mob, reducing east-west tensions in North Carolina.[18] The Regulators' movement symbolized the east-west, coastal-backcountry divide. Presbyterianism and patriotism also were inextricably interwoven: "'Presbyterian' and 'Episcopalian' were frequently used as synonyms for 'rebel' and 'loyalist.'"[19] The religious contrast paralleled other dichotomies such as coastal or backcountry, and slaveholding or slave-free.

Rumblings and Early War Years

In 1774, William Davidson became a member of the Rowan County Committee on Correspondence. By 1775, at age nineteen, he was captain of the Rowan County Militia. In September 1775, the Continental Congress authorized two North Carolina regiments with James Moore and Robert Howe as colonels.[20] Colonel, later General, Griffin Rutherford commanded the North Carolina Militia in the backcountry. Rutherford made Captain Davidson adjutant of the western county "Minutemen."

Near the North Carolina coast, Scottish Highlanders settled in the southeast, where Fayetteville (then Cross Creek) stands today. Unlike the Scots-Irish of the backcountry, the newly arrived Scots were Loyalists.[21] The crown had granted them land after they had taken an oath of allegiance.[22] Fourteen hundred Cross Creek Scots marched southeast: "A number were armed [only] with Claymores, traditional Highland swords."[23] Eighteen miles upriver from Wilmington, militia forces vanquished the loyalists (Chapter 4).[24] Colonel Rutherford led his troops east to participate but he, Davidson, and the force arrived too late.

In April 1776, the Continental Congress authorized six additional North Carolina regiments, commanded by Francis Nash, Alexander Martin, Jethro Sumner, Thomas Polk, Edward Buncombe, and Alexander Lillington. William Davidson became major (third in command), 4th North Carolina Line.[25]

A False Alarm, a Leave, and a Journey North

The false alarm came in spring 1776. Two British fleets with armies aboard sailed into the Cape Fear estuary, downriver from Wilmington, North Carolina's principal port.[26] After Moore's Creek, the British never disembarked and soon departed.

In the meanwhile, though, the Continental Congress had ordered six North Carolina regiments, including Major Davidson's, to converge on Wilmington.[27] The specter of a cataclysmic battle was averted.

Davidson's leave of absence came in summer 1776. His Continental Regiment released Davidson to participate with the militia and Colonel Griffith Rutherford in another campaign against the Cherokees, who were raiding, marauding, scalping, and killing settlers in the state's western reaches.[28] Rutherford led 2,000 militia, with soldiers from North Carolina, Virginia, South Carolina, and Georgia serving under him.[29] The force "burned at least thirty-six Cherokee towns."[30] As Chalmers Davidson recounted, "The Indians had their villages burned [and] their cornfields leveled.... Rutherford left in his wake only the ashes of wigwams and the stubble of maize fields. The Cherokees were never again a serious menace to Carolinians."[31] The excursion complete, Major Davidson returned to service with the 4th North Carolina.

In April 1777, Francis Nash, promoted to brigadier some months earlier, succeeded upon James Moore's death to become head of the North Carolina forces. The Continental Congress created the 7th, 8th, and 9th North Carolina regiments, to be commanded by Colonels James Hogun, James Armstrong, and John Williams. Congress followed with another directive, ordering all nine North Carolina regiments north to the Middle Department. Brigadier Nash led the Carolina contingent. Once in the north, Washington kept the North Carolina regiments in reserve, the Carolinians being "virtual spectators" at Brandywine on September 11, 1777. With the rest of the army, the Carolina regiments marched and countermarched. It was at Germantown on October 4, 1777, that the North Carolina contingent lost its second commanding general: "Francis Nash [Chapter 19] fell in action and died a few days later."[32]

Much Ado About Nothing: Service with the Middle Department

In December 1777, George Washington took his army, crestfallen after Brandywine and Germantown but heartened by Saratoga, into the Valley Forge encampment. Davidson endured the winter without major event. As has been seen, he did become friendly with the famous Virginians, Light-Horse Harry Lee and Daniel Morgan.[33] Before breaking camp, George Washington re-organized his army into three divisions under Major Generals Charles Lee, Adam Stephen, and Nathanael Greene. As part of the preparations, Congress telescoped the nine North Carolina regiments into three. Lt. Colonel Davidson became second-in-command of the 3rd North Carolina, under Colonel Jethro Sumner. In June 1778, Sumner, Davidson, and their troops formed the Philadelphia garrison after the British had vacated the city. Otherwise, Davidson's movements during spring and summer 1778 were "almost impossible to map correctly."[34]

Return Home

After two years in the North, Davidson returned to North Carolina, taking leave to visit his family. On May 1, 1780, Davidson left his family and the backcountry, journeying from central North Carolina to join his regiment on the coast at Charles Town, South Carolina. In South Carolina, Davidson could not penetrate the British blockade. Charles Town surrendered a few weeks later on May 12, 1780. "The fall of Charleston ... released many 'Huzza for King George from long repressed Tories. Loyalists in western North Carolina [included] the peace-loving Germans who were grateful to the British government for a haven from strife ... and a remnant of the Regulators ... who felt bound by the oaths of allegiance which Governor Tyron had exacted for forgiving their rebellious past."[35] Differences thought to have dissipated had not done so completely.

Deprived of his continental command because of his regiment's capture, Davidson returned to the backcountry, taking up command of militia. In early July, Davidson was shot in stomach leading 200 troops at Colson's Mill near where the Yadkin River joins the Pee Dee, southeast of Salisbury. He and his force skirmished with a British force twice the size. From the middle of July until the first of September, Davidson recuperated.[36]

On August 31, the North Carolina Legislature decreed General Davidson commander, Western Carolina Militia, replacing General Griffin Rutherford, whom the British had captured at Camden. Although "Davidson held a Continental Commission and was a veteran of Washington's army," thereafter he commanded militia.[37]

Then, the defeat of the American forces at Camden, South Carolina, on August 16, 1780, occurred "so soon after Charleston's fall turned doubtful Whigs into triumphant Tories." As Chalmers Davidson wrote, "The counties east of Mecklenburg [Charlotte] and Rowan [Salisbury] had shown themselves as yet unweaned from King George ... in all sections there was disaffection."[38] Yet, as Professor Davidson continued in *Brigadier William Lee Davidson*, "To frontier Scots England had been an invader for generations. They detested her religion, despised her dukes and earls, and considered her Redcoats the private prey of any sharpshooter."[39]

On August 31, 1780, Congress promoted William Lee Davidson to Brigadier General.

Openings of the British Southern Campaign

The British now imagined that a southern strategy was the pathway to victory.[40] The northern strategy had come to naught with Saratoga and the defeat of Burgoyne coming down from Canada. In the Middle Department, despite numerous losses (Brooklyn, White Plains, Brandywine, Germantown) and smaller successes (Trenton, Princeton, the draw at Monmouth Courthouse), the Americans had done enough in the mid–Atlantic to preserve the quest for independence. Middle department strategy represented a draw, the equivalent of success for the patriots. Now the British command initiated a third focus, to the south, early on achieving successes at Savannah, Charles Town, Waxhaw, and Camden. But thereafter, the British force's peregrinations lengthened supply lines, entered increasingly hostile territory, and suffered surprising defeats at Kings Mountain and Cowpens.

In September 1780, Lord Cornwallis came seventy miles north from Camden,

South Carolina, to occupy the village of Charlotte. In command, Davidson "found himself faced with a bellicose, turbid mob of about 400 frontiersmen." These backcountry frontiersmen had "one unique advantage in arms. Hunts and Indian wars had led to the importation of the rifle ... whereas the coastal regiments and the British began the war [and continued] with their main dependence on the smooth-bored musket."[41] With their "Kentucky Rifles," Davidson's men resembled Daniel Morgan's Virginia Rifle Corps.

Cornwallis came north from Camden with 1,200 British regulars and probably half as many Loyalists, the latter having sprung up from South Carolina regions. As he came north, Cornwallis sent a large party, a few regulars and mostly Tories under Colonel Patrick Ferguson, to the west. Several things then occurred. One, Davidson and his men's increasing hit-and-run tactics against Cornwallis in Charlotte plagued the British to no end. Two, on October 7, 1780, American militia, commanded by Virginian William Campbell, defeated Colonel Ferguson and his party of now 1,100 men at Kings Mountain, southwest of Charlotte, a few miles below the North Carolina border (Chapter 22).[42] Although not present at Kings Mountain, Davidson passed on news of the victory to his superiors: "[British] Colonel Ferguson fell in the action besides 150 of his men—810 were made prisoners ... 1500 Stands of arms fell into our Hands.... We lost about 20 men. ... The Blow is great and I give you Joy upon the Occasion."[43] If only temporarily, the tide had turned. After embarrassing losses at Charles Town and Camden, the Americans at Kings Mountain had achieved a measure of redemption.[44]

In North Carolina, "Meanwhile, Cornwallis was finding Charlotte an inhospitable hostess. Every able-bodied Whig in the vicinity did his bit to make his lordship uncomfortable." Fifty horses were wrestled from Tory camps; over twenty-five barrels of gun powder were filched from a British camp; a supply train coming up from Camden was stopped in its tracks and raided; and an estimated fifty messengers to Cornwallis were fired upon, wounded, or killed before reaching British headquarters. Davidson's militia "made life miserable for the British soldiers." Nervous British sentries fired at the smallest sound. Foraging parties sent out to collect food were ambushed, attacked by small patriot groups. Detachments of troops sent to guard grist mills were harassed. Snipers hid in the trees, picking off careless British soldiers. According to Hugh Rankin, bright red coats made good targets.[45] "The bushwhacking proclivities of the backwoods-men were beating down the morale of the [supposed] conquerors."[46]

Forage for both men and horses was not to be had in the Charlotte area. Ferguson's defeat at Kings Mountain resulted in Cornwallis's left flank being unprotected. On October 12, 1780, the British began leaving Charlotte, bound back to South Carolina from whence they had come.

Contest with Cornwallis

Lord Cornwallis retreated slowly. The fall rains impeded the British withdrawal; their baggage train moved with difficulty. "Rain fell for several days without intermission," the rivers and streams were swollen, and the red clay roads turned into quagmires.[47] "The laboring and lumbering [British] column was harassed almost continuously by little groups under colonel [William] Davie and Davidson."[48] By the end of October, Cornwallis and his "bedraggled" force reached Winnsboro, South Carolina, a village seventy miles south of Charlotte. There, Cornwallis took his army into winter quarters to rest. On the American side, on December 2, 1780, Major General Nathanael Greene arrived in Charlotte, relieving the disgraced General Horatio Gates. Gates had become known as "Horatio the Helpless," since at Camden he had deserted his troops and fled 150 miles to the rear.

The British posts at Ninety-Six and at Camden in South Carolina were well guarded and had Cornwallis's back. The British still "held the delusion that a large number of North Carolina Loyalists would flock to their standard once they entered the state," as groups of Loyalists had been expected to do in South Carolina. The British began the trek north again in mid–January 1781.

Cornwallis sent ahead his prized British Legion commanded by the dashing, give-no-quarter Colonel Banastre Tarleton. On January 17, General Daniel Morgan and his men administered "a devil of a whipping" at Cowpens.[49] Davidson missed the opportunity of participating. After the battle, Davidson gave Morgan wholehearted applause, writing, "You have in my opinion paved the way for the Salvation of this Country."[50]

In the Carolina backcountry, General Davidson "was using all his powers of persuasion to bring in the militia. This, in the piedmont, was the time that tried men's souls."[51] Cornwallis and the British were coming with a vengeance. Americans suffered war fatigue as the seventh anniversary of Lexington and Concord—April 1774 to April 1781—approached.

Davidson's Final Chapter: The Crossing at Cowan's Ford

Deeply chagrined at the utter defeat of his crack troops, Lord Cornwallis ordered his men to stockpile all but weapons, ammunition, and half rations, a slimming down Cornwallis himself undertook. He then pursued Morgan at more than a double-quick march, seeking to overtake and exact revenge for Cowpens. After a feint toward Charlotte, Morgan and his men veered to the northeast in the direction of Hillsboro, near the Virginia border. In Morgan's wake, the Catawba River above present-day Charlotte, and the Yadkin River, west of Salisbury, approached flood stage. The swirling waters made crossing difficult if not impossible. Cornwallis and his men found it necessary to pause.

It was Nathanael Greene's opinion that the enemy would attempt to cross the rivers, "probably sending their cavalry at night by some private ford," rather than crossing on a well-used route.[52] He thought Lord Cornwallis also might attempt a diversion by sending units toward various river fords. Davidson had about 800–1,000 militia under his immediate command, including Graham's cavalry, who rode plow horses rather than sleek steeds.[53] General Greene "assigned Davidson and his North Carolina militiamen the unenviable task of contesting the [pursuing] British at the fords of the Catawba."[54]

General Davidson distributed his force along the east banks of the Catawba to guard private fords. At Cowan's Ford, however, there were two fords: a wagon ford and a horse ford. The latter was shallower, going straight across the river. The wagon ford started at the same point on the right bank but proceeded diagonally, probably because wagons were less able to take the river's current head on. The wagon ford reached the left (east) bank a quarter mile below the horse ford's terminus. Davidson himself "paraded at the horse ford," where he placed a contingent of troops. Later, at the sounding of alarm, he rode to the wagon ford, lightly guarded because Davidson and his officers had not believed the British would attempt crossing there.[55] "General Davidson, a confident thirty-five-year-old of Continental experience at Germantown, awaited the redcoat advance.... Davidson coolly awaited the enemy as if he still led a Continental regiment."[56]

Lord Cornwallis himself led the Brigade of Guards, the Royal Welsh Fusiliers, and the Hessian von Bose Regiment into the river. On the opposite shore, upriver, Davidson sat his mount, having just arrived to rally the wagon ford sentries and a contingent of militia cavalry, such as they were, on the crest of the hill behind him. According to Rankin, "The [river's] waters were swift and the sentries soon heard the splashing of water as the British struggled along, trying to maintain their footing … [o]ut on the river, the British were experiencing rough going … roped together to prevent being swept away by the current."[57] A patriot shot hit Lord Cornwallis's horse. For the British, "Some men and horse had been swept away by river current, and some had been killed or wounded by the first [American] volley. [British infantry] were up to their breasts in the rapid stream."[58]

On the American-held riverbank, an officer with Davidson, colonial Colonel William Polk, shouted, "Fire away, boys. There is help at hand!" For a moment, having arrived at a gallop, "Davidson stared in the direction of the man with the smoking gun. Then, without a sound, he fell from his horse. Davidson was hit by a musket ball in the chest … he died instantly. Without their leader the patriots ran."[59] Davidson lay dead of a wound near the nipple of his left breast. The musket ball had pierced his heart.[60] General Davidson's battlefield death set off "a confused and precipitous Colonial retreat."[61] "[T]he death of General Davidson was akin to catastrophe, creating panic among his followers, who fled in wild disorder, all thought of further resistance disappearing."[62]

A Partisan's Contribution

Upon consideration, "Measured by the contemporary criterion of a great soldier, Davidson fails to qualify." He neither commanded nor participated in any critical encounter throughout the Revolution. Measured by subjective criteria, however, "There was no more completely adored soldier in North Carolina."[63] In the backcountry, "[t]he militia of the Salisbury District would do for him what they would do for no other man." Davidson was rough-hewn senior officer, "a backwoodsman who won the allegiance of such ambitious and self-assured Princetonians as Harry Lee, William Davie, and Waightstill Avery. ... It was, however, [Davidson's] hold on the plain men of dirt farms ... that made him important."[64]

25

Route to Yorktown

The Battle of Guilford Courthouse

Brigadier Davidson and his ragged militia had Brigadier Daniel Morgan's back, at least for a few hours, by holding up the British Catawba crossing. On February 4, 1781, Morgan marched his troops into Guilford Courthouse (present day Greensboro, North Carolina), having pushed his men 47 miles east in the last 48 hours.[1] Lord Cornwallis stood behind, with his army now in the center of the state, waiting for the Yadkin River's flood stage to subside.

Cornwallis had been out-generaled and embarrassed, so much so that he ranted about Morgan and American forces. According to David Lee Russell, "Cornwallis swore that he would retake Morgan … at any cost."[2] Adding to Cornwallis's chagrin, the British effort to recruit Carolina Tories had failed, culminating with the annihilation of the Tory force, such as it was, and the British cadre (Major Ferguson and staff) at Kings Mountain. Then, at Cowpens, the jewel of Cornwallis's force, the British Legion under dashing Lt. Colonel Banastre Tarleton, lost 350 men killed or wounded and 600 captured, again, "a blow from which the British in the South never recovered," William Powell opined in his North Carolina history.[3] Seeking retribution for Cowpens, when river levels subsided, Cornwallis renewed his pursuit. His force crossed North Carolina diagonally, from the Charlotte area in the south toward Hillsborough in the north. Thirty-three miles short of Hillsborough, at Guilford Courthouse, Cornwallis and his men joined issue with a colonial force under Major General Nathanael Greene in the Battle of Guilford Courthouse. They did so, however, only after both sides' five weeks' peregrinations.

The Race to the Dan

General Nathanael Greene raced westward 125 miles in three days, from Cheraw in eastern North Carolina to meet Morgan and his force, along with General William Davidson (Chapter 23), on the eastern bank of the Catawba, where Greene tasked Davidson with his mission. Morgan's force was then only a day ahead of Cornwallis. After meeting with General Greene, on February 4, 1781, Morgan left the Catawba behind, expanding the lead to 25 miles ahead of the stranded Cornwallis.[4] William Powell says of the retreat across North Carolina and then across the Dan River into Virginia, "Greene's management of this retreat entitled him to a high rank among soldiers of his time.⁵ [H]e used every means possible of moving his own army and delaying the enemy."⁶

After meeting with Morgan and Davidson, Greene himself rode east to Salisbury, later rejoining the retreat and accompanying it to Guildford Courthouse (present-day Greensboro, North Carolina). While in Salisbury, Greene gave General Isaac Huger and his Continentals orders to come westward to Salisbury, later amending the order to direct a right-hand turn to rendezvous with Morgan. After a pause, the combined militia-regular American force (Morgan's and Huger's commands) resumed their march, 70 miles northeast to Irwin's Ferry on the Dan River, thence north across the river into Virginia. Having commandeered all the flatboats and other vessels in the vicinity, the combined force of 2,046 Americans crossed the Dan on February 14, 1781, having marched 230 miles and averaging 27 miles per day crossing North Carolina's Piedmont.⁷ Cornwallis and his force arrived four hours after Light Horse Harry Lee, Colonel Otho Holland Williams, and the last of the American rear guard had crossed the Dan.⁸

With no boats or other means to cross the river, Cornwallis and his men back tracked southeast to Hillsborough: "I proceeded by easy marches to Hillsborough". His men were tired, 230 miles from their original home base of Charles Town, 200 miles from Camden, and 150 miles from their nearest supply base in Wilmington, North Carolina. They rested in Hillsborough, cleaning and repairing equipment. The weary Americans also rested in Virginia until early March, when they re-crossed the Dan. In the interim, in a game of cat and mouse, skirmishes and ambushes mostly by American detachments had taken place, but no major engagements had ensued. Once back across the Dan, patriot reinforcements from Virginia to the north and those from the south swelled Greene's force to 4,400 men, of whom 1,762 were Continental regulars.⁹

The Deployments at Guilford Courthouse

Once back south of the Dan and in North Carolina, General Greene mimicked Daniel Morgan's array of troops at Cowpens. Morgan was beset by sciatica, rheumatism, and other ailments so severe that he could no longer mount a horse and was traveling prone in a covered wagon. Although he had decamped for recuperation at his home in Virginia (Chapter 22), he wrote to Greene urging him to follow the recipe Morgan had devised at Cowpens. Greene chose to follow this advice, with differences that later became apparent.

The prospective battleground was laid from the Guilford Courthouse south to a point two-thirds of a mile along the New Garden Road, a track running from Salisbury to Hillsborough. The topography consisted of slightly rising ground with a clearing around the courthouse itself, a band of woods, and another clearing. The Americans had the courthouse at their back. Beyond the far clearing would come the British advance, up from the south.

In the lowest clearing, as a first line of defense, Greene stationed 1,000 North Carolina militia behind a split-rail fence, in the words of one combatant, "a cover too insignificant to inspire confidence."[10] Major General Green instructed militia soldiers to fire three rounds, then peel off retreating through gaps in the second line of defense. "Three rounds, my boys, and then you fall back," intoned Greene, sounding as if he were Daniel Morgan.[11] For the second defensive line, brigadiers Robert Lawson and Edward Stevens (Chapter 26) commanded 1,200 Virginia militia. Beyond the band of woods, on the slope in front of the courthouse stood the third and final line consisting of nearly 1,400 Continental regulars from Maryland, Delaware, and Virginia. On the American flanks, at the edges of the woods, stood the remainder of the American force: William Washington's cavalry, Light Horse Harry Lee's cavalry, and Colonel William Campbell's 400 Virginia riflemen.

The British display was less complicated. First, Cornwallis's army was smaller, about 2,000 effectives, as the British army had been reduced by 237 men due to desertions in January and a further 210 due to sickness and combat-related causes in February.[12] Cornwallis had begun the British march in South Carolina with 2,440 men.[13] Second, and in contrast, the British force consisted entirely of battle-hardened professional soldiers: kilt-wearing Scottish Highlanders, green-coated cavalry, and red coated infantry). On the British side, unlike the American, there were no militia troops or greenhorn, first-time combatants. "About 1:30 P.M. on 15 March 1781, the head of the British column appeared on the New Garden Road and with measured tread and to the beat of drums, [tunes played on] fifes, and Highland bagpipes' [unique sound], the British troops marched across a brook and spread out in both directions on the edge of the cleared area," John Buchanan described in *The Road to Guilford Courthouse*.[14] Upon reaching that first clearing, the British "displayed" into two rows spanning the clearing, soon thereafter beginning their advance.

Battle Commences

Some militia in the first American line fired muskets across a cleared cornfield then retreated to the rear as Greene ordered, while others panicked and ran. The American second line stood 350 yards distant, too far away to replicate Morgan's Cowpens strategy. After penetrating the first American line but beyond shooting range for the second, the British had an interval in which they could catch their breath and regroup before marching on, escalating to quick step and then "double quick step," in the classic British bayonet charge maneuver. After firing, the American second line, particularly to the right of the road, began to collapse, swinging "back to the road like an open door." With an inviting road before them, the militia troops took the opportunity to flee northward. The troops left of the road now had their flank exposed. They had to retreat as of necessity because, had they not, the British would roll them up, forming a T, enabling the British to bring a full line's firepower against the American file.

The third line of Continental regulars never gave way. "Twice the British were turned back with heavy losses," as William Powell wrote.[15] But satisfied with the damage the Americans had inflicted, General Greene ordered a retreat with his force intact enough to fight another day.[16] Exhausted, the British did not pursue.

Historians record the battle as a victory for the British because, at the end of the day, they controlled the battlefield. The victory, though, was a Pyrrhic one as the British "paid dearly." Of a 2,000-man force, Lord Cornwallis lost a quarter of his men (532, with 93 killed and 439 wounded). By contrast, with a 4,400-man force, General Greene lost only six percent of his troops (78 killed and 183 wounded).[17]

Critiques of the American Effort

General Greene did not pay close enough attention to what Morgan had done at Cowpens. First, Greene's lines were too far apart, as has been seen, allowing the British to regroup before resuming their advance. Second, the distances between lines and the copse of woods between the second and third lines hindered communication and coordination of the overall effort. Third, the battlefield commander, Greene, was a thousand yards in the rear, his view blocked by thickets of trees. He could not see, let alone react to, developments as they occurred. In his defense, General Greene did not realize that the field of battle at Guilford Courthouse was much larger than it had been at Cowpens, as John Buchanan observed in *Guilford Courthouse*.[18]

Performance of the American force varies. The response of the North Carolina Militia, populating the first American line, has been a particular subject for debate. "Part of them began a fire, but a considerable part of them left the ground without firing at all; some fired once, and some twice," was General Greene's assessment.[19] British officers had a decidedly more positive view: "Colonel Dugald Stuart said that 'one half of his Highlanders dropt [sic] on the spot.'" Sir Thomas Saumarez, an officer of the Royal Fusiliers, "remembered 'a more galling and destructive fire'" from the American front.[20] When the British advance came close, however, the line did break. The time had come for a bayonet finish to the advance, a British hallmark, "not their [the Americans'] way of fighting," much feared by patriot militia. "Almost 1,000 terror-stricken men stampeded for the rear [dropping] weapons, ammunition boxes, knapsacks [and] canteens."[21]

The second line held steady for a time, putting up a withering fire but eventually gave way, as has been described. The third line, the line populated by Continental regulars, never gave way, instead repulsing two British attacks. Overall, General Greene was satisfied that his men had delivered a devastating blow to Lord Cornwallis's force, despite the Americans' abandonment of the battlefield. The latter, a British victory of sorts, only became possible because of the dogged British advance, its willingness to take losses, and its commanders several times stopping, reforming, and continuing to advance. The battle-seasoned British regulars were bulldogs.

Southern Brigadiers

Although the Battle of Guilford Courthouse took place in the South, the conduct of no brigadier, Southern or otherwise, rose to the level of having been "mentioned in the dispatches." In fact, only one brigadier general, Edward Stevens of Culpepper, Virginia, merited mention. General Stevens had been a general in command of several Continental regiments. He resigned his regular commission and returned to Culpeper, where the Virginia governor commissioned Stevens as a general in the militia (*see generally* Chapter 26). He led Virginia militia at Camden and Guildford Courthouse.

At the latter, Stevens was wounded in battle, his thigh shattered by a British musket ball. Before the battle, embarrassed by his men's rout at Camden, Stevens determined to forestall a repeat of Camden. He stationed forty sharpshooters to the Virginia militia's rear, with instructions to shoot deserters who attempted fleeing.[22] He broadcast the deployment to his men.

The Road to Yorktown

In summer 1781, Lord Cornwallis stayed within the South but went north, from North Carolina to Virginia. His force harassed Richmond briefly, forcing the Virginia Assembly to flee west to Charlottesville and Staunton. Cornwallis then took his footsore, weary force down the York Peninsula, where he expected a Royal Navy task force to evacuate his men and retire them to British New York. From August 13, 1780, when they left Charles Town, to early June 1781, when they marched down the York Peninsula, the British had zigged and zagged, tracing a large inverted "V." Charles Town was to the south and Yorktown to the north as the bases, and Charlotte at the apex. Carrying heavy muskets and with packs on their backs, British soldiers marched a thousand miles, probably more.[23]

Although in the South, Yorktown (more accurately the siege of Yorktown) did not feature Southern commanders or Southern troops. General Washington and the army of the Middle Department, assisted by Major General Marquis de Lafayette, marched south, conducting the siege.

Recovered from his wound at Guilford Courthouse, Brigadier Edward Stevens was present. No record of any participation by him in the siege exists. Of the Continental regulars, Brigadier Peter Muhlenberg did participate in the siege. A minority view holds that he, and not Lafayette, led the assaulting force that took the second British redoubt (Chapter 18). Across the York River, at Gloucester Point, George Weedon, whose resignation Congress had not accepted, commanded a force intended to tighten the American noose, cutting off any attempt to escape by British crossing the York River and fleeing northward. Weedon, however, was not present at the October 1781 ceremony when Lord Cornwallis surrendered, his men stacked their arms, and a British military band played "The World Turned Upside Down."

The war had not ended completely. Among other things, the British alliance with certain of the Indian tribes in the "Ohio country" continued to wreak havoc and present a threat to the emerging nation.

PART VIII

British Foment Among and Alliances with Native Americans

26

Attempts to Neutralize the Northwest Territory

George Rogers Clark of Virginia

In the Revolutionary War, America faced British threats from the north (Canada), from the east (along the Atlantic coast), from the south (British East Florida), and out of the west. From the west, the alliance of the British with Native American warriors could mushroom into a threat to the fledging nation. The British were stirring up trouble, as the French had twenty years previously. Historians have researched and written about the first two threats, less about the third, and about the fourth—scarcely at all. Two Southern brigadiers—George Rogers Clark and Lachlan McIntosh (Chapter 6)—played prominent roles in the army's effort to quell the threat, or at least to hold the Native Americans at bay.[1]

To hold the western threat in check, in late 1777, Congress sent a Virginian, George Rogers Clark, with a small number of soldiers west into today's Ohio, Indiana, and Illinois.[2] Clark fulfilled the mission assigned, earning the sobriquet "Conqueror of the Old Northwest."[3] It was an apt choice.

Many of the Southern brigadiers had in their youth been surveyors, but in nearby precincts. For example, Andrew Lewis and George Washington surveyed near-western Virginia, wilderness but still close by the Shenandoah Valley. By contrast, Clark's surveying ventures took him far west.[4] By 1772, Clark, "the rugged red-headed explorer," had surveyed the Kanawha River region of today's West Virginia. After mapping the Kanawha region, George Rogers Clark pushed west into Kentucky, where in the late 1760s, bands of settlers were beginning to populate the frontier. The tall, lanky surveyor, known for his "flashing black eyes," aided in pacifying the far west of that day.

The Original Colonies' Outsized Territorial Claims

Earlier the French had laid claim to the land west of the mountains, most of which they ceded to Britain by the Treaty of Paris (1763) ending the French & Indian War. Twenty years later, by 1783's (Second) Treaty of Paris, the British had ceded the wildness expanse to the United States, that expanse becoming known as the Northwest Territory.[5]

26. Attempts to Neutralize the Northwest Territory

Although it lay over the Allegheny Mountains from the major theaters of war, the Northwest Territory was known to be rich in forests, game, and arable land. The Native Americans—Shawnees, Mingos, Delawares, Miami, Pawnees, Wyandots, and Ottawas—resented encroachments into what they perceived as their territory. To partner with the native people, the British maintained a fort and a 300-man garrison at Detroit captained by deputy governor of Quebec Province, Harry Hamilton. Throughout the region, the British supported smaller fortifications such as at Vincennes on the Wabash River in present-day Indiana. Those British sought and formed trading and military alliances with the Native Americans, principally to counteract American claims to the territory. The British supported native raids in Ohio, Indiana, and south into Kentucky.[6] "Most Indians," though, "agreed that the British were vital trading partners—yet hardly considered them as the rulers of North America."[7] Still, in all, the British confederation with various native tribes was something that the Americans had to counter.

George Rogers Clark, by James Barton Longacre. Clark led American forces in the least remembered sector of the war, namely the west, where for the duration of the war British-inspired Indian raids threatened the new nation and its survival (National Portrait Gallery US).

East Rather than West

George Rogers Clark was one of six sons of John and Ann Rogers Clark, born near Charlottesville, on Virginia's piedmont, in the center of the colony.[8] While George was still a young boy, John and Ann Rogers Clark moved their family from Charlottesville to the east rather than to the west. The Clarks settled on 400 acres at the head of the Northern Neck between the Rappahannock and Potomac Rivers, in Caroline County, not far from Fredericksburg. Eventually, the Clarks amassed 2,000 acres.[9]

Rather than becoming a Virginia planter, George trained as a surveyor. At age 19, Clark set out on a surveying expedition to western Virginia. From there, as previously stated, Clark penetrated wilderness to map the northwest region of what in 1863 became West Virginia. Resuming a westward journey, Clark surveyed settlements in far western Virginia (Kentucky). One band of settlers there established a propriety colony known as Transylvania. But a single colony was not sufficient. After formation of several colonies, Kentuckians petitioned Virginia to assert sovereignty over the region. In 1776, Virginia Governor Patrick Henry did so. Along with the General Assembly, Governor Henry decreed the Virginia region beyond the Alleghenies the County of Fincastle, later Kentucky, the Union's fifteenth state.[10]

Clark's Military Career

In 1776, George Rogers Clark had traveled east to Williamsburg to petition Governor Henry for recognition of Kentucky. At the time of creating the new county, Governor Patrick Henry commissioned Clark a major in the Kentucky Militia, a unit within the Virginia Militia. "Clark convinced Governor Henry ... to provide powder to protect the state's western region. With black eyes flashing, he had succinctly stated, 'If a Country is not worth protecting, it is not worth claiming.'"[11] Emulating his brothers, Clark's military career began. His older brother Jonathan Clark was Continental Army major in the Revolutionary War.[12] Later, as an army colonel, younger brother William Clark co-captained the 1804 Corps of Discovery commissioned by President Jefferson to explore 1803's Louisiana Purchase.[13]

With his contingent of 200 men and promoted from major to lieutenant colonel, George Rogers Clark ranged far and wide in the Northwest Territory. On July 4, 1777, the Kentucky Militia under Clark raided the settlement at Kaskaskia, 100 miles "through thick forests" far into the Illinois Territory, in southwestern Illinois on the Mississippi River. Next, Clark and his men raided the settlement of Cahokia, once a center of the Illini Indian Nation, across the Mississippi from modern day St. Louis and a hundred miles north of Kaskaskia.[14]

Vincennes, Indiana, had begun existence as a principal French settlement in 1732, growing to a population of 600. After the French and Indian War, the British made Vincennes a center of their activities. Vincennes sat on the Indiana side of the Wabash River that today constitutes the southern 120 miles of the boundary between Indiana and Illinois. The British had a fortification there, Fort Sackville, named after British secretary of state for the American Colonies, Lord George Germain, who as a peer took the name First Viscount Sackville. After a 72-day march across the Illinois country, Clark and 170 Americans laid siege to the fort in February 1778. Two days later, the British surrendered. Clark's Americans captured Harry Hamilton, British governor of the Northwest Territory, who in December 1777 had arrived from his headquarters in Detroit with plans to reconstruct Fort Sackville as a sturdier outpost. Clark rechristened the fort as Fort Patrick Henry, after the Virginia governor who had sent him west.[15]

General Clark sent the "notorious" Hamilton back to Virginia where the colonials imprisoned him. "News of the indiscriminate murder of women and children and the cruel atrocities by Indians preceded Hamilton's arrival in Williamsburg where a curious crowd gathered to stare at him and his subordinates." Hamilton's "policy of giving rewards for scalps had earned him the name 'Hair-buyer' and the fear and hatred of local citizens."[16]

Clark's Achievements Generate Lasting Fame

Thus, by 1778, the American flag flew over three distant British forts. Virginia's legislators were "delighted to hear Clark's dispatch describing the three captures."[17] Clark returned to the Falls of the Ohio, in Indiana across from the site of Louisville, where Clark made a home on the Indiana side. But the British-inspired Native America raids continued. In June 1780, a combined native force of Shawnee, Wyandot, and Delaware raided into Kentucky, overtaking two settlements, capturing 200 women and children destined to become enslaved.[18] In August of that year, Clark led a force northward from Kentucky into Ohio, overrunning the Shawnee village of Peckuwe, at the site of present-day Springfield, twenty miles northeast of Dayton, Ohio. In 1781, George Rogers Clark became a brigadier general.

Native American raids continued while fighting in the east had ceased, by and large, after Yorktown in October 1781. In November 1782, General Clark again led a military force northward along the Miami River, flowing north from just west of Cincinnati, where the Miami flows into the Ohio River. Northward into the Ohio country went the Clark expedition, destroying native villages. The force reached as far north as Piqua, a native village. According to Professor Harry Ward, Henry Clay, later a United States senator and secretary of state from Kentucky ("the Great Compromiser"), as a young man served in Clark's campaigns.[19]

In 1786, after the Revolutionary War had long come to an end, native raids continued. General Clark led another large force of 1,200 northward from Kentucky father west, along the Wabash River. During that several weeks' foray, Clark's subordinates reported that he had been drinking heavily and was often drunk on duty. Clark asked for a board of inquiry, but the Virginia governor refused to convene one.

Retirement as an Indian Fighter

Clark again returned to the Falls of the Ohio, where he built a grist mill. There Clark drank heavily, struggling the remainder of his life with alcohol. His creditors besieged him for debts arising from his personal finance of various military excursions. He lost much of the land he owned in southern Indiana, where he once had 150,000 acres that Virginia settled upon him for his military service.

Due to the ravages of diabetes, Clark had a leg amputated. He could no longer operate the grist mill. He moved across the Ohio River to the town of Locust Grove, near Louisville, where he lived out his life in the home of his sister Lucy and her husband, Major William Croghan. George Rogers Clark died in 1818.

Ironies

Scholars have penned biographies, often obscure, about generals who were in the thick of Revolutionary War combat. For example, there are single volumes about George Weeden, William Davidson, or Charles Scott. About Andrew Lewis or Edward Stevens, for example, there are none. By contrast, historians have penned a dozen George Rogers Clark biographies.[20] Historical works contain lengthy passages devoted to Clark.[21]

The Midwest abounds with memorials, including statues of Clark, in Massac County, Illinois; Piqua, Ohio; Springfield, Ohio; Vincennes, Indiana; Indianapolis, Indiana (Monument Circle); Louisville, Kentucky (Riverfront Plaza); and Quincy, Illinois (Riverview Park). In addition, Fredericksburg, Virginia, and Charlottesville, Virginia (on the University of Virginia's grounds) have George Rogers Clark memorials. Illinois, Indiana, Kentucky, Ohio, and Virginia have counties named after Clark. Cities and towns include a Clarksville in Georgia, Indiana, Tennessee, and West Virginia. One of Chicago's main thoroughfares is Clark Street. Ships and major bridges have been named after General Clark.[22]

Why such lopsided historical treatment? An adage is that all politics are local. Much of history is local as well. Citizens can visit the sites at which George Rogers Clark had an impact, that is, in Kentucky, Ohio, Indiana, and Illinois. Clark's posthumous titles are intriguing, including "Conqueror of the Northwest," "Hannibal of the West," "Father of Louisville," and "George Washington of the West." Yet George Rogers Clark was another Revolutionary War general whose career plummeted after reports of excessive drinking destroyed his life but not his memory.

27

Postscript
Post War Biographies

John Ashe

Ashe commanded the North Carolina Militia 1776–1779. Prior thereto, as a senior militia officer, he led the men who captured the British Fort Johnson on the Cape Fear River, below Wilmington, North Carolina. As a brigadier, in 1779 he led North Carolina forces into Georgia, forcing Augusta's abandonment by British and Loyalist units. Ashe and his men gave pursuit, only to be surprised at the Battle of Brier's Creek, where the British inflicted 150 casualties while suffering only 16. Superiors threatened Ashe with a court martial for failure to post sentries. The court never took place, but Ashe surrendered his command. In 1780, becoming active again, Ashe was captured by the British in early 1781. On October 24, 1781, Ashe died of smallpox contracted while a prisoner of war. His remains were buried in the Ashe family plot on John Sampson's farm in Clinton, Sampson County, North Carolina.[1]

Richard Caswell

Richard Caswell was North Carolina's first governor, serving 1776–1780. He served in the Continental Army, but after taking umbrage over the appointment of William Smallwood, a Marylander, to command North Carolina's forces, Caswell resigned his commission and returned once more to political pursuits. In 1785, he became the state's fifth governor, serving until 1787. He died on November 10, 1789, in Fayetteville, North Carolina. His remains were removed to Kinston, Lenoir County, North Carolina, and interned in the Caswell Family Cemetery.

George Rogers Clark

Descending deeper and deeper into alcohol's clutches, General Clark lived out his penultimate days on a southern Indiana small holding. Nearer the end, he moved across the Ohio River to live with a daughter south of Louisville, Kentucky. George Rogers Clark died 13 February 1818. His grave is in Cave Hill Cemetery, Louisville, Kentucky.

William Lee Davidson

Brigadier Davidson died of a single musket wound to the chest in the early morning of February 1, 1781, leading militia impeding Lord Cornwallis's river crossing and foray into central North Carolina. After fording the Catawba River, British soldiers stripped Davidson's body of clothing, shoes, and weapons, leaving the corpse naked on the ground. Officers of the North Carolina forces removed his body to a tavern in Salisbury, North Carolina. He was buried in the grounds of Hopewell Presbyterian Church, Beattie's Road, Huntsville, North Carolina, north of Charlotte.

Isaac Huger

Somewhat of a rarity, Huger was of Huguenot rather than English, Scottish, or Irish stock, his family settling in Beaufort, South Carolina. He obtained early military experience under Colonel Thomas Middleton in the 1761 Cherokee Wars in the western Carolinas. In the Revolutionary War, he commanded the Fifth South Carolina. Congress promoted him to brigadier early in 1779. On June 20, 1779, he was wounded at Stono Ferry, and on March 15, 1781, he was wounded again at Guilford Courthouse. He was able to participate in the latter despite taking part in the earlier defense of Charles Town in April-May 1780. At Charles Town, he and his men were tasked with holding the last escape route from Charles Town. British Lt. Colonel Banastre Tarleton and his cavalry defeated Huger at Monck's Corner on the Cooper River above Charleston. As a result, Huger was not able to return to the city where, in that event, the British would have captured him. He died October 17, 1797, and was buried in a private cemetery at Huger Bridge, East Fork of the Cooper River, north of Charleston.

Andrew Lewis

After resigning his commission in April 1777, General Lewis continued to serve. He was a commissioner for treaty negotiations with Native American tribes, travelling to Pittsburgh for that purpose. In 1780, Virginia Governor Thomas Jefferson appointed General Lewis to the Governor's Council. While returning from a Council meeting in Richmond, Virginia Lewis fell ill near Bedford, and died on September 26, 1781. His remains were interred, finally, at East Hill Cemetery, in Salem, Virginia.

Lachlan McIntosh

Freed from captivity by the British in Charles Town and transported to Philadelphia, Brigadier McIntosh returned to Georgia when the war ended. He found his plantation in costal Georgia in ruins. He and his family relocated to Savannah where they owned a home. Lachlan McIntosh died on September 27, 1805. He is buried in the Colonial Park Cemetery, Savannah.

Hugh Mercer

The delegates to the Continental Congress remembered the dead during their Spring 1777 session. Army representatives bought General Hugh Mercer's body to Philadelphia, burying the hero with full military honors at Christ Church. On April 8, Congress approved monuments to the two patriot physicians who had "died in defense of freedom." One was to General Joseph Warren of Massachusetts, who had died at Bunker Hill in 1775, to be placed in Boston. The other was to General Hugh Mercer of Virginia, who in 1777 had died at Princeton, to be placed in Fredericksburg. In a further tribute, Congress stipulated "that the eldest son of General Warren and the youngest son of General Mercer be educated ... at the expense of the United States." George Weedon, the young Mercer's guardian, oversaw the matriculation and graduation of Hugh Mercer, Jr., from the United States Military Academy, West Point, New York.

Daniel Morgan

The "Old Waggoner," aged 45 or 46 but old beyond his years, journeyed to his home in Winchester, Virginia, after Cowpens (January 17, 1781). Morgan suffered various aches and rheumatism from his youth as a brawler and laborer. These afflictions laid General Morgan low, at times rendering him bed-ridden, but he rose again with vigor. In Virginia, he built a new larger home, Saratoga, east of Winchester.

Astonished by losses by Major General Arthur St. Clair to midwestern Native American tribes, President Washington announced formation of a super army to settle the frontier. Daniel Morgan wished to lead the new, larger expedition, but Washington appointed General "Mad Anthony" Wayne, imagining Morgan to be too fond of drink. In August 1794, feeling remorse and reconsidering his decision, President Washington called upon Morgan to lead a substantial element of the 12,500-man force set to quell the Whiskey Rebellion in Western Pennsylvania. Small-scale distillers had resorted to violence in protest over the federal excise tax on whiskey. Quickly quelled, the revolt subsided, and the federal troops marched home. They left behind General Daniel Morgan and his corps as the nominal occupation force, with Morgan becoming the de facto military governor. Morgan was a highly effective governor, administering and running government's affairs smoothly, discovering that he possessed political savvy.

Back in Virginia, Morgan, a Federalist, ran for Congress against Republican incumbent Robert Rutherford ("Old Robin"). Daniel Morgan ran twice, lost twice, and then on March 20, 1797, won the election. Morgan served one term only, abandoning Philadelphia because of perennial outbreaks of yellow fever in that city. Morgan returned to his older, smaller house, Soldier's Rest, near Berryville, Virginia. In 1800, his health failing him, Morgan moved into Winchester, there to live with his daughter Betsey and her husband Major Heard. General Daniel Morgan died on July 6, 1802. He is buried in Mount Hebron Cemetery, Winchester, Virginia.

William Moultrie

A British prisoner following the 1780 investiture of Charles Town, Brigadier Moultrie returned to his beloved Charles Town after regaining his freedom. He served as president, South Carolina Chapter, the Society of the Cincinnati. In 1785, he became governor of the state. He died on September 27, 1805. A state historical marker on Middle Street, Sullivan's Island, South Carolina, marks his final resting place.

Peter Gabriel Muhlenberg

Following the war, in 1783, Congress promoted Muhlenberg to major general, as Congress did for other brigadiers. In the same year, Major General Muhlenberg became a founding member of the Society of the Cincinnati, serving as president, Virginia Chapter. In 1783, he moved his family from Woodstock, Virginia, to his ancestral home of Trappe, Pennsylvania. General Muhlenberg did so because the abolishment of an official church in Virginia meant cessation of the governmental support for Church of England parishes, as had existed in colonial Virginia.

General Muhlenberg's political career began with his appointment as the commissioner to distribute grants of bounty lands to Virginia veterans of the war. In Pennsylvania, in 1785, he became a member of Supreme Executive Council of Pennsylvania, elevated to vice-president in 1787. Pennsylvanians elected Muhlenberg to the First, Third, and Sixth U.S. Congresses. In between the latter two terms, Muhlenberg lost elections to the United States Senate (in those days, elected by states' legislatures). Finally, during the Sixth Congress, the Commonwealth Assembly voted Muhlenberg a senator, albeit one who served two days. He resigned from the Senate to take the position of federal supervisor of revenue for Pennsylvania and later head of customs for the Port of Philadelphia. Upon receipt of the federal offices, General Muhlenberg sold his holding in Trappe and moved to Philadelphia.

General Peter Muhlenberg died on October 1, 1807. He is buried in Augustus Lutheran Cemetery, Trappe, Pennsylvania. The gravestone inscription reads, "Brave in the field, faithful in the cabinet, honorable in all his transactions, a sincere friend, an honest man."

Francis Nash

Struck by an errant British cannonball at Germantown on October 4, 1777, Francis Nash lingered for several days before dying on October 7, 1777. He was buried in the churchyard of Towamencin Mennonite Meetinghouse, twenty-two miles northwest of Philadelphia. Congress appropriated funds for a memorial honoring Nash's service, but the memorial was never built. The capital of Tennessee was named in Brigadier Nash's honor as were towns in several states.

Andrew Pickens

Another refugee from Pennsylvania, Pickens, his parents, and the Pickens family emigrated to Virginia's Shenandoah Valley. Several years later, they migrated again to the Waxhaw region on the North Carolina–South Carolina border, thirty miles east of Charlotte. As an adult, Pickens and his family journeyed further south, founding Hopewell Plantation in Abbeville County, South Carolina, in the far western part of the state, on the Cherokee lands border. There Pickens became a successful planter.

Later in the war, Pickens became a high-raking officer, later a brigadier, in the South Carolina Militia. A severe-countenanced, devout Presbyterian, his troops and others called him the "Fighting Elder." Tall, gaunt, and balding, he possessed a stern visage with an elongated head reminiscent of an El Greco painting or a scary movie villain. He tolerated no imbibing of alcoholic drink or cursing among his men. At Cowpens, Pickens led the militia that acquitted themselves so well. He also led South Carolina Militia at Kettle Creek, the siege of Ninety-Six, Eutaw Springs, and Charleston. He and his men operated with Brigadier Frances Marion, the fabled Swamp Fox whose hit-and-run raids became the stuff of legend.[2]

After the war, citizens elected him to the United States House of Representatives. He died on August 1, 1817. His burial site is in Old Stone Churchyard in Clemson, South Carolina.

Griffith Rutherford

Born in Ireland in 1731, Griffith Rutherford emigrated at age eleven, landing in America as an orphan as both parents died on the Atlantic crossing. He spent time in Philadelphia before heading south where in 1753 he put down roots in Rowan County, North Carolina. In the early 1760s, he led expeditions against the Cherokees in western Carolina, with future brigadier William Davidson serving as a junior officer under Rutherford. By May 1776, Rutherford was a brigadier in the North Carolina Militia, leading a large 2,400-man force against the Cherokees, this time stirred up and otherwise heavily assisted by the British. In June 1780, he led militia in the Battle of Ramsour's Mill, North Carolina, achieving victory over an armed Loyalist force. A short time later, in August 1780, he was wounded and then captured by the British at the Battle of Camden, South Carolina. Imprisoned at St. Augustine, capital of British East Florida, Brigadier Rutherford engineered an exchange approximately a year after his capture. After a short political career, in 1792 Rutherford relocated over the Appalachians to Sumner County (Gallatin), Tennessee. He died on August 10, 1805, and was buried in the Shiloh Presbyterian Church Cemetery, Rogana, in Sumner County, Tennessee.

Charles Scott

Obtaining parole from imprisonment at Charles Town, in 1785, General Scott led his family westward from Virginia, over the Blue Ridge and the Allegheny Mountains. Scott settled on the Kentucky River, in the middle of the Commonwealth, near the present-day site of Versailles, Kentucky. Once settled, General Scott led several successful militia expeditions against the Native Americans in the Ohio Country to the north as well as in Kentucky. "Our obligations to our country never cease but with our lives," John Adams observed, and Charles Scott evidently believed. In 1808, at age 69, General Scott ran for and was elected governor of the Commonwealth of Kentucky. He served a four-year term. Scott died on October 22, 1813. He is buried in Frankfort Cemetery in Frankfort, Kentucky.

Edward Stevens

Edward Stevens commanded a Virginia regiment in the Second Continental Line but resigned after the Battle of Germantown in 1777. He returned to his home in Culpepper, Virginia, where he had started out with the Culpepper Minutemen. From Culpepper, Stevens received gubernational appointment as brigadier general in the Virginia Militia, leading the Virginia regiment in the Battles of Camden and Guilford Courthouse. Wounded at the latter, he made his way back north to Charlottesville, Virginia, near Culpepper, where he recuperated. Later, he led a contingent of 750 Virginia Militia at Yorktown.

General Stevens returned to Culpepper, living until August 17, 1820. He is buried in the Masonic Cemetery in Culpepper, Virginia.[3]

Jethro Sumner

Born and raised in Virginia, where his family settled in 1691, Sumner was a subaltern in the Virginia complement in the French and Indian War, serving under George Washington. With Fort Duquesne neutralized and the war concluded in 1763, sometime thereafter Sumner struck out for Bute County, North Carolina (now Warren County, renamed after Brigadier Joseph Warren). There Sumner acquired extensive landholdings. At the formation of the North Carolina Line in 1776, the North Carolina Legislature commissioned Sumner colonel of the 3rd Carolina Regiment, and later Congress promoted him to brigadier.

Although not "mentioned in the dispatches," Sumner and his men fought at Brandywine and Germantown, retiring to Valley Forge. There Sumner became ill and was granted leave to return to North Carolina. After recovering, he led a North Carolina brigade at Stono Ferry. He then became ill once more. In 1780, the North Carolina Board of War combined regular and militia forces in the state. Further, they commissioned William Smallwood of Maryland commanding officer of the combined force. As with Richard Caswell, Jethro Sumner expressed extreme displeasure at not receiving the command and resigned. Still later, Sumner resurrected himself long enough to command the American right wing at the Battle of Eutaw Springs, the last major engagement of the war.

In retirement, Sumner became the first president of the North Carolina Chapter of the Society of the Cincinnati. He died on March 18, 1785, and was buried in the Guilford Courthouse Battlefield Memorial Park in Greensboro, North Carolina.

Thomas Sumter

Born in 1734, the "Fighting Gamecock" grew up in Hanover County, Virginia. He served in the Virginia contingent accompanying the British in 1755 on General Edward Braddock's failed expedition. In 1762, with Henry Timberlake escorting three Cherokee chiefs who desired to meet the king, Sumter traveled to England, where he stayed for three months, returning with the Native Americans to Charles Town. Destitute, Sumner returned to Virginia only to be incarcerated in a debtors' prison in Staunton. Having had enough of Virginia, Sumter migrated to Stateburg in South Carolina, where Sumner became a planter in the high hills of the Santee. In 1776, he became lieutenant colonel of the 2nd South Carolina, later commissioned a brigadier of militia in 1780. He saw no action in any major battles of the war, but he and his men harassed British and Loyalist units in South Carolina. He troops prevailed at Hanging Rock, South Carolina in August 1780, and against Banastre Tarleton at the Battle of Blackstock's Farm in November 1780, where Sumter was severely wounded in the shoulder. Tarleton uttered the compliment, he "fights like a gamecock." After the war, Sumner served four terms (not all consecutive) in the House of Representatives, 1789–1801, and just shy of two terms in the Senate, 1801–1810. Thomas Sumter died on June 1, 1832, at age 97, and is buried Thomas Sumter Memorial Park in Sumter County, South Carolina. Sumter outlived all Southern Revolutionary War major and brigadier generals.

George Weedon

Following Yorktown, General George Weedon returned to Fredericksburg, Virginia, where at his tavern he hosted a post-victory celebration that George Washington attended. Weedon served a term as mayor of Fredericksburg and another as president, Virginia Chapter, the Society of the Cincinnati. Having no children, General Weedon and his wife Catharine devoted considerable effort to the education of Hugh Mercer's five children. General Weedon died on November 11, 1793. He is buried in the Masonic Cemetery in Fredericksburg.

William Woodford

The British captured Brigadier Woodford at the fall of Charles Town. General Woodford was unable to work an exchange or obtain parole. Several months later, the British transported Woodford to New York City and imprisoned him, possibly aboard a prison ship in Wallabout Bay on the East River. General Woodford died on November 13, 1780, as a result of the harsh conditions of his confinement. He is buried in Trinity Churchyard, his grave unmarked and its location unknown.

Summary

These men exhibited extraordinary heroism in the war. Seven southern brigadiers died: John Ashe, William Davidson, James Hogun, Hugh Mercer, James Moore, Francis Nash, and William Woodford. Twelve of nineteen were wounded. The group's post–war achievements were also remarkable. Four became governors of the states they inhabited: Richard Caswell in North Carolina, William Moultrie in South Carolina, Thomas Nelson in Virginia, and Charles Scott in Kentucky, with Daniel Morgan serving as military governor in western Pennsylvania. In addition, two high-ranking militia colonels—Isaac Shelby and John Sevier (Chapter 22)—became governors of Kentucky and Tennessee, respectively.

Peter Muhlenberg served three terms in the House of Representatives as well as a brief term in the U.S. Senate. Daniel Morgan of Virginia and Andrew Pickens of South Carolina served in the House of Representatives. Thomas Sumter of South Carolina served four terms in the House of Representatives and not quite two terms in the Senate. George Weedon became the mayor of Fredericksburg, Virginia.

These brigadiers wore their records of Revolutionary War service and heroism like a valuable and cherished coat, acclaimed by the citizenry, and many times leading to political office or government service. It was said of veterans returning from the Civil War that "they were heroes all their days." In an earlier time, these men, the Revolution's brigadier generals, were doers, movers, and shakers. They too were heroes all their days.

28

Society of the Cincinnati

As their post-war records show, southern brigadiers were founders, presidents of state chapters, and otherwise active members of the Society.[1] What was, and is (it remains in existence), the Society?

With the British surrender at Yorktown in October 1781, General Washington removed the main army northward to Newburgh, 55 miles north of New York City, on the Hudson's west bank. There and across the river in Peekskill, Revolutionary War officers created the Society of the Cincinnati meant to be, among other things, a fraternal organization.

To the south of Newburgh, the City of New York remained the British army's American headquarters. American commanders' worries still existed, concerned that a British force could descend from Canada, as General Burgoyne's had in 1777, linking up with a British force coming north from the city. The combined British contingent could, belatedly, split the fledging nation in two.[2] Then, too, "There was always the chance that Britain would renew the struggle," Walter Isaacson observed in his Benjamin Franklin biography.[3] The American army's post–Yorktown positions along the Hudson, including Fishkill and Peekskill on the Hudson's east bank, permitted a quick American response should any do-over of the Burgoyne strategy take place. The do-over, though, never occurred. American military did engage in skirmishes with British troops, garrisoned outposts serving as pickets for the major American camps and patrolled the territory.[4] The war had not ended, despite Prime Minister Lord North's remark upon news of Lord Cornwallis's Yorktown defeat, "Oh, God! It's all over."[5]

American camps, though, were not beehives of activity. Days of idleness facilitated lengthy discussion and grumbling. Two major outgrowths were the Newburgh Addresses and the birth of the Society of the Cincinnati.[6]

The Newburgh Addresses

Not having received pay from Congress for two years, American officers banded together. In March 1783, the inner circle circulated draft letters intimating officers would invoke military force should Congress continue to ignore requests for back pay. The letters called for a meeting on March 10, 1783, to consider the letter and other resolutions.[7] George Washington learned of the proposed convocation: "Washington banned the meeting."[8] He shared the grumbling officers' sentiments but summoned the officer corps before him for an alternate forum a few days later, on March 13, at Newburgh's Temple of Virtue. In no uncertain terms, the Commanding General set down the superiority of civilian government over the military, the government for which the officers and soldiers had fought.[9] Author John Fitzpatrick described Washington, normally a paragon of self-control, as "sensibly agitated."[10] "How unmilitary! How subversive of all order and discipline!" General Washington condemned "the blackest designs" and "most insidious purposes" behind the cabal. To act against the government of the United States, would "cast a shade over that glory which has been so justly acquired, and tarnish [the] reputation of the army."[11]

"George Washington rarely addressed his officers as a group, but he showed himself a natural at it," Washington's biographer Ron Chernow found. Washington pulled from his pocket a letter from a Congressional representative who expressed sympathy for the army's plight. As Washington began to read the letter, he paused to pull his reading glasses from his pocket: "Gentlemen, you will permit me to put on my spectacles, for I have grown not only gray, but almost blind, in the service of my country." Washington's performance drew tears.[12] The Newburgh conspiracy dissipated, "averted," according to Chernow, "by Washington's succinct but brilliant, well-timed oratory."[13]

Historians cite Washington's Inaugural Address for his pronouncement of the superiority of civil authority over the military.[14] Some years earlier, General Washington's quick and decisive action in quashing the Newburgh Conspiracy firmly asserted civilian rule's primacy.[15]

The Society of the Cincinnati—Origins

The prime mover behind the Society of the Cincinnati's formation was General Henry Knox, the rotund Boston book seller who had served as General Washington's commander of artillery through the war.[16] "For some years" in the latter stages of the war, "Knox had been thinking about a ribbon that veterans might wear to show that had fought for the liberty of their nation. He envisaged a badge ... that could be passed from generation to generation," Edwin Hoey wrote.[17] Following the Newburgh letters' demise, in May 1783, a group of officers met at Varplanek House in Fishkill, New York, across the river from Newburgh. The house sheltered Major General Baron Friedrich von Steuben, who spearheaded the draft of the new organization's charter.

In part, the Society was to be a labor federation, given the backdrop of agitation for back pay. In part, the society was a fraternal organization to keep close those who bought about creation of the new nation and, in Edwin Hoey's words, "to preserve the camaraderie established by the war." And, in part, the Society was created to be the issuer of a credential and badge signaling to the public that the wearer had fought for liberty.

Yet, "some said [the Society's formation] was treason." Edwin Hoey continued, "The Society of Cincinnati ... would touch off an international furor and shake the wobbly foundations of the new American Republic. Along the way it would embarrass George Washington, distress John Adams, alarm Thomas Jefferson, amuse Benjamin Franklin, and in some way stir the lives of all leading Americans."[18]

The society's founders named the organization after the Roman General Lucias Quinctius Cincinnatus (519–430 BC), a retired general turned farmer who left his fields to lead once again Roman legions against an invasion. After having vanquished the threat, Cincinnatus returned to his farm. He is considered a legendary figure of civic virtue, a shining example of the citizen-soldier.[19] The Society's motto, "*Omnia reliquit servare republicam*" ("He relinquished everything to save the Republic"), honors Lucias Quinctius Cincinnatus's memory.

Ben Franklin Weighs In

Criticism swirled around the Society's charter provision that membership pass from veteran officers to first-born sons and thereafter to first-born sons in successive generations. This was primogeniture, in England the device used in both testamentary and intestate successions to pass peerages and titles to first-born sons and first-born sons only (*see* Chapter 17). Primogeniture was a central ingredient of the English system of classes and hereditary peerages that Americans found distasteful. Benjamin Franklin labeled the Society's embrace of primogeniture as creation of a new "order of heredity knights." Any form of hereditary nobility was, Franklin declared, "in direct opposition to the solemnly declared sense of their [Revolutionary Army officers'] country."[20] Further, said Franklin, "If honor had to be assigned in families, it ought to be handed *up* to parent rather than down to children."[21] Children, here the line of first-born sons, tending toward infinity, could neither take nor receive credit for the ancestor's service.[22]

George Washington's Ambivalence

Washington's views ranged from obdurate to ambivalent, with various gradations in between. In 1783, Washington consented to serve as the society's first president, "imagining himself signing on to a fraternal organization that was charitable in intent and incontrovertibly good."[23] Membership passed down through eldest sons, though, created a firestorm, engendering hostility toward aristocracy. To many Americans, primogeniture in a quasi-military organization raised the specter of a military caste that had as its intent domination of political life.

The Society's secretary general, Henry Knox, explained opposition to the society, telling Washington, "The [critics'] idea is that [the Society] has been created … to change our form of government."[24] The Marquis de Lafayette, head of the Society's French chapter, reported that in France, "Most of the Americans here are indecently violent about our association." Washington, though, could not merely wash his hands of the Cincinnati. Historian Ron Chernow wrote on Washington's predicament, "His first public act since the war had backfired, and it had engulfed him in a flaming controversy. Since the group's power derived largely from its identification with Washington, he lacked the option of staying aloof."[25]

At the Society's first general meeting, Washington was "fiery and outspoken." He advocated removal of political words and phrasings from the charter, elimination of hereditary succession to the first-born, and curtailment of admissions to honorary members. His efforts to purge the Society of features he thought objectionable were, by and large, unsuccessful.[26] Washington also wanted the Society to discard national meetings, relying on state-by-state assemblies. However, "Openly opposing him, the delegates voted to retain the general gatherings, and several state chapters refused to accept the alterations [proposed] ... leaving the hereditary feature intact."[27]

In 1786, Washington journeyed to Philadelphia to attend the Constitutional Convention. The Society of the Cincinnati's second triennial week-long general gathering was scheduled to precede the Constitutional Convention, also to be held in Philadelphia. Washington was in "a knotty predicament vis-à-vis the Society of the Cincinnati," for he had time to attend the annual meeting. Reluctant to become more involved with an association whose basic tenets, or some of them, he disagreed with, Washington came up with what Chernow termed "a clever alternative. Instead of attending meetings, he dined on May 15 with twenty members of the society, thus preserving a self-protective distance."[28]

Nevertheless, three days later, on May 18, Washington accepted a second three-year term as Society of the Cincinnati president. With respect to the society, he appears to have straddled the fence the remainder of his life. An example surfaced, at times, in his prominent wearing of the Society's insignia.[29]

Another Naysayer: John Adams

John Adams of Massachusetts "[a]damantly opposed hereditary monarchy and hereditary aristocracy in America, as well as all hereditary titles, honors, or distinctions of any kind."[30] Adams went overboard in this respect because his entire his life and political career were dogged by accusations that he was a closet monarchist. Adams "strongly opposed the Society of the Cincinnati, [an] association restricted to Continental Army officers, which had a hereditary clause in its rules whereby membership passed on to eldest sons."[31]

A Third Important Objector: Thomas Jefferson

Thomas Jefferson of Virginia followed John Adams as president. Like Franklin and Adams, Jefferson wholeheartedly opposed the Society. The society's "elitist character" squarely contradicted the notion of Jeffersonian democracy that contemplated farmers and tradesmen as equal participants in a republican form of government. After having consented to be the Society's first president, George Washington asked Jefferson, a fellow Virginian, what stand Washington should take vis-à-vis the new association. By letter, Jefferson replied that the Society "was contrary to the spirit of American institutions ... and that Washington's association with the Cincinnati sullied his character and renown."[32]

Jefferson opposed monarchy, seeing the Society as a handmaiden to potential imposition of a monarch and royalty in the United States. "In later years, Jefferson stated that it had 'always been believed' that some army officers, especially von Steuben and Knox, had offered a crown to Washington and started the Cincinnati only when he rejected it."[33] Von Steuben and Knox hoped "the hereditary order would be engrafted into the future frame of government and placing Washington at the head." Jefferson's vision of a potential monarchy was the strongest criticism yet of the Society and the danger it posed for the new nation.[34]

The Legal Framework

Founders of the Society operated in a new nation governed by the Articles of Confederation (1781). That document provided that no person "holding any office of profit or trust under the United States ... shall accept any present, emolument, office, or title of any kind whatsoever from any King, Prince, or foreign state; nor shall the United States in Congress assembled ... grant any title of nobility."[35] The Articles of Confederation clause had antecedents as old as the Dutch Laws of 1651.[36] And the prohibition, more broadly stated, carried over into the United States Constitution (1787): "No title of Nobility shall be granted by the United States."[37]

Neither under its wording, nor pursuant to a good faith argument for the prohibition's extension, did the potentially relevant provision affect the Society's practices. Instead, the Constitutional provision reflected the milieu of the times, the deep-seated distrust of any non-egalitarian organization that could easily tip over into a prohibited organization of titles and hereditary aristocracy.[38] Widespread at the time was a feeling that the Society could easily shade over into areas forbidden by the new Constitution.

The Society of Cincinnati Today

Today, existing as fourteen chapters (the thirteen original colonies plus France), there has been relaxation of the Society's eligibility rules. Some chapters have deleted the first-born requirement, while others retain it. The club's headquarters are at Anderson House, a Romanesque mansion on Massachusetts Avenue, just off Dupont Circle and at the start of Washington's "Embassy Row." Anderson House contains the office of the Society's permanent secretariat which, in conjunction with the chapters, conducts symposia and other presentations about aspects of the Revolutionary War.[39]

Chapter Notes

Introduction

1. Bertolt Brecht, *Life of Galileo* (New York, Grove Press, reprint, 1984).

2. North Carolina's James Moore died early in the war, from natural causes described as "gout of the stomach."

3. *See, e.g.*, H. W. Brands, *Our First Civil War: Patriots and Loyalists in the American Revolution* (New York, Doubleday, 2021).

4. See Chapter 8. After the fact, Congress did award many brigadiers with promotions to major general but did so based upon past accomplishment and toward or after the war's conclusion.

5. *See generally* Rod Andrews, Jr., *The Life and Times of General Andrew Pickens: Revolutionary War Hero, American Founder* (Chapel Hill, NC, University of North Carolina Press, 2017); William R. Reynolds, *Andrew Pickens: South Carolina Patriot in the Revolutionary War* (Jefferson, NC, McFarland, 2012); Craig Campbell, *General Francis Marion: Irregular Life of an Irregular Warrior* (Seattle, WA, Create Space, 2016); William James, *Swamp Fox: General Francis Marion and His Guerilla Fighters in the American Revolutionary War* (Whitefish, MT, Kessinger Publishers, 2010).

6. *See generally* Nell Moore Lee, *Patriot Above Profit: A Portrait of Thomas Nelson, Jr., Who Supported the Revolution with His Purse and His Sword* (Nashville, TN, Rutledge Hill Press, 1989).

7. See, *e.g.*, Emory G. Evans, *Thomas Nelson and the Revolution in Virginia*, 28 (Williamsburg, VA, Virginia Bicentennial Commission,1978): "Most [Virginians] had little or no military experience." Professor Evans was chair, Department of History, University of Maryland. So, too, in New England where some Revolutionary War officers (Generals John Stark, Moses Hazen, and Israel Putnam, for instance) had gained military experience in the French and Indian War, fighting with Roger's Rangers. *See, e.g.*, Richard V. & John F. Polhemus, *Stark: The Life and Wars of John Stark*, 43–79 (Delmar, NY, Black Dome Press, 2014).

8. Aside from Virginia's Muhlenberg, the other outlier was Lachlan McIntosh, the brigadier from Georgia.

9. George Washington to John Augustine Washington, August 5, 1777.

10. Henry Muhlenberg, *The Life of Major-General Peter Muhlenberg of the Revolutionary Army*, 454–455 (Philadelphia, PA, C. Sherman Painter, 1818, republished 1849) lists 58 brigadier generals and 28 major generals. He lists William Moultrie as a major general although Congress did not promote Moultrie until October 1782. Including Moultrie as a brigadier brings the brigadier headcount to 59.

11. The British imprisoned five of the nine (Brigadiers Moultrie, McIntosh, Hogun, Scott, and Woodford) in one fell swoop, upon the surrender of Charles Town in May 1780. *See, e.g.*, Chapter 10.

12. To obtain parole, a prisoner had to sign and execute an oath that he would never again bear arms against the British. Exchange involved no such restriction. If a prisoner could identify an officer of roughly equivalent rank for a proffered exchange, say a major for a lieutenant colonel, after the exchange the officers would return to combat roles.

13. Lynne Cheney, *The Virginia Dynasty: Four Presidents and the Creation of the American Nation* (New York, Viking, 2020).

14. *Virginia Dynasty*, IV.

15. Winston Groom, *The Patriots: Alexander Hamilton, Thomas Jefferson, John Adams, and the Making of America* (Washington, DC, National Geographic, 2020), reviewed by Jonathan Jordan, "Founding Brothers," *Wall Street Journal*, January 9, 2021, C-12.

16. *See generally* H.W. Brands, *The First American: The Life and Times of Benjamin Franklin* (New York, Doubleday, 2000).

17. *See, e.g.*, Stacy Schiff, *The Revolutionary: Samuel Adams* (Boston, MA, Little Brown & Co, 2022)(Sam Adams and Thomas Paine), reviewed by Adam Gopnik, "Finding the Founders: How Samuel Adams Helped Ferment a Revolution," *The New Yorker*, October 31, 2022, 62; Stephen Fried, *Rush: Revolution, Madness, and the Visionary Doctor Who Became a Founding Father* (New York, Crown Books, 2018); Harlow Giles Unger, *Benjamin Rush: The Founding Father Who Healed a Wounded Nation* (New York, Da Capo, 2018).

18. The terminology, "founding brothers" as opposed to "founding fathers," comes from Joseph F. Ellis, *Founding Brothers: The Revolutionary Generation* (New York, Vintage, 2002) (Hamilton,

Burr, Jefferson, Franklin, Washington, Adams, and Madison).

19. *The Life of Major-General Peter Muhlenberg, of the Revolutionary Army*, 2, 4.

20. *See. e.g.*, Albert Louis Zambone, *Daniel Morgan: A Revolutionary Life*, 309 (Yardley, PA. Westholme, 2018): "Today ... Morgan remains obscure" and, compared to Daniel Boone and Davy Crockett, Morgan suffers "from continuing obscurity." A library search reveals no less than twelve Morgan biographies. A list includes North Callahan, *Daniel Morgan: Ranger of the Revolution* (Arms PR, Inc., 1961); Michael Cecere, *A Good and Valuable Officer: Daniel Morgan in the Revolutionary War* (Berwyn Heights, MD, Heritage Books, 2019); Daniel Morgan, Nathanael Greene, et al., *The Battle of Cowpens: Primary and Secondary Accounts* (Regiment Press, 2019); James Graham, *The Life of General Daniel Morgan: Of the Virginia Line with Portions of His Correspondence* (1856) (republished by Andesite Press, 2015); Ronald Hamilton, *Daniel Morgan Forgotten Hero* (Seattle, WA, Create Space Publishing, 2015); Bob Hampton and George Schember, *Walking in the Footsteps of General Daniel Morgan* (Seattle, WA, Create Space—Amazon Publishing, 2016); Don Higginbotham, *Daniel Morgan: Revolutionary Rifleman* (University of North Carolina Press, 1979); Patrick K. O'Donnell, *Washington's Immortals: The Story of an Elite Regiment Who Changed the Revolution* (New York, Grove Press, 2017); James Kenneth Swisher, *Daniel Morgan: An Inexplicable Hero* (Virginia Beach, VA, Koehler Books, 2019); and Andrew Louis Zambone, *Daniel Morgan: A Revolutionary Life* (Yardley, PA, Westholme, 2019).

21. The latest is John Oller, *The Swamp Fox: How Frances Marion Saved the American Revolution* (New York, DeCapo, 2016, reprinted Hachette Books, 2020). Other biographies include Robert Bass, *The Life and Campaigns of General Francis Marion* (Kipara, New Zealand, Papamoa Press, 2017); Craig Campbell, *General Francis Marion: Irregular Life of an Irregular Warrior* (Seattle WA, Create Space, 2016); Cecil P. Hartley, *Heroes of the South; The Life of Francis Marion* (Seattle, WA. Create Space, 2012); General P. Horry and Parson M.L. Weems, *The Life of General Francis Marion: A Celebrated Partisan Officer, in the Revolutionary War, Against British and Tories in South Carolina* (Quantico, VA, Marine Corps Staff College, 2021); William D. James, *Swamp Fox: General Francis Marion and His Guerilla Fighters in the American Revolutionary War* (Whitefish, MT, Kessinger Publishers, 2010); and William Gilmore Simms, *The Life of Frances Marion: The Swamp Fox* (New York, Suzette Enterprises, 2019).

Chapter 1

1. *See, e.g.*, Patrick O'Donnell, *Washington's Immortal: The Story of an Elite Regiment Who Changed the Course of the Revolutionary War* (New York, Atlantic Monthly Press, 2016). Marylanders "were animated by the crown's brutal repression of Boston's rebellious citizens"; Serena Zabin, *The Boston Massacre: A Family History* (New York, Houghton Mifflin Harcourt, 2020). Seminal events for the revolution were in Boston.

2. *See* Ethel Armes, *Stratford Hall: The Great House of the Lees*, 113 (Garden City, NJ, Doubleday Doran, 1937).

3. *See also* Rick Atkinson, *The British Are Coming*, Chapters 1 "God Himself Our Captain" and 2 "Men Came Down from the Clouds", 35–82 (New York, Henry Holt, 2019). In Volume One of his trilogy, Mr. Atkinson devotes the entire opening discussion of pre-war events to Boston and New England. Only much later in his treatment does Atkinson deal with Virginia, beginning only with December 1775 and "Lord Dunmore's War." *See The British Are Coming*, 182–194.

4. *See, e.g.*, Mark G. Spencer, "Boston Tinderbox," *Wall Street Journal*, April 28, 2020, A-13.

5. *Our First Civil War*, 108.

6. Keep in mind that the entire American population was 2.5 million, including 800,000 held in slavery. Benjamin Franklin's estimate was three million residents in America's thirteen colonies. Isaacson, *Ben Franklin*, 303 (1775 letter from Benjamin Franklin to Joseph Priestly).

7. American Battlefield Trust, American Revolution FAQs, http://www.battlefields.org (visited December 19, 2019). The fourth largest city was Charleston, SC, (12,000 residents) and the fifth Newport, RI (11,000).

8. Oscar H. Darter, *Colonial Fredericksburg and Neighborhood in Perspective*, 106 (New York, Twayne Publishing, 1957).

9. Half in 1764 and half in 1773. See Charles L. Hamerick, *A Bag of Nails: The Ledger of George Weedon's Tavern in Fredericksburg Virginia*, IX (Athens, GA, New Papyrus, 2007).

10. *Colonial Fredericksburg*, 106.

11. John Goolrick, *Hugh Mercer*, 37 (New York, Neale Brothers, 1906).

12. George H. S. King, "General George Weedon," 20, *Wm. & Mary Quarterly* 237, no. 244 (1940):

13. Henry Augustus Muhlenberg, *The Life of Major-General Peter Muhlenberg, of the Revolutionary Army*, 42 (1818) (re-published, Philadelphia, PA, Carey & Hart, 1849).

14. *See* Nell Moore Lee, *Patriot Above Profit: A Portrait of Thomas Nelson, Jr.*, 235 (Nashville, TN, Rutledge Hill Press, 1989).

15. *John Adams*, 291.

16. The statute was one of the three achievements of which Jefferson was most proud. The other achievements Mr. Jefferson desired noted on his headstone were author of the Declaration of Independence and founder of the University of Virginia. At Jefferson's grave, nothing indicates that he was president of the United States, secretary of state, and governor of Virginia.

17. Hamerick, *Bag of Nails*, IX.

18. Joseph W. Waterman, *With Sword and Lancet: The Life of General Hugh Mercer*, 67 (Richmond, VA, Garrett & Massie, 1941) (Kessinger Reprint).
19. *Bag of Nails*, I.
20. King, "General George Weedon," 244.
21. Harry M. Ward, *Duty, Honor or Country: Gen. George Weedon and the American Revolution*, VII (Philadelphia, Am. Philosophical Society, 1979).
22. No traces of Weedon's tavern exist in Fredericksburg. The building was demolished years ago. The house George and Catherine Weedon built after the war, named the Sentry Box, still stands in east Fredericksburg, but, as previously noted, is in private hands, occupied, and may not be visited. Conversation by the author with Danelle Rose, Visitor Center Manager, City of Fredericksburg, Economic Development & Tourism, January 24, 2020.
23. *Life of Major General Peter Muhlenberg*, 42.
24. "The Boston Tinderbox," *supra*.
25. *See, e.g.*, Nell Moore Lee, *Patriot Above Profit*, 28.
26. That focus even intensified as Indian raids increased both in number and boldness after the abysmal failure of Braddock's expedition in 1755. *The First American*, 256.
27. Unlike certain other colonies, ruled by the crown and its ministers, Pennsylvania was ruled by the proprietors, William Penn and his successor, Thomas Penn. They vetoed any attempt to tax their vast land holdings. Extracting secret promises from their gubernatorial appointees, the proprietors obtained vetoes of all tax legislation purporting to govern or affect the proprietors (the Penns). "For the first twenty years of his political life [Benjamin] Franklin had fought the powers that be in Pennsylvania; now [in 1773] the contest with Parliament superseded the struggle with the Penns." *The First American*, 455.
28. *Our First Civil War*, 313–314.
29. *The First American*, 430.
30. As Pennsylvania and other colonies' representative in London, Ben Franklin had a "low opinion" of Lord Hillsborough as "proud, supercilious, extremely conceited (moderate as they are) of his political knowledge and abilities, fond of every one that can stoop to flatter him, and inimical to all that dare tell him disagreeable truths." Benjamin Franklin, quoted in *The First American*, 436.
31. Nikole Hannah-Jones, "The 1619 Project," *Sunday Magazine, New York Times*, August 14, 2019.
32. Nikole Hannah-Jones, quoted in Jake Silverstein, "A Nation of Argument: The 1619 Project and the Long Contentious History of American History," *Sunday Magazine, New York Times*, November 14, 2021, 42, 46, pointing out that editors added "some of" before "colonists."
33. Williamsburg had already become hotbeds of revolution fervor. Dunmore had dissolved the House of Burgesses and Virginia Assembly in June 1774. In May, the second of the five Virginia Conventions that replaced the Assembly passed resolutions for a day of fasting and prayer on June 1, 1774, offending Governor Dunmore. In April 1775, Dunmore ordered confiscation of gunpowder, stored by putative revolutionaries in a Williamsburg basement. Patrick Henry as well as others led revolutionary bands toward the Virginia capitol, Henry with 150 armed men from Hanover County. In early May, Dunmore issued a proclamation condemning Henry and his followers. Only after all these events did Dunmore issue his proclamation, after he had fled the capital city down the James River toward Norfolk. *See generally The British Are Coming*, 182–194. *See also* the discussion of Lord Dunmore's War in connection with Generals William Woodford (Chapter 8) and Andrew Lewis (Chapter 18).
34. Alexis Coe, *You Never Forget Your First: A Biography of George Washington* (New York, Viking, 2020). As noted, one early source of the theory was the *New York Times*'s "1619 Project." *Cf.* Peter R. Henriques, *First and Always: A New Portrait of George Washington* (Charlottesville, VA, University of Virginia Press, 2020).
35. *See generally* "The 1619 Project, https://www.nytimes.com/interactive/2020/2/1212/magazine/1619-project (visited September 17, 2020).
36. *See, e.g.*, Jason L. Riley, "Critical Race Theory Is a Hustle," *Wall Street Journal*, July 14, 2021, A-17.
37. Nikole Hannah-Jones, Caitlin Roper, Ilene Silverman & Jack Silverstein, editors, *The 1619 Project: A New Origin Story* (New York, Random House, 2021).
38. Woody Holton, *Liberty Is Sweet: The Hidden History of the Revolution* (New York, Simon & Schuster, 2021).
39. *A Nation of Argument*, 52.
40. Adam Kirsch, "What's Really at Stake in America's History Wars," *Wall Street Journal*, February 12, 2022, C-1.
41. Adam Rowe, in Rowe, "Liberty Is Sweet," *Wall Street Journal*, January 15, 2022, C-7.
42. *See Out First Civil War*, 24.
43. The thirteenth, Georgia, had a very small population at the time.
44. *See* "Populations of Great Britain and United States (1775)," http://www.encyclopedia.com (visited January 10, 2022). Massachusetts had 280,166 persons (4,595 enslaved). Relevant figures for Pennsylvania were 282,166 (6,769 enslaved) and for New Hampshire 81,300 (656 enslaved).
45. "What's Really at Stake in America's History Wars," C-2.
46. Ada Ferrer, *An American History—Cuba* (New York, Scribner & Sons, 2021).
47. *See, e.g., Cuba*, 91 ("[T]he Monroe Doctrine kept Great Britain—... the world's newest crusader against the slave trade—out of Latin America), 94 (the Monroe Doctrine "bolstered slavery and protected a wide rage if U.S. investments"), and 111 (similar).

48. *See, e.g.,* Patrick Spero, *Frontier Rebels: The Fight for Independence in the American West, 1765–1776* (New York, Norton, 2018); Woody Hilton, *"Forced Founders": Indians, Debtors, Slaves, and the Making of the American Revolution in Virginia* (Chapel Hill, NC, University of North Carolina Press, 1999).

49. Philip Vickers Fithian, *The Journal and Letters of Philip Vickers Fithian, A Plantation Tutor in the Old Dominion*, 110–111 (Williamsburg, VA, Colonial Williamsburg Press, 1957).

Chapter 2

1. John F. D. Smyth, in 1772, quoted in Darter, *Colonial Fredericksburg*, 62.

2. *See, e.g.,* Emory G. Evans, *Thomas Nelson and the Revolution in Virginia*, 28 (Williamsburg, VA, Virginia Bicentennial Commission,1978): "most [Virginians] had little or no military experience." Professor Evans was chair, Department of History, University of Maryland.

3. So, too, in New England where some Revolutionary War officers (Generals John Stark, Moses Hazen, and Israel Putnam, for instance) had gained military experience in the French and Indian War, fighting with Roger's Rangers. *See, e.g.,* Richard V. & John F. Polhemus, *Stark: The Life and Wars of John Stark*, 43–79 (Delmar, NY, Black Dome Press, 2014).

4. *See, e.g.,* David McCullough, *The Pioneers: The Heroic Struggle of the Settlers Who Brought The American Ideal West*, 33 (first settlers went by "wagon to the headwaters of the Ohio") and 40 (upon reaching the rivers, the pioneers "built a large roofed galley, forty-five feet in length and twelve feet wide … capable of carrying fifty tons" in order to navigate down the Ohio River) (New York, Simon & Schuster, 2019)

5. *See generally* Harry W. Ward, *Duty, Honor or Country: General George Weedon and the American Revolution*, 6–8 (Philadelphia, PA, American Philosophical Society, 1979). Weedon and troops under his command, 18 in number, joined others to form an eighty-man force. Led by Major Andrew Lewis (Chapter 8), himself a future Revolutionary War general, the Virginia soldiers marched westward, over the Piedmont and the Blue Ridge, into the wide Shenandoah Valley to Fort Loudon at Winchester, seventy-five miles from Fredericksburg. There Weedon and his recruits joined a larger force under Colonel Adam Stephen, also destined to become a Revolutionary War general.

6. *Duty, Honor or Country*, 13.

7. King, "General George Weedon," 241.

8. *Duty, Honor or Country*, 46.

9. *Duty, Honor or Country*, 45–47.

10. *Bag of Nails*, VII. A cadet in the Third Virginia Regiment was future president James Monroe.

11. *See generally* John J. Gallagher, *The Battle of Brooklyn 1776* (Edison, NJ, Castle Books, 2002).

12. George Weedon to John Page, September 20, 1776.

13. Ron Chernow, *Washington: A Life*, 254 (New York, Penguin, 2010).

14. *Duty, Honor or Country*, 60.

15. Described as a "a hotbed of English loyalism." *John Adams*, 294.

16. George Weedon to John Page, July 23, 1789.

17. *Duty, Honor or Country*, 70.

18. *Duty, Honor or Country*, 75. Soldier James Monroe was wounded in the assault.

19. George Weedon to John Page, December 29, 1776.

20. *Duty, Honor or Country*, 80.

21. *See generally* John T. Goolrick, *The Life of General Hugh Mercer* (New York, Nealie Publishing, 1906).

22. *See, e.g., Cabal*, 4: "True, Washington had stunned the British at Trenton and Princeton, but imperial forces were anything but defeated, and the Continental Army was still young and struggling to reorganize and replenish its ranks." *See also* Robert J. Schiller, *Irrational Exuberance* (Princeton, NJ, Princeton University Press, 3rd ed., 2016).

23. The other promotions were Poor, Glover, Patterson, Wayne, Varnum, De Haas, Muhlenberg, Cadwalader, and Woodford. On April 1, 1777, Congress also promoted Hand, Scott, and Learned to brigadier.

24. George Weedon to John Page, March 27, 1777.

25. Weedon and Greene were to form a close friendship that continued after the war concluded.

26. *See, e.g.,* Mark Edward Lender, *Cabal: The Plot Against General Washington*, 15 (Yardley, PA, Westholme Publishing, 2019).

27. Site of present-day Elkton, Maryland.

28. Louis Gottaschalk, *Lafayette Joins the American Army*, 40 (Chicago, IL, 1937).

29. *Cf.* Michael Cecere, *General William Woodford of Virginia, Revolutionary War Patriot*, 143 (Berwyn Hts., MD, Heritage Books, 2019 (Lord Cornwallis's force consisted of 8,000 British and Hessian troops).

30. Long Island involved 41,000 combatants while Brandywine involved 30,000. Third was the final battle of the war, Yorktown, which involved 27,000 men at arms. See FAQs, http://www.battlefields.org (visited January 12, 2020).

31. Almond's Remembrancer, *quoted in* Catesby Willis Stewart, Vol. 2, *The Life of Brigadier General William Woodford of the American Revolution*, 810 (Richmond, VA, 1973).

32. Harry M. Ward, *Major General Adam Stephen and the Cause of American Liberty*, 181 (Charlottesville, VA, University of Virginia Press, 1989); *see also* Michael Cecere, *General William Woodford of Virginia*, 145: "Over a third of the [3rd Virginia] regiment was lost in the fight, killed, wounded or captured."

33. Henry Lee, *The Revolutionary War Memoirs of General Henry Lee*, 89–90 (New York, De Capo Press, 1979).

34. *Washington: A Life*, 375.
35. *Duty, Honor or Country*, 106.
36. George Weedon to John Page, October 4, 1777.
37. George Weedon to John Page, October 8, 1777.
38. "Weedon's first introduction [his Quaker hosts] was a haughty display of his imperious temper, driving the poor, fatigued, and famished [soldiers] from the house [in which Weedon was to board] striking some of them with the flat of his sword ... calling them impious names for entering the house ...." Henry Woodman, *The History of Valley Forge*, 49–52 (Philadelphia, PA, Oaks, 1922).
39. *See Patriot Above Profit*, 326.
40. Douglas S. Freeman, Vol. 4, *George Washington*, 594 (Washington, DC, 1949). See *also* Ford, *Journals of the Continental Congress*, Vol. 10, 63 (Washington, DC, 1937).
41. *See, e.g.*, Ward, *Major General Adam Stephen*, 199.
42. As Stephen R. Taaffe in *Washington's Revolutionary Generals*, 150 (Norman, OK, University of Oklahoma Press, 2019) describes the events:
Because Woodford was not in the Continental army when Congress acted [ranking ten brigadiers], he became the most junior brigadier ... Woodford formally complained that he deserved to be senior to Muhlenberg and Weedon. Woodford had served as a colonel in the Continental army in 1775–76 before resigning in a dispute over [promotion of] Hugh Mercer [and Adam Stephen].
"Listening to the squeaky wheel," the Continental Congress "made Woodford the most senior brigadier, followed by Muhlenberg, Weedon, and Scott."
43. For example, earlier in 1777, New Hampshire's most celebrated Revolutionary War general, John Stark ("Live Free or Die") resigned his commission when Congress had promoted another New Hampshire officer, Colonel Joseph Reed, ahead of Stark. Stark wrote to Congress, "There are so many officers in the Continental army promoted before me that neither seniority or merit entitles them to and never was in an army until they joined the Continental service." Colonel John Stark, quoted on Richard V. Polhemus & John F. Polhemus, *Stark: The Life and Wars of John Stark—French and Indian War Ranger, Revolutionary War General*, 203 (Delmar, NY, Black Dome Publishing, 2014).
44. *See generally Stark*, 237–268.
45. George Washington to George Weedon, March 15, 1778.
46. *See, e.g., Major General Adam Stephen*, 210.
47. General George Weedon to Henry Lee, April 12, 1778.
48. Weedon and his wife Catherine had no children.
49. One hundred and seventy years later, the United States encountered the same expiring enlistments problem at the advent of World War II. In the original draft, in fall 1940, authorities signed enlistees to one-year terms of service that would have expired before the U.S. had even entered the war. President Roosevelt and General George Marshall, "in a paroxysm of political maneuvering," persuaded Congress to amend the statutes authorizing a draft. *See, e.g.*, Paul Dickson, *The Rise of the G.I. Army, 1940–41* (New York, Atlantic Monthly Press, 2020), reviewed in Peter Cozzens, "The Race to Get Ready to Fight," *Wall Street Journal*, July 16, 2020, A-15.
50. *Patriot Above Profit*, 385.
51. General Thomas Nelson, Jr., to General George Weedon, November 22, 1780.
52. *See generally Patriot Above Profit*, 390–392.
53. General Thomas Nelson, Jr., to General George Weedon, November 3, 1780.
54. Nell Moore Lee, in *Patriot Above Profit*, 391.
55. Relations between Lauzun and Weedon "were strained even before the two met." According to Weedon's biographer, Harry Ward, "Lauzun viewed Weedon as the boorish leader of a peasant army, while Weedon considered the dandyish aristocrat, who had obtained rank and influence at the French royal court, as nothing more than a snob." *Duty, Honor or Country*, 220.
56. George Weedon to George Washington, October 3, 1781.
57. Quoted in Rupert Hughes, Vol. 3, *Washington: The Savior of the States, 1771–1781*, 661 (New York, 1930). In another missive, Lauzun called Weedon "a coward and a sloth" and American militia "all cowards."
58. Andrew Zambone, *Daniel Morgan: A Revolutionary Life*, 159–160.
59. George Weedon to Nathanael Greene, February 17, 1781.

Chapter 3

1. South Carolina had a markedly smaller regulator-like movement. As David Russell explains, though, "The basis of the conflict" in South Carolina was "much like it was for its northern neighbor ... and was centered in the difference between the Lowcountry and Upcountry regions." Author Russell expands: "In the Lowcountry were the aristocracy with their plantations, their capital, their Charles Town, slaves, rice and indigo crops, Anglican religion, wealth, and a heritage of English peoples." By contrast, "The Upcountry was populated with small farmers, of moderate means and [with] few slaves, from Scotch-Irish and German families with some English .... These people were poorly educated and lacked the social standing of the Tidewater Lowcountry populace." David Lee Russell, *The American Revolution in the Southern Colonies*, 22 (Jefferson, NC, McFarland, 2000).
2. David K. Wilson, *The Southern Strategy: Britain's Conquest of South Carolina and Georgia, 1775–1780*, 21 (Columbia, SC, University of South Carolina Press, 2005), describes colonial North Carolina as composed of three sections: the tidewater, the piedmont, and the frontier.

3. "The piedmont or backcountry [was] a vast, relatively flat inland region between the tidewater and the mountains." The mountain region was "almost entirely patriot." Other regions were mixed. *Southern Strategy*, 21

4. *The American Revolution in the Southern Colonies*, 19. *See also* Hugh Owen Nash, Jr., *Patriot Sons, Patriot Brothers*, 16 (Nashville, TN, Westview Publishing, 2006): in 1764 "[a] group of North Carolina insurgents began to protest abuses of power by public officials and what was considered to be 'the ruling class' in North Carolina."

5. Again, South Carolina had more "political harmony but with a social fabric of significant contrasts." *See* John Richard Alden, *The South in the Revolution, 1763–1789*, 6 (Baton Rouge, University of Louisiana Press, 1957).

6. For example, in 1770, the colony's western regions had only 15 of 81 representatives in the General Assembly even though western counties accounted for one third of the population. *American Revolution in the Southern Colonies*, 19.

7. *Cf.* Joe A. Mobley, *North Carolina Richard Caswell: Founding Father and Revolutionary Hero*, 36 (Charleston, SC, The History Press, 2016): "The Regulator revolt cannot be interpreted as a direct defiance of king and Parliament and, as such, a prelude to the American Revolution,"

8. William Powell, *The War of the Regulators and the Battle of Alamance*, 5–6 (Raleigh, NC, North Carolina Division of Archives and History, 1975).

9. Quoted in *Patriot Sons*, 17.

10. Majoleine Kars, *Breaking Loose Together*, 157–158 (Chapel Hill, NC, University of North Carolina Press, 2002).

11. *Breaking Loose Together*, 159.

12. Powell, *War of Regulation*, 17.

13. *Patriot Sons*, 27.

14. *Breaking Loose Together*, 199–203.

15. *War of Regulation*; *North Carolina Governor*, 34.

16. *The American Revolution in the Southern Colonies*, 43.

17. *The Southern Strategy*, 23.

18. *North Carolina Governor*, 52.

19. *See generally* Mark M. Boatner, *Encyclopedia of the American Revolution*, 732–733 (Mechanicsburg, PA, Stackpole Books, 1996).

20. *The American Revolution in the Southern Colonies*, 59.

Chapter 4

1. In 1648, Oliver Cromwell and his supporters enacted a statute, the Self-Denying Ordinance, that barred altogether members of the House of Commons and House of Lords from serving in any military capacity. Cromwell excoriated military service by "members of the Commons and the Lords" because Cromwell thought "they were prosecuting the war incompetently and perhaps deliberately refusing to bring it to a quick end 'lest their own power should [terminate] with it.'" Barton Swaim, "A Plain Man, Warts and All," *Wall Street Journal*, December 28, 2001, A-15, quoting Ronald Hutton, *The Making of Oliver Cromwell* (New Haven, CT, Yale University Press, 2021). Of course, no such statute was in force at the times of Caswell's switches back and forth between political and military roles.

2. *The American Revolution in the Southern Colonies*, 47. When Royal Governor Josiah Martin refused to call the General Assembly to consider the election of delegates, "Speaker John Harvey went into a rage and proclaimed that the people would call an assembly without the governor." Showing further spunk, "The delegates felt it was better to meet right under the governor's nose in New Bern." Powell, *North Carolina Through Four Centuries*, 171. The delegates chosen were William Hooper, Joseph Hewes, and Richard Caswell.

3. *See, e.g.*, Joe A. Mobley, *North Carolina's Governor Richard Caswell; Founding Father and Revolutionary Hero*, 14–15 (Charleston, SC, The History Press, 2016).

4. *North Carolina's Governor Richard Caswell*, 95.

5. *See also* Chapter 8.

6. *See generally* Max Mintz, *The Generals of Saratoga: John Burgoyne and Horatio Gates* (New Haven, CT, Yale University Press, 1990); Richard John Alden, *General Charles Lee: Traitor or Patriot?* (Baton Rouge, LA, Louisiana State University Press, 1951); Dominick Mazzagetti, *Charles Lee: Self Before Country* (New Brunswick, NJ, Rutgers University Press, 2013); Phillip Pappas, *Renegade Revolutionary: The Life of General Charles Lee* (New York, New York University Press, 2014).

7. *See generally* Harry M. Ward, *Major General Adam Stephen and the Cause of American Liberty* (Charlottesville, VA, University of Virginia Press, 1989), and R.W. Dick Phillips, *Arthur St. Clair: The Invisible Patriot* (iUniverse, 2014).

8. After recovering from a bout of ill health, the father and the remainder of the family migrated to North Carolina as well. *North Carolina's Governor Richard Caswell*, 82.

9. Ron Chernow, *George Washington: A Life*, 147–148 (New York, Penguin Press, 2011).

10. *North Carolina's Governor Richard Caswell*, 22.

11. Further details may be found in Clayton B. Alexander & W. Keats Sparrow, *The First of Patriots and the Best of Men: Richard Caswell in Public Life*, 14 et. seq. (Kingston, NC. Lenoir County Colonial Commission, 2007).

12. *See* Malcom Ross, *Cape Fear*, 106–107 (New York, Holt, Rinehart & Winston, 1965).

13. *The American Revolution in the Southern Colonies*, 80.

14. In October 1775, the Provincial Congress had elected Moore as colonel of the First Continental Regiment of North Carolina. *The American Revolution in the Southern Colonies*, 80.

15. *See generally The Southern Strategy*, 25. (The battle site is seventeen miles above Wilmington.)

16. The Battle of Moore's Creek enjoys an out-sized account in many of the history books. *See, e.g.,* Chapter Six, "Moore's Creek Bridge," in *The American Revolution in the Southern Colonies*, 78–86; Chapter Three in *Southern Strategy*, 19–34; *Patriot Sons*, 48–52; and, of course, Chapter Three, in *North Carolina's Governor Richard Caswell*, 37–58.

17. *The Southern Strategy*, 27.

18. Creek's dimensions are from *North Carolina's Governor Richard Caswell*, 53.

19. *The Southern Strategy*, 27.

20. There exists some dispute about the size of the loyalist force at that point (1,600?, 1,400?, fewer?). *See* Hugh F. Rankin, *The Moore's Creek Bridge Campaign, 1776*, 33 (1980) (Currie, NC, Eastern National, reprint edition 1998). *See also The Southern Strategy*, 28: "The Loyalist army was in bad shape due to rampant desertions …. The loyalist army was now reduced to only six hundred Highlanders and one hundred or two hundred Regulators."

21. Colonel Alexander Lillington's Wilmington Minutemen (150) and Colonel John Ashe's New Hanover Rangers (100) had joined Caswell and the New Bern Militia at Moore Creek. *See Southern Strategy*, 33–34.

22. *The Southern Strategy*, 29.

23. *The Southern Strategy*, 30; *North Carolina's Governor Richard Caswell*, 55.

24. *See, e.g., Patriot Sons*, 50.

25. Colonel James Moore, quoted in Henry Steele Commager & Richard B. Morris, *The Spirit of Seventy-Six*, 115 (1958) (New York, Harper and Row, reprint edition 1998).

26. Reported by William Powell in *North Carolina Through Four Centuries*, 180 (Chapel Hill, NC, University of North Carolina Press, 1989).

27. *See, e.g., Patriot Sons*, 49.

28. Hugh Rankin, an eminent scholar of North Carolina's wartime experience, maintains that "the real hero of the campaign was James Moore, although he was not a participant in the ultimate battle. It was Moore, with all the finesse of a master chess player, who maneuvered his troops in such a fashion to effectively seal off the loyalists from their objective and force them to do battle on ground of his choosing." Hugh Rankin, *The North Carolina Continentals*, 53–54 (Chapel Hill, NC, University of North Carolina Press, 2d edition, 2005).

29. *Southern Strategy*, 91, 251.

30. *North Carolina's Governor Richard Caswell*, 55.

31. *The Southern Strategy*, 33.

32. *Patriot Sons*, 53.

33. *See* Staff, "Chronology of North Carolina's Governors," available at http://www/ncpedia.org (visited December 22, 2021).

34. *North Carolina's Governor Richard Caswell*, 68.

35. *North Carolina Through Four Centuries*

36. *North Carolina's Governor Richard Caswell*, 60.

37. *North Carolina's Governor Richard Caswell*, 70.

38. *North Carolina's Governor Richard Caswell*, 74.

39. Rankin, *North Carolina Continentals*, 235.

40. *North Carolina's Governor Richard Caswell*, 75–76.

41. Dean Snow, *1777: Turning Point at Saratoga*, 18. Ron Chernow, in *Washington: A Life*, 182, was perhaps less charitable, describing Gates as "a ruddy, thickset man, with a large aquiline nose and long hair flowing over his shoulders from a receding hairline." Presaging the commander-in-chief's later assessment, Chernow writes, "As Washington was to discover, Gates had more than a trace of egotism and duplicity in his character."

42. *The Battle of Camden*, 13.

43. Hoffman Nickerson, *The Turning Point of the Revolution: Burgoyne in North America*, 277, 282 (Boston, MA, Houghton Mifflin, 1928).

44. On the other side of the ledger, examining several generals of the Revolution, historian Lynn Montross found that from 1778 onward, "There was a campaign of character assassination [against Gates] that has few parallels in American history." Gates "was attacked at every opportunity." Lynn Montross, *Ragtail and Bobtail: The Story of the Continental Army, 1775–1783*, 222 (NY, 1952).

45. *The American Revolution in the Southern Colonies*, 163

46. M.F. Treacy, *Prelude to Yorktown, the Southern Campaign of Nathanael Greene, 1780–1781*, 25 (Chapel Hill, NC, University of North Carolina Press, 1963).

47. *Our First Civil War*, 302.

48. Ortho Holland Williams, "A Narrative of the 1780 Campaign by Ortho Holland Williams, Adjutant General," in *The Papers of General Nathanael Greene*, Vol. 1, 486 (Charleston, SC, 1822).

49. Rankin, *North Carolina Continentals*, 242.

50. The actual number of "effectives" in Gates's "Grand Army," as he called it, beginning the march to Camden was 3,052 according to one source. *See Road to Guilford Courthouse*, 161.

51. *Road to Guilford Courthouse*, 153, 157–158.

52. *Road to Guilford Courthouse*, 161.

53. Williams, *Narrative*, 494–495.

54. *Road to Guilford Courthouse*, 163.

55. General Horatio Gates to the Continental Congress, August 20, 1780.

56. Garret Wats, quoted in John C. Dann, *The Revolution Remembered: Eyewitness Accounts of the War for Independence*, 194 (Chicago, IL, University of Chicago Press, 1980).

57. *North Carolina's Governor Richard Caswell*, 78. Compare the quotation with the following: "Caswell made three attempts to rally his men and establish an orderly withdrawal." *North Carolina's Governor Richard Caswell*, 79.

58. *Road to Guilford Courthouse*, 172.
59. *North Carolina's Governor Richard Caswell*, 83.
60. *See* Staff, "Chronology of North Carolina's Governors," available at http://www/ncpedia.org (visited December 29, 2021).
61. John Buchanan in *Road to Guilford Courthouse*, 172.
62. *See* C.B. Alexander, "Richard Caswell: Versatile Leader of the Revolution," *North Carolina Historical Review*, April 1946, 23.
63. *North Carolina's Governor Richard Caswell*, 123.
64. Rankin, *North Carolina Through Four Centuries*.

Chapter 5

1. *See* "Population of Great Britain and America, 1775," available http://www.encylopedia.com (visited January 23, 2022).
2. Coleman, *The Revolutionary War in Georgia*, 96–100.
3. *This Cursed War*, 10–11.
4. On Georgia's radicals versus conservatives of those times, *see generally* Daniel McDonald Johnson, *This Cursed War: Lachlan McIntosh in the American Revolution*, 39–75 (Allendale, SC, self-published, 2018); *Politics of Revolutionary Georgia*, 21 et seq.
5. Martha Condray Searcy, *The Georgia-Florida Contest in the American Revolution, 1776–1778*, 56, 61–62 (Tuscaloosa, AL, University of Alabama Press, 1985). *See also* Coleman, *The American Revolution in Georgia*, 102.

Chapter 6

1. Mark Van Doren, editor, *The Travels of William Bartram*, 39–40 (Amazon CreateSpace, Scotts Valley, CA, 2016). Bartram was an American naturalist who travelled through the South and among Native tribes, 1773–1777.
2. *See, e.g.*, the McIntosh portrait on the cover of Harvey H. Jackson, *Lachlan McIntosh and the Politics of Revolutionary Georgia*, 118 (Athens, GA, University of Georgia Press, 1979).
3. Quoted in *Lachlan McIntosh and the Politics of Revolutionary Georgia*, 118.
4. *Politics of Revolutionary Georgia*, 111
5. Many brigadier generals, especially southern ones (William Woodford, Charles Scott, Peter Muhlenberg, Jethro Sumner), entangled themselves in disputes over promotions, seniority, and actual resignations (George Weedon, Muhlenberg, Sumner). Pronounced senses of honor precipitated extreme reactions to perceived slights. *See, e.g.*, Chapter 20. Another characteristic of such snits and perceived maltreatment, though, was that, by and large, they originated within and remained within the Continental Army's four corners.
6. *Our First Civil War*, 137.
7. Charles W. Heathcote, "General Lachlan McIntosh," Historic Valley Forge, 1, available https://www.ushistory.org/valleyforge/served/mcintosh.html: "Laurens would become a very good friend ... wield[ing] an unusual influence over the maturing life of Lachlan McIntosh."
8. *See generally Revolutionary Georgia*, 33–37.
9. Recorded in *Revolutionary Georgia*, 5.
10. Percy Scott Flippin, "Royal Government in Georgia. 1752–1776: The Land System," 1926 *Georgia History Quarterly* 1, no. 25 (March 1926).
11. For instance, the piedmont and Shenandoah Valley in Virginia, around Salisbury in North Carolina, or Camden and vicinity in South Carolina.
12. Conservatives centered on Christ Church Parish and the Savannah area. "Radicals" were centered in mid coastal Georgia (St. John's Parish) extending north to Sunbury, once a town of 1,000 persons that no longer exists. *See, e.g.*, Paul McIlvaine, *The Dead Town of Sunbury* (self-published, 1971).
13. *See, e.g., Politics of Revolutionary Georgia*, 21: "By 1760 the colony's older areas, particularly along the coast and up the Savannah River [Savannah and the surrounding Christ Church Parish], had fashioned a political coalition based upon family ties, economic conditions, and social compatibility." The coalition members tended to be whigish, if not Tory. They termed themselves conservatives," although elements of the populace termed them the "merchant party" or "the city party."
14. *See generally* E. Merton Coulter, *Georgia: A Short History*, 130–135 (Chapel Hill, NC, University of North Carolina Press, 1960). *See also* Kenneth Coleman, *The American Revolution in Georgia*, 82–89 (Athens, GA, University of Georgia Press, 1958).
15. *This Cursed War*, 44.
16. *Politics of Revolutionary Georgia*, 24.
17. *See generally* Charles F. Jenkins, *Button Gwinnett*, 21–69 (New York, Doubleday & Page, 1926).
18. Jenkins, *Button Gwinnett*, 31.
19. *Politics of Revolutionary Georgia*, 33.
20. *Politics of Revolutionary Georgia*, 38.
21. Martha Condray Searcy, *The Georgia-Florida Contest in the American Revolution, 1776–1778*, 56, 61–62 (Tuscaloosa, AL, University of Alabama Press, 1985). *See also* Coleman, *The American Revolution in Georgia*, 102.
22. *See, e.g.*, Heathcote, "General Lachlan McIntosh," 2.
23. *Politics of Revolutionary Georgia*, 55.
24. Coleman, *The Revolutionary War in Georgia*, 82–89. *See also* Coulter, *Georgia: A Short History*, 134–135.
25. *This Cursed War*, 47.
26. *This Cursed War*, 60.
27. Lachlan McIntosh to South Carolina's Henry Laurens, May 30, 1777, reproduced in Jenkins, *Button Gwinnett*, 254–255.
28. *Revolutionary Georgia*, 61.
29. *Revolutionary Georgia*, 61.

30. *Revolutionary Georgia*, 58–64.
31. Jenkins, *Button Gwinnett*, 108–110.
32. Coleman, *Revolution in Georgia*, 103. See also Jenkins, *Button Gwinnett*, 218–219.
33. William Belcher, ed., 1777, on file Rare Bookroom, Library of Congress, Washington, D.C.
34. The dueling episode is described in Jenkins, *Button Gwinnett*, 229–240. The duel has been termed "the most famous duel in Georgia history." March 5, *Today in Georgia History*, available https://www.todayingeorgiahistory.org/content/lachlan-mcintosh (visited July 6, 2021).
35. *This Cursed War*, 60.
36. Coleman 87–89; Coulter 134–135.
37. *Revolutionary Georgia*, 65–66.
38. See generally *This Cursed War*, 64–67.
39. Reproduced in *Revolutionary Georgia*, 71.
40. Although Professor Stephen Taaffe, in *Washington's Revolutionary War Generals*, 132–133 (Norman, OK, University of Oklahoma Press, 2019) gives scant mention to Lachlan McIntosh, he does label McIntosh "a troublesome general." Congress, Professor Taaffe writes, "authorized [General Howe] to relieve one troublesome general, Brig. Gen. Lachlan McIntosh, and send him to Washington's army."
41. *This Cursed War*, 75.
42. *Washington's Revolutionary War Generals*, 153. Cf. *Washington's Revolutionary War Generals*, 132 (McIntosh was "one troublesome general"). Author Taaffe's depiction of Lachlan McIntosh seems inaccurate and unjustified.
43. See Hugh F. Rankin, *The North Carolina Continentals*, 139 (Chapel Hill, NC, University of North Carolina Press, republished 2005).
44. George Washington to Lachlan McIntosh, May 26, 1778, reproduced in Heathcote, "General Lachlan McIntosh," 3. McIntosh's biographer termed the posting assignment "the greatest responsibility of McIntosh's career." *This Cursed War*, 79.
45. *Our First Civil War*, 11.
46. As John Sugde wrote in his biography of Shawnee chieftain, *Tecumseh*, "In the American settlements of the old Northwest there were many who charged the British with encouraging Indian hostility to the United States and furnishing angry warriors with arms." Native American chief "[Blue Jacket] remembered how Indians ... had been used as pawns by both the French and the British." John Sugde, *Tecumseh: A Life*, 4 & 5 (New York, Henry Holt, 1997).
47. Washington "whose vision of the future on the United States included western expansion," and who himself owned title or claims to vast tracts of Ohio River Valley lands, chose a Southerner because "he wanted a commander who could remain neutral." Besides opposing the British as well as the Shawnee, Patowamies, Kickapoos, Miamis, Wyandots, Chippewas, Mingos, and a dozen other tribes, the new commander would be buffeted by "competing claims by land companies, speculators, colonizers, and state officials from Pennsylvania and Virginia." *Politics of Revolutionary Georgia*, 74–75.
48. Brodhead consistently second-guessed McIntosh's decisions, becoming a thorn in McIntosh's side. See Louise Phelps Kellogg, *Frontier Advance on the Upper Ohio, 1778–1779*, 15, 61–88 (Madison, WI, Collections of the State Historical Society, 1916)
49. See generally Edward G. Williams, "General Lachlan McIntosh's Expedition, 1778," 43 *Western Pennsylvania Historical Magazine*, 282–288 (1960).
50. Kellogg, *Frontier Advance on the Upper Ohio, 1778–1779*, 256–257.
51. Kellogg, *Frontier Advance on the Upper Ohio, 1778–1779*, 240–242.
52. Kellogg, *Frontier Advance on the Upper Ohio, 1778–1779*, 185.
53. Quoted in Kellogg, *Frontier Advance on the Upper Ohio, 1778–1779*, 210
54. Kellogg, *Frontier Advance on the Upper Ohio, 1778–1779*, 208.
55. "General McIntosh ...[is] universally hated by every man in this department, both civil and military. [W]hatever his capacity may be for conducting another campaign, I fear he will not have it in his power to do anything salutary .... There is not an officer who does not appear to be exceedingly disgusted" with McIntosh. Daniel Brodhead to General George Washington, January 16, 1779, reproduced in Kellogg, *Frontier Advance on the Upper Ohio, 1778–1779*, 200. A source of Brodhead's disenchantment with McIntosh was Brodhead's belief that McIntosh consistently favored Virginia's interests over Pennsylvania's. Reasons for Washington's rapid dismissal of such accusations was that not only was Washington a Virginian and fellow Southerner, he also was a friend of McIntosh's, a fellow planter, a fellow member of the coastal aristocracy. In addition, Washington was more than cross wise with Major General Thomas Mifflin, Brodhead's brother-in-law, who had been an instigator of the 1777–1778 Conway Cabal whose aim was to replace Washington as commander-in-chief, possibly with Major General Horatio Gates.
56. *Politics of Revolutionary Georgia*, 91.
57. *Politics of Revolutionary Georgia*, 94.
58. See Benjamin Kennedy, Ed., *Muskets, Cannon Balls & Bombs: Nine Narratives of the Siege of Savannah in 1779*, 188 (Savannah, GA, Beehive Press, 1974). See also Alexander A. Lawrence, *Storm Over Savannah: The Story of Count d'Estaing and the Siege of the Town in 1779* (Athens, GA, University of Georgia Press, 1951).
59. See generally *This Cursed War*, 110–114.
60. *Politics of Revolutionary Georgia*, 100.
61. See *This Cursed War*, 126.
62. Edward Cashin & Heard Robertson, *Augusta and the American Revolution: Events in the Georgia Back Country, 1773–1783*, 5–9 (Darien, GA, Ashantilly Press, 1975).
63. See generally Lawrence A. Alexander, "General Lachlan McIntosh and His Suspension from

Continental Command During the Revolution," 38, *Georgia Historical Quarterly*, No. 2, 101–102 & 101–141.

64. Continental Congress President Samuel Huntington to General Lachlan McIntosh, February 15, 1780.

65. *See also Politics of Revolutionary Georgia*, 105.

66. *See generally* Carl P. Borick, *A Gallant Defense: The Siege of Charleston, 1780*, 104–126 (Columbia, SC, University of South Carolina Press, 2003).

67. See Vol. 2 William Moultrie, *Memoirs of the American Revolution*, 116–118 (1802) (re-published, New York, New York Times and Arno Press, 1968).

68. *Politics of Revolutionary Georgia*, 149.

69. *This Cursed War*, 159.

70. Lawrence, *Suspension from Continental Command During the Revolution*, 132.

71. Edward G. Williams, Editor, "A Revolutionary Journal and the Orderly Book of General Lachlan McIntosh's Expedition, 1778," 1960, *Western Pennsylvania Historical Magazine*, 157, 162.

72. No fewer than ten books memorializing Button Gwinnett exist. *See, e.g.,* Denny Magic, *Button Gwinnett: The Making of a Statesman* (San Francisco, CA, Independent, 2018); Colin Gwinnett Sharp, *Button Gwinnett: Failed Merchant, Plantation Owner, Mountebank, Opportunistic Politician and Founding Father* (Shrewsbury, UK, YouCaxton, 2015); William Montgomery Clemens, *Button Gwinnett, Man of Mystery: Member of the Continental Congress: Signer of the Declaration of Independence* (Andesite Press, 2015); D.J. Drewien, *Button Gwinnett: A Historiography of the Georgia Signer of the Declaration of Independence* (Pittsburgh, PA, Dorrance Publishing, 2007); Charles Francis Jenkins, *Button Gwinnett, Signer of the Declaration of Independence* (New York, Doubleday, Page & Co., 1926). *See also* Joseph Edward Fields, *The Known Signatures of Button Gwinnett* (Commission, 1950).

73. Further evidence is that Atlanta, Georgia's most populous, well-known suburban county is Gwinnett, with a 2019 population of 936,250. One of Georgia's smallest (population 14,378) counties, located on the southwest Georgia coast, is McIntosh County, with the county seat at Darien.

74. In 1780, a letter by Georgia Governor Walton and his Council capsulating an alleged legislative resolution issued forth to the Continental Congress. The letter read, "Georgia has such a Repugnance to General McIntosh ... [Georgians] would not turn out under his Command." McIntosh's detractors therefore requested that McIntosh be employed in some other department. Continuing, the letter deemed it "highly necessary that Congress would while General McIntosh was in the service of the United States direct him to some distant field for the exercise of his abilities." Council Resolution in Lilla M. Hawes, Papers of Lachlan McIntosh, 83 (Savannah, GA, Georgia Historical Society, 1957). Upon learning of the letter, Speaker of the Georgia Assembly, William Glasscock, who supposed had been the signatory, declared the letter "a flagrant forgery." He avowed that McIntosh had served Georgia well and that McIntosh "ought to receive the Grateful testimonials of Publick approbation, instead of the malicious insinuations of Private Slander." Affidavit of William Glasscock, Hawes, Papers of Lachlan McIntosh, at 124–125. The exchange represents one more set of unfair and libelous utterances and accusations that must have seemed to McIntosh and others as having no end in sight. The lengthy chain of criticisms and accusations also reflected the state of that era's Georgia politics, schizophrenic at best, with a dominant personality pursuing parochial interests and petty quarrels rather than a dedication to the emerging new nation and independence from Britain.

Chapter 7

1. Rice, *Allegheny Frontier*, 80

2. Reported to be a 1,000-warrior force in *Adam Stephen and the Cause of American Liberty*, 110.

3. *See generally* Phillip Sturm, "The Battle of Point Pleasant," *West Virginia Encyclopedia* (2016), available https://www.wvencyclopedia.org (visited October 18, 2020). *See also* "Lord Dunmore's War and the Battle of Point Pleasant," available https://www.OhioHistoryCentral.org (visited October 18, 2020).

4. Professor Harry Ward, in *Adam Stephen and the Cause of American Liberty*, 110.

5. *West Virginia Roots*, 2.

6. The poem many school children learn is the "Concord Hymn" by Ralph Waldo Emerson

By the rude bridge that arched the flood,
Their flag unfurled by the April breeze,
Here once the embattled farmers stood,
And fired the shot heard round the world.

See, e.g., http://poets.org/poem/concord-hymn (visited January 27, 2022). No comparable poems memorialize Point Pleasant.

Chapter 8

1. Quoted in Livia Simpson-Proffenbarger, "The Battle of Point Pleasant; A Battle of the Revolution," *Point Pleasant Star-Gazette*, October 10, 1974.

2. Quoted in Nathan Zipfel, "The Battle of Point Pleasant," in *West Virginia Roots*, available www.wv-roots.org/index.php/book-and-journal-archives/80-the-battle-of-point-pleasant-of-the-revolution/55-o1 (visited October 8, 2020).

3. "Andrew Lewis," 4, http://www.madeofcotton.com/family/andrew_lewis.html

4. Jeff Dacus, "The Neglected Andrew Lewis," *Journal of the American Revolution*, September 28, 2015.

5. *See* Alicia Petska, "Andrew Who? The Famous Virginian You Might Not Know," *Richmond Times-Dispatch*, February 19, 2017 ("[H]is name hasn't carried over to the history books. There isn't a whole lot known about him," quoting John Long, Director, Salem, Virginia, Museum and Historical Society).

6. Robert S. Conte. *The History of the Greenbrier: America's Resort*, 2 (White Sulphur Springs, WV, Greenbrier Publishing, 10th ed., 2016).

7. *See, e.g.*, "Andrew Lewis," 5, available https://www.madeofcotton.com/family/andrew_lewis.html/ (visited October 10, 2020). A statue of Andrew Lewis, kneeling to light a fuse firing a cannon at Lord Dunmore's Fleet, setting of the 1776 battle of Gwynn's Island, stands in front of the Salem, Virginia, Civic Center. Roanoke has an Andrew Lewis Middle School (formerly the Andrew Lewis High School), Andrew Lewis Grade School, and Lewis Baptist Church. The first exit for Roanoke, Virginia, off Interstate 81, is the Andrew Lewis Parkway.

8. The other figures are George Mason, Thomas Jefferson, Thomas Nelson, Jr., and Patrick Henry. *See* "The Neglected Andrew Lewis," 6, note 9. Thomas Nelson, Jr., predominantly a politician and later governor of Virginia, became a militia general late in the war but never saw combat. *See generally* Nell Moore Lee, *Patriot Without Profit* (Nashville, TN, Rockledge Hill Press, 1988).

9. Chapter 4 contains a representative list of Revolutionary brigadiers with Irish and Scots backgrounds. Thomas Conway, of the infamous Conway Cabal, was Irish born. New Hampshire's General John Sullivan was the son of Irish immigrants. Richard Montgomery, who died in the Siege of Quebec, was Dublin born. From Scotland came Adam Stephen, Alexander McDougal, Hugh Mercer, and Arthur St. Clair. William Smallwood of Maryland, Lord Stirling, bore the latter name because he believed himself heir apparent to the Scottish title, Earl of Stirling.

10. *The History of the Greenbrier*, 2.

11. *See, e.g.*, Profile, General Andrew Lewis—American Revolutionary War Veteran, 1, available https://www.waymarking.com/waymarks/WMV_General_Andrew_Lewis (visited October 8, 2020).

12. *See The History of the Greenbrier*, 2: "It was Lewis, some say, who named the major river 'Greenbrier' after the profusion of tangled and clinging vines that stood in his way." As to the secret presidential bunker, *see also The History of the Greenbrier*, 193–200 (Chapter 12. "Project Greek Island").

13. Salem, for instance, is home to two highly regarded liberal arts colleges: Salem College and Roanoke College. *See, e.g.*, http://roanokecollege.edu (visited January 27, 2021).

14. *See, e.g.*, Ward, *Adam Stephen and the Cause of American Liberty*, 19.

15. Accounts of George Washington and James MacKay Concerning the Capitulation, *Maryland Gazette*, August 19, 1754.

16. *Adam Stephen and the Cause of American Liberty*, 35.

17. *See, e.g.*, W. H. Loudermilk, *A History of Cumberland, Maryland*, 210–212 (Washington, DC, 1878).

18. *See* Hugh Cleland, *George Washington in the Ohio Valley*, 164 (Pittsburgh, PA, University of Pittsburgh Press, 1955).

19. Loudermilk, *Cumberland*, 221–222; *Adam Stephen and the Cause of American Liberty*, 54–55.

20. "The Neglected Andrew Lewis," 2.

21. George Washington, quoted in "Andrew Who? The Most Famous Virginian You Might Not Know," 4.

22. "Andrew Lewis," 3, available https://www.revwartalk.com/andrew-lewis (visited October 10, 2020).

23. *The British Are Coming*, 345.

24. Andrew Lewis, RevWarTalk, 4

25. Ward, *Major General Adam Stephen and the Cause of American Liberty*, 138–139.

26. Dr. Benjamin Rush, quoted in McCullough, *John Adams*, 141.

27. *See, e.g.*, Dumas Malone, Volume 1, *Jefferson: The Virginian*, 390 (Boston, MA. Little, Brown & Co., 1948) ("inevitable death from the smallpox … then raging in Lord Cornwallis's camp").

28. *See* McCullough, *John Adams*, 142.

29. Not until 1796 did English Doctor Edward Jenner develop a safe and effective smallpox vaccine. *See, e.g.*, George Smith, *The Man Who Saved the World from Smallpox: Doctor Edward Jenner* (London, IUniverse, 2004).

30. *The British Are Coming*, 259, 284.

31. *The British Are Coming*, 292.

32. *The British Are Coming*, 294.

33. Other generals such as John Stark resigned after Congress promoted lower ranked, in seniority, over him. *See General Washington's Revolutionary Generals*, 80.

34. Letter from General George Washington to Andrew Lewis, March 25, 1777, recorded in Frank E Gizzard, Jr., ed., Vol. 8, *The Papers of George Washington*, 500 (Charlottesville, VA, University of Virginia Press, 1998).

35. *See generally* "The Neglected Andrew Lewis," 4.

36. Letter from Andrew Lewis to George Washington, November 1777, recorded in David Hoth, ed., Vol. 16, *The Papers of George Washington*, 273–274 (Charlottesville, VA, University of Virginia Press, 2006).

37. The five men promoted in February 1777 were Lord Stirling (William Alexander) of Maryland, Thomas Mifflin, and Arthur St. Clair of Pennsylvania, Adam Stephen of Virginia, and Benjamin Lincoln of Massachusetts. *See* "The Neglected Andrew Lewis," 1.

38. Later, as Governor of the Northwest Territory, Arthur St. Clair led forces against the Native Americans, with disastrous results and his relief from that command. *See generally* Kevin Patrick Kopper, "Arthur St. Clair and the Struggle for

Power in the Old Northwest" (unpublished doctoral dissertation, Kent State University, 2005).

39. *See generally* Paul David Nelson, *Lord Stirling: Washington's Noble General* (Tuscaloosa, AL, University of Alabama Press, 2003).

40. In the *Journal of the American Revolution*, historian William Welsh rated Thomas Mifflin seventh on his list of the Revolution War's ten worst generals. Welsh, "The 10 Worst Continental Army Generals," *Journal of the American Revolution*, October 22, 2013: "His work as quartermaster general was disastrous, being largely responsible for the suffering at Valley Forge. He was also active as a behind the scenes plotter [and] perhaps leader of the Conway Cabal" to replace George Washington with Horatio Gates.

41. *See, e.g.*, Chapter 14.

42. Letter from Andrew Lewis to George Washington, August 1778, in David Hoth, Ed., *The Letters of George Washington Revolutionary War Series*, vol. 8, 500 (Charlottesville, VA, University of Virginia Press, 2006).

43. Brigadier General Andrew Lewis, http://www.gewi.com/people/brigadier-andrew-lewis-contonental-army (visited October 10, 2020).

44. For instance, in his schematic for a sound government, the "'Council,' as [John] Adams called it, would be given 'free and independent judgment' on all acts of legislation." McCullough, *John Adams*, 103.

45. "Andrew Who? The Most Famous Virginian You Might Not Know," 3.

Chapter 9

1. *See, e.g.*, *Washington's Revolutionary War Generals*, 32.

2. Quoted in *Duty, Honor and Country*, 166.

3. *The British Are Coming*, 332.

4. *The British Are Coming*, 333; *Washington's Revolutionary War Generals*, 32.

5. Attributed to Captain Clement Lampriere, a well-regarded American privateer, in *The Southern Strategy*, 45.

6. William Moultrie, *Memoirs of the American Revolution*, Volume 1, 141 (1802, reprinted New York, Arno Press, 1968).

7. *The Southern Strategy*, 49.

8. After wet cement has been in place for a time, it becomes hardened and resistant to change. *See, e.g.*, Burrow, "The Treachery of Charles Lee," 1: "[H]e repelled a British assault at Fort Moultrie." In fact, Lee recommended just the opposite: rather than stand and fight, that the defenders should abandon the fort.

9. Adam Gopnik, "Original Gangsters: The New York Mob," *New Yorker*, December 7, 2020, 65, 67. The myth was "that gangsters were melancholic men of honor… legendary and, in a black way, lovable."

10. "Privately Rutledge advised Moultrie, "General Lee wishes you to evacuate [Fort Sullivan]. You will not without an order from me. I would sooner cut off my hand than write one." Quoted in *The British Are Coming*, 333–334.

11. *See, e.g.*, Hugh O. Nash, Jr., *Patriot Sons, Patriot Brothers*, 57 & n. 6 (Nashville, TN, Westview Publishing, 2006) ("Lee liked Nash and considered him to be the best candidate to replace Moultrie as Commander of the Fort"). *See also American Revolution in the Southern Colonies*, 91. "The night before the battle, Lee told Francis Nash he would relieve Moultrie the following day."

12. *See Andrew Pickens: South Carolina Patriot*, 60, quoting A. L. Pickens, who characterized Lee as "eccentric [and] selfishly ambitious … offensively superior, [who] sought to discourage Moultrie who, in spite of Lee …won a glorious victory."

13. A hogshead is a larger cask for wine or beer holding 63–64 gallons. A traditional wine cask holds 60 gallons.

14. *American Revolution in the Southern Colonies*, 91.

15. *See* Henry Lumpkin, *From Savannah to Yorktown*, 17 (New York, Paragon House Publishers, 1981).

16. South Carolina Governor John Rutledge to Colonel William Moultrie, June 1776, quoted in Oller, *Swamp Fox*, 39; Edward McGrady, *The History of South Carolina, 1775–1780*, 144 (New York, Russell & Russell, 1901, reprinted 1969). In additional to criticizing Moultrie's failure to act with alacrity in construction of the fort, Charles Lee also "sized up Moultrie as too easy of a commander to put up much of a fight."

17. *See American Revolution in the Southern Colonies*, 93.

18. *Savannah to Yorktown*, 16. *See also Crescent Moon Over Carolina*, 81.

19. *American Revolution in the Southern Colonies*, 94.

20. As a result of the 1776 victory, "The state now had new symbol—the palmetto tree—an emblem that would endure as a central element of the state seal and the state flag." E. Stanley & Robert H. Woody, *Christopher Gadsden and the American Revolution*, 160–161 (Knoxville, TN, University of Tennessee Press, 1982).

Chapter 10

1. William Hollinshead, *A Discourse Commemorative of the Late Major-Gen. William Moultrie*, 14 (Charleston, SC, Peter Freeman, 1805).

2. Oller, *Swamp Fox*, 39.

3. *Crescent Moon Over Carolina*, 12.

4. Criticism of Major General Charles Lee, reproduced in *Crescent Moon Over Carolina*, 68.

5. *See, e.g.*, Oller, *Swamp Fox*, 4, "General William Moultrie [was] Marion's mentor"); 36, "Marion's mentor, William Moultrie [made] colonel of the 2nd [South Carolina} Regiment;" and 148, "Moultrie still identified as Marion's mentor" in 1780, Swamp Fox designated as "Moultrie's protege".

6. C.L. Bragg, *Crescent Moon Over Carolina: William Moultrie & American Liberty*, 86 (Columbia, SC, University of South Carolina Press, 2013).

7. Alexander Garden, *Anecdotes of the American Revolution, Illustrative of the Talents and Virtues of Heroes and Patriots*, 7 (Charleston, SC, Miller Publishing, 1828).

8. *Crescent Moon Over Carolina*, 87 ("the other two being Saratoga and Kings Mountain").

9. See David Lee Russell, *The American Revolution in the Southern Colonies*, 60 (Jefferson, NC, McFarland, 2000).

10. *See, e.g., Crescent Moon Over Carolina*, 14. These divides had their genesis in English rule of the colonies. Under British regulation, Scots had to swear the oath of abjuration—forswearing the right of any of House of Stuart to accede to the English throne. Moreover, actual and suspected Catholics had to swear a "declaration against transubstantiation" to further isolate Catholics from civil rights other British citizens enjoyed.

11. Rod Andrew, Jr., *The Life and Times of General Andrew Pickens; Revolutionary War Hero, American Founder*, 166 (Chapel Hill, NC, University of North Carolina Press, 2017).

12. *See, e.g.*, William Reynolds, Jr., *Andrew Pickens: South Carolina Patriot in the Revolutionary War*, 38 (Jefferson, NC, McFarland, 2012). Tories outnumbered Whigs two-to-one in the backcountry as well.

13. Marvin R. Zahniser, *Charles Cotesworth Pinckney: Founding Father*, 34 (Chapel Hill, NC, University of North Carolina Press, 1967).

14. Nonetheless, Britain's royal governors acted surreptitiously "to provoke backcountry Loyalists ... to incite the Indians to 'lift the hatchet for the King.'" Walter Edgar, *South Carolina: A History*, 224–225 (Columbia, SC, University of South Carolina Press, 1998).

15. Among others, John Oller, in *The Swamp Fox: How Francis Marion Saved the American Revolution*, 26–29 (New York, DeCapo, 2016, reprinted Hachette Books, 2020), describes the 1759–1763 Cherokee wars. During the 1761 Cherokee War expedition, Francis "Marion [later famous as the Swamp Fox] was Moultrie's first lieutenant in the [South Carolina] provincial light infantry."

16. The Cherokees were not nomadic. They lived in 80–90 established villages on the piedmont or in the Appalachian foothills and mountains, cultivating crops and remaining largely stationary. The three principal Cherokee wars, 1759–1761, are described in, *inter alia*, *The Life and Times of Andrew Pickens*, 17–18; *Pickens: South Carolina Patriot*, 38–44. *See also Crescent Moon Over Carolina*, 15–22.

17. *The Life and Times of Andrew Pickens*, 17.

18. *Crescent Moon Over Carolina*, 18. *See also American Revolution in the Southern Colonies*, 90. "Moultrie had "military experience and a reputation as a leader of militia during the Indian fighting in the 1760s;" 160, "In the 1760s, Francis Marion, later christened the Swamp Fox," served under William Moultrie in the Cherokee Wars.

19. The need to be prepared to "live rough" explains, as the introduction points out, why so many of the senior officers in the revolution had been surveyors in their younger days. Their number included Anthony Wayne and Daniel Brodhead in Pennsylvania, Andrew Lewis and Charles Scott in Virginia, as well as George Washington himself, Richard Caswell in North Carolina, and Lachlan McIntosh in Georgia, to name several. Although not a surveyor by profession, William Moultrie spent significant time in the wilds trailblazing and surveying as one of South Carolina's two commissioners appointed to determine the boundary between the Carolinas on the piedmont and in the mountainous west. *See Crescent Moon Over Carolina*, 27.

20. Robert Gibbes Thomas, *A Memoir of James De Veau of Charles Town S.C.*, 17–25 (Legare Street Press, reprint, 2022).

21. *Crescent Moon Over Carolina*, 9, 11.

22. *American Revolution in the Southern Colonies*, 91.

23. Remarks of Thomas Ferguson, South Carolina Committee of Safety, October 1775.

24. *See, e.g.*, Hugh O. Nash, Jr., *Patriot Sons, Patriot Brothers*, 57 & n. 6 (Nashville, TN, Westview Publishing, 2006), "Lee liked Nash and considered him to be the best candidate to replace Moultrie as Commander of the Fort." *See also American Revolution in the Southern Colonies*, 91, "The night before the battle, Lee told Francis Nash he would relieve Moultrie the following day."

25. *Crescent Moon Over Carolina*, 70, 88.

26. In April 1777, another threat to Georgia and the South materialized, this time from the backcountry. Five or six hundred armed Loyalists, known as "Scophites" after their leader Joseph Scopol, rallied near Augusta. The mob crossed the Savannah River, pillaging and committing atrocities against the South Carolina populace. On April 19 and 20, Moultrie, now overall commander of the South Carolina Continentals, sent detachments to turn back the threat. Another alarm soon sounded a threat from Florida and the far south. In June 1777, intelligence came to light that British General Augustine Prevost with 1,200 British regulars and Creek Indians were preparing to invade Georgia. Now in command of the southern department, North Carolina's General Robert Howe personally led 2,500 men southward to meet the threat. Again, General Moultrie augmented the force, although he stayed in South Carolina. Six hundred Carolina regulars and 800 South Carolina militia constituted much of the total force. Lack of provisions and shelter dispirited the men. Malaria and other diseases affected the Carolinians, killing many and laying others extremely low. Equally affected by the same impediments, having reached the St. Mary's River in South Georgia, the threatening British Prevost expedition ended its foray. The British force reversed direction, returning 55 miles to St. Augustine.

27. *Crescent Moon Over Carolina*, 104.

28. Principal causes of Howe's downfall were his actions leading to development of a reputation as a womanizer and his ineffectual attempt to defend Savannah. *See generally* Charles E. Barnett & Donald R. Lennon, *Major General Robert Howe and the American Revolution*, 85–99 (Chapel Hill, NC, University of North Carolina Press, 1991).

29. *See, e.g., North Carolina Through Four Centuries*, 180, In late 1775, "Lord Charles Cornwallis with seven regiments would sail from Cork, Ireland." *See also* Wilson, *The Southern Strategy*, 45, Later, in 1776, at the failed siege of Charles Town, "Lord Cornwallis … headed up seven regiments that had come from Ireland."

30. Charles E. Barnett & Donald R. Lennon, *Major General Robert Howe and the American Revolution,* 96 (Chapel Hill, NC, University of North Carolina Press, 1991).

31. Quoted in *Major General Howe*, 98–99.

32. *Crescent Moon Over Carolina*, 114–117, recounts the Port Royal affair.

33. *Savannah to Yorktown*, 30.

34. General Moultrie and unidentified American officer quoted in *Crescent Moon Over Carolina*, 117.

35. *See generally The American Revolution in the Southern Colonies*, 106–107.

36. David K. Wilson, *The Southern Strategy: Britain's Conquest of South Carolina and Georgia, 1775–1780*, 101–102 (Columbia, SC, University of South Carolina Press, 2005).

37. *See, e.g.,* http://johnsislandsc.us (visited October 15, 2012); http://jamesislandsc.us (visited October 15, 2021).

38. Wilson, *Southern Strategy*, 269–270, describing the reversal at Stono River. *See also* McGrady, *The History of South Carolina, 1775–1780*, 359–360 (same); *American Revolution in the Southern Colonies*, 110–111 (same).

39. *Crescent Moon Over Carolina*, 159.

40. *Crescent Moon Over Carolina*, 138.

41. Moultrie, quoted, *inter alia*, in *American Revolution in the Southern Colonies*, at 108.

42. Recorded in Thomas, "William Moultrie," 330, on file, South Carolina Historical Society, Charleston, SC.

43. *See American Revolution in the Southern Colonies*, 108.

44. American *Revolution in the Southern Colonies*, 109.

45. *Southern Strategy*, 238–241, 241.

46. *Southern Strategy*, 211–213.

47. *Crescent Moon Over Carolina*, 174–175.

48. Carl P. Borick, *A Gallant Defense: The Siege of Charleston, 1780*, 132 (Columbia, SC, University of South Carolina Press, 2003).

49. Reported in Henry Steele Commager & Richard B. Morris, *The Spirit of Seventy-Six*, 110 (New York, Harper & Row, 1958). *See also A Gallant Defense*, 219; Wilson, *Southern Strategy*, 134.

50. *American Revolution in the Southern Colonies*, 147.

51. *Washington's Revolutionary War Generals*, 206.

52. *A Gallant Defense*, 177–178.

53. *A Gallant Defense*, 209.

54. General Moultrie's Memoirs, *Memoirs of the American Revolution So Far as it Related to the States of North- and South Carolina, and Georgia* (1802), quoted in *Crescent Moon Over Carolina*, 182.

55. *Crescent Moon Over Carolina*, 182.

56. *Washington's Revolutionary War Generals*, 206.

57. Described in Carl P. Borick, *Relieve Us of this Burden: American Prisoners of War in the Revolutionary South, 1780–1782*, 52 et seq. (Columbia, SC, University of South Carolina Press, 2012).

58. *Relieve Us of this Burden*, 58–59.

59. Robert Gibbes Thompson, "William Moultrie: Arms and Man" (1930), manuscript on file at South Carolina Historical Society, Charleston, SC.

60. *Washington's Revolutionary War Generals*, 246.

61. Oller, *Swamp Fox*, 235.

Chapter 11

1. Waterman, *With Sword and Lancet; The Life of General Hugh Mercer*, 103.

2. If travelers thought a portion of their journey might be after dark, they were wise to consult an almanac concerning "lunations." Night-time travel was safest, although never as safe as travel in daylight, under a three-quarters or full moon. Almanacs "charted the phases of the moon, which constituted essential intelligence for travelers … in an era before extensive artificial lighting." Brands, *The First American*, 122–123.

3. *See also* Atkinson, *The British Are Coming*, 542, reviewing the second Battle of Trenton and repeating British Lord Cornwallis' description of the trek from Princeton: "[In the dark] men tripped over the tree stumps studding the rough trace."

4. David McCullough, *The Pioneers: The Heroic Story of the Settlers Who Brought the American Ideal West*, 14 (New York, Simon & Schuster, 2019).

5. *See, e.g.,* Frederick B. Kegley, *Kegley's Virginia Frontier: The Beginnings of the Southwest, 1740–1783*, 64 (1938) (reprinted, Heritage Publishing, Jacksonville, FL, 2012).

6. *See, e.g.,* Emory G. Evans, *Thomas Nelson and the Revolution in Virginia*, 20 (Williamsburg, VA, Virginia Bicentennial Commission, 1978).

7. *See, e.g.,* Brands, *The First American*, 339.

8. *See, e.g., Sword and Lancet*, 14.

9. *See generally Major General Adam Stephen and the Cause of American Liberty*, 48–51.

10. *See, e.g., Daniel Morgan: A Revolutionary Life*, 51–52. Daniel Morgan's first position in government was as a road overseer, "the most minor of all public positions," in 1770 and again in 1774.

11. *See, e.g.,* Atkinson, *The British Are Coming*, 549 (15 miles in day after the Battle of Princeton);

Duty, Honor or Country, 7 (Andrew Lewis and George Weedon marched 80 recruits from Fredericksburg to Winchester, Virginia, a distance of 72 miles, in 4 days).

12. *See, e.g.,* Barbara W. Tuchman, *A Distant Mirror: The Calamitous 14th Century*, 267 (New York, Ballantine Books, 1978). On their 1,000-mile circuit of France in 1373, English forces under John of Gaunt "covered eight or nine miles a day in the usual three lines of march, the better to live off the country."

13. *A Distant Mirror*, 267.

14. *The Life of Major-General Peter Muhlenberg*, 56. The march entailed approximately 190 miles. See http://www.distancecalculator.net (visited March 26, 2020).

15. *See, e.g., Duty, Honor or Country: Gen. George Weedon and the American Revolution*, 57. The distance, via York, Pennsylvania, and then Philadelphia, to New York City, is 256.31 miles. See http://www.distancecalculator.net (visited March 26, 2020).

16. Jonathan Jordon, paraphrasing author O'Donnell, in "Maryland's Finest," *Wall Street Journal*, March 5, 2016, C-6.

17. Quoted in *Davidson on Davidson*, 41.

18. *See, e.g., Light-Horse Harry Lee*, 37 ('many [soldiers] had no shoes" on the mid-winter march from Trenton to Princeton early in 1777) and 52 (at Valley Forge in 1778 "their bleeding feet leaving crimson tracks in the snow").

19. *See, e.g., Major General Adam Stephen and the Cause of American Liberty*, 24.

20. Atkinson, *The British Are Coming*, 550.

21. *See Major General Adam Stephen and the Cause of American Liberty*, 17.

22. *The Pioneers: The Heroic Story of the Settlers*, 14.

23. *The Pioneers: The Heroic Story of the Settlers*, 18. Earlier, Rev. Cutler averaged 30 miles per day, traveling by carriage from Ipswich, Massachusetts, to Boston, then Providence, and onward to New York. *The Pioneers: The Heroic Story of the Settlers*, 13.

24. *Light-Horse Harry Lee*, 131.

25. *See generally* Chapter 15.

26. *See, e.g., 1777: Turning Point at Saratoga*, 89; "The windage of smooth-bored muskets made them inaccurate beyond fifty to seventy yards."

27. Breech-loading small arms were developed and perfected by Casimir LeFaucheax around 1835. *See* James H. Willbanks, *Machine Guns: Their History*, 15 (Santa Barbara, CA, ABC-CLIO, 2004).

28. Description of colonial weaponry is based upon an interview with Andrew E. Masich, President and CEO, Senator John Heinz History Center, Historical Society of Western Pennsylvania, Pittsburgh, PA, February 13, 2020.

29. Dean Snow, *1777: Turning Point at Saratoga*, 89–90 (New York, Oxford University Press, 2016).

30. *Turning Point at Saratoga*, 113.

31. *Turning Point at Saratoga*, 90.

32. Daniel Morgan, quoted in Johann Friedrich Sprecht, *A Military Journal of the Saratoga Campaign*, 79 (Mary C. Lynn, ed., Westport, CT, Greenwood Press, 1995).

33. *Military Journal of the Saratoga Campaign*, 79.

34. *Turning Point at Saratoga*, 113–114 (Battle of Freeman's Farm), 245–46 & 249–253 (Battle of Bemis Heights). Saratoga was two battles, as aforesaid, Freeman's Farm (September 19, 1777) and Bemis Heights (October 7, 1777).

35. In the October 1215 Battle of Agincourt, King Henry V and "his Band of Brothers" defeated a French force of four times greater size by coordinated use of infantry and archers (in those times akin to the Revolutionary War era's and Daniel Morgan's riflemen). With swords and pikes, at Agincourt, the tightly packed English infantry surrounded and fronted the English archers against the more loosely or even unorganized French troops. *See generally* the classic John Keegan, *The Face of Battle: A Study of Agincourt, Waterloo, and the Somme* (New York, Penguin, 1983).

Chapter 12

1. *Cf.* Daniel McDonald Johnson, *This Cursed War; Lachlan McIntosh and the American Revolution*, 15 (Self-Published, Allendale, SC, 2018): Continental troops at Darien, Georgia, received "a half pint of rum three times a week." The British measure of a gill, followed at that time and dating from the 14th Century, was five fluid ounces, amounting to five "shots," if a one ounce shot glass were used. *See, e.g.,* Amy Tikkman. "Gill," in *Encyclopedia Britannica*, available http://britannica.com/gill (visited April 5, 2020). The gill liquid measurement is no longer widely used, although the European Union's regulations provide that the amount of alcoholic beverage in a mixed drink must be one-sixth of a gill.

2. Dean Snow, *1777: Tipping Point at Saratoga*, 174 (New York, Oxford University Press, 2016). General Gates later rescinded the order.

3. *This Cursed War*, 95.

4. Ben Franklin, quoted in Walter Isaacson, *Benjamin Franklin: An American Life*, 170 (New York, Simon & Schuster, 2003).

5. At the 1780 Battle of Camden, General Gates led the Southern Army out of Hillsborough, North Carolina, before quartermasters could re-supply the army. On the eve of the battle, in lieu of the gill of rum customary before a major fight, Gates and commissary men substituted a gill of molasses for rum, with catastrophic intestinal results for the men (especially diarrhea—with soldiers constantly disappearing into the woods as they marched toward the engagement). "[I]t was unluckily conceived that molasses would be an acceptable substitute [for rum] .... [M]olasses ... operated so carthartically as to disorder the men, who were breaking ranks all night ... certainly much debilitated before the action commenced." Colonel

Ortho Holland Williams, quoted in Jim Piecuch, *The Battle of Camden*, 29 (Charleston, SC, The History Press, 2006).

6. *See, e.g., Fighting Parson*, 56 ("Sutlers selling liquor caused trouble" in army encampments).

7. Gordon S. Wood, "The Age That Made the Man," *Wall Street Journal*, September 26, 2020, C-7.

8. McCullough, *John Adams*, 36.

9. Barbara Tuchman, *A Distant Mirror: The Calamitous Fourteenth Century*, 112–114 (New York, Ballantine Books, 1978).

10. Of Revolutionary War encampments, Chalmers Davidson recorded much the same thing: "Roaring fires served to roast the belly while the buttocks froze." Davidson, *Piedmont Partisan: The Life and Times of Major General William Lee Davidson*, 48 (Davidson, NC, Davidson College, 1951).

11. George Washington, quoted in Jared Sparks, Vol. IV, *The Writings of George Washington*, 199–200 (Boston, MA, 1840).

12. *A Distant Mirror*, 54 & 141.

13. *See Major General Adam Stephen and the Cause of American Liberty*, 71–72 (Cherokee expedition) & 82–84 (Pontiac's War).

14. *See, e.g.,* Ron Chernow, *Washington: A Life*, 18–20 (New York, Penguin, 2010). "Surveying suited Washington's talents perfectly" and "toughened" him by experiences on the frontier.

15. *See* Chapter 6.

16. Richard V. Polhemus & John F. Polhemus, *Stark: The Life and Wars of John Stark*, 254–268 (Delmar, NY, Black Dome Press, 2014); Ben Z. Rose, *John Stark: Maverick General*, 114–124 (Waverly, MA, TreeLine Press, 2007).

17. Account of George Washington of the Capitulation, July 19, 1754, in Vol. 1, Papers of George Washington, 159–165 (Charlottesville, VA, University of Virginia Press). *See also Major General Adam Stephen and the Cause of American Liberty*, 11.

18. *Duty, Honor or Country: Gen. George Weedon and the American Revolution*, 119.

19. John Jakes, *Charleston*, 51 (New York, Dutton, 2002).

20. Quoted in Harry M. Ward, *Charles Scott and the Spirit of '76*, 19 (Charlottesville, VA, University of Virginia Press, 1988) (internal quotation marks omitted).

21. *Patriot Above Profit*, 348.

22. *Daniel Morgan: A Revolutionary Life*, 30.

23. *Daniel Morgan: A Revolutionary Life*, 38.

24. David McCullough, *The Pioneers: The Heroic Story of the Settlers Who Bought the American Ideal West*, 4–5 (New York, Simon & Schuster. 2019).

25. *See, e.g.,* Walter Isaacson, *John Adams: An American Life*, 8 (New York, Simon & Schuster, 2003). "They wanted to go even further and 'purify' the church of all Roman Catholic traces … lingering pollutants from the Church of Rome".

26. *See, e.g., A Distant Mirror*, 383: In defense of Ghent, in Flanders, "[t]he militia of [neighboring] Bruges … caroused through the night and staggered forth on the morrow, May 5 [1382] shouting and singing in drunken disorder.

27. Quoted in Atkinson, *The British Are Coming*, 49.

28. Benjamin Franklin, as a commissioner to negotiations with the Native Americans leading to the Carlisle Treaty of 1753, described the effect of alcohol on that occasion: "We found that they [the approximately 100 Natives in attendance] had made a great bonfire in the middle of the square. They were all drunk, men and women, quarreling and fighting … by the gloomy light of the bonfire, running after and beating one another with firebrands, accompanied by horrid yelling …." Ben Franklin, quoted in *The First American*, 227.

29. *See Charleston*, 91.

30. Francis Marion, the Swamp Fox, quoted in *Charleston*, 54.

31. Marquis de Lafayette, quoted in *Duty, Honor or Country: Gen. George Weedon and the American Revolution*, 201.

32. *Major General Adam Stephen and the Cause of American Liberty*, 75.

33. Atkinson, *The British Are Coming*, 552. A hogshead is a large cask, in terms of more precise measurement, a larger barrel containing 63 gallons.

34. General Charles Scott, quoted in *Charles Scott and the Spirit of '76*, 56–57.

35. Ron Chernow, *Grant*, 246 (New York, Penguin Press, 2017).

36. Cholera was another water-borne sickness, the third of the big three pandemics in history (the plague, smallpox, and cholera), caused by a bacteria (*Vibrio cholerae*) in the water. The first cholera pandemic, however, did not occur until 1817, in Calcutta, India, after the American Revolution had concluded. *See* Elizabeth Kolbert, "The Spread: Now Pandemics Shape Human History," *New Yorker*, April 6, 2020, 58, 60.

37. Jonathan W. Jordon, paraphrasing author Patrick O'Donnell, in "Maryland's Finest," *Wall Street Journal*, March 5, 2016, C-6

38. *Duty, Honor or Country: Gen. George Weedon and the American Revolution*, 59.

39. *Charles Scott and the "Spirit of '76,"* 20 & 22.

40. Congressman Charles Carroll to General George Washington, September 27, 1777.

41. *See Major General Adam Stephen and the Cause of American Liberty*, 182.

42. Dean Snow, *1777: Tipping Point at Saratoga*, 19, 249.

43. The court acquitted General Maxwell. Robert Lisle, "The Court Martial of Adam Stephen, Major General, Continental Army," 30. *Madison College Bulletin*, No. 3, 33, 37 & n. 18 (1972).

44. Reed at 230. Robert Lisle argues that Stephen's later court martial found only "inattention or want of judgment" along with drinking generally: "He has been frequently intoxicated since in the service, to the prejudice of good order and

military discipline," but no specific finding that Stephen was drunk or had been drinking at Germantown. *See, e.g.,* "The Court Martial of Adam Stephen," 36–38.

45. Jeff Dacus, "The Neglected Andrew Lewis," *Journal of American History*, September 28, 2015, text following note 8, available https://www.allthingsliberty.com/2015/09/the-neglected-andrew-lewis (visited September 8, 2020).

46. George Washington, quoted in *Charles Scott and the "Spirit of '76*, 120.

47. *Major General Adam Stephen and the Cause of American Liberty*, 191 (emphasis added).

48. In 1775, Stephen opened two new industries on his plantation: a distillery and a weapons manufactory. "Stephen viewed war as creating opportunities for profit." *Major General Adam Stephen and the Cause of American Liberty*, 123.

49. The story told of young U.S. Navy officers is that early in the eighteenth century, the U.S. Navy ceased flogging as a means of punishment, although until recently, confinement with limitation of nourishment to bread and water ("piss and punk") remained as a potential form of punishment for U.S. sailors. When Navy regulations eliminated flogging, the Navy extracted a *quid pro quo*. American sailors had to give up their entitlement to a daily grog ration, marking the beginning of the broader prohibition of alcohol in the armed services.

Chapter 13

1. Zambone, *Daniel Morgan: A Revolutionary Life*, 26.

2. *See* James Titus, *The Old Dominion at War: Society, Politics, and Warfare in Late Colonial Virginia*, 1–3 (Columbia, SC, University of South Carolina Press, 1991).

3. *See, e.g.,* Glenn F. Williams, *Dunmore's War: The Last Conflict of America's Colonial Era*, 108 (Yardley, PA, Westholme Publishing, 2017) (Governor Dunmore's 1774 expedition against Shawnees and Mingo's in the Ohio Country); *Daniel Morgan: A Revolutionary Life*, 56 ("A mustered company would be about twice the size" of the contingent ordered deployed).

4. *See Dunmore's War*, at 105. For unexcused absences from monthly musters, militia members could be fined five pounds, a considerable sum in those times. See also *Dunmore's War*, 105.

5. Davidson, *Piedmont Partisan*, 10.

6. Benjamin Franklin, for instance, recommended that wooden pikes make up for the shortages of muskets for the Pennsylvania Militia. *See* Isaacson, *Benjamin Franklin*, 302. Franklin even ventured the opinion that "that using pikes and bows and arrows compensate" for the colonial shortages of muskets and gunpowder.

7. *See* Michael Cecere, *Second to No Man but the Commander in Chief*, 51–52. Each militia member within six months was to procure '[a] good rifle [or] firelock, bayonet, pouch, [and] cartouch box .... [a member] shall constantly keep by him one pound of powder and four pounds of ball." Militia leaders were instructed to hold musters every two weeks except in December, January, and February.

8. *See* Richard D. & John F. Polhemus, *Stark: The Life and Wars of John Stark, French & Indian War Ranger, Revolutionary War General*, 247–249 (Delmar, NY, Black Dome Press, 2014).

9. George Washington to Enoch Poor, March 3, 1777.

10. Polhemus, *Stark, The Life and Wars of John Stark*, 247–249.

11. John Langdon, quoted in Howard Parker Moore, *A Life of General John Stark of New Hampshire*, 262 (New York, 1949).

12. *See, e.g.,* Herbert D. Foster & Thomas Streeter, "Stark's Independent Command at Bennington," 1905 Proceedings of the New York Historical Association, 26

13. *The Life and Wars of John Stark*, at 249, in Chapter 20, "The Road to Bennington," 237.

14. Quoted on historical marker at the Bennington battlefield site in southern Vermont. Also quoted in Dean Snow, *1777: Tipping Point at Saratoga*, 80.

15. Ward, *Duty, Honor or Country*, 195.

16. Edward Hocker, *The Fighting Parson*, 80.

17. Joseph Waterman, *With Sword and Lancet*, 115.

18. Cecere, *Second to No Man but the Commander in Chief*, 82.

19. *Piedmont Partisan*, 37.

20. Barboursville, Virginia, approximately ten miles northeast of Charlottesville, was named after the colonel's descendant, 19th Virginia governor and U.S. Senator, James Barbour. Another militia unit, Buck's Minutemen, formed up at Woodstock, Virginia, in 1776, soon thereafter incorporated by Congress into the Second Continental Line. The author's great, great, great grandfather, Lionel Branson, served as the ensign of Buck's Minutemen and, once in the Continental Line, fought for the duration of the war (until 1783).

21. *See* Ryan Cole, *Light-Horse Harry Lee: The Rise and Fall of a Revolutionary Hero*, 41 (Washington, DC, Regnery History Press, 2019).

22. George Weedon to Colonel William Fleming, November 18, 1780, reproduced in *Duty, Honor and Country*, 159.

23. General George Weedon to General George Washington, December 4, 1777.

24. Atkinson, *The British Are Coming*, 99.

25. Emory G. Evans, *Thomas Nelson and the Revolution in Virginia*, 37 (Williamsburg, VA, Virginia Bicentennial Commission, 1978).

26. General Thomas Nelson, Jr., quoted in *Thomas Nelson and the Revolution in Virginia*, 37.

27. David K. Wilson, *The Southern Strategy: Britain's Conquest of South Carolina and Georgia, 1775–1780*, 42–43 (Columbia, SC, University of South Carolina Press, 2005).

28. Chalmers Gaston Davidson, *Piedmont*

Partisan: The Life and Times of Brigadier-General William Lee Davidson, 37 (Davidson, NC, Davidson College, 1951).

29. General George Washington to John Hancock, September 2, 1776.

30. George Washington to the Continental Congress, September 24, 1776.

31. General George Washington to Thomas Nelson, Jr., September 2, 1777, in John C. Fitzpatrick, ed., Vol. 9, *Writings of George Washington*, 163–64 (Washington, DC, Government Printing Office, 1927).

32. General Hugh Mercer to the president of the Congress, September 4, 1776.

33. Colonel James Hendricks to General George Weedon, May 9, 1781.

34. Lt. Colonel Harry Lee, quoted in *Light-Horse Harry Lee*, 134.

35. Higginbotham, *Daniel Morgan: Revolutionary Rifleman*, 82.

36. Nell Moore Lee, in *Patriot Above Profit*, 400.

37. *See* James Wilkinson, *Memoirs of My Own Times*, Volume 1, 249.

38. Daniel McDonald Johnson, *This Cursed War: Lachlan McIntosh and the American Revolution*, 115 (Allendale, SC, Self-Published, 2018).

39. Zambone, *Daniel Morgan: A Revolutionary Life*, 226 (Yardley, PA, Westholme, 2019).

40. Gregory J.W. Urwin, "Renegade Revolutionary: The Life of General Charles Lee," 3, available https://armyhistory.org/renegade-revolutionary-the-life-of-general-charles-lee/ (visited August 7, 2020).

41. Lender, *Cabal*, 57.

42. *Cabal*, 58.

43. *Cabal*, 64.

44. Snow, *1777: Tipping Point at Saratoga*, 11: "It was a new kind of army. There was nothing like it in Europe. The men were all volunteers, mostly amateurs. [Many] had signed up to buy [their] way out of jail."

45. *See 1777: Tipping Point at Saratoga*, 201 & 340.

46. Quoted in *1777: Tipping Point at Saratoga*, 283.

47. *See Duty, Honor or Country*, 220.

48. Quoted in *Duty, Honor or Country*, 225.

49. Cowpens lies in the west of South Carolina's northern tier, 14 miles northeast of Spartanburg, South Carolina and 56 miles southwest of Charlotte, North Carolina.

50. John Buchanan, *The Road to Guilford Courthouse: The American Revolution in the Carolinas*, 316 (New York, Wiley & Sons, 1997).

51. *1777: Tipping Point at Saratoga*, 130.

52. *1777: Tipping Point at Saratoga*, 169.

53. *1777: Tipping Point at Saratoga*, 179.

54. *1777: Tipping Point at Saratoga*, 183. & 224.

55. *1777: Tipping Point at Saratoga*, 225.

56. *1777: Tipping Point at Saratoga*, 247–248 & 255 (tables of ring and left wings' compositions).

57. *1777: Tipping Point at Saratoga*, 261.

58. Following receipt of the news about Saratoga, the French entered the war, providing troops, ships, loans, armaments, and supplies. *See, e.g.*, Isaacson, *Benjamin Franklin*, 346 & 349. After news of Saratoga reached them, the French ministers told Franklin "that the King would assent to the treaties—one on friendship and trade, the other creating a military alliance … Franklin's diplomatic triumph would help seal the course of the Revolution." Ben Franklin was the principal of three American Commissioners sent to Paris to deal with the French King and ministers: "Franklin knew that power on the battlefield correlated to power at the bargaining table." *Benjamin Franklin*, 343.

59. *Duty, Honor or Country*, 227. His force of 2,000 consisted of Georgia, South Carolina, North Carolina, and Virginia militia along with several hundred seasoned Continental regulars. On January 17, 1781, Morgan-led force presented a weak center to draw in a 1,150 British infantry and cavalry assault, headed by the impetuous Colonel Banastre Tarleton. Again, Morgan instructed his "militia to form the first and second lines." The militia were "to fire two shots at the enemy, falling back to reload." The Americans then performed a double envelopment, flanking Tarleton and his men, who had been sucked into the vortex, killing 110, wounding 229, and capturing 700 British troops. It was the most decisive American victory of the war, in the words of one military historian, "a devil of a whipping."

Chapter 14

1. Or two of them. Earlier, in what could be termed the first Dunmore's War, Dunmore had called for and led a two-pronged expedition against Native Americans in the Ohio country. The actual fighting that occurred had taken place south of the Ohio River by a militia force led by Andrew Lewis (*see* Chapter 7). The Battle of Point Pleasant is thought by some to have been the first battle of the war, preceding Lexington and Concord by six months. For his part, Governor Dunmore and his contingent never showed for the rendezvous with Lewis. Instead, Dunmore led his force into the heart of the Ohio Country, some said because, like many others at the time, Dunmore was a land speculator and especially interested in Ohio.

2. Previously, he had been governor of New York Province for between one and two years.

3. Atkinson, *The British Are Coming*, 186.

4. *See generally* James Corbett David, *Dunmore's New World: The Extraordinary Life of a Royal Governor in Revolutionary America* (Charlottesville, VA, University of Virginia, 2013).

5. The second objective would be to restore a Catholic to the throne.

6. England observes each November 5 as Guy Fawkes Day with bonfires and fireworks. Children beg passers-by with a request of "Penny for Guy."

7. *See, e.g., Charles Scott and the "Spirit of '76,"* 11–12.

8. *Revolutionary War Patriot*, 50.
9. Cecere, *Revolutionary War Patriot*, 57–58.
10. See *Revolutionary War Patriot*, 59.
11. The title of Chapter Four, in *Revolutionary War Patriot*, 57. The Battle of Bunker Hill took place on June 17, 1775.
12. Future Chief Justice John Marshall was present as a member of the Culpepper Militia in which his father, Thomas Marshall, was a senior officer. Justice Marshall described the conflict in John Marshall, Vol. 2, *The Life of George Washington*, 132 et seq. (Fredericksburg, Va., Citizens Guild, 1926 ed.).
13. *Charles Scott and the "Spirit of '76,"* 20.
14. Report of the Virginia Committee on Safety, Vol. 3, *Naval Documents of the Revolution*, 132.
15. For an in-depth portrait of Governor Dunmore, *see* James Corbett David, *Dunmore's New World: The Extraordinary Life of a Royal Governor in Revolutionary America* (Charlottesville, VA, University of Virginia Press, 2013).
16. *See generally* "The Battle of Gwynn's Island," available http://www.virginiaplaces/military/gwynnbattle.html (visited February 4, 2022).
17. *See, e.g.*, Jack N. Rakove, "What Remains of Thomas Jefferson?" *Wall Street Journal*, July 2, 2022, C-1, C-2.

Chapter 15

1. Seventy-two brigadiers served under Washington. Henry Muhlenberg, in *The Life of Major General Peter Muhlenberg*, 453–455, lists 84 generals who served, 28 major-generals, and 56 brigadier generals. Excluding the 12 non-Americans who came to the United States only for the purpose of serving in the army yields 72, several of whom did not serve. The major generals in the "foreign" category included Lafayette, De Kalb, Du Coudray, Conway, Steuben, and Du Portail. The brigadier generals in the category included De Woedtke, de Fermay, de Barre, Pulaski, Armand, and Kosciusko. The U.S. generals who died included James Hogun, Hugh Mercer, Richard Montgomery, James Moore, Francis Nash, Enoch Poor, John Thomas, Joseph Warren, William Woodford, and Daniel Wooster. The generals from abroad who perished were De Kalb, De Woedtke, and Pulaski. *The Life of Peter Muhlenberg*, Appendix, 453–455.
2. *See generally* Harry M. Ward, *Charles Scott and the "Spirit of 76,"* 17 (Charlottesville, VA, University of Virginia Press, 1988).
3. Congress elevated Hugh Mercer to his new rank in March 1777. *See Washington's Revolutionary War Generals*, 30.
4. Michael Cecere, *General William Woodford of Virginia, Revolutionary War Patriot*, 115 (Berwyn Heights, MD, Heritage Books, 2019).
5. Colonel William Woodford to General George Washington, July 6, 1776, Vol. 5, *The Papers of George Washington* 228–30 (Charlottesville, VA, University of Virginia Press, 1993).
6. *Revolutionary War Patriot*, 121.
7. *George Washington: A Life*, 260.
8. George Washington to Samuel Washington, December 18, 1776, quoted in *George Washington: A Life*, 271.
9. *See Washington's Revolutionary War Generals*, 78. Of the four generals ranked last, three were the southerners of the group: Seventh: George Weedon (Virginia), Eighth: Peter Muhlenberg (Virginia), Tenth and last: William Woodford (Virginia).
10. *Revolutionary War Patriot*, 126 (footnote omitted).
11. General George Washington to William Woodford, March 3, 1777, Vol. 8, *The Papers of George Washington*, 507 (University of Virginia Press, 1998).
12. Douglas Southall Freeman, *George Washington*, vol. 4, 613 (New York, Scribner & Sons, 1952). *See also* Chapter 16.
13. Great military leaders often have "emphasized grinding rather than genius…. Winning the day of the battle is not enough, you have to win the campaign, then the year, then the decade." Cathal J. Nolan, *The Allure of Battle* (New York, Oxford University Press, 2017).
14. *See* William Woodford, Revolutionary War Biography, available http://www.battlefields.org/learn/biographies/william-woodfrod (visited March 22, 2020).
15. Library of Virginia, *William Woodford (1734-1780)*, available http://edu.lva.virginia.gov/online_classroom/william_woodford (visited March 23, 2020).
16. William Woodford, Encyclopedia, available http://www.encyclopedia.com/history/encyclopedias-almanacs-transcripts-and-maps/william-woodford (visited March 23. 2020).
17. Revolutionary Biography, 2
18. Woodford owned property in Fredericksburg as well. In June 1774, Fredericksburg citizens elected him to the Committee on Correspondence. As winds of war blew stronger, Woodford became one of five residents selected to serve on Caroline County's Non-Importation Committee. William Rind, *Virginia Gazette*, January 17, 1771, 2.
19. William Woodford, Encyclopedia, 1. *See also Revolutionary War Patriot*, 33–35.
20. Quoted in William Wirt, *Sketches of the Life and Character of Patrick Henry*, 139 (Philadelphia, PA, 1817).
21. *Revolutionary War Patriot*, 132.
22. *Revolutionary War Patriot*, 118.
23. Quoted in *Revolutionary War Patriot*, at 119 (shortly before Battle of Gwynn's Island).
24. Ward, *Charles Scott and the Spirit of '76*, 74.
25. Colonel John Neville to General Daniel Morgan, November 9, 1779.
26. *See generally* Cecere, 140–143.
27. *See Fighting Parson*, 69 ("It was then," at Woodstock, "his firm purpose to resign from the army" was abandoned).
28. *Duty, Honor or Country*, 88. *See also Duty,*

Honor or Country, at 123 (Woodford "appears to have been rather pompous and a dandy").

29. *See. e.g.*, Jim Piecuch, *The Battle of Camden*, 10–11 (Charleston, SC, The History Press, 2006).

30. *Revolutionary War Patriot*, 171–172.

31. Varying accounts of that June day exist, including one that a pullback by General Scott on the left precipitated what occurred. *See, e.g., Charles Scott and the Spirit of '76*, at

32. Cecere, *Revolutionary War Patriot*, 173–174.

33. Cecere, 176.

34. Major General Charles Lee faced a court martial that included Woodford sitting in judgment. The court found Lee guilty. Washington affirmed judgment on the verdict. Lee was cashiered from the army, returning to his estate in Berkeley County, Virginia.

35. *See, e.g., Charleston*, 489.

36. "You will put everything in train and march the whole with Tents & baggage as soon as possible to Philadelphia, where you will await further orders." George Washington to William Woodford, December 8, 1779, available, Vol. 23, *Papers of George Washington*, 559 (Charlottesville, VA, University of Virginia Press).

37. *Revolutionary War Patriot*, 212.

38. *Charleston*, 44.

39. *Revolutionary War Patriot*, 214.

40. *Charleston*, 45.

41. *See* Banastre Tarleton, *A History of the Campaigns of 1780-1781 in the Southern Provinces of North America*, 16 (Manchester, NH, Ayer Co., 1999, reprinting original 1787 edition).

42. Captain Hinrichs, describing the dire situation in May of 1780 in Charleston, quoted in John Jakes, *Charleston*, 7.

43. *See Charleston*, 46 (12,000 British force) & 64 (5,600 American troops).

44. *See generally* Carl P. Borick, *A Gallant Defense: The Siege of Charleston, 1780* (Columbia, SC, University of South Carolina Press, 1980).

45. After the surrender of Charleston, Brigadier James Hogun (born Hogan, in Ireland) died January 4, 1781, a British prisoner at Haddrell's Point.

46. French volunteer and engineering officer Louis Lebeque Duportail, quoted in *Charles Scott and the Spirit of '76*, 78 (footnote omitted).

47. The Pennsylvania Packet, December 16, 1780, quoted in Catesby Willis Stewart, *The Life of Brigadier William Woodford of the American Revolution*, Vol. 2, 1187 (Richmond, VA, Witten & Shepperson, 1973).

48. Polhemus, *The Life and Wars of John Stark*, 232.

49. *See Duty, Honor or Country*, 76.

50. *See* Polhemus, *The Life and Wars of John Stark*, 229.

51. Quoted in William M. Dwyer, *The Day Is Ours*, 269.

52. Recorded in James Curtis Ballagh, *The Letters of Richard Henry Lee*, 203–04 (New York, Macmillan, 1911).

53. On land, the DUMBO (Down Underneath the Manhattan and Brooklyn Bridge Overpasses) neighborhood lies south of the Brooklyn Navy Yard area. It has become a very trendy area.

54. A. Roger Ekirch, "Hell Afloat: Wallabout Bay," *Wall Street Journal*, August 23, 2017, A-13.

55. *See generally* Robert P. Watson, *The Ghost Ship of Brooklyn: An Untold Story of the American Revolution* (New York, Da Capo, 2017).

56. Colonial numbers were: 6,800 killed, 6,100 wounded, and 20,000 imprisoned. *See* http://www.battlefields.org/combat/deaths/revolutionary/war (visited April 30, 2020).

57. *See also* Edwin G. Burrows, *Forgotten Patriots: The Untold Story of American Prisoners During the Revolutionary War* (New York, Basic Books, 2008).

Chapter 16

1. *Washington: A Life* 281.

2. Militia Colonel Robert Byrd to Colonel Henry Bouquet, on Mercer's tenure in the Virginia Militia.

3. *With Sword and Lancet*, 56.

4. *See generally* Allan Massie, *The Royal Stuarts: A History of the Family that Shaped Britain* (New York, St. Martin's Griffin, 2013).

5. *See, e.g.*, Geoffrey Plank, *Rebellion and Savagery; The Jacobite Rising and the British Empire* (Philadelphia, University of Pennsylvania Press, 2005).

6. *See* John T. Goolrick, *The Life of General Hugh Mercer*, at Appendix "A," (1906). Mercer's mother was Ann Munro. "Revolutionary War Biography: Hugh Mercer," 1, available http://www.battlefields.org/learn/biographies/hugh-mercer (visited July 6, 2020).

7. Biography of Hugh Mercer, 2.

8. *See* Stuart Reid, *Culloden Moor 1746: The Death of the Jacobite Cause* (Oxford, UK, Osprey Publishing, 2002); Reid, *Like Hungry Wolves: Culloden Moor 16 April 1746* (London, Windrow & Greene, 2000).

9. *Cf. Second to No Man but the Commander in Chief*, 3, listing Mercer as an assistant surgeon's mate.

10. In addition, in return for loyalty oaths to the Crown, the King not only granted pardons but also bestowed grants of American land on a group of Highland Scots. They settled, forming a colony, on the Cape Fear River in southeastern North Carolina. Throughout the Revolution, the Scottish enclave remained loyalist, thoroughly Tories. *See* Joe A. Mobley, *North Carolina Governor Richard Caswell: Founding Father and Revolutionary Hero*, 51–53 (Charleston, SC, The History Press, 2016).

11. The area was the site of Fort Chambers (now Chambersburg, Pennsylvania), which founder Benjamin Chambers built for protection against Indian raids. *See* Waterman, *With Sword and Lancet: The Life of Hugh Mercer*, 8–9.

12. Author Cecere records Mercer as practicing

in the same general vicinity, along Conocoheague Creek, but in Cumberland County, abutting Franklin County to the east (seat: Carlisle).

13. *See, e.g.,* H.W. Brands, *The First American: The Life and Times of Benjamin Franklin,* 161 (In the Quaker dominated Pennsylvania Assembly, 'There remained an uneasiness with war and war preparations, especially when they entailed expense and risk"); Walter Isaacson, *Benjamin Franklin: An American Life,* 123 (when in 1747 Benjamin Franklin tried to organize a militia "in response to ongoing threats by the French and their Indian allies," … "The Assembly, dominated by pacifist Quakers, dithered and failed to authorize any defenses").

14. Quoted in Francis Packman, *Montcalm and Wolfe,* 195 (1884, republished Wentworth Press, 2019).

15. *With Sword and Lancet: The Life of Hugh Mercer,* 20.

16. Kittanning, which still exists, today is the seat of Armstrong County, Pennsylvania.

17. *Second to No Man but the Commander in Chief,* 15.

18. Henry Wadsworth Longfellow, *The Song of Hiawatha* (1855).

19. *Second to No Man but the Commander in Chief,* 14

20. *With Sword and Lancet,* 30.

21. New York *Mercury,* October 4, 1756.

22. *See generally Second to No Man but the Commander in Chief,* 8–16.

23. *With Sword and Lancet,* 38.

24. *See* Israel D. Rupp, *Early History of Western Pennsylvania,* 97 (republished, HardPress, 2019).

25. *See* Biography of Hugh Mercer, 2–3 (George Washington, Hugh Mercer, George Weedon, William Woodford, Fielding Lewis, Thomas Posey, Gutavus Wallace, and Marquis de Lafayette).

26. Biography of Hugh Mercer, 3.

27. *With Sword and Lancet,* 71.

28. George Weedon, as quoted in part in *With Sword and Lancet,* 91.

29. John T. Goolrick, *Historic Fredericksburg,* 33 (1922). Virginia drew a distinction between county militias that were of former stuff and county by county district militias that varied in their professionalism, mostly being of an unreliable nature.

30. *See* Volume 5, *William & Mary Quarterly,* 249.

31. *Second to No Man but the Commander in Chief,* 53.

32. *Second to No Man but the Commander in Chief,* 63

33. *See* Biography of Hugh Mercer, 3.

34. *See generally With Sword and Lancet,* 96 & 99–101.

35. Alfred Thayer Mahan, *The Influence of Sea Power Upon History: 1660–1783* (Boston, MA, Little, Brown & Co., 1890).

36. General Hugh Mercer to General George Washington, July 29, 1776.

37. For example, in August 1776, Mercer sent Smallwood's Marylanders, a battalion of Pennsylvania riflemen, and a battalion of Pennsylvania militia north to General Washington, then superintending defense of Brooklyn and Long Island. *See, e.g., With Sword and Lancet,* 83.

38. Biography of Hugh Mercer, at 4.

39. *Cf. With Sword and Lancet,* 134 (2,634 officers and men surrendered). This was an event that Greene lamented for the remainder of his career.

40. General Hugh Mercer to General George Washington, September 17, 1776.

41. *See, e.g., Second to No Man but the Commander in Chief,* 104–105.

42. Reproduced in Stephen Fried, *Rush: Revolution, Madness, and the Visionary Doctor Who Became a Founding Father* (New York, Crown Books, 2018). See also Harlow Giles Unger, *Benjamin Rush: The Founding Father Who Healed a Wounded Nation* (New York, Da Capo, 2018).

43. General Hugh Mercer to Colonel Durkee et al., reproduced in William S. Stryker, *The Battles of Trenton and Princeton,* 379 (1898, republished by Old Barracks Association, Trenton, NJ, 2001).

44. Quoted in Isaac Greenwood, *The Revolutionary Service of John Greenwood,* 39 (New York, 1922).

45. John Greenwood, of General John Sullivan's division, quoted in *The Revolutionary Service of John Greenwood,* 41.

46. Stryker, *The Battles of Trenton and Princeton,* 318. Hanover, in Germany's north, also provided mercenaries to the British.

47. Quoted in William M. Dwyer, *The Day Is Ours: An Inside View of the Battles of Trenton and Princeton,* November 1776-January 1777, 219 (New Brunswick, NJ, Rutgers University Press, 1998).

48. *With Sword and Lancet,* 149 & 151.

49. William Stryker, *The Battles of Trenton and Princeton,* 394, quoting General Lord Stirling to New Jersey Governor Robert Livingston.

50. *See generally* David Hackett Fischer, *Washington's Crossing* (New York, Columbia University Press, 2004).

51. Quoted in Colonel James Wilkinson, *Memoirs of My Own Times,* 146 (1816).

52. *With Sword and Lancet,* at 154.

53. *Second to No Man but the Commander in Chief,* 154–55.

54. *With Sword and Lancet,* 153–54.

55. Benson J. Lossing, *Pictorial Field Book of the Revolution,* 29 (1860)

56. Ron Chernow in *Washington: A Life,* 281. Historical accounts differ, although the differences amount to no more than a distinction without a difference. In another account, General Washington sent Mercer and his men as an advance party to secure the bridge at Stony Brook, which spans the Princeton Turnpike nearer Princeton than Trenton. The Mercer contingent left camp at one o'clock, in advance of the main American army.

57. Biography of Hugh Mercer, 4–5. A reproduction of the tree is the seal of Mercer County, New Jersey.

58. Benjamin Rush, *A Memorial Containing Travels Through Life of Sundry Incidents in the Life of Dr. Benjamin Rush*, 98 (Philadelphia, Louis Biddle, 1905).

59. General Hugh Mercer, quoted in George Washington Parke Custis, *Recollections and Memoirs of Washington*, 13 (1860).

60. *With Sword and Lancet*, 159.

61. Inscription on the General Hugh Mercer Monument, Fredericksburg, Virginia.

62. Tuchman, *A Distant Mirror*, 571, eulogizing the French Baron de Coucy.

Chapter 17

1. The Treaty of Lancaster, also the Treaty of 1744, between Britain and the Iroquois Six Tribes, sold to the British, thus making it part of the Virginia colony, all the land west of the Appalachians to the Pacific Ocean ('from sea to sea)," or in default, at least as far as the Ohio River extended, that is, to present-day Missouri. An earlier treaty, the Treaty of 1701, memorialized the sale by the Indians of all lands north of the Ohio and, roughly, west of Pennsylvania. *See generally* "The Treaty of 1744," http://www.visitlancaster.com/treatyof1744/ (visited December 24, 2020). *See also* http://www.unchartedlancaster.com/Treatyof1701 (visited December 24, 2020).

2. H. W. Brand, *The First American*, 229.

3. Kentucky's major river, the Kentucky River, flows north through the center of the state joining the Ohio River at Carrollton, KY. The river passes west of Lexington and flows through Frankfort (the state capital). The river rises in the coal country of southeastern Kentucky and then flows 460 miles through the bluegrass and horse country. *See, e.g.,* http://www.Britannica.com/places/Kentucky/River (visited May 5, 2020).

4. Recounted in Ward, *Charles Scott and the "Spirit of '76,"* 95–96.

5. *Charles Scott and the "Spirit of '76,"* 99.

6. Quoted in William Bane, *Excursions in the U.S. and Canada* (1824). *See also* Lewis Collins, *Historical Sketches of Kentucky*, 516 (Cincinnati, OH, 1847, republished Andesite Press, in 2 volumes, 2017–2018).

7. Serving as president for only a short time, Taylor died the July following his March 1849 inauguration, succeeded in office by vice-president Millard Fillmore of New York. *See, e.g.,* Michael Holt, "Zachary Taylor: Death of a President," available http://www.millercenter.org/presidents/taylor/death-of-a-president (visited February 10, 2022).

8. Anthony Wayne had been Scott's colleague and fellow brigadier in the Revolutionary War.

9. *Charles Scott and the "Spirit of '76,"* 147. "The battle of Fallen Timbers, as time passed, would increasingly be regarded as a great victory; in reality it was hardly a battle," with 30 Americans and 30 to 40 Native American lives lost.

10. Primogeniture requires "an inheritance that is given by law, custom, or usage to the eldest son." Its avowed purpose was "to preserve the integrity of inheritances." *See* http://www.bitannica.com/primogeniture (visited December 24, 2020).

11. *See* "Georgia Constitution Abolishes Primogeniture and Entail," available https://www.history.com/this-day-in-histrory/georgia-constitution-abolishes-primogentiure (visited January 23, 2021).

12. "Farmers and small business owners hold significant amounts of capital in the form of [illiquid] assets …. Concern for the impact of the federal estate tax in the ability to transfer the farm [or business] to the next generation has been primary factor in increasing [the] exemption …" Ron L. Durst, "The Effects of Federal Estate Tax on Farm Households" (2013), available https://www.choicesmagazine.org (visited January 23, 2021).

13. A Roll of Captain David Bell's Company, July 13, 1756.

14. The war did not formally conclude until the Treaty of Paris in 1763. *See generally* Fred Anderson, *Crucible of War: The Seven Years' War and the Fate of Its Empire in British North American, 1754–1766* (New York, Knopf, 2000). The French & Indian War also is known as the Seven Years' War, as well as Queen Anne's War.

15. Adam Stephen executed a peace treaty with the Native Americans on December 18, 1761.

16. *See generally* Richard T. Couture, *Powhatan: A Bicentennial History*, at 75–82 (Richmond, VA, Virginia Book Company, 1980).

17. *See, e.g., Charles Scott and the "Spirit of '76,"* 11–12.

18. Cecere, *Revolutionary War Patriot*, 57–58.

19. *See Revolutionary War Patriot*, 59.

20. *Charles Scott and the "Spirit of '76,"* 20.

21. Robert Beale, quoted in Dennis P. Ryan, "Robert B. Memoirs," in *A Salute to Courage: The American Revolution as Seen Through the Wartime Writings of Officers of the Continental Army and Navy*, at 56 (New York, Columbia University Press, 1979).

22. *See* http://www.revwartalk.com/charles-scott, 4 (visited May 9, 2020).

23. Michael Cecere, *Second to No Man but the Commander in Chief: Hugh Mercer, American Patriot*, 146 (Berwyn Heights, MD, Heritage, 2015), and 143–146 (Second Battle of Trenton generally).

24. Charles Scott, quoted in *Charles Scott and the "Spirit of '76,"* 27.

25. *See, e.g., Major General Adam Stephen and the Cause of American Liberty*, 155.

26. Until 1776, Perth Amboy and Burlington near Philadelphia were dual capitals for the New Jersey Colony, having survived the East Jersey and West Jersey merger into today's New Jersey (1702).

27. Lender, *Cabal*, 6, 4, & 7.

28. Recorded in Jared Lobdell, "Two Forgotten Battles," in volume 85 *New Jersey History*, 229–230 (1967).

29. During spring and early summer, 1777, Scott's light infantry several other times engaged British scouting and foraging parties.

30. *Stephen and the Cause of American Liberty*, 181.

31. *Stephen and the Cause of American Liberty*, 188.

32. *Stephen and the Cause of American Liberty*, 189.

33. Washington's initial design was that "fifteen hundred men under Brigadier General Charles Scott would harass the enemy." Chernow, *Washington: A Life*, 340.

34. *See, e.g., Revolutionary War Patriot*, at 171. *See also* http://www.revwartalk.com/charles-scott, 5–6 (visited May 9, 2020). *See, e.g., Stephen and the Cause of American Liberty*, 157–162.

35. *Charles Scott and the "Spirit of '76,"* 49–49.

36. *Charles Scott and the "Spirit of '76,"* 50.

37. Quoted in Michael Stephenson, *Patriot Battle: How the War of Independence Was Fought*, 188 (New York, HarperCollins, 2007).

38. Quoted in Theodore B. Lewis, "Was Washington Profane at Monmouth?" 89 *New Jersey History* 149, 162 (1971). *See also* http://www.revwartalk.com/charles-scott, 45. "Tradition holds that … Scott witnessed Washington excoriating Lee in a profanity-laden tirade." (visited May 9, 2020).

39. Quoted in Edward Lengel, *General George Washington: A Military Life*, 300 (New York, Random House, 2005).

40. Stephenson, *Patriot Battle*, 188.

41. Lender, *Cabal*, 12–13.

42. Letter dated December 13, 1776, from Charles Lee to Horatio Gates, available Volume II, Charles Lee Papers, 348 (Richmond, VA, State Library of Virginia).

43. *See* http://www.mountvernon.org/library/digitalhistory/digital-encyclopedia/article/battle-of-monmouth/ (visited May 12, 2020).

44. Quoted in James Flexner, *George Washington in the American Revolution, 1775–1783*, 305 (Boston, MA, Little, Brown, 1968).

45. As to the battle overall, *see generally* William S. Stryker, *The Battle of Monmouth* (Princeton, NJ, Princeton University Press, 1927).

46. General Charles Scott to General George Washington, October 21, 1778.

47. General George Washington to General Charles Scott, via General George Weedon at Fredericksburg, March 6, 1779.

48. *See, e.g.*, the material on General George Weedon and Peter Muhlenburg, Chapters 2 and 18.

49. Scott's colleagues, Generals Woodford and Hogun, obtained neither parole nor exchange. The British shipped Woodford to New York City where on November 13, he died in captivity. The second brigadier, North Carolina's James Hogun, became ill as well, dying at Haddrell's Point on January 4, 1781. *See, e.g., Revolutionary War Patriot*, 239.

50. A brevet rank is of a temporary nature but frequently one that is never revoked. *See. e.g.*, https://www.britannica.com/brevet/rank (visited November 20, 2020). "It carried with it the pay, right to command, and uniform of a higher grade. In the United States especially, brevet rank was widely bestowed as a reward for outstanding service." It was declared obsolete in 1922.

51. *Duty, Honor or Country*, 82.

52. Ryan Cole, *Light-Horse Harry Lee: The Rise and Fall of a Revolutionary Hero*, 77–78 (Washington, DC, Regnery History, 2019).

53. General Charles Scott to Colonel Benjamin Harrison, August 3, 1777.

54. *See Duty, Honor or Country*, at 53–54. *See also Charles Scott and the "Spirit of '76,"* 33–34. Weedon, of course, left the army despite General Washington's entreaties for Weedon to stay. *See generally* Chapter 2.

55. *See generally Charles Scott and the "Spirit of '76,"* 85.

Chapter 18

1. Henry A. Muhlenberg, *The Life of Major General Peter Muhlenberg*, 33 (Philadelphia, PA, Carey & Hart, 1849).

2. *See generally* Arthur J. Mekeel, *The Relation of the Quakers to the American Revolution* (Washington, D.C., University Press of America, 1979).

3. Albert Louis Zambone, *Daniel Morgan: A Revolutionary Life*, 8 (Yardley, PA, Westholme Publishing, 2018), citing Pierre Marambaud, *Byrd of Westover*, 51 & 250 (Charlottesville, VA, University of Virginia Press, 1971).

4. The northern end of the Valley near Woodstock, Winchester, and Front Royal, stretching into what today is the panhandle of West Virginia, is lower than the southern portion (Staunton, Lexington, Roanoke, etc.) so under a view prevalent then, the upper area was known as the "lower valley," that is, lower in elevation. The east and west branches of the Shenandoah then flow north, that is, downhill, merging and then turning toward the east where the Shenandoah flows into the Potomac at Harper's Ferry, West Virginia.

5. Edward W. Hocker, *The Fighting Parson of the American Revolution: A Biography of General Peter Muhlenberg*, 44 (Mechanicsburg, PA, Sunbury Press, 1936).

6. Bruce Catton, *Stillness at Appomattox*, 307 (Garden City, NY, Doubleday, 1962).

7. *Life of Major General Peter Muhlenberg*, 53. Accord: *The Fighting Parson of the American Revolution*, 45 (the sermon was based upon Ecclesiastics, Chapter 3, Verse 1).

8. Bill Federer, "Sometimes Even Pastors Must Go to War," *World Net Daily*, September 30, 2019, available, https://wnd.com/2019/9/sometimes-even-pastors-must-go-to-war, 2 (visited February 2, 2020).

9. Muhlenberg's brother, Frederick Augustus Muhlenberg, later to serve in Congress with his sibling, "did not approve of [brother Peter] going into the army until the British burned down his church, Christ Lutheran in New York City in front of him. Then Frederick joined the military himself." American War History, "Peter Muhlenberg,"

available http://www.revwartalk.com/peter-muhlenberg (visited February 3, 2020).

10. *Cf. Life of Major General Peter Muhlenberg*, 50: "[The incident] shows of what sterling metal the patriots of old time were formed."

11. The 2,200 student Allentown, Pennsylvania, college is named after Peter Muhlenberg's father, Reverend Henry Melchior Muhlenberg, rather than after the Revolutionary War general. *See, e.g.,* http://www.Muhlenberg.edu (visited February 6, 2020). Henry Melchior Muhlenberg, who emigrated from Eimbeck, Germany, in 1742, is considered the patriarch of Lutheran churches in America. "He exercised superintendence for many years over virtually all of the Lutheran congregations of Pennsylvania, New Jersey, Maryland, and Virginia." He is considered "the founder of the Lutheran Church in America," frequently termed "the venerated Father Muhlenberg." *Life of Major General Peter Muhlenberg*, 17 & 40.

12. Each state of the Union has placed two statutes in Statuary Hall of the U.S. Capitol. Pennsylvania's first choice is a statue of Robert Fulton, inventor of the steamboat. Pennsylvania's other choice is a statue of General Peter Muhlenberg. Again, the statute depicts General Muhlenberg in clerical garb, open to reveal a Virginia officer's Revolutionary War uniform. See "Sometimes Even Pastors Must Go to War," 5.

13. Further, Pennsylvania labored under a double disability. While the Crown and Parliament ruled other colonies, the proprietors (William Penn and later Thomas Penn) ruled Pennsylvania, with the Crown and Parliament in the background. The proprietors did not permit any taxation whatsoever on their vast land holdings, even entering secret non-taxation pacts with the colonial governors appointed by and beholden to the Penns. So, even had the Pennsylvania Assembly voted a tax, the royal governors would veto it. Even if the Quaker-dominated Assembly conceded the need for defense against Indian raids, which it eventually did, the colony lacked ability to fund a defense. *See generally* Brands, *The First American*, 37 & 211.

14. *Fighting Parson*, 7.

15. *See, e.g.,* www.bioguide.congress.gov/scripts/biodisplay.pl?/index=M001066 (visited February 2, 2020).

16. Quoted in *The Life of Major-General Peter Muhlenberg*, 27–28.

17. *The Life of Major-General Peter Muhlenberg*, 25.

18. *Fighting Pastor*, 13.

19. His descendent, Henry A. Muhlenberg, omits any biographical reference to an indenture by the ancestor, maintaining instead that after leaving Halle, a young Peter became a dragoon in German regiment. *See generally Life of Major General Peter Muhlenberg*, 29–30.

20. Until 1702, as aforesaid, the territory consisted of two colonies, East Jersey and West Jersey, with separate capital cities of Perth Amboy, across from Staten Island, and Burlington, across the Delaware River from Philadelphia. The unified colony retained dual capital cities after East and West Jersey combined.

21. Just turned age 24, Muhlenberg married on November 6, 1770, to Anna Barbara Meyer. Upon completing theological studies, Minister Muhlenberg's assignments were in the New Jersey Raritan River valley, including Bedminster and New Germantown, New Jersey. Church records list Peter Muhlenberg assistant pastor or pastor *pro tem*.

22. *See, e.g., With Sword and Lancet*, 9.

23. Benjamin Franklin had tried repeatedly to form and arm a militia that would protect against Native American forays and brutal raids into areas even east of the frontier, which in the 1750's and 1760's existed not far beyond Lancaster and York, a distance east of the Alleghenies. "The theology of the Quakers," who controlled the colony, "had attenuated over time; pacifism was not as central to the self-conception of the third generation of Friends in America as it had been to William Penn's contemporaries. Yet there remained an uneasiness with war and war preparation." H.W. Brands, *The First American: The Life and Times of Benjamin Franklin*, 161 (New York, Doubleday, 2000). Later, after the Assembly's refusal to pay for equipment of a militia, Franklin organized a lottery to do so. "Many of the same persons who objected on pacifist grounds to buying weapons for the province now objected on anti-gambling grounds to a lottery." *The First American*, 184.

24. *The Life of Major-General Peter Muhlenberg*, 33. "For many years, German inhabitants of the Middle States commenced emigrating in considerable numbers to Virginia, settling principally in the Valley of the Blue Ridge".

25. Letter from James Wood, Esq., to Peter Muhlenberg, May 4, 1777.

26. *American War History*, "Peter Muhlenberg," 2. "Since the Anglican Church was the state church of Virginia, he was required to be ordained in the Anglican Church in order to serve a congregation in Virginia."

27. *Fighting Parson*, 31–32.

28. *Life of Major General Peter Muhlenberg*, 44 (Committee of Safety and Correspondence).

29. *See generally Fighting Parson*, 38–41.

30. *The Life of Major General Peter Muhlenberg*, 47.

31. Author Rick Atkinson in *The British Are Coming*, 565, reports that the HMS (His or Her Majesty's Ship) designation did not come into regular use "until several years after the American Revolution had ended." I have continued to use the HMS designation on the theory that its descriptive value outweighs the historical inaccuracy.

32. *The Life of Major-General Peter Muhlenberg*, 56.

33. *See generally* Rick Atkinson, *The British Are Coming: The War for American Lexington to Princeton, 1775–1777*, 324 et seq. (New York, Henry Holt, 2019).

34. *The British Are Coming*, 330.

35. *See, e.g.*, Henry Lumpkin, *From Savannah to Yorktown*, 11 & 17 (New York, Paragon Publishers, 1981).
36. Russell, *American Revolution in the Southern Colonies*, 94.
37. *Fighting Parson*, 51.
38. Quoted in *The Life of Major-General Peter Muhlenberg*, at 62.
39. *Fighting Parson*, 62.
40. *The Life of Major-General Peter Muhlenberg*, 71.
41. *The Life of Major-General Peter Muhlenberg*, 77–78.
42. *Fighting Parson*, 57.
43. *Cf.* Ward, *Adam Stephen*, 180. "The Virginia troops distinguished themselves. The 3rd Regiment in Weedon's brigade (Greene's division) was the last to leave the field, and most of its officers were killed."
44. *The Life of Major-General Peter Muhlenberg*, 96.
45. Quoted in *Fighting Parson*, 60.
46. Ward, *Adam Stephen*, 185. *See generally Adam Stephen*, 184–89.
47. *Fighting Parson*, 63.
48. Nathanael Greene, quoted in *Adam Stephen*, 188.
49. *The Life of Major-General Peter Muhlenberg*, 114.
50. *See generally* Bob Drury & Tom Clavin, *Valley Forge* (New York, Simon & Schuster, 2018).
51. *Fighting Parson*, 68. To the British, especially strong incentives existed for Muhlenberg's capture. "The British would surely have been delighted to lay their hands on him, for in view of his having been a parson of the established Church of England, his treason was looked upon as especially heinous."
52. *The Life of Major-General Peter Muhlenberg*, 124.
53. *Adam Stephen*, 197.
54. George Washington to Peter Muhlenberg, April 10, 1778, quoted in Henry Augustus Muhlenberg, *The Life of Major-General Peter Muhlenberg*, 131.
55. By contrast, in summer 1777, the disgruntled George Weedon retired, seemingly on a permanent basis, to Fredericksburg. *See* Chapter 2.
56. *The Life of Major-General Peter Muhlenberg*, 149, records that General Anthony Wayne dissented from an otherwise unanimous vote not to attack Philadelphia.
57. *See The Life of Major-General Peter Muhlenberg*, 156. "Although the Virginians fought with their usual steadiness and gallantry [and] although [General Muhlenberg] displayed the same skill and impetuous ardour … the actions of this particular body of troops were lost in those of the main force. They did their duty … but more cannot be claimed."
58. At White Plains, General Muhlenberg commanded a body of picket troops that undertook reconnaissance in the direction of the enemy's lines. Later in the year, General Washington, having sent Nathanael Greene to the southern campaign, commanded Muhlenberg and his troops across the Hudson where they were stationed at West Point. Muhlenberg and his men spent winter encampments in 1778 at West Point, New York, in 1779 at Middlebrook, New Jersey, and in 1780 at Morristown, New Jersey, the latter of which was without General Muhlenberg whom Washington had sent south to superintend the defense of Virginia. *The Life of Major-General Peter Muhlenberg*, 157 & 176.
59. *Fighting Parson*, 76.
60. Friedrich Kapp, *The Life of Frederick von Steuben, Major General of the Revolutionary* Army, 60 (republished, Create Space. 2015).
61. *The Life of Major-General Peter Muhlenberg*, 205.
62. *The Life of Major-General Peter Muhlenberg*, 210.
63. *The Life of Major-General Peter Muhlenberg*, 220–221.
64. *See generally Fighting Parson*, 77–81.
65. An interesting sidelight: The traitor Arnold questioned a captured colonial. Arnold asked, "What would be my fate if the Americans captured me?" The colonial soldier replied, "We would cut off the shortened leg wounded at Quebec and Saratoga and bury it with the honors of war, and hang the rest of you." Recounted in *Fighting Parson*, 78.
66. *See* Henry P. Johnston, *The Yorktown Campaign and the Surrender of Cornwallis, 1781*, 33–34 (Arlington, VA, Honford House, 1975).
67. *See Fighting Parson*, 83.
68. *See, e.g.*, Russell, *American Revolution in the Southern Colonies*, 289 (noting only that Muhlenberg, with 700 troops, was present at Yorktown) & 296 (Hamilton commanded the force attacking the British redoubt).
69. *Washington's Revolutionary War Generals*, 236.
70. Eighty-five years later another minister or priest, Leonidas Polk, left behind his miter and crozier to enter the military. Polk left his position as an Episcopal bishop to accept a commission as a general in the Confederate army in the War Between the States, as many southerners term the Civil War. *See* Ron Chernow, *Grant*, 153–154 (New York, Penguin Press, 2017)
71. Reproduced in William Holmes McGuffey, *McGuffey's Fifth Eclectic Reader*, 200–04 (Cincinnati, OH, Van Antwerp & Bragg, rev. ed., 1979), also available https://www.AmericanMinute.com (visited February 11, 2020); Friedrich Kapp, *The Life of Frederick von Steuben, Major General of the Revolutionary* Army, 60 (republished, Create Space. 2015).

Chapter 19

1. Three representative historical works devoid of any mention of Francis Nash are Billias,

Washington's Generals (De Capo Press, 1994); Ferreiro, *Brothers at Arms* (Knopf, 2016); and A. J. Langguth, *Patriots: The Men Who Saved the American Revolution* (Simon & Schuster, 1988). See also James Swisher, *The Revolutionary War in the Southern Backcountry* (Pelican Publishing 2008) (same).

2. *See, e.g.*, Taaffe, *Washington's Generals*, 78. "Congress expected Nash to recruit much of North Carolina's allotment of troops in the western part pf the state and then march them northward to join Washington's army."

3. Yet both Ohio and Tennessee have a Nashville, the latter being the state's capital city. *See, e.g.*, http://en.wikipedia.org/Nashville/Tenessee (visited November 5, 2012). The city was founded in 1779, named after Revolutionary War hero Francis Nash.

4. Recorded in A. N. Waddell, "Gen. Francis Nash," Dedication of Guilford Courthouse Battlefield, July 4, 1906.

5. Stephen R. Taaffe, *Washington's Revolutionary War Generals*, 78, quoting Congressional delegate Charles Carroll (Norman, OK, University of Oklahoma Press, 2019).

6. *See generally* Hugh Owen Nash, Jr., *Patriot Sons, Patriot Brothers*, 17 (Nashville, TN, Westview Publishing, 2006).

7. John Luster Brinkley, *On This Hill: A History of Hampden-Sydney College, 1774–1994*, 10 (Hampden-Sydney, 1994).

8. *Patriot Sons*, 7–11. Francis married Sarah Moore, who gave birth to daughters Anna and Sarah. Only Sarah survived to adulthood.

9. *See* Archibald Henderson, *Conquest of the Old Southwest*, 177 (New York, Century Co., 1920).

10. Reed, "Tragic Sword, A Biography of Brigadier Francis Nash of North Carolina," 18 Montgomery County (PA) Historical Society, 241 (1972).

11. *See* William S, Powell, *North Carolina Through Four Centuries*, 17 (Chapel Hill, NC, University of North Carolina Press, 1989).

12. Majoleine Kars, *Breaking Loose Together*, 157–158 (Chapel Hill, NC, University of North Carolina Press, 2002).

13. Powell, *North Carolina Through Four Centuries*, 167.

14. *See generally* Russell, *American Revolution in the Colonies*, 45 et seq.

15. Letter from Governor Martin to Lord Dartmouth dated March 10, 1775, reproduced in Hugh Nash, *Southern Sons*, 37–38.

16. Nash, *Patriot Sons, Patriot Brothers*, 40.

17. These events are recounted in Lindley S. Butler, *North Carolina and the Coming of the Revolution, 1763–1776*, 60 et seq. (Raleigh, NC, Division of Archives and History, 1976).

18. On November 28, 1775, the Continental Congress took North Carolina's regiments into the Continental Line, making them answerable to the Congress rather than the North Carolina's Provincial Congress. *See generally* Nash, *Patriot Sons*, 46–47.

19. A more detailed rendition of the battle may be found, *inter alia*, in Hugh F. Rankin, Chapter II, "The Battle at Moore's Creek Bridge," *North Carolina in the American Revolution*, 10–20 (Raleigh, NC, North Carolina Division of Archives and History, 1959, 7th ed., 2001).

20. They then greased the skids, so to speak, greasing the trusses ("sleepers") arching over the waterway. The Black itself is a tributary of the Cape Fear River.

21. *See, e.g.*, Rankin, *North Carolina in the American Revolution*, 18. "Two massive logs had been thrown across the creek .... The Whigs had removed most of the planks and had coated the bare logs with soap and tallow. It was almost impossible [for the Scots] to maintain a footing on the greasy, round logs."

22. Based upon what occurred at Moore's Creek, the British, with troops awaiting aboard transports in the Cape Fear Estuary, called off a planned invasion. *See, e.g.*, Powell, *North Carolina Through Four Centuries*, 180–181. *See also* Chapter 4.

23. Just as the appointment of Francis Nash to the lieutenant colonel rank marked the end of Nash's political and civic career and the beginning of a military one, Moore's Creek marked the opposite for Richard Caswell. His leadership and heroics in the battle marked the end of his military career, to be followed by a political one. Richard Caswell became North Carolina's first governor, sitting from early 1777 to 1780. *See, e.g.*, Joe A. Mobley, *North Carolina Governor Richard Caswell: Founding Father and Revolutionary Hero*, Chapter Four, "Governor in the Struggle for Independence," 59–74 (Charleston, SC, The History Press, 2016) (Governor January 1777 to April 1780).

24. David Lee Russell, *The American Revolution in the Southern Colonies*, 90–91 (Jefferson, NC, McFarland, 2000).

25. *Southern Patriots*, 57.

26. Russell, *American Revolution in the Southern Colonies*, 90.

27. Hugh F. Rankin, *The North Carolina Continentals*, 88 (Chapel Hill, NC, University of North Carolina Press, 1971).

28. *Southern Patriots*, 63.

29. John F. Reed, *Campaign to Valley Forge*, 49 (St. Paul, MN, Pioneer Press, 1980).

30. *Campaign to Valley Forge*, 78.

31. Quoted in Bruce E. Mowday, *September 11, 1777: Washington's Defeat at Brandywine Dooms Philadelphia*, 127–128 (Shippensburg, PA, White Mane Books, 2002).

32. Today incorporated within Philadelphia. Rand McNally, *2022 Road Atlas*, at 90 (Chicago, IL, Rand McNally Publishers. 2021).

33. Witherspoon's father, John Witherspoon, was the president of Princeton University and a New Jersey signatory to the Declaration of Independence. *See, e.g.*, *Patriot Sons*, 78 & n. 57.

34. *Campaign to Valley Forge*, 229.

35. *See* Thomas J. McGuire, *The Surprise of Germantown*, 394–395 (Philadelphia, PA. Cliveden

Press, 1994), who records that the errant cannon ball struck the horse first, then Nash, and finally Witherspoon.

36. *Tragic Sword*, 285–286; Rankin, *The North Carolina Continentals*, 115.
37. *Tragic Sword*, 287–288.
38. *Tragic Sword*, 288–290; *Surprise at Germantown*, 90–91.
39. *See, e.g., Patriot Sons*, 196.

Chapter 20

1. John Adams to Abigail Adams, May 22, 1777, available Massachusetts Historical Society, *Adams Family Papers*, available http://www.masshist.org/digitaladams/ (visited October 21, 2020). See also *John Adams*, 169 (same).
2. Richard V. Polhemus & John F. Polhemus, *Stark: The Life and Wars of John Stark*, 238 (Delmar, NY, Black Dome Press, 2014).
3. Ulysses Grant quoted in Ron Chernow, *Grant*, 357 (New York, Penguin Press, 2017).
4. In the modern military, promotion of others thought less deserving and recognition of seniority in others deemed less capable may cause grumbling by those who think they have been left behind, but nothing more.
5. Professor Rod Andrews, Jr., *The Life and Times of General Andrew Pickens*, Preface, xv (Chapel Hill, University of North Carolina Press, 2017).
6. *See generally* Chapter 7.
7. Michael Cecere, *General William Woodford of Virginia, Revolutionary War Patriot*, 115 (Berwyn Heights, MD, Heritage Books, 2019).
8. Colonel William Woodford to General George Washington, July 6, 1776, Vol. 5, *The Papers of George Washington* at 228–30 (Charlottesville, VA, University of Virginia Press, 1993).
9. George Washington to George Weedon, March 15, 1778, quoted at length in Chapter 2.
10. *See, e.g., Major General Adam Stephen*, 210.
11. General George Weedon to Henry Lee, April 12, 1778.
12. *Washington's Revolutionary War Generals*, 151.
13. *Washington's Revolutionary War Generals*, 151.
14. General Charles Scott to General George Washington, October 21, 1778.
15. *See, e.g.*, Chapter 15. Saratoga was a turning point because the victory motivated the French to aid the American cause.
16. Colonel Daniel Morgan to President, Continental Congress, July 18, 1779.
17. General Horatio Gates to President John Hancock, October 12, 1777.
18. Graham, *Life of Morgan*, 53
19. *See generally* Chapter 12. Horatio Gates, the overall commander of American forces at Saratoga, deserves a share of the blame. Eight generals under his command fought valiantly and well, with Morgan clearly in the ascendancy. Rather than single out one or the other of his generals from the eight, Gates made no recommendations at all. A fair inference might be that the prospect of his own fame and capitalization on it, rather than credit for battlefield exploits, preoccupied Gates after Saratoga.
20. *See* Chapter 17.
21. *Life and Wars of John Stark*, 239.
22. *Washington's Revolutionary War Generals*, 78. Poor was a capable officer who served at Trenton, Princeton, Saratoga, and Monmouth, after which he was killed in dual with a French officer. *See generally* Amos T. Akerman, "The Military Career of General Enoch Poor," Manchester, NH, 1878, on file, New Hampshire Historical Society (NHHS), Concord, NH. *See also* M.H. Cannon, "General Enoch Poor, 1736–1780," Exeter, NH, 1966, unpaginated monograph on file with NHHS: Poor "was conspicuous at the Battle of Monmouth"; Reginald McMahon, "The Death and Burial of General Enoch Poor," Proceedings of the Bergen County (NJ) Historical Society (1992).
23. *Stark: Maverick General*, 89.
24. Howard P. Moore, *A Life of General John Stark of New Hampshire*, 252 (New York, 1949).
25. *Stark: Maverick General*, 99.
26. *Life and Wars of John Stark*, 239.
27. Resignation letter of John Stark, dated March 22, 1777, reproduced in *Stark: Maverick General*, 100. He continued, quite eloquently for a New Hampshire lumberman, "I should have served with the greatest pleasure; more especially at this important Crisis when our Country calls for the Utmost Exertions of every American."
28. *See Turning Point at Saratoga*, 80 & 84. Earlier, in response to the Congressional snub, New Hampshire had responded by creating a state-only army of firmer stuff than an ordinary militia unit, appointing Stark as a brigadier general to lead the 1,500-man unit. It was this New Hampshire army that Stark led to victory over the Hessians at the Battle of Bennington, thereby protecting Horatio Gates's right flank, Gates's force then to the west on the Hudson's right bank, below the village of Saratoga. Stark, though, following Bennington, awash with praise and glory, remained petulant. For one, following his resignation from Continental service, he had also pledged never to take orders from a Continental Army officer. He refused, after Bennington, to join forces with the Northern Army on the far side of the Hudson.
29. Charles W. Heathcote, "General Ebenezer Learned: Courageous Patriot and Friend of George Washington," *Picket Post*, 1958, available at https://www.ushistory.org/valleyforge/served/learned.html, 9 (visited January 23, 2023). "In the spring of 1778, Learned's health failed and he was forced to resign his commission."
30. *Washington's Revolutionary War Generals*, 190 & 244.
31. Stephen Taaffe, in *Washington's Revolutionary War Generals*, 177.

32. McCullogh, *Pioneers*, 117.
33. *See generally* http://www.ncpedia.com/James-Moore (visited February 25, 2021).
34. *Piedmont Partisan*, 93. In turn, General Smallwood (Maryland) resigned after Nathanael Greene appointed Baron von Steuben over Smallwood. *See Piedmont Partisan*, 100.
35. Mobley, *Richard Caswell: Founding Father and Revolutionary Hero*, 81.
36. *Piedmont Partisan*, 125.
37. Abraham Lincoln, quoted in Christopher Klein, "How Lincoln and Grant's Partnership Won the Civil War," available https://www.history.com/how-Lincoln-and Grant's-partnership-won-the-civil-war (2017) (visited September 30, 2020). *See also Grant*, 211 (same).
38. For example, the American encampment at Valley Forge began on December 19, 1777, and continued to June 19, 1778, although planning for the 1778 campaign took place several weeks before the camp broke.
39. In the best of times, moving men and equipment took weeks. Feints and other strategies delayed or prevented altogether the cataclysmic battles. The major American conflicts 1775–1779 were as follows:

Bunker Hill	June 17, 1775
Long Island (Brooklyn)	August 27, 1776
White Plains	October 18, 1776
Trenton	December 26, 1776
Princeton	January 3, 1777
Brandywine	September 11, 1777
Germantown	October 4, 1777
Monmouth Court House	June 21, 1778

The mode was two months between engagements. The Battles of Trenton and Princeton were an exception, occurring seven days apart. All other exceptions involved intervals greater than two months. The interval between Bunker Hill and Long Island was fourteen months. Nine months separated Princeton and Brandywine; nine-and-one-half months separated Germantown and Monmouth Courthouse.

40. Max M. Mintz, *The Generals of Saratoga*, 87.
41. *Se, e.g.,* John Buchanan, *The Road to Guilford Courthouse*, 147–148.
42. Zambone, *Daniel Morgan: A Revolutionary Life*, 167–168. Author Zambone continued, "Washington succeeded in outwaiting and outwitting the plot." Gates and those in support of him did not succeed. *See generally* Mark Edward Lender, *Cabal: The Plot Against General Washington* (Yardley, PA, Westholme Publishing, 2019). After his disgrace for fleeing midst the Battle at Camden, Gates turned once again to his belief that he could manipulate the system. He lobbied Congress, successfully, for an inquiry to hear Gates's side of the story. Two years later, however, Congress rescinded the resolution calling for the inquiry.
43. George Washington to Anthony Wayne, September 6, 1780, quoted in Stephen R. Taaffe, *Washington's Revolutionary War Generals*, 210 (Norman, OK, University of Oklahoma Press. 2019).

Chapter 21

1. *Cuba*, 50 (views of General Ulysses H. Grant).
2. "General Roche de Femoy," in Robert P. Broadwater, *American Generals of the Revolutionary War: A Biographical Dictionary* (Jefferson, NC. McFarland, 2007).
3. *See* https://en.wikipedia.org/wiki/Frederick_William_Baron_de_Woedtke (visited February 16, 2022).
4. *See* Ken Alder, *Engineering the Revolution: Arms and Enlightenment in France* (Chicago, IL, University of Chicago Press, 2010).
5. *See* https://fr.wikipedia.org/wiki/Philippe_Hubert_Preudhomme_de_Borre (visited February 16, 2022).
6. *Life and Wars of John Stark*, 238.
7. Ben Z. Rose, *John Stark: Maverick General*, 99 (Waverly, MA, TreeLine Press, 2007). *See also* Jonathan G. Rossie, *The Politics of Command in the American Revolution*, 139 (Syracuse, NY, Syracuse University Press, 1975).
8. *See generally* Stephen Brumwell, *Turncoat: Benedict Arnold and the Crisis of American Liberty* (New Haven, CT, Yale University Press, 2018); James K. Martin, B*enedict Arnold: Revolutionary War Hero—An American Warrior Reconsidered*, 306 (New York, New York University Press, 1997).
9. His name also is forever twinned to a plot (some say just a few letters, a whispering campaign, or some idle thoughts, but not a plot) to replace George Washington with Horatio Gates or Conway himself. The Conway Cabal is described in, *inter alia*, in Lender, *Cabal*. Contrary to previous accounts, *see Cabal*, xiii, Professor Lender arguing that "the challenge to Washington's leadership of the Continental Army was broader, deeper, and more serious."
10. Douglas S. Freeman, Vol. 4, *George Washington*, 594 (Washington, DC, 1949). See *also* Ford, *Journals of the Continental Congress*, 10, no. 63 (Washington, DC, 1937).
11. George Washington was "incensed to learn about [Irishman Thomas] Conway's impending promotion" to major general, Ron Chernow wrote. The Continental Congress was set to and did award a promotion whereby Conway "would be jumped over twenty more senior [and American] brigadiers." Chernow, *Washington: A Life*, 317.
12. Brand, *The First American*, 535 (description of supplicants to Benjamin Franklin who composed "[a] small army of young men—some not so young—[who] besieged [him] seeking commissions in the American army").
13. *See generally* Milton C. Van Vlack, *Silas Deane: Revolutionary War Diplomat and Politician* (Jefferson, NC, McFarland, 2013).
14. Benjamin Franklin, quoted in Isaacson, *Ben*

Franklin, 340. Franklin's screening and recommendations did bear some fruit. The Maquis de Lafayette, Baron von Steuben, and Count Pulaski came to the attention of the American Congress via Franklin. *Benjamin Franklin*, 341.

15. Jimmy Dick, "Silas Deane: Forlorn and Forgotten Patriot," *Journal of the American Revolution*, October 2013.

16. George Washington, paraphrased in *The First American*, 536–537.

17. Quoting Benjamin Franklin, in *The First American*, 537.

18. *The First American*, 536.

19. *See generally The First American*, 536. Mentioned less frequently was another French officer, promoted to general only at Yorktown in October 1781; Colonel Charles Armand Tuffin, Marquis de la Rouerie, commanded American cavalry at, among other engagements, New York, Brandywine, Germantown, Whitemarsh, Monmouth Court House, and Camden. Similar to Marquis de Lafayette, Armand became close to George Washington. Until his death in 1793, again like Lafayette, Armand carried on an active correspondence with General Washington. Later, Armand was a major actor in the French Revolution. *See generally* Christian Bazin, *The Marquis de Rouerie "Colonel Armand" in the American War* (Paris, Perrin, 1990). Armand was a colorful and controversial figure about whom considerable biographical material exists but, for the most part, in French.

20. Reported by Amos T. Akerman, "The Military Career of General Enoch Poor," Manchester, NH, 1878, on file, New Hampshire Historical Society (NHHS), Concord NH. *See also* M.H. Cannon, "General Enoch Poor, 1736–1780," Exeter, NH, 1966, unpaginated monograph on file with NHHS. Poor "was conspicuous at the Battle of Monmouth."

21. Cannon, "General Enoch Poor" (conclusion).

22. Poor was buried "with all the pomp and respect that loving comrades ... could give one who had lead thousands in fierce charges against his country's foes," wrote Reginald McMahon, in "The Death and Burial of General Enoch Poor," Proceedings of the Bergen County (NJ) Historical Society (1992).

23. Quoted in Charles E. Bennett & Donald R. Lennon, *A Quest for Glory: Major General Robert Howe and the American Revolution*, 58 (Chapel Hill, NC, University of North Carolina Press, 1999). Neither man was wounded in the duel. They became friends afterward.

24. *Cabal*, 213.

25. Or government representatives from accepting titles or gifts from foreign sources. *United States Constitution*, Article 1, Section 9, Clause 8 reads, "No title of nobility shall be granted by the United States: And no person holding any Office of Profit or Trust under [the United States] shall, without the consent of Congress, accept any present, Emolument, Office, or Title, of any kind whatever, from any King, Prince, or foreign state."

26. *See, e.g.*, Tuchman, *A Distant Mirror*, 64. "More than a code of manners in war and in love, chivalry was a moral code governing the whole of a noble life .... It developed at the same time as the great crusades of the 12th century." Noted historian Tuchman added, "Honor and loyalty ... were the ideals of chivalry."

Chapter 22

1. Thomas Jefferson, quoted in *The American Revolution in the Southern Colonies*, 200.

2. President Herbert Hoover, Remarks on Dedication of Kings Mountain National Park, October 7, 1930.

3. "From Wilderness Battle to National Park," National Park Service, Department of the Interior, *Kings Mountain* (undated brochure) (National Park, visited December 11, 2021).

4. *Kings Mountain*, 1.

5. Major Patrick Ferguson, quoted in "The American Revolution Moves South," in National Park Service, Department of the Interior, *Overmountain Victory* (undated brochure).

6. Powell, *Four Centuries*, 200.

7. Kentucky became the fifteenth state to join the union. Tennessee became the sixteenth.

8. "Carolina Backwoodsmen," Historical Marker, Kings Mountain National Park (visited December 11, 2021).

9. "Over-the-Mountain-Men," Historical Marker, Kings Mountain National Park (visited December 11, 2021).

10. *Kings Mountain*, 2.

11. *Revolutionary Rifleman*, 102.

12. *See generally* John Buchanan, *The Road to Guilford Courthouse: The American Revolution in the Carolinas* (New York, Wiley & Sons, 1997); David K. Wilson, *The Southern Strategy: Britain's Conquest of South Carolina and Georgia, 1775–1780* (Columbia, SC, University of South Carolina Press, 2005).

13. Reviewed previously, *see* Chapter 12.

14. General Horatio Gates to Daniel Morgan, October 17, 1780.

15. *Revolutionary Rifleman*, 120.

16. Another hero of the Revolutionary War, in February 1781, General Davidson was later killed in action at Cowan's Ford across the Catawba River in North Carolina. North Carolina's Davidson College, north of Charlotte, is named after General Davidson. *See generally* Chalmers Gaston Davidson, *Piedmont Partisan: The Life and Times of General William Lee Davidson* (Davidson, NC, 1951, reprinted, Literary Licensing, 2011).

17. Lawrence E. Babits, *A Devil of a Whipping: The Battle of Cowpens*, 84 (Chapel Hill, NC, University of North Carolina Press, 2011).

18. *A Devil of a Whipping*, 40–42. *See also* Mobley, *Richard Caswell: Founding Father and Revolutionary Hero*, 85 ("Hannah's Cowpens").

19. *Washington's Revolutionary War Generals*, 230. The Battle of Cowpens has been a favorite subject for historians. Besides Lawrence Babits's *Devil of a Whipping*, accounts and analyses include Robert W. Brown, Jr., *Kings Mountain and Cowpens: Our Victory Was Complete* (Charleston, SC, The History Press, 2009); Thomas J. Fleming, *Cowpens: "Downright Fighting"—The Story of Cowpens* (Washington, DC, National Park Service,1989); Christine Sager, *Come to the Cowpens* (Spartanburg, SC, Hub City Press, 2002); U.S. Army General Staff College, *American Revolution: the Battle of Cowpens* (Seattle, WA, Create Space, 2016).

20. See *A Devil of a Whipping*, 84.

21. For a complete description of Morgan's deployment of troops, see *A Devil of a Whipping*, 40–42 & 79.

22. *Daniel Morgan: A Revolutionary Life*, 227.

23. Daniel Morgan, quoted in Robert Middlekauff, *The Glorious Cause: The American Revolution, 1763–1789*, 471 (New York, Oxford University Press, 2005).

24. See *A Devil of a Whipping*, 137–138.

25. Daniel Morgan, quoted in *Daniel Morgan: A Revolutionary Life*, 231.

26. General Daniel Morgan, at Cowpens, on January 16, 1781, quoted in Graham, *The Life of Daniel Morgan*, 297 & 309.

27. Daniel Morgan to William Snickers, January 16, 1781. See also *A Devil of a Whipping*; *The Life of Daniel Morgan*, 469.

28. Buchanan, *The Road to Guilford Courthouse*, 285.

29. Quoted in *Green Dragon*, 160.

30. *A Devil of a Whipping*, 133–134.

31. *Revolutionary Rifleman*, 145.

32. William S. Powell, *North Carolina Through Four Centuries*, 202 (Chapel Hill, NC, University of North Carolina Press, 1989). Cowpens was in South Carolina, a short distance over the border from North Carolina.

Chapter 23

1. See, e.g., James Graham, *The Life of General Daniel Morgan, with Portions of His Correspondence, Etc.* (New York, Derby & Jackson, 1856); George Henry More, *Mr. Lee's Plan—March 29, 1777: The Treason of Charles Lee, Major General, Second in Command in the American Army of the Revolution* (Port Washington, NY, Kennikat Press, 1860); Henry A. Muhlenberg, *The Life of Major General Peter Muhlenberg* (Philadelphia, PA, Carey & Hart, 1849); Jared Sparks, *Lives of Charles Lee and Joseph Reed* (Boston, MA, C.C. Little & J. Brown, 1846).

2. A list of Daniel Morgan biographies includes North Callahan, *Daniel Morgan: Ranger of the Revolution* (Arms PR, Inc., 1961); Michael Cecere, *A Good and Valuable Officer: Daniel Morgan in the Revolutionary War* (Berwyn Heights, MD, Heritage Books, 2019); Daniel Morgan, Nathanael Greene, et al., *The Battle of Cowpens: Primary and Secondary Accounts* (Regiment Press, 2019); James Graham, *The Life of General Daniel Morgan: Of the Virginia Line with Portions of His Correspondence* (1856) (republished by Andesite Press, 2015); Ronald Hamilton, *Daniel Morgan Forgotten Hero* (Seattle, WA, Create Space Publishing, 2015); Bob Hampton & George Schember, *Walking in the Footsteps of General Daniel Morgan* (Seattle, WA, Create Space—Amazon Publishing, 2016); Don Higginbotham, *Daniel Morgan: Revolutionary Rifleman* (University of North Carolina Press, 1979); Patrick K. O'Donnell, *Washington's Immortals: The Story of an Elite Regiment Who Changed the Revolution* (New York, Grove Press, 2017); James Kenneth Swisher, *Daniel Morgan: An Inexplicable Hero* (Virginia Beach, VA, Koehler Books, 2019); Andrew Louis Zambone, *Daniel Morgan: A Revolutionary Life* (Yardley, PA, Westholme, 2019).

3. *Cf.* Albert Louis Zambone, *Daniel Morgan: A Revolutionary Life*, 309 (Yardley, PA, Westholme, 2018). "Today … Morgan remains obscure" and, compared to Daniel Boone and Davy Crockett, Morgan suffers "from continuing obscurity."

4. Buchanan, *The Road to Guilford Courthouse*, 285.

5. *Daniel Morgan: A Revolutionary Life*, XV.

6. *Daniel Morgan: A Revolutionary Life*, 37.

7. A teamster often rode on the left side horse closest the wagon, the "wheel horse," both to be close to the animals and close to the brake lever, usually near the wagon's left front wheel.

8. *Daniel Morgan: A Revolutionary Life*, 37.

9. *Daniel Morgan: A Revolutionary Life*, 66.

10. See, e.g., Donald Higginbotham, *Daniel Morgan, Revolutionary Rifleman*, 9. "No one could ride better than he or out distance him in a foot race—in his fortieth year he outran sturdy men half his age. In wrestling, he excelled."

11. *Daniel Morgan, Revolutionary Rifleman*, 1.

12. See, e.g., Warren R. Hofstra, *The Planting of New Virginia: Settlement and Landscape in the Shenandoah Valley*, 56–57 & 61 (Baltimore, MD, Johns Hopkins University Press, 2004).

13. *The Life of General Daniel Morgan*, 29.

14. On the Braddock expedition, Morgan got to know Adam Stephen, second-in-command to George Washington, who led the Virginia regiment accompanying Braddock's force. Stephen, of course, became an American major general in the Revolutionary War who campaigned with Morgan.

15. Forty or more of the author's ancestors are buried in the Winchester Quaker cemetery. Bransons migrated to Virginia from West Jersey in the 1720s.

16. See, e.g., *Revolutionary Rifleman*, 11. "Informal unions were not uncommon on the Virginia frontier."

17. *Revolutionary Rifleman*, 11.

18. See generally Graham, *The Life of General Daniel Morgan*, 33–34; *Revolutionary Rifleman*, 7.

19. There Morgan's troops joined other forces, including those of George Rogers Clark (Chapter

27), another militia leader who like Morgan was destined for fame as a regular, to form a battalion.

20. Dunmore's army had a southern force as well, led by Andrew Lewis, *see* Chapter 17, marching from Greenbrier County in southwest Virginia northwest up the Kanawha River. Near the confluence of the Kanawha with the Ohio, Lewis and his men met a Native American force led by Shawnee warrior Cornstalk in the Battle of Point Pleasant. The Virginians prevailed but suffered losses Lewis felt would have been minimized had the northern battalion come to his aid, as had been the plan. *See generally* Glenn F. Williams, *Dunmore's War: The Last Conflict of America's Colonial Era*, 105–108 (Yardley, PA, Westholme, 2017); Reuben G. Thwaites and Louise P. Kellogg, eds., *A Documentary History of Dunmore's War* (Madison, WI, University of Wisconsin Press, 1905).

21. *Daniel Morgan: A Revolutionary Life*, 76.

22. *Revolutionary Rifleman*, 19 (internal quotation marks omitted).

23. Quotation by Don Higginbotham, in *Revolutionary Rifleman*, 36.

24. *See. e.g.*, Arthur Lefkowitz, *Benedict Arnold's Army: The 1775 American Invasion of Canada During the Revolutionary War* (Savas Beatie, 2008); James M. LeMoine, *The Assault of Brigadier-General Richard Montgomery and Colonel Benedict Arnold on Quebec in 1775: A Red Letter Day for Canada* (Trans Royal Society, 1899); Kenneth Roberts, *March to Quebec* (New York, 1940); Justin Harvey Smith. *Arnold's March from Cambridge to* Quebec (New York, 1903, reprinted Surry Hills, NSW, AU, Wentworth Press, 2018).

25. *See generally* Perry Keese, *The Story of General Richard Montgomery: The Tale of the Invasion of Canada* (London, UK, Forgotten Books, 2016).

26. *Revolutionary Rifleman*, 33.

27. *March to Quebec*, 137. *See also March to Quebec*, 216, 329, & 335–36 (journal comments of Senter, Henry, and Morrison).

28. *See, e.g.*, Christopher Ward, *War of Revolution*, 450 (New York, Konecky & Konecky, 1950); *Revolutionary Rifleman*, 36.

29. *Revolutionary Rifleman*, 50.

30. *Daniel Morgan: A Revolutionary Life*, 108.

31. *See* James K. Martin, *Benedict Arnold, Revolutionary Hero: An American Warrior Reconsidered*, 143–145 (New York, New York University Press, 1997).

32. *See generally* Willard Wallace, *Traitorous Hero: The Life and Fortunes of Benedict Arnold*, 83–84 (New York, Harper, 1954).

33. Graham, *The Life of Daniel Morgan*, 97–98.

34. *Revolutionary Rifleman*, 46.

35. *See, e.g., Revolutionary Rifleman*, 44.

36. *Life of Daniel Morgan*, 102; *Revolutionary Rifleman*, 46.

37. *Life of Daniel Morgan*, 103. *See also Revolutionary Rifleman*, 49; *Daniel Morgan: A Revolutionary Life*, 107.

38. *See, e.g., Life of Daniel Morgan*, 110–112.

39. Daniel Morgan to British Captain Joseph Graham, as quoted in *Daniel Morgan: A Revolutionary Life*, 261.

40. *Revolutionary Rifleman*, 60–61.

41. *Daniel Morgan: A Revolutionary Life*, 132.

42. Reproduced in James Thacher, *Eyewitness to the American Revolution: The Battles and Generals as Seen by an Army Surgeon*, 85–86 (republished Longmeadow Press, 1994). The surrender of Ticonderoga is described in, *inter alia*, *Stark: The Life and Wars of John Stark*, 253–256. In 1775, of course, Seth Warner, Ethan Allen, and the "Green Mountain Boys" from Vermont had captured the fort from the British. Loss of the fort two years later was a blow to colonial forces' morale, leading to heavy criticism of St. Clair.

43. *See, e.g.*, American Battlefield Trust, "Oriskany," available http://www.battlefields.org (visited July 27, 2020).

44. *See generally* "The Battle of Bennington: A Continual Thunderclap," Chapter 21, in *Stark: The Life and Wars of John Sark*, 254–268.

45. *Revolutionary Rifleman*, 63.

46. Zambone in *Daniel Morgan: A Revolutionary Life*, 62.

47. *Revolutionary Rifleman*, 20.

48. Works describing and critiquing the battles are numerous. *See, e.g.*, Richard Ketchum, *Saratoga: Turning Point of America's Revolutionary War* (New York, Henry Holt, 1997); John Luzader, *Saratoga: A Military History of the Decisive Campaign of the American Revolution* (Philadelphia, PA, Casemate, 2008); Hoffman Nickerson, *Turning Point of the Revolution, or Burgoyne in America* (republished Whitefish, MT, Kessinger Publishing, 2010); and Dean Snow, *1777, Tipping Point at Saratoga* (New York, Oxford University Press, 2016).

49. *See generally* Lloyd A, Brown & Howard H. Peckham, *The Revolutionary War Journals of Henry Dearborn, 1775–1783* (Chicago, IL, 1939, republished by Heritage Books, 2019).

50. Dean Snow, in *1777, Tipping Point at Saratoga*, 72.

51. *Turning Point of the Revolution, or Burgoyne in America*, 311.

52. *Revolutionary Rifleman*, 69.

53. *See Daniel Morgan: A Revolutionary Life*, 190.

54. There were approximately 4,400 participants in the battle of Freeman's Farm, approximately 2,200 per side, at least until later in the afternoon. In his battle plan, General Burgoyne had directed Baron von Riedesel and his Hessians down the river road, feinting a frontal assault on American positions. With 2,000 plus troops, General Simon Fraser was to attempt a flanking movement to the west, around the American lines. Late in the afternoon, General Burgoyne ordered von Riedesel to reinforce General Fraser. Inexplicably, the Baron came with only half his troops. He pushed the American line back, but it was "too little, too late."

55. *Daniel Morgan: A Revolutionary Life*, 141 & 142. "After three weeks—an exhausted British

army that still knew little about either the terrain or the disposition of Gates's army."

56. James Wilkinson, *Memoirs of My Own Times*, 268 (Philadelphia, PA, Abraham Small, 1816).

57. *Daniel Morgan: A Revolutionary Life*, 149 & 151.

58. *See Revolutionary Rifleman*, 73–74. Simon Fraser University is a principal Canadian university, located in Vancouver, British Columbia, named however for a Canadian explorer with the same name as the general. Another principal Canadian university, located in Ottawa, is Carlton University, named after Governor and General Guy Carlton.

59. Instead, hardship resulted from the paucity, or absence, of clothing, foodstuffs, horses, forage, blankets, and other suppliers. The Quartermaster General, Thomas Mifflin, did little or nothing, as the rudderless quartermaster department failed absolutely. *See, e.g.*, Kenneth R. Rossman, *Thomas Mifflin and the Politics of the American Revolution*, 109–110 (Chapel Hill, NC, University of North Carolina Press, 1952); Stephen Taffee, *Washington's Revolutionary War Generals*, 155 (Norman, OK, University of Oklahoma Press, 2021). "The quartermaster department quickly disintegrated" for want of "the presence of its head." Eighteen hundred men died at Valley Forge that winter.

60. *See, e.g., Daniel Morgan: A Revolutionary Life*, 173.

61. *See* Chapter 14.

62. *Revolutionary Rifleman*, 87.

63. General George Washington to Colonel Daniel Morgan, June 28, 1778.

64. *Daniel Morgan: A Revolutionary Life*, 180.

65. William S. Stryker, *The Battle of Monmouth*, 155–156 (Princeton, NJ, Princeton University Press, 1927).

66. Colonel Daniel Morgan to President, Continental Congress, July 18, 1779.

67. *See, e.g., Revolutionary Rifleman*, 93.

68. General Horatio Gates to President John Hancock, October 12, 1777.

69. Graham, *Life of Morgan*, 53

70. *Daniel Morgan: A Revolutionary Life*, 169.

71. George Washington Park Custis, Recollections and Private Memoirs of George Washington, 320–21 (New York, 1860).

72. General George Washington to President John Jay, June 30, 1779.

73. *Daniel Morgan: A Revolutionary Life*, 193.

74. Fitzpatrick, Volume XIX, *The Writings of Washington*, 225.

75. Daniel Morgan was, of course, from Virginia. Washington was rigidly proper when Virginia officers were engaged in questions of rank and seniority, as they frequently were. He feared accusations of favoritism to officers from his own colony. With officers from other states, he was, according to authorities, "more flexible." *See* Howard Swiggett, *The Great Man*, 13 (New York, 1953). There can be suggested additional causes for Washington's faint praise and failures to reciprocate. He was covering up for the error he realized he had made in choosing Wayne over Morgan as commander of the new light infantry unit. Or, Washington was red-faced in the lack of attention he had given to Morgan's requests for promotion to brigadier general, given that Morgan's combat experience and tactical genius greatly exceeded any other brigadier or colonel.

76. L.N. Barton, *Men and Events of the Revolution in Winchester and Frederick County* (Winchester, VA, Winchester-Frederick Historical Society, 1975).

77. William Hill, Sermon concerning Daniel Morgan, July 6, 1802, reproduced in *Daniel Morgan: A Revolutionary Life*, 308.

Chapter 24

1. Chalmers Gaston Davidson, *The Life and Times of Brigadier General William Lee Davidson*, 87 (Davidson, NC, Davidson College, 1951).

2. Ryan Cole, *Light-Horse Harry Lee: The Rise and Fall of a Revolutionary Hero*, 52 (Washington, DC, Regnery History, 2019).

3. Henry Lee, *Memoirs of the War in the Southern Department* Vol. 2, 399 (Philadelphia, PA, 1812) (internal quotation marks omitted).

4. James K. Swisher, *The Revolutionary War in the Southern Backcountry*, 277 (Gretna, LA, Pelican Publishing, 2008).

5. *See, e.g.*, "Fast Facts," https://www.davidson.edu/fast-facts (visited August 3, 2021).

6. Davidson's name also is absent in historical accounts of the Revolution. *But see* David L. Russell, *The American Revolution in the Southern Colonies*, 166 (Jefferson, NC, McFarland, 2000), noting in passing that "after Camden [1780] Gates did not have the support of the most courageous and brave Southern leaders such as colonels Davidson, Polk, or Davie."

7. *Revolution in the Southern Backcountry*, 175–176: "[P]artisan activities [became] a critical part of that effort in the lower south."

8. *Davidson on Davidson*, 3.

9. *See, e.g.*, Walter Isaacson, *Benjamin Franklin: An American Life*, 156–157 & 154. "The Quakers opposed military spending on principle, and the Penns (acting through a series of appointed lackey governors) opposed anything that would cost them money or subject their land to taxes"; H.W. Brands, *The First American: The Life and Times of Benjamin Franklin*, 160, "Horror stories of women and children being slaughtered by fiendish red men, provoked and provisioned by the French …. [In the] theology of the Quakers there remained an uneasiness with war and war preparation …."; & 209, "Failure of the politicians to provide defense … demonstrated that politicians could not be trusted to accomplish what needed to be done …"

10. *See, e.g.*, Chapter 18.

11. *Davidson on Davidson*, 15.

12. *Davidson on Davidson*, 7.
13. Governor William Tyron to Earl of Shelburne, July 8, 1767.
14. *See* Steven Beauregard Weeks, *Church and State in North Carolina*, 43 (Baltimore, MD, 1893, republished Wentworth Press, NSW Australia, 2019). A description of Davidson at the time: "Davidson was a son of the frontier ... He was open-hearted, sympathetic, and a trifle credulous. He was physically brave to the point of fool-heartedness. To his thinking, arms and a man were inseparable. He respected authority, political or religious .... Throughout his life he remained a personable, gregarious extrovert." *Davidson on Davidson*, 27.
15. Christine R. Swager, *Heroes of Kettle Creek, 1779–1782*, 13(West Conshohocken, PA, Infinity Publishing, 2008).
16. William R. Reynolds, Jr., *Andrew Pickens: South Carolina Patriot in the Revolutionary War*, 104 (Jefferson, NC, McFarland, 2012).
17. What the literature universally refers to as the backcountry conjures up visions of mountain cabins and rough-hewn frontiersman. The backcountry then was around Salisbury and Charlotte, the seats respectively of Rowan and Mecklenburg Counties that lie in central North Carolina's southern tier. Beyond Charlotte, a traveler must transit at least three additional counties before reaching the Appalachians and what today's observer might term "backcountry." Rand McNally, Inc., *2022 Road Atlas*, 74 (Chicago, IL, Rand McNally, 2021).
18. For a detailed description of regulator movement, see Robert O. DeMond, *The Loyalists of North Carolina during the Revolution*, 23–33 (Durham, NC, Duke University Press, 1940, republished Greenville, SC, Southern Historical Press, 2019).
19. *Davidson on Davidson*, 29.
20. Charles E. Bennett & Donald R. Lennon, *Major General Robert Howe and the American Revolution: A Quest for Glory*, 28 (Chapel Hill, NC, University of North Carolina Press, 1991).
21. *See* Hugh F. Rankin, *North Carolina in the American Revolution*, 12 (Raleigh, NC, North Carolina Division of Archives and History, 1959): "In 1746 [this group of Highlanders] had revolted against the King of England and led by "Bonnie Prince Charlie," they had been defeated in the Battle of Culloden. After that, and before they migrated to the New World, they had taken an oath of allegiance to the King. Highlanders were people who believed in keeping their word. They settled in eastern North Carolina around Cross Creek ..."
22. Joe A. Mobley, *North Carolina Governor Richard Caswell: Founding Father and Revolutionary Hero*, 52 (Charleston, SC, History Press, 2016) (land grants).
23. Mobley, *Caswell: Founding Father and Revolutionary*, 52.
24. *See generally* J.D. Lewis, "The Battle of Moore's Creek Bridge," available https://www.carolina.com/revolution_battle_of_moores_creek_bridge (visited August 16, 2021). *See also* Rankin, *North Carolina in the American Revolution*, 10–19.
25. *Davidson on Davidson*, 37.
26. Rankin, *North Carolina in the American Revolution*, 11; Mobley, *Caswell: Founding Father and Revolutionary*, 51.
27. Although none of the states ever filled the troop quota Congress assigned them, North Carolina had a particularly difficult time because "[a] large part of the population were loyalists unwilling to fight against the Crown." Mobley, *Caswell: Founding Father and Revolutionary*, 60. At its peak, "North Carolina supplied ten regiments—6,086 to 7,663 soldiers—to the Continental Line in the Revolution. [The militia] was not as competent a fighting force as the regular army, although 10,000 North Carolinians served in its ranks during the war." Mobley, 60. *Cf.* Rankin, *North Carolina in the American Revolution*, 73: "It has been estimated that nearly 22,000 North Carolinians (continental and militia) saw service during the War of the Revolution."
28. Described by historian James Swisher as "crusty old Gen. Griffith Rutherford ... a warrior, the veteran of many a backwoods fight." *Revolutionary War in the Southern Backcountry*, 71. He "was not a great military mind but he was a leader of focus and will." He was badly wounded at the Battled of Camden, captured by the British, and exchanged by the Americans, in 1781. *Revolutionary War in the Southern Backcountry*, 151.
29. *See* Mobley, *Caswell: Founding Father and Revolutionary*, 66.
30. Rankin, *North Carolina in the American Revolution*, 28.
31. *Davidson on Davidson*, 39.
32. *North Carolina Through Four Centuries*, 192.
33. Cole, *Lee: The Rise and Fall of a Revolutionary Hero*, 52
34. *Davidson on Davidson*, 51.
35. *Davidson on Davidson*, 60.
36. *See, e.g.*, William A. Graham, *General Joseph Graham and His Papers on North Carolina Revolutionary History*, 238 (Raleigh, NC, 1904)
37. *American Revolution in the Southern Colonies*, 178.
38. *Davidson on Davidson*, 65.
39. *Davidson on Davidson*, 69.
40. *See, e.g.*, Rankin, *North Carolina in the American Revolution*, 31: "In 1779 the British government made a major change in its military strategy. From now on ... they would concentrate their primary efforts in the southern states."
41. *Davidson on Davidson*, 71–72.
42. *See generally* Rankin, *North Carolina in the American Revolution*, 41–44.
43. William Davidson to General Horatio Gates, October 10, 1780.
44. *See generally* Editors, Battlefieds.org, "Battle of Kings Mountain," available https://www.history.com/the-day-in-history/battle-of=kings-

mountain (visited August 19, 2021); L.C. Draper, *Kings Mountain and Its Heroes* (Cincinnati, OH, 1881): "The victory ranks with Saratoga and Yorktown as one of decisive engagements of the Revolution."

45. Rankin, *North Carolina in the American Revolution*, 40.

46. *Davidson on Davidson*, 82.

47. *See, e.g.*, John Buchanan, *The Road to Guilford Courthouse: The American Revolution in the Carolinas*, 242 (New York, Wiley & Sons, 1997) (quoting Charles Stedman, an officer under Cornwallis). The British had a reputation for moving very slowly when in force. The pace was deemed attributable to British soldiers and their mercenary colleagues' (Hessians and Brunswickers) proclivity to range six and eight miles either side of the main force, looting, marauding, raping, and burning crops, farm buildings, and houses. *See, e.g.*, Hilary Mantel, *Wolf Hall*, 108 (New York, Picador, 2009):

The English will never be forgiven for the talent for destruction they have always displayed when they get off their own island. English armies laid waste to the land they moved through. [S]ystematically, they perform every act proscribed by the code of chivalry, and broke every one of the laws of war. The battles were nothing; it was what they did between the battles that left its mark. They robbed and raped for forty miles around the line of their march. They burned the crops in the fields, and the houses with people in them.

Ministers premised the southern strategy on the plurality or even majority of loyalists and closet sympathizers who lived there. A fruitful exercise might be research into how the British army's lack of discipline contributed to reversal of Loyalist sympathizer attitudes, not only in the South but throughout the colonies.

48. Rankin, *North Carolina in the American Revolution*, 44.

49. The definitive account of Cowpens is Lawrence E. Babbits, *A Devil of a Whipping: The Battle of Cowpens* (Chapel Hill, NC, University of North Carolina Press, 2011).

50. General William Davidson to General Daniel Morgan, January 21, 1781.

51. *Davidson on Davidson*, 102.

52. *Davidson on Davidson*, 113.

53. *Compare* Graham, *Revolutionary North Carolina History*, 257 (250 men) *with* Lee, *War in the Southern Department*, 398 (300 men).

54. *Revolution in the Southern Backcountry*, 275. *See also American Revolution in the Southern Colonies*, 218: "Greene put General Davidson in charge of slowing Cornwallis at the fords."

55. Swisher, *The Southern Back Country*, 10 & 275–277, recounts events at Cowan's ford.

56. *Revolution in the Southern Backcountry*, 277.

57. Rankin, *North Carolina in the American Revolution*, 50.

58. John S. Pancake, *This Destructive War*, 163 (Tuscaloosa, AL, University of Alabama Press, 1985).

59. *American Revolution in the Southern Colonies*, 219.

60. *See generally* Robert Henry, *Narrative of the Battle at Cowan's Ford* (Greensboro, NC, 1891).

61. Swisher, *The Southern Back Country*, 10.

62. *Revolution in the Southern Backcountry*, 278.

63. Editor, "Davidson College," Watchman of the South, Richmond, Virginia, March 23, 1843: "[He was] a man of influence, and, as tradition says, more beloved than any other man in the country."

64. *Davidson on Davidson*, 129.

Chapter 25

1. *The American Revolution in the Southern Colonies*, 221.

2. *The American Revolution in the Southern Colonies*, 214.

3. *See* William S. Powell, *North Carolina Through Four Centuries*, 202 (Chapel Hill, NC, University of North Carolina Press, 1989).

4. *The Road to Guildford Courthouse*, 330.

5. The Dan River flows north to south through the area where the city of Danville now lies in southern Virginia. A short distance beyond the state line into North Carolina, the river bends in an easterly direction.

6. *North Carolina Through Four Centuries*, 203.

7. *The American Revolution in the Southern Colonies*, 224.

8. *Cf. The American Revolution in the Southern Colonies*, 223 (one hour). Author Buchanan terms the rear guard "the screening force."

9. *The Road to Guildford Courthouse*, 372. *Cf. The American Revolution in the Southern Colonies*, 228 (4,000 men including 1,600 Continentals).

10. Quoting William Richardson Davie, in *The Road to Guildford Courthouse*, 372.

11. Quoted by Daniel R. Morrill, in *Southern Campaign of the American Revolution*, 152 (Baltimore, MD, Nautical & Aviation Publishers, 1993).

12. *See The American Revolution in the Southern Colonies*, 216 (January) & 228 (February leaving "about 2,000" overall). *See also North Carolina Through Four Centuries*, 203.

13. *The Road to Guildford Courthouse*, 352.

14. *The Road to Guildford Courthouse*, 374.

15. *North Carolina Through Four Centuries*, 204.

16. Which they did at the Battle of Eutaw Springs (South Carolina on September 8, 1781), the last major engagement of the war before Yorktown. Leaving Guildford Courthouse and detecting no British pursuit, Greene and his men rested three miles west of the battlefield. After resting, the Americans turned southwest toward Wilmington, North Carolina.

17. *North Carolina Through Four Centuries*, 204–05.

18. *The Road to Guildford Courthouse*, 373.

19. Quoted in Hugh Rankin, *The North Carolina Continentals*, 311.

20. Quoted in *The Road to Guildford Courthouse*, 375.

21. *The Road to Guildford Courthouse*, 376.

22. *See, e.g.,* The American Revolution in the Southern Colonies, 228.

23. By the author's calculation totaling 970 miles, computed as follows: Charlestown to Camden, 110 miles; Camden to Waxhaw and return, 100 miles; Camden to Charlotte, NC, 70 miles; Charlotte to Winnsboro and return, 150 miles; Charlotte to Hillsborough, 120 miles; Hillsborough to Irwin's Ferry and return, 140 miles; Hillsborough to Guildford Courthouse, 40 miles; Guilford Courthouse (Greensboro, NC) to Richmond, VA, 165 miles; and Richmond to Yorktown, VA, 65 miles.

Chapter 26

1. Lachlan McIntosh's expeditions against the Native American tribes are described in Chapter 6.

2. McIntosh's expeditions went straight west from the Forks of the Ohio (Pittsburgh) into present-day Ohio, reaching only 130 miles into that territory.

3. *See, e.g.,* Michael DuVal, *George Rogers Clark: Conqueror of the Old Northwest* (1969). *See also* James Fisher, "A Forgotten Hero Remembered, Revered, and Revised," *Indiana Magazine of History*, June 1996, 109–132.

4. George Washington, Lachlan McIntosh, William Moultrie, Andrew Pickens, William Davidson, Daniel Brodhead, Charles Scott, Anthony Wayne, and several other brigadier generals had been surveyors.

5. The Northwest Territory became today's Ohio, Michigan, Indiana, Illinois, and Wisconsin. *See, e.g.,* McCullough, *The Pioneers: The Heroic Struggle of the Settlers Who Brought the American Ideal West* (2020).

6. *See, e.g.,* http://www.battlefields.org/Harry/Hamilton (visited April 16, 2020).

7. Kathleen DuVal, "The Revolution Out West," *Wall Street Journal*, December 19, 2018, A-17, reviewing Patrick Spero, *Frontier Rebels: The Fight for Independence in the American West* (2018).

8. Outside of the Midwest (Indiana, Kentucky, Ohio), George Rogers Clark is better known as the older brother of William Clark, with Meriwether Lewis co-leader of the Voyage of Discovery (1804–05), known as the Lewis and Clark Expedition. *See generally* Stephen Ambrose, *Undaunted Courage: Meriwether Lewis, Thomas Jefferson, and the Opening of the American West* (New York, Simon & Schuster, 1997).

9. *See* James H. Madison & Lee Ann Sandweiss, *Hoosiers and the American Story*, 35–39 (Indianapolis, IN, Indiana Historical Society Press, 2014).

10. *See* http://www.factmonster.com/states/by/order/of/entry/into/union (visited May 4, 2020). Vermont was the fourteenth state.

11. *See* Robert Douthat Meade, *Patrick Henry*, Vol. 2, 134 & 206–08 (Philadelphia, PA, J.B. Lippincott Co., 1969).

12. As had the careers of his brothers Jonathan and William. Elder brother Major Jonathan Clark, "a seasoned patriot and soldier," led Virginia infantry in support of Light-Horse Harry Lee's capture of the British fort at Paulus Hook, New York in 1779. *See* Ryan Cole, *Light-Horse Harry Lee: The Rise and Fall of a Revolutionary Hero*, 70 (Washington, DC, Regnery History, 2019).

13. *See, e.g.,* Stephen Ambrose, *Undaunted Courage*, 41.

14. *See, e.g.,* Lee, *Patriot Above Profit*, at 363.

15. In Vincennes, an impressive memorial—a rotunda of Indiana limestone—is dedicated to George Rogers Clark. The memorial is included in and surrounded by a small national park, sitting beneath the levee constraining the Wabash, just below the bridge crossing the river to Illinois.

16. Recorded in Claude G. Bowers, *The Young Jefferson, 1743–1789*, 244–250 (Boston, MA, Houghton Mifflin, 1945).

17. Alf J. Mapp, Jr., *The Virginia Experiment: The Old Dominion's Role in the Making of America, 1607–1781*, 472–474 (Richmond, VA, Dietz Press, 1957).

18. Legendary frontiersman Daniel Boone participated in one or both excursions. Natives had kidnaped Boone's daughter, spiriting her away from Kentucky to Ohio. *See, e.g.,* Robert Morgan, *Boone: A Biography* (Charlotte, MD, Recoded Books, 2008).

19. Ward, *Charles Scott and the "Spirit of '76,"* 165. Clay was not born until 1777, which would have made him far too young for Clark's earlier exploits against the Native Americans.

20. *See, e.g.,* Temple Bodley, *George Rogers Clark: His Life and Public Services* (Boston, MA, Houghton Mifflin, 1926); Linda C. Gugin & James E. St. Clair, *The People Who Shaped the Hoosier State* (Indianapolis, IN, Indiana Historical Society Press, 2015); Michael DuVal, *George Rogers Clark: Conqueror of the Old Northwest* (1969); James Fisher, "A Forgotten Hero Remembered, Revered, and Revised," *Indiana Magazine of History*, June 1996, 109–132; James Alton James, *The Life of George Rogers Clark* (Chicago, IL, University of Chicago Press, 1928); James H. Madison, *Hoosiers: A New History of Indiana* (Bloomington & Indianapolis, IN, Indiana University Press, 2015); James Madison & Lee Ann Sandweiss, *Hoosiers and the American Story* (Indianapolis, IN, Indiana Historical Society, 2014); Frederick Palmer, *Clark of the Ohio: A Life of George Rogers Clark* (Kessinger Publishing, 2008).

21. *See, e.g.,* June Greif-Glory, *Faith and Fancy: Outdoor Sculpture in Indiana* (Indianapolis, IN, Indiana Historical Society Press, 2005); Steve Schneider, "The View from Here: The Story of the George Rogers Clark Statue in Quincy, Illinois," *Journal of the Illinois State Historical Society*, Winter 2007–08, 360–382.

22. The main bridge spanning the Ohio River at Louisville, Kentucky, is the George Rogers Clark Memorial Bridge. The SS George Rogers Clark was commissioned in 1942 and scrapped in 1965.

Chapter 27

1. John Ashe was a militia rather than Continental Line general. In the main, this book limits itself to regular army generals even though several militia generals such as Ashe fought long and hard prosecuting the war.

2. Like John Ashe of North Carolina, Andrew Pickens served as a general of the South Carolina Militia.

3. Stevens obtained a brigadier's commission early in the war but soon resigned. He became a general in the Virginia Militia. He led troops at the Battles of Camden and Guilford Courthouse, among other engagements.

Chapter 28

1. For example, George Weedon served a term as president of the Virginia Chapter while Peter Muhlenberg served another. From South Carolina, both Andrew Pickens and William Moultrie were enthusiastic members and presidents of the South Carolina chapter, as was Lachlan McIntosh of Georgia.

2. *See, e.g.*, Charles E Bennett & Donald R. Lennon, *Major General Robert Howe and the American Revolution: A Quest for Glory*, 124 (Chapel Hill, NC, University of North Carolina Press, 1991): "By early April [1780], General Washington was concerned that a British attack up the Hudson was imminent."

3. Isaacson, *Benjamin Franklin*, 399.

4. For instance, Colonel John Laurens of South Carolina, who had served as aide-de-camp to George Washington and was a son of Continental Congress President Henry Laurens, died August 27, 1782, shot in a skirmish at Combahee River, South Carolina. He thus died in combat nearly a year after Yorktown. *See, e.g.*, https://www.britancia.com/biography/john-laurens (visited November 5, 2020).

5. Lord North, quoted in McCullough, *John Adams*, 267.

6. Besides inactivity and idleness, causes were the Continental Congress's fiscal irresponsibility in not providing payment of officers' and men's salaries (meager as they were); the advanced state of poverty in which officers and men found themselves after a lengthy war; and a desire for an enduring benevolent mechanism to continue after the war and recognize the bravery and fellowship that had emerged from seven years' combat.

7. A behind-the-scenes agitator was Major General Horatio Gates, whom Washington had summoned from semi-retirement in Virginia (*See* Chapter 11). Gates warned the Society of Cincinnati founders and other plotters that without protections, come peace, they would "grow old in poverty, wretchedness, and contempt." *See, e.g., Washington: A Life*, 433 (attributing authorship to Gates's aide-de-camp, John Armstrong, Jr.). In reference to the Newburgh letters, Gates advised the officers to "assume a bolder tone—and suspect the man who would advise to more moderation and longer forbearance," the latter probably a poke at George Washington. Quotations from John Rhodehamel, *George Washington: Writings*, 239 (New York, Library of America, 1997).

8. Ron Chernow, *Washington: A Life*, 434 (New York, Penguin, 2010).

9. *See generally* H.W. Brands, *The First American*, 687–688 (New York, Doubleday, 2000). Another detailed account can be found in Chernow, *Washington: A Life*, at 433–436.

10. John C. Fitzpatrick, *The Writings of George Washington*, Vol. 26, 239 (Washington, DC, 1931–1944).

11. George Washington, quoted in *The First American*, 668.

12. George Washington, quoted in *The First American*, 668.

13. *Washington: A Life*, 436.

14. For instance, writing in his recent book, *The First Inauguration (George Washington and the Invention of the Republic)*, history professor Stephen Browne singles out newly sworn President George Washington's 1789 address: "That Americans have been spared the trauma of the military coup d'état is owing in no small measure to a general [George Washington] insistent on the privilege of civil authority …." Professor Browne asks, "Can there be any stronger proof than the Inauguration Day of Washington's continued relevance?" Stephen Howard Browne, *The First Inauguration (George Washington and the Invention of the Republic)* (College Park, PA, Pennsylvania State University Press, 2020).

15. *But see* Stephen Howard Browne, *The Ides of War: George Washington and the Newburgh Crisis* (Columbia, SC, University of South Carolina Press, 2016).

16. Knox, of course, had become a universally admired hero early on, when "in a feat of unimaginable daring and difficulty," he and his men dragged 58 cannons, on sleds, over the snowy Berkshire mountains in western Massachusetts, enabling the fortification of Dorchester Heights and success for the siege of Boston. *See, e.g.*, David McCullough, *John Adams*, 73.

17. Edwin A. Hoey, "A New and Strange Order of Men," *American Heritage*, Vol. 19, Issue 5 (August 1968).

18. "A New and Strange Order," 1.

19. *See generally* Gary Forsythe, *A Critical History of Rome: From Prehistory to the First Punic War* (Berkeley, CA, University of California Press, 2006). Many have asserted that George Washington's example, as the planter from Mount Vernon in Virginia who left his farm to command the

revolutionary forces, inspired the founders' choice of Cincinnatus in naming their society.

20. Walter Isaacson, *Benjamin Franklin: An American Life*, 422 (New York, Simon & Schuster, 2003)

21. *The First American*, 688.

22. Benjamin Franklin, quoted in *The First American*, 688. To illustrate the connection's tenuousness as generation after generation succeeded to membership, Ben Franklin applied mathematical analysis. "A man's son, for instance, is but half of his family, the other half belong to the family of his wife. His son, too, marrying into another family, [the ancestor's] share of the grandson is but a fourth. And so on," onto the ninth or tenth generation. The ancestor's contribution to the remote descendant's genetic material is a 256th after eight generations and a 512th after nine generations. With the tenth generation, the fraction's numerator is one, the denominator is over one thousand.

23. Chernow, *Washington: A Life*, 497.

24. Henry Knox, quoted in *Washington: A Life*, 498.

25. *Washington: A Life*, 498.

26. Later, Washington said of his acceptance of a three-year term as the Society's initial president, that it was "much against my inclination." George Washington to Theodore Bland, November 18, 1786, recorded in W.W. Abbot & Dorothy Twohig, *The Papers of George Washington: Confederation Series*, Vol. 6, 478 (Charlottesville, VA, University of Virginia Press, 1992–1997).

27. *Washington: A Life*, 499.

28. *Washington: A Life*, 527.

29. The French engineer Pierre-Charles L'Enfant designed a metal for the Society featuring a bald eagle and hanging from a pale blue and white ribbon. When officers first gave Washington the insignia, he put it in a drawer. Later Washington retrieved it. "[Artist John] Ramage depicted a notably dour Washington in a uniform adorned by the badge of the Society of the Cincinnati." In two Washington portraits, artist Edward Savage "portrayed him in uniform with the badge of the Society of the Cincinnati pinned to his left lapel." See *Washington: A Life*, 614.

30. David McCullough, *John Adams*, 375.

31. *John Adams*, 375–376.

32. Thomas Jefferson to George Washington, quoted by Merrill D. Peterson, *Thomas Jefferson & the New Nation: A Biography*, 286 (New York, Oxford University Press, 1970).

33. Ron Chernow, *Washington: A Life*, 497.

34. Author Chernow added, "There was absolutely no evidence whatsoever that Steuben and Knox ever contemplated such an offer." *Washington: A Life*, 498.

35. Articles of Confederation, Article VI, Paragraph 1.

36. *See* Brian Duignan, "What Is the Emoluments Clause?" available https://www.britannica.com (visited November 4, 2020).

37. United States Constitution, Article I, Section 9, Clause 8.

38. Closer to a prohibition applicable to the Society of the Cincinnati was the Commonwealth of Massachusetts Constitution of 1777: "No man… or association of men [shall have] … any title to obtain advantages or particular and exclusive privileges distinct from those of the community." Quoted in McCullough, *John Adams*, 222. The late Mr. McCollough pointed out, "The constitution of the Commonwealth of Massachusetts is the oldest functioning written constitution in the world." *John Adams*, 225.

39. Anderson House programs in 2020 included "Sealed With Blood: Gratitude for Revolutionary Veterans and American National Identity," January 23, 2020 (Sarah Parker, I.F. Parker Professor of History, Grinnell College); "The Soldier's Two Bodies: Military Sacrifice and Popular Sovereignty in the Revolutionary War—Veteran Narratives," February 13, 2020 (James M. Greene, Assistant Professor of English, Indiana State University); "Captives of Liberty: Prisoners of War and the Politics of Vengeance in the American Revolution," February 27, 2020 (T. Cole Jones, Assistant Professor of History, Purdue University); and "1774: The Long Year of the Revolution," March 5, 2020 (Mary Beth Norton, Mary Donlon Alger Professor of History Emerita, Cornell University). *See generally* http:///www.societyofthecincinnati.org/events/public (visited November 2, 2020).

Bibliography

Abbot, W.W. & Dorothy Twohig, *The Papers of George Washington: Confederation Series* (Charlottesville, VA, University of Virginia Press, 1992–1997).

Alder, Ken, *Engineering the Revolution: Arms and Enlightenment in France* (Chicago, IL, University of Chicago Press, 2010).

Alden, John Richard, *General Charles Lee: Traitor or Patriot?* (Baton Rouge, LA, Louisiana State University Press, 1951).

_____, *The South in the Revolution, 1763–1789* (Baton Rouge, LA, University of Louisiana Press, 1957).

Alexander, Clayton B. & W. Keats Sparrow, *The First of Patriots and the Best of Men: Richard Caswell in Public Life* (Kinston, NC, Lenoir County Colonial Commission, 2007).

Ambler, Charles H., *Washington and the West* (republished by Kessinger Publishing, Whitefish, MT, 2010).

Ambrose, Stephen, *Undaunted Courage: Meriwether Lewis, Thomas Jefferson, and the Opening of the American West* (New York, Simon & Schuster, 1997).

Anderson, Fred, *Crucible of War* (New York, Vintage, 2001).

Andrews, Rod, Jr., *The Life and Times of General Andrew Pickens: Revolutionary War Hero, American Founder* (Chapel Hill, NC, University of North Carolina Press, 2017).

Armes, Ethel, *Stratford Hall: The Great House of the Lees* (Garden City, NJ, Doubleday Doran, 1937, republished Literary Licensing, 2012).

Atkinson, Rick, *The British Are Coming* (New York, Henry Holt, 2019).

Babits, Lawrence E., *A Devil of a Whipping: The Battle of Cowpens* (Chapel Hill, NC, University of North Carolina Press, 1998).

Ballagh, James Curtis, *The Letters of Richard Henry Lee* (New York, Macmillan, 1911).

Barnett, Charles E. & Donald Lennon, *Major General Robert Howe and the American Revolution* (Chapel Hill, NC, University of North Carolina Press, 1991).

Barton, L.N., *Men and Events of the Revolution in Winchester and Frederick County* (Winchester, VA, Winchester-Frederick Historical Society, 1975).

Bass Robert, *The Life and Campaigns of General Francis Marion* (Kipara, New Zealand, Papamoa Press, 2017).

Bazin, Christian, *The Maquis de Rouerie "Colonel Armand" in the American War* (Paris, Perrin, 1990).

Bennett, Charles E. & Donald R. Lennon, *Major General Robert Howe and the American Revolution: A Quest for Glory* (Chapel Hill, NC, University of North Carolina Press, 1991).

Billias, George Athan, *George Washington's Generals and Opponents: Their Exploits and Leadership* (New York, Morrow, 1964, republished New York, De Capo, 1994).

Boatner, Mark M., *Encyclopedia of the American Revolution* (Mechanicsburg, PA, Stackpole Books, 1996).

Bodley, Temple, *George Rogers Clark: His Life and Public Services* (Boston, MA, Houghton Mifflin, 1926).

Borick, Carl P., *A Gallant Defense: The Siege of Charleston, 1780* (Columbia, SC, University of South Carolina Press, 1980).

_____, *Relieve Us of this Burden: American Prisoners of War in the Revolutionary South* (Columbia, SC, University of South Carolina Press, 2012).

Bowers, Claude G., *The Young Jefferson, 1743–1789* (Boston, MA, Houghton Mifflin, 1945).

Boyd, Thomas, *Mad Anthony Wayne* (New York, Scribner & Sons, 1929).

Bragg, C. L., *Crescent Moon Over Carolina: William Moultrie & American Liberty* (Columbia, SC, University of South Carolina Press, 2013).

Brands, H.W., *The First American: The Life and Times of Benjamin Franklin* (New York, Doubleday, 2000).

_____, *Our First Civil War: Patriots and Loyalists in the American Revolution* (New York, Doubleday, 2021).

Brecht, Bertolt, *Life of Galileo* (New York, Grove Press, reprint, 1984).

Brinkley, John Luster, *On This Hill: A History of Hampden-Sydney College, 1774–1994* (Hampden-Sydney, VA, Hampden-Sydney College, 1994).

Broadwater, Robert P., *American Generals of the Revolutionary War: A Biographical Dictionary* (Jefferson, NC, McFarland, 2007).

Brown, Lloyd A. & Howard H. Peckham, *The*

Revolutionary War Journals of Henry Dearborn, 1775–1783 (Chicago, IL, 1939, republished by Heritage Books, 2019).

Brown, Jr., Robert W., *Kings Mountain and Cowpens: Our Victory Was Complete* (Charleston, SC, The History Press, 2009).

Browne, Stephen Howard, *The First Inauguration (George Washington and the Invention of the Republic)* (College Park, PA, Pennsylvania State University Press, 2020).

———, *The Ides of War: George Washington and the Newburgh Crisis* (Columbia, SC, University of South Carolina Press, 2016).

Brumwell, Stephen, *Turncoat: Benedict Arnold and the Crisis of American Liberty* (New Haven, CT, Yale University Press, 2018).

Buchanan, John, *The Road to Guilford Courthouse: The American Revolution in the Carolinas* (New York, Wiley & Sons, 1997).

Burnett, Edmund Cody, *The Continental Congress* (New York, W.W. Norton, 1941).

Burrows, Edwin G., *Forgotten Patriots: The Untold Story of American Prisoners During the Revolutionary War* (New York, Basic Books, 2008).

Butterfield, Lyman H., *Diary and Writings of John Adams*, Vol. 2 (Cambridge, MA, Harvard University Press, 1961).

———, *Letters of Benjamin Rush* (Princeton, NJ, Princeton University Press, 1951).

Callahan, North, *Daniel Morgan: Ranger of the Revolution* (Arms PR, Inc., 1961).

Campbell, Craig, *General Francis Marion: Irregular Life of an Irregular Warrior* (Seattle, WA, Create Space, 2016).

Cashin, Edwin & Heard Robertson, *Augusta and the American Revolution: Events in the Georgia Back Country, 1773–1783* (Darien, GA, Ashantilly Press, 1975).

Catton, Bruce, *Stillness at Appomattox* (Garden City, NY, Doubleday, 1962).

Cecere, Michael, *General William Woodford of Virginia: Revolutionary War Patriot* (Berwyn Heights, MD, Heritage Books, 2019).

———, *A Good and Valuable Officer: Daniel Morgan in the Revolutionary War* (Berwyn Heights, MD, Heritage Books, 2019).

———, *Second to No Man but the Commander in Chief: Hugh Mercer, American Patriot* (Berwyn Heights, MD, Heritage Books, 2019).

Charlton, Thomas Usher Pulaski, *The Life of Major General James Jackson* (Augusta, GA, 1809, republished London, Forgotten Books, 2018).

Cheney, Lynne, *The Virginia Dynasty: Four Presidents and the Creation of the American Nation* (New York, Viking, 2020).

Chernow, Ron, *Alexander Hamilton* (London, UK, Penguin, 2008).

———, *Grant* (New York, Penguin, 2020).

———, *Washington: A Life* (New York, Penguin, 2010).

Cleland, Hugh, *George Washington in the Ohio Valley* (Pittsburgh, PA, University of Pittsburgh Press, 1955).

Clemens, William Montgomery, *Button Gwinnett, Man of Mystery: Member of the Continental Congress: Signer of the Declaration of Independence* (Andesite Press, 2015).

Coe, Alexis, *You Never Forget Your First: A Biography of George Washington* (New York, Viking, 2020).

Cohen, Stan, *Historic Springs of Virginia* (Charleston, WV, 1981).

Cole, Ryan, *Light-Horse Harry Lee: The Rise and Fall of a Revolutionary Hero* (Washington, DC, Regnery History, 2019).

Coleman, Kenneth, *The American Revolution in Georgia, 1763–1789* (Athens, GA, University of Georgia Press, 1958).

Collins, Lewis, *Historical Sketches of Kentucky* (Cincinnati, OH, 1847, republished in two volumes, Andesite Press, 2017–2018).

Commager, Henry Steele & Richard B. Morris, *The Spirit of Seventy-Six* (New York, Harper & Row, 1958).

Conte, Robert S., *The History of the Greenbrier: America's Resort* (White Sulphur Springs, WV, Greenbrier Publishing, 10th ed., 2016).

Coulter, E. Merton, *Georgia: A Short History* (Chapel Hill, NC, University of North Carolina Press, 1960).

Couture, Richard T., *Powhatan: A Bicentennial History* (Richmond, VA, Virginia Book Company, 1980).

Custis, George Washington Parke, *Recollections and Private Memoirs of George Washington* (New York, 1860).

Dann, John C., *The Revolution Remembered: Eyewitness Accounts of the War for Independence* (Chicago, IL, University of Chicago Press, 1980).

Darter, Oscar H., *Colonial Fredericksburg and Neighborhood in Perspective* (New York, Twayne Publishing, 1957).

Davidson, Chambers G., *Piedmont Partisan: The Life and Times of General William Lee Davidson* (Davidson, NC, 1951).

DeMond, Robert O., *The Loyalists of North Carolina during the Revolution* (Durham, NC, Duke University Press, 1940, republished Greenville, SC, Southern Historical Press, 2019).

Dickson, Paul, *The Rise of the G.I. Army, 1940–41* (New York, Atlantic Monthly, 2020).

Draper, L.C., *Kings Mountain and Its Heroes* (Cincinnati, OH, 1881).

Drewien, D. J., *Button Gwinnett: A Historiography of the Georgia Signer of the Declaration of Independence* (Pittsburgh, PA, Dorrance Publishing, 2007).

Drury, Bob & Tom Clavin, *Valley Forge* (New York, Simon & Schuster, 2018).

DuVal, Michael, *George Rogers Clark: Conqueror of the Old Northwest* (1969).

Dwyer, William, *The Day Is Ours: An Inside View of the Battles of Trenton and Princeton, November 1776–January 1777* (New Brunswick, NJ, Rutgers University Press, 1998).

Ellis, Joseph, *Founding Brothers: The Revolutionary Generation* (New York, Vintage, 2002).

Evans, Emory G., *Thomas Nelson and the Revolution in Virginia* (Williamsburg, VA, Virginia Bicentennial Commission, 1978).

Evans, Willis F., *History of Berkeley County* (Martinsburg, WV, 1928).

Ferreiro, Larrie D., *Brothers at Arms* (New York, Knopf, 2016).

Ferrer, Ada, *An American History—Cuba* (New York, Scribner & Sons, 2021).

Fields, Joseph Edward, *The Known Signatures of Button Gwinnett* (Commission Publishing, 1950).

Fischer, David Hackett, *Washington's Crossing* (New York, Columbia University Press, 2004).

Fisher, James, "A Forgotten Hero Remembered, Revered, and Revised: The Legacy and Ordeal of George Rogers Clark," *Indiana Magazine of History*, June 1996, 109–132.

Fithian, Philip Vickers, *The Journal and Letters of Philip Vickers Fithian, a Plantation Tutor in the Old Dominion* (Williamsburg, VA, Colonial Williamsburg Press, 1957).

Fitzpatrick, John C., Ed., Vols. 9 & 26, *Writings of George Washington* (Washington, DC, Government Printing Office, 1927).

Fleming, Thomas J., *Cowpens: "Downright Fighting"—The Story of Cowpens* (Washington, DC, National Park Service, 1989).

Flexner, James, *George Washington in the American Revolution, 1775–1783* (Boston, MA, Little Brown, 1968).

Ford, Washington Chauncey, *Journals of the Continental Congress*, Vol. 10 (Washington, DC, 1937).

Forsythe, Gary, *A Critical History of Rome: From Prehistory to the First Punic War* (Berkeley, CA, University of California Press, 2006).

Freeman, Douglas Southall, *George Washington*, Vol. 4 (New York, Scribner & Sons, 1952).

Fried, Stephen, *Rush: Revolution, Madness, and the Visionary Doctor Who Became a Founding Father* (New York, Crown Books, 2018).

Gallagher, John J., *The Battle of Brooklyn 1776* (Edison, NJ, Castle Books, 2002).

Gavin, James M., *On the Road to Berlin: Battles of an Airborne Commander, 1943–1946* (New York, Viking, 1978).

Gizzard, Frank E., Jr., ed., *The Papers of George Washington*, Vol. 8 (Charlottesville, VA, University of Virginia Press, 1998).

Goolrick, John, *Historic Fredericksburg* (1922).

_____, *The Life of General Hugh Mercer* (New York, Neale Brothers, 1906).

Gottaschalk, Louis, *Lafayette Joins the American Army* (Chicago, IL, 1937).

Graham, James, *The Life of General Daniel Morgan, with Portions of His Correspondence, Etc.* (New York, Derby & Jackson, 1856).

Graham, William A., *General Joseph Graham and His Papers on North Carolina Revolutionary History* (Raleigh, NC, North Carolina Department of Archives and History, 1904).

Greif-Glory, Judy, *Faith and Fancy: Outdoor Sculpture in Indiana* (Indianapolis, IN, Indiana Historical Society Press, 2005).

Groom, Winston, *The Patriots: Alexander Hamilton, Thomas Jefferson, John Adams, and the Making of America* (Washington, DC, National Geographic, 2020).

Grove, Max W., *Reconstructed Census of Berkeley County, Virginia* (Colesville, MD, 1970).

Gugin, Linda C. & James E. St. Clair, *The People Who Shaped the Hoosier State* (Indianapolis, IN, Indiana Historical Society Press, 2015).

Hamerick, Charles L., *A Bag of Nails: The Ledger of George Weedon's Tavern in Fredericksburg, Virginia* (Athens, GA, New Papyrus, 2007).

Hamilton, Robert, *Daniel Morgan: Forgotten Hero* (Seattle, WA, Create Space Publishing, 2015).

Hampton, Bob, & George Schember, *Walking in the Footsteps of General Daniel Morgan* (Seattle, WA, Create Space, Amazon Publishing, 2016).

Hannah-Jones, Nikole, Caitlin Roper, Ilene Silverman, & Jack Silverstein, editors, *The 1619 Project: A New Origin Story* (New York, Random House, 2021).

Harley, Gail E., *Jack Jouett's Ride* (New York, Viking, 1973).

Hartley, Cecil P., *Heroes of the South; The Life of Francis Marion* (Seattle, WA, Create Space, 2012).

Hawes, Lilla M., *Papers of Lachlan McIntosh* (Savannah, GA, Georgia Historical Society, 1957).

Henderson, Archibald, *Conquest of the Old Southwest* (New York, Century Co., 1920).

Henriques, Peter R., *First and Always: A New Portrait of George Washington* (Charlottesville, VA, University of Virginia Press, 2020).

Henry, Robert, *Narrative of the Battle at Cowan's Ford* (Greensboro, NC, 1891).

Higginbotham, Don, *Daniel Morgan: Revolutionary Rifleman* (Chapel Hill, NC, University of North Carolina Press, 1979).

_____, ed., *The Papers of John Iredell* (Raleigh, NC, North Carolina Division of Archives, 1976).

Hilton, Woody, *"Forced Founders": Indians, Debtors, Slaves, and the Making of the American Revolution in Virginia* (Chapel Hill, NC, University of North Carolina Press, 1999).

Hocker, Edward W., *The Fighting Parson of the American Revolution: A Biography of General Peter Muhlenberg* (Mechanicsburg, PA, Sunbury Press, 1936).

Hofstra, Warren R., *The Planting of New Virginia: Settlement and Landscape in the Shenandoah Valley* (Baltimore, MD, Johns Hopkins University Press, 2004).

Hollinshead, William, *A Discourse Commemorative of the Late Major-Gen. William Moultrie* (Charleston, SC, Peter Freeman, 1805).

Holton, Woody, *Liberty Is Sweet: The Hidden History of the Revolution* (New York, Simon & Schuster, 2021).

Horry, General P. & Parson M. L. Weems, *The Life*

of General Francis Marion: A Celebrated Partisan Officer, in the Revolutionary War, Against British and Tories in South Carolina (Quantico, VA, Marine Corps Staff College, 2021).

Hoth, David, Ed., *The Letters of George Washington Revolutionary War Series*, Vol. 8 (Charlottesville, VA, University of Virginia Press, 2006).

Hughes, Rupert, *Washington: The Savior of the States, 1771-1781* Vol. 3, (New York, 1930).

Isaacson, Walter, *Benjamin Franklin: An American Life* (New York, Simon & Schuster, 2003).

Jackson, Harvey H., *Lachlan McIntosh and the Politics of Revolutionary Georgia* (Athens, GA, University of Georgia Press, 1979).

Jakes, John, *Charleston* (New York, Dutton, 2002).

James, Alfred P., *Writings of General John Forbes* (Menasha, WI, 1938).

James, James Alton, *The Life of George Rogers Clark* (Chicago, IL, University of Chicago Press, 1928).

James, William, *Swamp Fox: General Francis Marion and His Guerilla Fighters in the American Revolutionary War* (Whitefish, MT, Kessinger Publishers, 2010).

Jenkins, Charles F., *Button Gwinnett, Signer of the Declaration of Independence* (New York, Doubleday, Page & Co., 1926).

Johnson, Daniel McDonald, *This Cursed War: Lachlan McIntosh in the American Revolution* (Allendale, SC, Self-published, 2018).

Kapp, Friedrich, *The Life of Frederick von Steuben, Major General of the Revolutionary Army* (republished, Seattle, WA, Create Space, 2015).

Karels, Carol, *A Disobedient Servant: The Revolutionary War and the Times that Tried Men's Souls* (Cheltenham, UK, The History Press, 2007).

Kars, Majoleine, *Breaking Loose Together* (Chapel Hill, NC, University of North Carolina Press, 2002).

Keese, Perry, *The Story of General Richard Montgomery: The Tale of the Invasion of Canada* (London, UK, Forgotten Books, 2016).

Kegley, Frederick B., *Kegley's Virginia Frontier: The Beginnings of the Southwest, 1740–1783* (1938, reprinted by Heritage Publishing, Jacksonville, FL, 2012).

Kennedy, Benjamin, Ed., *Muskets, Cannon Balls & Bombs: Nine Narratives of the Siege of Savannah in 1779* (Savannah, GA, Beehive Press, 1974).

Ketchum, Richard, *Saratoga: Turning Point of America's Revolutionary War* (New York, Henry Holt, 1997).

Langguth, A. J., *Patriots: The Men Who Saved the American Revolution* (New York, Simon & Schuster, 1988).

Lawrence, Alexander A., *Storm Over Savannah: The Story of Count d'Estaing and the Siege of the Town in 1779* (Athens, GA, University of Georgia Press, 1951).

Lee, Henry, *The Revolutionary War Memoirs of General Henry Lee* (New York, Da Capo Press, 1979).

Lee, Nell Moore, *Patriot Above Profit: A Portrait of Thomas Nelson, Jr.* (Nashville, TN, Rutledge Hill Press, 1989).

Lefkowitz, Arthur, *Benedict Arnold's Army: The 1775 American Invasion of Canada During the Revolutionary War* (El Dorado Hills, CA, Savas Beatie, 2008).

LeMoine, James M., *The Assault of Brigadier-General Richard Montgomery and Colonel Benedict Arnold on Quebec in 1775: A Red Letter Day for Canada* (Trans Royal Society, 1899).

Lender, Mark Edward, *Cabal: The Plot Against George Washington* (Yardley, PA, Westholme Publishing, 2019).

———, & Garry Wheeler Stone, *Fatal Sunday: George Washington, the Monmouth Campaign, and the Politics of Battle* (Norman, OK, University of Oklahoma Press, 2016).

Lengel, Edward, *General George Washington: A Military Life* (New York, Random House, 2005).

Lingley, Charles R., *The Transition in Virginia from Colony to Commonwealth* (New York, 1910).

Lint, Gregg, Ed., *The Papers of John Adams* (Cambridge, MA, Belknap Press, 1996).

Longacre, Edward G., *Pickett Leader of the Charge: A Biography of General George Pickett, C.S.A.* (Shippensburg, PA, White Mane, 1998).

Lossing, Benson J., *Pictorial Field Book of the Revolution* (1860).

Loudermilk, W. H., *A History of Cumberland, Maryland* (Washington, DC, 1878).

Lumpkin, Henry, *From Savannah to Yorktown* (New York, Paragon House Publishers, 1981).

Luzader, John, *Saratoga: A Military History of the Decisive Campaign of the American Revolution* (Philadelphia, PA, Casemate, 2008).

Madison, James H., *Hoosiers: A New History of Indiana* (Bloomington & Indianapolis, IN, Indiana University Press, 2015).

———, and Lee Ann Sandweiss, *Hoosiers and the American Story* (Indianapolis, IN, Indiana Historical Society Press, 2014).

Magic, Denny, *Button Gwinnett: The Making of a Statesman* (San Francisco, CA, Independent, 2018).

Mahan, Alfred Thayer, *The Influence of Sea Power Upon History: 1660–1783* (Boston, MA, Little Brown & Co., 1890).

Malone, Dumas, *Jefferson: The Virginian*, Vol. 1 (Boston, MA. Little Brown & Co., 1948).

Mantel, Hillary, *Wolf Hall* (New York, Picador, 2009).

Marambaud, Pierre, *Byrd of Westover* (Charlottesville ,VA, University of Virginia Press, 1971).

Martin, James K., *Benedict Arnold, Revolutionary Hero: An American Warrior Reconsidered* (New York, New York University Press, 1997).

Massie, Allen, *The Royal Stuarts: A History of the Family that Shaped Britain* (New York, St. Martin's Griffin, 2013).

Mazzagetti, Dominick, *Charles Lee: Self Before Country* (New Brunswick, NJ, Rutgers University Press, 2013).

McBurney, Christian, *George Washington's Nemesis: The Outrageous Treason and Unfair Court-Martial of Charles Lee During the Revolutionary War* (El Dorado Hills, CA, Savas Beatie, 2020).

McCullough, David, *John Adams* (New York, Simon & Schuster, 2001).

———, *The Pioneers: The Heroic Struggle of the Settlers Who Brought the American Ideal West* (New York, Simon & Schuster, 2018).

McGrady, Edward, *The History of South Carolina, 1775-1780* (New York, Russell & Russell, 1901, reprinted 1969).

McGuffey, William Holmes, *McGuffey's Fifth Eclectic Reader* (Cincinnati, OH, Van Antwerp & Bragg, rev. ed., 1979).

McGuire, Thomas J., *The Surprise of Germantown* (Philadelphia, PA. Cliveden Press, 1994).

McIlvaine, Paul, *The Dead Town of Sunbury* (self-published, 1971).

McIlwaine, H. R., *Legislative Journals of the Convention of Virginia*, Vol. 3 (Richmond, VA, 1918-19).

Meade, Robert Douthat, *Patrick Henry*, Vol. 2 (Philadelphia, PA, J.B. Lippincott Co., 1969).

Mekeel, Arthur H., *The Relation of the Quakers to the American Revolution* (Washington, DC, University Press of America, 1979).

Middlekauff, Robert, *The Glorious Cause: The American Revolution, 1763-1789* (New York, Oxford University Press, 2005).

Mintz, Max, *The Generals of Saratoga: John Burgoyne and Horatio Gates* (New Haven, CT, Yale University Press, 1990).

———, *The Seeds of Empire: The American Revolutionary Conquest of the Iroquois* (New York, New York University Press, 2001).

Mobley, Joe A., *North Carolina's Governor Richard Caswell: Founding Father and Revolutionary Hero* (Charleston, SC, The History Press, 2016).

Montross, Lynn, *Rag, Tag, and Bobtail: The Story of the Continental Army, 1775-1783* (New York, Harper, 1952).

Moore, George Henry, *Mr. Lee's Plan—March 29, 1777: The Treason of Charles Lee, Major General, Second in Command in the American Army of the Revolution* (Port Washington, NY, Kennikat Press, 1860).

Moore, Howard Parker, *A Life of General John Stark of New Hampshire* (New York, 1949, republished Isha Books, 2013).

Morgan, Daniel, Nathanael Greene, et al., *The Battle of Cowpens: Primary and Secondary Accounts* (Regiment Press, 2019).

Morgan, Robert, *Boone: A Biography* (Charlotte, MD, Recoded Books, 2008).

Morrill, Daniel R., *Southern Campaign of the American Revolution* (Baltimore, MD, Nautical & Aviation Publishers, 1993).

Morris, Edmund, *The Rise of Theodore Roosevelt* (New York, Random House Trade, reprint, 2001).

Morton, Louis, *Robert Carter of Nomini Hall: A Virginia Tobacco Planter of the Eighteenth Century* (Charlottesville, VA, University of Virginia Press, 1969).

Moultrie, William, *Memoirs of the American Revolution*, Vols. 1 & 2 (1802, reprinted New York, Arno Press, 1968).

Muhlenberg, Henry Augustus, *The Life of Major-General Peter Muhlenberg, of the Revolutionary Army* (1818, re-published, Philadelphia, PA, Carey & Hart, 1849).

Nash, Hugh Owen, Jr., *Patriot Sons, Patriot Brothers* (Nashville, TN, Westview Publishing, 2006).

Neilson, Charles, *An Original, Compiled, and Corrected Account of Burgoyne's Campaign* (Port Washington, NY, Kennikat Press, 1970).

Nelson, Paul David, *Lord Stirling: Washington's Noble General* (Tuscaloosa, AL, University of Alabama Press, 2003).

Nickerson, Hoffman, *Turning Point of the Revolution, or Burgoyne in America* (republished Whitefish, MT, Kessinger Publishing, 2010).

Nolan, Cathal J., *The Allure of Battle* (New York, Oxford University Press, 2017).

O'Donnell, Patrick, *Washington's Immortal: The Story of an Elite Regiment Who Changed the Course of the Revolutionary War* (New York, Atlantic Monthly Press, 2016).

Oller, John, *The Swamp Fox: How Frances Marion Saved the American Revolution* (New York, DeCapo, 2016, reprinted Hachette Books, 2020).

Palmer, Frederick, *Clark of the Ohio: A Life of George Rogers Clark* (Kessinger Publishing, 2008).

Palmer, John McAuley, *General Von Steuben* (New Haven, CT, Yale University Press, 1937).

Pancake, John S., *This Destructive War* (Tuscaloosa, AL, University of Alabama Press, 1985).

Pappas, Phillip, *Renegade Revolutionary: The Life of General Charles Lee* (New York, New York University Press, 2014).

Parkman, Francis, *Montcalm and Wolfe* (1884, republished 2019, Wentworth Press).

Patterson, Samuel White, *Knight Errant of Liberty: The Triumph and Tragedy of General Charles Lee* (New York, Lantern Press, 1958).

Peterson, Merrill D., *Thomas Jefferson & the New Nation: A Biography* (New York, Oxford University Press, 1970).

Phillips, R.W. Dick, *Arthur St. Clair: The Invisible Patriot* (Bloomington, IN, iUniverse, 2014).

Piecuch, Jim, *The Battle of Camden* (Charleston, SC, The History Press, 2006).

Plank, Geoffrey, *Rebellion and Savagery: The Jacobite Rising and the British Empire* (Philadelphia, PA, University of Pennsylvania Press, 2005).

Polhemus, Richard V. & John F. Polhemus, *Stark: The Life and Wars of John Stark—French and Indian War Ranger, Revolutionary War General* (Delmar, NY, Black Dome Publishing, 2014).

Powell, William S., *North Carolina Through Four Centuries* (Chapel Hill, NC, University of North Carolina Press, 1989).

Preston, David L., *Braddock's Defeat: The Battle of

Monongahela and the Road to Revolution (New York, Oxford University Press, 2015).

Rankin, Hugh F., *The Moore's Creek Bridge Campaign, 1776* (Currie, NC, Eastern National, 1980, reprint edition 1998).

———, *The North Carolina Continentals* (Chapel Hill, NC, University of North Carolina Press, republished 2005).

———, *North Carolina in the American Revolution* (Raleigh, NC, Office of Archives and History, 1959).

Reid, Stuart, *Culloden Moor 1746: The Death of the Jacobite Cause* (Oxford, UK, Osprey Publishing, 2002).

———, *Like Hungry Wolves: Culloden Moor 16 April 1746* (London, UK, Windrow & Greene, 2000).

Reynolds, William R., *Andrew Pickens: South Carolina Patriot in the Revolutionary War* (Jefferson, NC, McFarland, 2012).

Rhodehamel, John, *George Washington: Writings* (New York, Library of America, 1997).

Roberts, Kenneth, *March to Quebec* (New York, 1940).

Robinson, Jr., James L., *General A.P. Hill: The Story of a Confederate Warrior* (New York, Random House, 1987).

Robinson, William P., *The Revolutionary Sketches of William R. Davie* (Chapel Hill, NC, University of North Carolina Press, 1976).

Rose, Ben Z., *John Stark: Maverick General* (Waverley, MA, TreeLine Press, 2007).

Ross, Malcom, *Cape Fear* (New York, Holt, Rinehart & Winston, 1965).

Rossie, Jonathan G., *The Politics of Command in the American Revolution* (Syracuse, NY, Syracuse University Press, 1975).

Rossman, Kenneth R., *Thomas Mifflin and the Politics of the American Revolution* (Chapel Hill, NC, University of North Carolina Press, 1952).

Rupp, Israel D., *Early History of Western Pennsylvania* (republished, HardPress Publishing, 2019).

Rush, Benjamin, *A Memorial Containing Travels Through Life of Sundry Incidents in the Life of Dr. Benjamin Rush* (Philadelphia, PA, Louis Biddle, 1905).

Ryan, Dennis P., *A Salute to Courage: The American Revolution as Seen Through the Wartime Writings of Officers of the Continental Army and Navy* (New York, Columbia University Press, 1979).

Sager, Christine, *Come to the Cowpens* (Spartanburg, SC, Hub City Press, 2002).

Sanderson, John, *Signers of the Declaration of Independence*, Vol. 7 (Philadelphia, PA, W. Brown & C. Peters, Publishers, 1928).

Schenck, David, *Being A History of the Invasion of the Carolinas by the British Army Under Lord Cornwallis in 1780–81* (republished Alpha Editions, 2015).

Schiff, Stacy, *The Revolutionary: Samuel Adams* (Boston, MA, Little Brown & Co, 2022).

Schiller, Robert J., *Irrational Exuberance* (Princeton, NJ, Princeton University Press, 3rd ed., 2016).

Schneider, Steve, "The View from Here: The Story of the George Rogers Clark Statue in Quincy, Illinois," *Journal of the Illinois State Historical Society*, Winter 2007–08, 360–382.

Searcy, Martha Condray, *The Georgia-Florida Contest in the American Revolution, 1776–1778* (Tuscaloosa, AL, University of Alabama Press, 1985).

Sharp, Colin G., *Button Gwinnett: Failed Merchant, Plantation Owner, Mountebank, Opportunistic Politician and Founding Father* (Shrewsbury, UK, YouCaxton, 2015).

Shelton, Hal T., *General Richard Montgomery and the American Revolution* (New York, New York University Press, 1994).

Simms, William Gilmore, *The Life of Frances Marion: The Swamp Fox* (New York, Suzette Enterprises, 2019).

Smith, George, *The Man Who Saved the World from Smallpox: Doctor Edward Jenner* (London, IUniverse, 2004).

Smith, Justin Harvey, *Arnold's March from Cambridge to Quebec* (New York, 1903, reprinted Surry Hills, NSW, AU, Wentworth Press, 2018).

Snow, Dean, *1777: Tipping Point at Saratoga* (New York, Oxford University Press, 2016).

Sparks, Jared, *Lives of Charles Lee and Joseph Reed* (Boston, MA, C.C. Little & J. Brown, 1846).

———, *The Writings of George Washington*, Vol. IV (Boston, MA, 1840).

Spero, Patrick, *Frontier Rebels: The Fight for Independence in the American West, 1765–1776* (New York, Norton, 2018).

Sprecht, Johann Friedrich, *A Military Journal of the Saratoga Campaign* (Mary C. Lynn, ed., Westport, CT, Greenwood Press, 1995).

Stanley, E., & Robert W. Woody, Robert, *Christopher Gadsden and the American Revolution* (Knoxville, TN, University of Tennessee Press, 1982).

Stewart, Catesby Willis, *The Life of Brigadier General William Woodford of the American Revolution*, Vols. 1 & 2 (Richmond, VA, Witten & Shepperson, 1973).

Stryker, William S., *The Battle of Monmouth* (Princeton, NJ, University of Princeton Press, 1927).

———, *The Battles of Trenton and Princeton* (1898, republished by Old Barracks Association, Trenton, NJ, 2001).

Stephenson, Michael, *Patriot Battle: How the War of Independence Was Fought* (New York, HarperCollins, 2007).

Sugde, John, *Tecumseh: A Life* (New York, Henry Holt, 1997).

Swager, Christine R., *Heroes of Kettle Creek, 1779–1782* (West Conshohocken, PA, Infinity Publishing, 2008).

Swiggett, Howard, *The Great Man* (New York, 1953).

Swisher, James Kenneth, *Daniel Morgan: An Inexplicable Hero* (Virginia Beach, VA, Koehler Books, 2019).

———, *The Revolutionary War in the South Backcountry* (Pelican Publishing, 2008).

Syrett, Harold G., *The Papers of Alexander Hamilton* (New York, Columbia University Press, 1961).

Taaffe, Stephen R., *Washington's Revolutionary Generals* (Norman, OK, University of Oklahoma Press, 2019).

Tarleton, Banastre, *A History of the Campaigns of 1780-1781in the Southern Provinces of North America* (Manchester, NH, Ayer Co., 1999, reprinting 1787 edition).

Tarter, Brent, *The Grandees of Virginia: The Origin and Persistence of Undemocratic Politics in Virginia* (Charlottesville, VA, University of Virginia Press, 2013).

Thacher, James, *Eyewitness to the American Revolution: The Battles and Generals as Seen by an Army Surgeon* (republished Longmeadow Press, 1994).

———, *A Military Journal During the American Revolutionary War* (Plymouth, MA, 1823).

Thayer, Theodore, *The Making of a Scapegoat: Washington and Lee at Monmouth* (Port Washington, NY, Kennikat Press, 1976).

Thwaites, Reuben G., and Louise P. Kellogg, eds., *A Documentary History of Dunmore's War* (Madison, WI, University of Wisconsin Press, 1905).

Titus, James, *The Old Dominion at War: Society, Politics, and Warfare in Late Colonial Virginia* (Columbia, SC, University of South Carolina Press, 1991).

Tuchman, Barbara, *A Distant Mirror: The Calamitous Fourteenth Century* (New York, Ballantine Books, 1978).

Unger, Harlow Giles, *Benjamin Rush: The Founding Father Who Healed a Wounded Nation* (New York, Da Capo, 2018).

U.S. Army General Staff College, *American Revolution: The Battle of Cowpens* (Seattle, WA, Create Space, 2016).

Van Doren, Mark, Ed., *The Travels of William Bartram* (Scotts Valley, CA, Amazon CreateSpace, 2016).

Van Vlack, Milton C., *Silas Deane: Revolutionary War Diplomat and Politician* (Jefferson, NC, McFarland, 2013).

Wallace, Willard, *Traitorous Hero: The Life and Fortunes of Benedict Arnold* (New York, Harper, 1954).

Ward, Christopher, *War of Revolution* (New York, Konecky & Konecky, 1950).

Ward, Harry W., *Charles Scott and the Spirit of '76* (Charlottesville, VA, University of Virginia Press, 1988).

———, *Duty, Honor or Country: General George Weedon and the American Revolution* (Philadelphia, PA, American Philosophical Society, 1979).

———, *Major General Adam Stephen and the Cause of American Liberty* (Charlottesville, VA, University of Virginia Press, 1989).

Waterman, Joseph W., *With Sword and Lancet: The Life of General Hugh Mercer* (Richmond, VA, Garrett & Massie, 1941).

Watson, Robert P., *The Ghost Ship of Brooklyn: An Untold Story of the American Revolution* (New York, Da Capo, 2017).

Weeks, Steven Beauregard, *Church and State in North Carolina* (Baltimore, MD, 1893, republished Wentworth Press, NSW Australia, 2019).

Whittemore, Charles P., *A General of the Revolution: John Sullivan of New Hampshire* (New York, Columbia University Press, 1961).

Wilkinson, Colonel James, *Memoirs of My Own Times* (Self-published, 1816).

Wilkinson, Lauren, *American Spy* (New York, Random House, 2019).

Willbanks, James H., *Machine Guns: Their History* (Santa Barbara, CA, ABC-CLIO, 2004).

Williams, Glenn F., *Dunmore's War: The Last Conflict of America's Colonial Era* (Yardley, PA, Westholme Publishing, 2017).

Wilson, David K., *The Southern Strategy: Britain's Conquest of South Carolina and Georgia, 1775-1780* (Columbia, SC, University of South Carolina Press, 2005).

Wirt, William, *Sketches of the Life and Character of Patrick Henry* (Philadelphia, PA, 1817).

Woodman, Henry, *The History of Valley Forge* (Philadelphia, PA, Oaks, 1922).

Zabin, Serena, *The Boston Massacre: A Family History* (New York, Houghton Mifflin Harcourt, 2020).

Zahniser, Marvin R., *Charles Cotesworth Pinckney: Founding Father* (Chapel Hill, NC, University of North Carolina Press, 1967).

Zambone, Albert Louis, *Daniel Morgan: A Revolutionary Life* (Yardley, PA, Westholme Publishing, 2018

Index

Numbers in ***bold italics*** indicate pages with illustrations

abolitionism 11
Adam Stephen (Ward) 140
Adams, John 83, 93, 156, 161–162, 214, 234n44; Society of Cincinnati and 218–220
Adams, Samuel 3
alcohol, intoxication and 60, 209, 236n5, 237n1, 238n28, 238n33, 238n44, 239n49; drunkenness and 1, 19, 85–88, 139, 142, 162; of Morgan, D. 85, 176–177, 187; of Scott 85–87, 124; taxation on 211
Altamaha River 37–38, 43
An American History—Cuba (Ferrer) 11
The American Revolution in the Southern Colonies (Russell) 33, 68, 72
Andrew, Rod 67, 156
Anecdotes of the American Revolution (Garden) 66
Anglican Church 1, 29, 119, 136–137, 190–191, 246n26
Arbuthnot, Mariot 72, 132
Armand Tuffin, Charles 251n19
Armstrong, John 116, 123, ***141***
Arnold, Benedict 21, 74, 88, 131, 144, 164, 179–181, 247n65
Arthur Kill 128–129, 139
Articles of Confederation (1781) 221
Arundel, Dohickey 102
Ashe, John 2, ***4***, 31, 209, 229n21, 258ch27n1
Assunpink Creen 122, 127–128
Atkinson, Rich 58, 63
Augusta, Georgia 47–48, 71, 209
Augustine, John 104

Babits, Lawrence 174
backcountry (piedmont), backcountry settlers and 1–3, 24, 27, ***34***, 67, 151, 192–193, 196–197, 199

Bag of Nails (Goolrick) 6
Balfour, Nisbet 74
Barbour, James 90–91, 239n20
Barboursville, Virginia 239n20
Battle of Agincourt (1215) 237n35
Battle of Alamance 191
Battle of Assunpink Creek 127–128
Battle of Bemis Heights 183–185
Battle of Bennington 84, 90, 159, 182–183
Battle of Blackstock's Farm 215
Battle of Brandywine 17–18, 87, 106, 129–130, 140–142, ***141***, 152, 226n30, 250n39
Battle of Brier's Creek 209
Battle of Bunker Hill 90, 211, 250n39
Battle of Camden (1780) 189, 213–214, 255n28, 258ch28n3; Gates at 33–36, 81, 237n5, 250n42
Battle of Charles Town 63, ***64***, 65, 66
Battle of Cowpens 94–95, 171–174, 176, 195, 252n19
Battle of Culloden 29, 255n21
Battle of Drake's Farm 128
Battle of Eutaw Springs 214–215, 256n16
Battle of Fallen Timbers 124–125, 244n9
Battle of Fort Moultrie 66
Battle of Freeman's Farm 19, 92, 94, 183–185, 253n54
Battle of Germantown 17, 19, 140–142, 147, ***153***, 212–213, 250n39
Battle of Great Bridge 30, 90–91, 99–102, ***101***, 126
Battle of Guilford Courthouse 22, 198–202, 214, 258ch27n3
Battle of Gwynn's Island 56, 58, ***101***, 102, 138, 144, 159, 233n7

Battle of Harlem Heights 16
Battle of Kings Mountain 168–171, 175
Battle of Lexington and Concord 31, 52–53, 178, 195, 240n1
Battle of Long Island (Battle of Brooklyn) 14–15, 18, 87, 250n39
Battle of Monmouth Courthouse 108, 130–131, 143, 157–158, 186, 250n39
Battle of Monongahela 56
Battle of Moore's Creek 26–27, 28, 30–31, 62, 150, 229n16, 248nn20–23
Battle of Oriskany 182
Battle of Point Pleasant 52–53, 55–56, 159, 240n1, 253n20
Battle of Princeton 80, 86, 111, 122–123, 128, 250n39
Battle of Ramsour's Mill 213
Battle of the Rice Boats 41–42
Battle of Trenton 16
Battle of White Plains 15
Battle of Yorktown 95, 255n44, 256n16
Battles of Saratoga 82, 83, 94–95, 183–185; *see also* Saratoga
Battles of Trenton 127, 162, 250n39
bayonets 82, 111, 122–123, 139, 200–201
Beale, Robert 127
Bedford, Pennsylvania 14, 57, 210
Belgium 238n27
Bell, Daniel 125–126
Bennett, Charles 70
black death 58
Black River 30, 150
Blue Ridge River 134–135
Boone, Daniel 257n18
Borick, Carl 48, 73–74
Boston, Massachusetts 6–7, 10, 12, 20, 178–179

269

Boston Massacre (1770) 98, 149
Boston Tea Party (1773) 6, 98, 149
Botetour (Baron) 98
Bouquet, Henry 14, 57
Bowman, Herman 124
Braddock, Edward 80–81, 177, 190; Braddock expedition 13, 56–57, 115–117, 215, 252*n*14
Bragg, C.L. 66, 72
Brands, H.L. 3, 6, 40, 124, 164
Branson, Lionel 239*n*20
Breyard, Mary 190
brigadier generals, southern *see specific topics*
Brigadier William Lee Davidson (Davidson, C.) 193
Bristol (HMS) 138
The British Are Coming (Atkinson) 58, 63
British army 24–25, 223*nn*11–12, 240*n*59, 247*n*51, 253*n*55, 255*n*40, 256*n*47; alcohol consumption by 85; attempts to take Charles Town 69–71; mode of warfare 81–82; Native American alliances with 46, 204–206; Philadelphiia abandoned by 107, 130, 143, 185; Savannah occupied by 71–72, 109–110; Southern Strategy 107, 168; surrender at Yorktown 61, 95, 217; *see also* prisoners of war; *specific battles*
British East Florida 37–39, 41–43, 68–69, 129–139, 151, 204, 213
Brodhead, Daniel 46, 231*n*48, 231*n*55
Brown, Thomas 37
Browne, Stephen 258*n*14
Brunswick, New Jersey 17, 127–128
Buchanan, John 34–35, 94, 176, 200–201
Buck's Minutemen 239*n*20
Bulloch, Archibald 38–38, 42
Burgoyne, John 19, 93, 159 182–185, 217, 253*n*54
Burr, Aaron 165
Burton (brig) 74
Byrd, Robert 114, 126

Cadwalader, John 130
Campbell, William 170–171, 194
Canada 59, 107, 118, 158, 179–182, 193, 217
Cape Fear River 30–31, 150
the Caribbean 40, 67, 74, 107
Carlisle Treaty (1753) 238*n*28
Carlton, Guy 158, 180–181

Carlton University 254*n*58
Caroline County Militia 105
Caswell, Richard 34, 36, 62, 214, 228*n*8, 248*n*23; as governor of North Carolina 25, 28, 31–32, 35, 79, 209, 216; North Carolina Militia commanded by 29–33, 150
Catawba River 175, 195, 198–199, 210
Catholicism 114–115, 238*n*25, 240*n*5
Catton, Bruce 135
Cerere, Michael 157
Charles Edward (Prince) 114
Charles Town, South Carolina 1, 21–22, 40, 62, 108, 129–130, 132, 138, 150–151, 242*n*45; Battle of Charles Town 63, **64**, 65, 66; Lincoln, B., at 47, 60, 109–110; Moultrie in **64**, 65, 66–75, 150–151; surrender of 32, 48–49, 72–75, 171, 193, 223*n*11
Cheney, Lynne 3
Chernow, Ron 29, 86, 104, 114, 218–220, 243*n*56, 259*n*34
Cherokee Indians 31–32, 67–68, 190, 192, 213, 215, 235*n*18, 235*nn*15–16; Cherokee Wars 2, 14, 210
Chesapeake Bay **8**, 13, 17, 22, 58, *101*, 139
Christ Church Parish 29, 40–41, 230*nn*12–13
Church of England 85, 135, 137, 190–191, 212, 247*n*51
Cincinnatus, Lucias Quinctius 219
Civil War, U.S. 3, 86, 216, 247*n*70
Clark, George Rogers 84, 204–208, **205**, 209, 252*n*19, 257*n*8
Clark, Jonathan 257*n*12
Clark, William 122
Clay, Henry 207
Clinton, Henry 26, 62–63, **64**, 69, 73, 107–109, 132, 138, 185; in Virginia 143–144
Coe, Alexis 9
Cole, Ryan 81, 189
'Common Sense' (Paine) 10
"Concord Hymn" (Emerson) 232*n*6
Congress, U.S. 227*n*49, 241*n*3, 250*n*42, 255*n*27; *see also* Continental Congresses; promotions, brigadier
Connecticut 163
Connecticut Militia 94–95
Constitution, U.S. 166, 221, 251*n*25
Continental Army (Continental Line) 17, 28, 89–95, 120, 209, 211, 226*n*22, 227*n*42, 250*n*11; Middle Department 79, 121, 143, 185, 192, 202; Southern Department 32–33, 39, 60, 62–63, **64**, 65, 69–74, 108, 138, 150–151, 158; Western Department 45–46; *see also specific battles; specific ranks*
Continental Congresses 2, 14, 19–20, 40, 48, 149, 162–165, 232*n*74, 248*n*18, 258*n*6; Hancock as president of 45, 91; Newburgh Conspiracy and 217–218; Pendleton as president of 105; *see also* seniority
Conway, Thomas 20, 163–164, 250*n*11
Conway Cabal (1777–1778) 33, 60, 231*n*55, 234*n*40, 250*n*9
Cook, Thaddeus 94
Coombs, Joseph 85
Cooper River 66–67, 73, 109–110, 138, 210
Cornstalk (Shawnee warrior) 52–53, 56, 253*n*20
Cornwallis, Charles 16, 18, **64**, 69–70, 93–94, 120, 169–171, 210, 236*n*3, 236*n*29; at the Battle of Assunpink Creek 127–128; at the Battle of Brandywine 106, 129, *141*; at the Battle of Camden 34; at the Battle of Guilford Courthouse 199–201; at the Battle of Princeton 122; Greene opposing 21–23, 195–196, 199–201; Morgan anticipating 174–175; in North Carolina 193–196; Yorktown defeat of 95, 144–145, 217
Coudray, Charles Tronson du 162–163
Craik, James 117–118, 152–153
Cross Creek, North Carolina 26–27, 29–30, 32, 150, 191
Culpepper Militia 103, 201–202, 214
Curry, Abagail 178
Cutler, Manasseh 81

Dan River 256*n*5
Darien, Georgia 40–41
Dartmouth (Lord) 69, 185
Davidson, Chalmers 90, 189, 192–193, 238*n*10, 251*n*16, 254*n*6, 255*n*14, 256*n*63
Davidson, William Lee **4**, 172, 175, 189–197, 198–199, 210, 213
Deane, Silas 164
Dearborn, Henry 184

Index

deaths, casualties and 1, 223*n*1, 242*n*45, 242*n*56, 244*n*7, 245*n*49, 247*n*43, 254*n*59, 258*n*4
Battle of Cowpens 174; Battle of Guilford Courthouse 201; Battle of Gwynn's Island 102; Battle of Point Pleasant 53; Battle of the Rice Boats 41; of Braddock 56; of Clark, G., 207; of Davidson, W., 196; of foreign appointments 164–165; Fort Laurens 46; at Fort Washington 15; by friendly fire 140; in Georgia 38; of Gwinnett 39, 44, 165; Indian raids 8; of Mercer **4**, 17, 123, 211; of Montgomery 181; of Moore 151, 192; of Morgan, D., 188, 211–212; of Nash, F., 4, 32, 152–154, 212–213; Native American 116; of prisoners of war 3, 74, 110–111, 156–157; Regulator movement 26; small pox 58–59, 209; of Sumner 215; Virginia Third Regiment 18; of Weedon 23; of Woodford **4**, 110, 203, 216
Declaration of Independence, U.S. 2, 10, 38, 102
De Kalb, Johann 35, 164–165, **165**
Delaware River 16, 107–108, 120–122, 127, 139, 143
desertions 23, 30, 90, 229*n*20
D'Estaing (Count) 47
Detroit, Michigan 45–46
A Devil of a Whipping (Babits) 174
dissenters 13, 92–93, 190
A Distant Mirror (Tuchman) 84
Dobbs, Arthur 25
drunkenness, drinking and *see* alcohol, intoxication and
duels 39, 44, 165–166, 231*n*34, 251*n*23
Dunmore (Governor) (John Murray) 10, 42, **99**, 126, 137–138, 225*n*33, 240*n*1; at the Battle of Gwynn's Island 56, 58; Gun Powder Affair and 98–102, 119; House of Burgesses dissolved by 57, 98, 147, 225*n*33
Dunmore's Wars 19, 52, 56–58, 98–102, **101**, 138–139, 159, 240*n*1
Dutch Laws (1651) 221

East River 15, 111
education 136, 215
Edward, Matthew 132
Eighth Virginia Regiment 134, 138–140
Elbert, Samuel 41
Emerson, Ralph Waldo 232*n*6
England *see* Great Britain, British rule and
English forces 237*n*12
Episcopalians 67, 99, 135, 137
Ethiopian Brigade, Dunmore's 10, 100
Evans, Emory G. 2, 91

Fauquier, Francis 177–178
Fawkes, Guy 99
Fenwick, John 137
Ferguson, Patrick 168–171, 175, 194
Ferguson, Thomas 69
Fermoy, Matthias de Roche 127, 162
Ferrer, Ada 11
Few, James 26
Fifth Virginia Regiment 127–128
The Fighting Parson (Hocker) 136, 138
Fillmore, Millard 244*n*7
The First American (Brands) 3
Fishkill, New York 217–218
Fitzpatrick, John 217
flogging 177–178, 239*n*49
Florida, British East 37–39, 41–43, 68–69, 138–139, 151, 204, 213
Florida Rangers 37–38
"flying camp," Continental Army 120
footwear, colonial 79–80, 82, 237*n*18
Forbes, John 14, 57, 117
Forbes expedition 13, 117
Forsyth, Robert 128
Fort Barrington 37
Fort Cumberland 14, 126
Fort Dobbs 190
Fort Duquesne 13–14, 56, 80–81, 115–118, 177
Fort Johnson 66–67, 72, 209
Fort Laurens 46
Fort Lee 16, 120
Fort Loudon 105
Fort Loyalhanna 57
Fort McIntosh 38, 46
Fort Moultrie 109, 132
Fort Pitt 14, 45–46, 52, 60, 118
Fort Sullivan 63, **65**, 66, 69
Fort Ticonderoga 60, 182
Fort Washington 15–16, 104, 120
"founding fathers," "founding brothers" and 3, 223*n*18
France, French forces and 47, 57, 116–117, 162–163, 237*n*12, 237*n*35, 240*n*58, 251*n*19; alcohol consumption in 84; Battle of Saratoga and 82, 185; Prince Charles Edward exiled in 114; Society of Cincinnati in 219, 221; at Yorktown 95, 145; *see also* French and Indian War
Franklin, Benjamin 3, 83, 225*n*27, 225*n*30, 238*n*28, 239*n*6, 243*n*13, 246*n*23, 250*n*14, 259*n*22; on Braddock 115; in France 164, 240*n*58; Society of Cincinnati and 218–219
Fraser, Simon 95, 185, 253*n*54
Fredericksburg, Virginia 6–7, **8**, 12–14, 23, 129, 215–216, 225*n*22, 241*n*18; Mercer in 99, 118–119
Freeman, Douglas 105
French and Indian War (1755–1763) 11–12, 13–14, 68, 78–81, 118, 147, 159, 204–205, 214; alcohol abuse during 85; Lewis, A., in the 56; Morgan, D., during 2, 178; Scott during the 125–126; Virginia Militia during 91; Woodford in the 105
French Revolution 251*n*19
friendly fire 140, 152

Gadsden, Christopher 165–166
Garden, Andrew 66
Gates, Horatio 1, 16, 131, 195, 229*n*41, 229*n*44, 229*n*50, 249*n*19, 258*n*7; at the Battle of Camden 33–36, 81, 237*n*5, 250*n*42; Morgan, D., and 158, 171; at Saratoga 19, 32–33, 83, 93–95, 161, 186–187, 249*n*19; as Southern Department Commander 32–33, 158
General Assembly 228*n*2, 228*n*6
The Generals of Saratoga (Mintz) 161
George III (King) 24, 69, 102
George Washington (Chernow) 114
Georgia 1, **4**, 125, **169**, 209–211, 225*n*43, 230*n*4, 235*n*26, 237*n*1; conservatives 40–41, 230*nn*12–13; Council of Safety 37–38, 42–43; McIntosh, L., in 37–38, 39–44, 47–49; Muhlenberg, P., in 138–139, 151; Scott in 131–132; *see also specific cities*
Georgia Assembly 41, 44, 48, 232*n*74
Germain, George 26–27, 69, 107

German immigrants 134–137, 246*n*24
gill (liquid measurement) 83, 86, 236*n*5, 237*n*1
Gist, Mordecai 35
Glasscock, William 48, 232*n*74
Glorious Revolution 114
Gloucester Point 22–23, 86, 94, 202
Glover, John 160
Goolrick, John 66
Gordon, Isabella 118–119
Gosport shipyard, Virginia 21, 24, 132
Graham, James 177
Grant (Chernow) 86
Grant, James 57, 117
Grant, Ulysses 156, 161
Great Britain, British rule and 9–12, 24, 98–100, 225*n*30, 228*n*7, 235*n*10, 235*n*14, 240*n*6, 244*n*1, 246*n*13; *see also* royal governors
Green Dragon (tavern) 7, 10
Greene, Nathanael 15, 17, 108, 120, 132, 226*n*25, 243*n*39, 247*n*58, 256*n*16; at the Battle Brandywine 140, **141, 153**; Cornwallis opposing 21–23, 195–196, 199–201; in North Carolina 171–172, 175, 199–201
Grey, Charles 19
Groom, Winston 3
Gun Powder Affair 98–102, 119
Gwinnett, Button 38, 39–44, 49, 165

Haddrell's Point 48–49, 74, 109–110, 132, 138, 150, 242*n*45, 242*n*49
Hall, Lyman 44
Hamilton, Alexander 91 165
Hamilton, Harry 205–207
Hancock, John 45, 91
Hand, Edward 45, 122, 127
Hannah-Jones, Nikole 9–10
Harger, George 170
Henry, Joseph 180
Henry, Patrick 14, 99, 105, 206, 225*n*33
Herkimer, Nickolas 182
Hessian forces 15–16, 18, 72, 79, 90, 109–110, 122, 182–183
Hillsborough, North Carolina 25–26, 33, 81, 150, 175
Hinchinbrook (British warship) 41–42
Hinrichs (Captain) 109
"hit-and-run" raids 92, 194, 213
HMS (His or Her Majesty's Ship) designation 246
Hocker, Edward 136, 138
Hoey, Edwin 218–219

Hogun, James **4**, 110, 242*n*45, 245*n*49
Hollinshead, William 66
Holton, Woody 10
Hooker, Edward 139
Hooper, William 149
Hoover, Herbert 168
horses, horseback travel and 78–81, 122, 131, 162–163, 176–177, 185, 187, 196
House of Burgesses, Virginia 57, 98, 147, 225*n*33
House of Representatives, U.S. 187–188, 213, 215–216
Howe, Robert 18–19, 27, 69, 128–129, 139, 165–166, 235*n*26, 236*n*28; at the Battle of Brandywine 106, 141; at the Battle of Great Bridge 30; as a major general 1, 43; on McIntosh, L., 45; North Carolina Second commanded by 150; Woodford and 103–104
Howe, William 15, 17, 26, 129, 139, 182, 185
Hubert, Philippe 163
Huger, Isaac 199, 210
Hughston, Earle 85
Huntington, Jedediah 163
Huntington, Samuel 48

Illini Indian Nation 206
Indian raids 8–9, 12, 31–32, 57–58, 207, 225*n*26, 246*n*13, 246*n*23; in Georgia 37, 40; Kittanning raid 116–117; in Pennsylvania 135–136, 190; Western frontier 45–46
Indian Wars (1790s) 124–125
Indiana 204–208
indigo farming 62, 67
The Influence of Sea Power Upon History (Mahan) 120
Irish descended troops 28–29, 54–55, 189–190, 213, 233*n*9
Isaacson, Walter 164, 217

Jackson, Harvey 39–40, 42–43
Jacobean Revolution 26–27
Jacobite Rebellion 114–115
Jamaica 42, 48
James River **8**, 21, 99–100, **101**, 126, 138, 143–145
Jasper, William 65
Jefferson, Thomas 7, 91, 102, 218–221, 224*n*16; as governor of Virginia 2, 20–21, 60–61, 210
Jenner, Edward 233*n*29
Jim Crow laws 11
Johnston, George 127
Julien, Damaris de 68, 168

Kanawha River 52–53, 204, 253*n*20
Kentucky 124, 170, 205–208, 214, 216, 244*n*3, 251*n*7
Kirsch, Adam 10–11
Knox, Henry 218–219, 221, 258*n*16, 259*n*34
Kosciuszko, Tadeus 164

land grants 11–12, 14, 212, 242*n*10
Langdon, John 90
Laurens, Henry 40, 43, 46
Laurens, John 72, 258*n*4
Lauzun (Duc de) 22–23, 94, 228*n*55
Lawrence, Alexander A. 49
Lawson, Robert 200
Learned, Ebenezer 94–95, 160
Lee, Charles 1, 58, 60, 92, 108, 133, 234*n*8, 234*n*12, 234*n*16, 235*n*24, 242*n*34; at the Battle of Monmouth Courthouse 130–131; Moultrie and 63, **64**, 65, 69, 150–151, 235*n*24; as a prisoner of war 16, 142; Southern Department commanded by 62–63, **64**, 65, 69, 138, 150–151
Lee, Light Horse Harry 81, 92, 192, 199–200
Lee, Nell Moore 21
Lee, Richard Henry 110–111, 121
LeFaucheax, Casimir 237*n*27
L'Enfant, Pierre-Charles 259*n*29
Lennon, Donald 70
Leslie, Alexander 21, 143–144, 165
Leslie, Phillip 100–101
Lewis, Andrew **4, 55**, 58, 84, 126, 226*n*5, 233*n*7, 233*n*12, 240*n*1, 253*n*20; at the Battle of Gwynn's Island 102; at the Battle of Point Pleasant 52–53, 54–55, 159; Native Americans and 53, 56–57, 60–61, 210; resignation of 59–60, 159
Lewis, John 55
Liberty Is Sweet (Holton) 10
Liberty Society 43–44
The Life and Times of General Andrew Pickens (Andrews Jr.) 156
Life of General John Stark (Moore, H.) 149
Lillington, Alexander 31, 229*n*21
Lincoln, Abraham 161
Lincoln, Benjamin 17, 22, 32, 39, 47–48, 131–132, 171; Southern Army commanded by 60, 69–74, 108–109

Index

Long Island, New York 14–15, 120, 226n30
Lowell, James 92–93
Loyalhanna Creek 57, 117
Loyalists 9, 27, 69, 100, 168–171, **169**, 191, 226n15, 229n20, 235n14, 235n26; Florida Rangers as 37–38; in Georgia 40, 209; Native Americans and 46; in North Carolina 29–32, 100, 197, 213, 242n10, 255n21, 255n27; Scottish 62, 191
Ludwig, Mary ("Molly Pitcher") 108
Lutheran churches 134–137, 246n11
Lyttelton expedition 67

MacArthur, Douglas 132–133
MacKenzie, Frederick 85
Magdalena (British man-of-war) 99
Magna Carta 10
Mahan, Alfred Thayer 120
Maine 179
major generals 1, 13, 20, 28–29, 43, 75, 129, 145, 163–164; *see also specific generals*
marches 30, 108–109, 143, 237n12, 237n14, 237n18, 237n23, 256n47, 257n23; colonial roads and 78–82, **80**; by Nash 151–152; night 34, 236nn2–3; to Quebec 179–181; Virginia Regiment 14, 138–139, 141
Marion, Francis 2–3, 85, 213; Moultrie and 66, 234n5, 235n15, 235n18
Marquis de Lafayette 22, 86, 91–92, 108, 130, 144–145, 219, 250n14, 251n19
Marshall, John 18, 54, 241n12
Martin, Josiah 26–27, 149–150, 228n2
Maryland **8**, 29, 126
Massachusetts 6–7, 9–12, 20, 37, 98, 149, 159, 178–179, 259n38
Massachusetts Militia 94–95
Mathew, Edward 20–21
Matthews, George 141
Maxwell, William 87, 130, **153**
McClean, Alex 26–27
McClellan, George 161
McClure, Alexander 161
McCullough, David 85
McCullough, Roderick 13
McDonald, Donald 26, 30
McDowell, Charles 170
McGuire, Thomas 152
McIntosh, George 42–44, 47–48

McIntosh, Lachlan **40**, 92, 165, 223n8, 231n40, 231n44, 232n74, 257n2; Brodhead and 231n48, 231n55; in Charles Town 48–49, 71; in Georgia 37–38, 39–44, 47–49; Native Americans and 204; as a prisoner of war **4**, 48–49, 210; Western Department commanded by 45–46; whiskey provided by 83
McIntosh, William 42–43
McLeod, Donald 26
Mercer, Hugh 7, 14, 90–91, 99, 114, **115**, 215, 241n3, 242n6, 242n12, 243n37; at the Battle of Princeton 111, 122–123; death of **4**, 17, 123, 211; during the Kittanning raid 116–117; in Philadelphia 115–116; promotion of 103–104, 119–120, 126, 157; reconnaissance by 16–17, 122; at Trenton 121–122; Washington and 16–17, 117–119, 123, 243n56
Mercury (newspaper) 117
Mexican War 124
Middle Department, Continental Army 79, 121, 143, 185, 192, 202
Middleton, Thomas 210
Mifflin, Thomas 60, 231n55, 234n40, 254n59
militia units 89–95, 170–171; militia generals 1–2, 20, 93, 258ch27n1; *see also specific militias*
Mintz, Max 161
Mobley, Joe 35–36
"Molly Pitcher" (Mary Ludwig) 108
Monroe, James 118, 150, 226n10, 226n18
Monroe Doctrine (1823) 11, 225n47
Montgomery, Richard 179–181
Montreal, Canada 118, 179–180
Montross, Lynn 229n44
Moore, Howard Parker 149
Moore, James 30–31, 151, 192, 223n1, 229n28
Morgan, Daniel 3, 92, **175**, 216, 224n20, 236n10, 252n3, 252n10, 252n14, 252n19, 254n75; at the Battle of Guilford Courthouse 198–199; in Cowpens 171–174, 176, 195, 200–201; death of 188, 211–212; during the French and Indian War 2, 178; intoxication of 85, 176–177, 187; Jefferson and 20; marching to Quebec

179–181; as a prisoner of war **4**, 181–182; at Saratoga 82, 94–95, 158–159, 172, 174, 183–187; Washington and 174, 183, 185–188, 192, 254n75; Whiskey Rebellion and 187–188, 211
Morgan, George 46
Moultrie, William **8**, 216, 223n10, 234n10, 234n16, 235n19, 235n26; in Charles Town **64**, 65, 66–75, 150–151; Lee, C., and 63, **64**, 65, 69, 150–151, 235n24; Marion and 66, 234n5, 235n15, 235n18; Muhlenberg, P., and 138–139; as a prisoner of war **4**, 74–75, 212
Muhlenberg, Henry Melchior 36, 140, 246n11
Muhlenberg, Peter 23, **136**, 245n9, 246n12, 246n19, 246n21, 247n51, 247nn57–58; Church of England and 135, 137; Eighth Virginia Regiment headed by 134, 138–140; in Georgia 138–139, 151; in Germany 136–137; in the House of Representatives 216; major general promotion for 145–146, 212; militias and 90, 93; on seniority 142–143; at Valley Forge 107, 157; in Virginia 134, 143–145; Weedon and 20–21; Woodford and 109
Murphy, Timothy 185
Murray, John *see* Dunmore
muskets 81–82, 94, 106, 180–181, 183–185, 202, 237n26
Muskingum River 46
musters, militia 89, 239n4, 239n7

Nash, Abner 32, 148
Nash, Francis 25, 148–151, **153**, 235n24, 248n8, 248nn2–3, 249n35; death of **4**, 32, 45, 147, 152–154, 212–213
Nashville, Tennessee 154, 213, 248n3
Native Americans 3, 122, 184, 213–214, 231n46, 231n47, 233n38, 238n28, 244n1, 244n15, 257nn18–19; alcohol consumption by 85; backcountry settlers and 24; in the Battle of Fallen Timbers 244n9; in the Battle of Point Pleasant 52–53, 240n1, 253n20; Braddock ambushed by 116; British alliances with 204–206;

Cherokees 235*n*18, 235*nn*15–16; Indian Wars 124–125; Lewis, A., and 53, 56–57, 60–61, 210; Morgan, D., and 177–178; in Northwestern Virginia 134–135; St. Clair and 211; *see also* Indian raids; *specific tribes*
Navy, Royal 22, 100, 120, 138, 144–145, 202
Navy, U.S. 65, 88, 239*n*49
Nelson, Thomas 2, 21, 91, 216, 233*n*8
Neville, John 106
New Bern, North Carolina 24–26, 29–31, 149–150, 190, 229*n*21
New England 6, 9, 37, 85, 182
New Hampshire 11, 90, 92, 159, 182–183, 185, 249*n*28
New Jersey 16, 80, 90, 185, 244*n*26, 246*n*20; *see also specific cities*
New York 6, 87, 143, 202, 237*n*15, 242*n*53, 245*n*9; *see also specific cities*
New York Militia 94–95, 182–184
Newburgh, New York 217
Nickerson, Hoffman 33
night-time travel 34, 236*nn*2–3
North Carolina 1, *4*, 160, **169**, 193–196, 227*nn*1–2, 228*nn*3–4, 237*n*5, 248*n*18, 255*n*17; Battle of Moore's Creek 229*n*16, 248*nn*20–23; Battle of Ramsour's Mill 213; Board of War 214; Caswell as governor of 25, 28, 31–32, 35, 79, 209, 216; Davidson, W., in 192–193; enslaved people in 11; Loyalists in 29–32, 100, 197, 213, 242*n*10, 255*n*21, 255*n*27; Nash in 148–149; Regulator movement 9, 24–27, 30, 147, 191; royal governors of 24–27, *34*, 149; *see also specific cities*
North Carolina Assembly 35, 160
North Carolina Brigade 45, 152, 214
North Carolina Militia 23, 28–35, 150–154, 191–192, 201, 213
North Carolina Through Four Centuries (Powell) 149
Northwest Territory 160, 204–206

O'Donnell, Patrick 79
Ohio River 13, 46, 52–53, 178, 207, 258*n*22
"Ohio Territory," Ohio and 11–12, 124–125, 178, 204

Our First Civil War (Brands) 3, 6, 40

pacifism 8–9, 246*n*23, 254*n*9
Page, John 15
Paine, Thomas 3, 10
palmetto trees 63, 65, 234*n*20
Parliament, British 24, 98–100, 225*n*30, 228*n*7, 246*n*13
The Patriots (Groom) 3
Patriots, patriotism and 1, 27–31, 42–44, 72, 120–122, 156, 170, 191; *see also* Continental Army
Peekskill, New York 108, 217
Pendleton, Edmund 105
Penn, William 115, 225*n*27
Pennsylvania 11, 212, 216, 225*n*27, 237*n*15, 242*n*11, 246*nn*11–13; Indian raids in 135–136, 190; *see also* Philadelphia; Quakers
Pennsylvania Assembly 8–9, 118, 243*n*13, 246*n*13
Pennsylvania Militia 83, 92, 116–118
Perth Amboy, New Jersey 17, 128–129
Philadelphia, Pennsylvania 6, 17–18, 115, 140, 152–153, 220; British abandonment of 107, 130, 143, 185
physicians 29, 59, 115, **115**, 117–119, 152–153, 211
Pickens, Andrew 2, 67–68, 213, 234*n*12, 258*n*2
The Pioneers (McCullough) 85
Pitt, William 48
plantations 13, 48–49, 62, 67, 105, 239*n*48
planters, wealthy coastal 1–2, 25, *40*, 41–42, 48, 103, 105; enslaved labor of 62, 67
Polhemus, John 156
Polhemus, Richard 156
The Politics of Revolutionary Georgia (Jackson) 42–43
Polk, Leonidas 247*n*70
Polk, William 196
Poor, Enoch 90, 94–95, 159, 165, 184, 249*n*78, 251*n*22
Port Royal, South Carolina 70, 72
potato famine, Irish 189
Potomac River *8*, 13–14, 119, 177
Powell, William 36, 149, 175, 198, 200
pre-Revolution 6–12, 14–15
Presbyterians 1, 67, 114–115, 119, 189–190
Prevost, Augustine 47, 71, 235*n*26

primogeniture 125, 219–221, 244*n*10
Princeton, New Jersey 16–17, 127
prisoners of war: captured brigadiers and 1, 57, 181–182, 209, 213; at Haddrell's Point 48–49, 74, 109–110, 132, 242*n*45, 242*n*49; Lee, C., as 16, 142; Lincoln, B., as a 60, 171; McIntosh as a *4*, 48–49, 210; Moultrie as a *4*, 74–75, 212; parole for 3, 49, 74–75, 132, 182, 214, 223*n*12; Scott as a *4*, 131–132; Woodford as a *4*, 103, 109–110, 156–157, 215–216
promotions 193, 226*n*23, 227*nn*42–43, 230*n*5, 233*n*33, 233*n*37, 249*n*4, 251*n*19; to major general 20, 59–60, 75, 145–146, 163–164, 212, 223*n*4, 223*n*10, 241*n*3, 250*n*11; of Mercer 103–104, 119–120, 126, 157; of Morgan, D. 158–159, 171, 176; of Moultrie 65; of Nash 147, 192; of Scott 128; of Stark 159; Washington and 57–58, 90, 104–105, 156, 163, 254*n*75; Weedon and 19–20, 133; Woodford on 105–107, 126, 156–157; *see also* rank and; seniority, *specific brigadiers*
Provost, Mark 71
Pulaski, Casimir 164–165
Putnam, Israel 17, 91

Quakers 123, 134, 190, 227*n*38, 243*n*13, 252*n*15; pacifism of 8–9, 115, 246*n*23, 254*n*9
Quebec, Canada 11–12, 118, 158, 179–181, 188, 205

The Raleigh (tavern) 7, 10
rank and seniority *see* promotions, brigadier
Rankin, Hugh 36, 151, 194, 196, 229*n*28
Rappahannock River 6, 13, 118
Raritan River 128, 246*n*21
Rawdon, Francis 33–34 174
Read, Thomas Buchanan 145–146
Reed, Alexander 54
Reed, James 90, 159
Reed, John F. 152
Reed, Joseph 227*n*43
Regulator Movement 9, 24–27, 30, *34*, 147, 191
Relieve Us of This Burden (Borick) 74
religion 67, 85, 114–115, 134–137,

190–191; *see also specific denominations*
Revolutionary War *see specific topics*
Rhode Island 160
rice farming 40–43, 49, 62, 67
Richmond, Virginia **8**, 22, 54, 147
rifles 81–82, 178–180, 183–186, 194
The Rise and Fall of a Revolutionary Hero (Cole) 189
"The Rising" (Read, Thomas Buchanan) 145–146
Rising Sun (tavern) 10
The Road to Guilford Courthouse (Buchanan) 200–201
roads, colonial 78–82, **80**
Roanoke, Virginia 56, 233n7
Rochambeau, Jean-Baptiste 22 94
Rose, Ben 159
Route 30, U.S. (Lincoln Highway) 78
royal governors 42; of North Carolina 24–27, **34**, 149; of Virginia 52, 98–102, 126
rum 83, 85–87, 236n5, 237n1
Rush, Benjamin 3, 58, 121–123
Russell, David 24, 33, 65, 68, 72, 198, 227n1
Rutherford, Griffith **4**, 32, 191–193, 213, 255n28
Rutherford, Robert 211
Rutledge, John 48, 65, 72

St. Andrew's Parish 40–41
St. Augustine, Florida 43–44, 69
St. Clair, Arthur 16, 29, 60, 158, 177, 182, 186, 211, 233n38
St. John (British warship) 41–42
St. John's Parish 40–41, 43–44
Salem, Virginia 56, 233n13
Saratoga, New York 91, 182–183, 237n34, 240nn58–59, 255n44; Gates at 19, 32–33, 83, 93–95, 161, 186–187, 249n19; Morgan, D., at 82, 94–95, 158–159, 172, 174, 183–187
Saumarez, Thomas 201
Savannah, Georgia 1, 21–22, 44, 47–49, 131; British occupation of 71–72, 109–110
Savannah River 41–42, 47, 69–70, 108–109, 132
Scammell, Alexander 94
Schiller, Robert 17
Schuyler, Philip 161, 179, 182
Scopol, Joseph 235n26
Scott, Charles 100–102, 122, **125**, 125–128, 187, 242n31, 244n9, 244n29, 245n33; at Battle of Brandywine 106; in Charles Town 108–109, 129–130; in Georgia 131–132; intoxication 85–87, 124; in Kentucky 124, 216; as a prisoner of war **4**, 131–132; Washington and 128–133, 157–158, 245n33, 245n38
Scottish descended troops 26–30, 54–55, 110–111, 114–119, 150, 191, 233n9
Second Battle of Trenton 127, 162
Second Continental Line 214, 239n20
Second Virginia Regiment: Virginia Regiment 100, 103–105, 126
Self-Denying Ordinance 228n1
Senate, U.S. 212, 215–216
seniority, rank and 60, 133, 156–161, 227n43, 230n5, 233n33, 249n4, 254n75; Muhlenberg on 142–143; Weedon on 19–20; Woodford on 103–105, 107, 109
Sergeant, Jonathan Dickinson 92–93
Sevier, John 170, 216
Shelby, Isaac 170, 216
Shenandoah River, Shenandoah Valley and 134–135, 137, 145, 171, 190
Simcoe, John 22
slavery, slave trade and 9–11, 13, 58, 100, 102, 138, 225n47; coastal planters and 1, 62
small arms 81–82, 237n27
smallpox 58–59, 162, 209, 233n29
Smallwood, William 28, 35, 209, 214
Smyth, John F.D. 13
Snow, Dean 33, 95
Society of the Cincinnati 23, 95, 215, 258ch28n1, 258n7, 259n38; founding of 212, 217–219; Washington and 217–221, 258n19, 259n26, 259n29
Sons of Liberty 6, 9
South Carolina 1, **4**, 11, 67, **169**, 215–216, 227nn1–2, 228n5–6, 235n19, 240n49; Battle of Camden 213, 237n5, 250n42, 255n28, 258ch27n3; Cowpens 170–174, 195, 198, 200–201, 211, 213, 252n32; ; *see also specific cities*
South Carolina Militia 213
Southern Brigadiers *see specific topics*
southern colonies, the South and 1–3, 6–9, **8**; Loyalists in 69, 168–171; *see also specific colonies*
Southern Department, Continental Army 32–33, 39, 60, 62–63, **64**, 65, 69–74, 108, 138, 150–151, 158
Southern Strategy (Wilson) 23, 31, 71
Spain 37
Spence, Joseph 15
Stamp Act (1765) 11
Stanwix, John 118
Stark, John 84, 86, 159, 227n43, 233n33, 249n27; New Hampshire army led by 90, 92, 182–183, 185, 249n28
Staten Island, New York 14
Stephen, Adam 17, 29, 52, 57, 104, 126, 226n5, 239n44, 239n48, 244n15, 252n14; at the Battle of Brandywine 106, 140–141, **141**, 152, **153**; in the Cherokee Wars 14, 84; court martial for 129–130, 142; inebriation and 19, 84, 86–87, 129, 140–141; as a major general 1, 60; Scott and 129–130, 133
Steuben, Baron Friedrich von 144, 164–165, 218, 221
Stevens, Edward 34, 59, 200–202, 214, 258ch27n3
Stirling (Lord) (William Alexander) 17, 60, 87, **141**, **153**
Stono River 71–72, 210, 214
Stuart, Dugald 201
sugar, sugar trade and 107, 185
Sugde, John 231n46
Sullivan, John 16, 18, 87, 140, **141**, 159, 201
Sumner, Jethro 214–215
Sumter, Thomas 215
Surprise of Germantown (McGuire) 152
surrenders 15–16, 23, 84–85, 132, 185, 209, 243n39, 253n42; of the British at Yorktown 61, 95, 217; of Charles Town 32, 48–49, 72–75, 171, 193, 223n11
surveyors 2–3, 12, 22, 29, 52, 84, 116, 204–206, 238n14; Lewis, A., as a 55; Scott as a 125
Susquehanna River 17, 118
The Swan (tavern) 7
Swisher, James 255n28

Taaffe, Stephen 45, 145, 147, 157, 172
Tarleton, Banastre 22, 73, 109, 172–174, **173**, 210, 215, 240n59

taverns 6–7, 12, 14, 23, 118, 152; *see also specific taverns*
taxation, taxes and 10, 115, 211, 225n27, 246n13, 254n9; estate 125, 244n12; Regulator movement on 24–26
Taylor, Zachary 124, 244n7
teamsters 78, 252n7
Tennessee 154, 170, 213, 248n3, 251n7
Thacher, James 182
Third Virginia Regiment 13–14, 16, 18, 86–87, 103, 119, 226n10
Thomas, John 59
Thomas Nelson and the Revolution in Virginia (Evans) 2
Thompson, Robert 74
Thornton, Mary 105
Timberlake, Henry 215
tobacco 13, 21, 126
Tories, Tory sympathizers and 1, 31–32, 48, 92, 198; Georgia 43; North Carolina 100; South Carolina 67, 194; Virginia 9, 138; *see also* Loyalists
Townes, Thomas 58
Treaty of Charlotte 53
Treaty of Lancaster (Treaty of 1744) 244n1
Treaty of Paris (1763) 37, 204–205, 224n14
Treaty of Paris (1783) 23
Trenton, New Jersey 16, 86–87, 121–122, 127–128
Treulen, John Adam 44
Tryon, William 25–26, **34**, 149, 190
Tuchman, Barbara 84, 123

United States (U.S.) 224n6, 246n12; Civil War 3, 86, 216, 247n70; Constitution 166, 221, 251n25; Declaration of Independence 2, 10, 38, 102; House of Representatives 187–188, 213, 215–216; Navy 65, 88, 239n49; Senate 212, 215–216; western expansion 11–12, 205–206, 231n47; *see also specific colonies; specific states*
Urwin, Gregory 92

Valley Forge 19, 84, 142 185, 189, 192, 214, 250n38, 254n59; intoxication at 85; McIntosh, L., at 45; Weedon at 157; Woodford at 107
Varnum, Andrew 160
Vermont 239n14, 257n10
veterans 74–75, 212, 216, 218–219

Virginia 1, **4**, 7, **8**, 137–138, **169**, 216, 243n29, 246n26; Committee on Safety 100, 137; enslaved people in 10–11; House of Burgesses 57, 98, 147, 225n33; Jefferson as governor of 2, 20–21, 60–61, 210; Nelson as governor of 2; Northwestern 134–135; royal governors of 52, 98–102, 126; Second Continental Line 214, 239n20; Tories 9, 138; The Treaty of Lancaster 244n1; *see also specific cities*
Virginia Assembly 225n33
Virginia Conventions 14, 225n33
The Virginia Dynasty (Cheney) 3
Virginia Gazette 14, 128
Virginia Militia 2, 53, 89–91, 119, 178–179, 214, 258ch27n3
Virginia Regiment 115, 125, 141, 183; Eighth Virginia Regiment 134, 138–140; Fifth Virginia Regiment 127–128; Second Virginia Regiment 100, 103–105, 126; Third Virginia Regiment 13–14, 16, 18, 86–87, 103, 119, 226n10

Wabash River 205–207
Waddell, Hugh 26
Wadsworth, Jeremiah 163
Wagner, Jonathan 94
Wall Street Journal 10
Wallabout Bay 110–111, 215–216
Walton, George 48, 232n74
Ward, Artemas 89
Ward, Harry 57, 87, 106, 140, 207
Warren, Joseph 211
Washington, George 32, 95, 226n22, 231n47, 250n42, 258ch28n2, 258n14; Battle of Brandywine and 141–142; Battle of Long Island and 14–15; at the Battle of Monmouth Courthouse 130–131; Braddock and 13, 115–116; brigadiers under 1–3, 241n1; Conway Cabal and 33, 231n55, 234n40, 250n9; French and Indian War and 214; Lee, C., and 63, 108; Lewis, A., and 56–60; Mercer and 16–17, 117–119, 123, 243n56; Morgan, D., and 174, 183, 185–188, 192, 254n75; Muhlenberg and 142–143, 145; Nash and 151–154; in Newburgh 217–218; in Philadelphia 17–18; on

prisoners of war 110–111; on promotions 57–58, 90, 104–105, 156, 163, 254n75; Scott and 128–133, 157–158, 245n33, 245n38; Society of Cincinnati and 217–221, 258n19, 259n26, 259n29; surrender at Fort Necessity by 84–85; surveying by 29, 84, 238n14; in Trenton 127; at Valley Forge 45; Weedon and 17, 20, 22–23, 91, 157, 245n54; Woodford and 104–106, 242n36
Washington's Immortals (O'Donnell) 79
Washington's Revolutionary War Generals (Taaffe) 45, 145
water, potable 83, 86, 110
Waterman, Joseph 7, 116, 123
Wayne, Anthony 18–19, 111, 130, 142, 152, 186, 211, 244n8, 247n56
weaponry, colonial 81–82, 237nn26–28, 239nn6–7
Weedon, George **23**, 225n22, 225n25, 226n5, 227n38, 228n55, 247n43, 247n55; Battle of Brandywine and **141**; Battle of Harlem Heights and 16; Battle of Long Island and 14–15; Continental Congress and 19–20; Fredericksburg tavern of 6–7, 12, 14; in the French and Indian War 13–14, 118; marches by 79; as mayor of Fredericksburg 215–216; militias and 90–91, 93, 119, 139, 144; resignation of 23, 59, 143, 157, 202; Washington and 17, 20, 22–23, 91, 157, 245n54
Welsh, William 234n40
Welsh immigrants 147
West Virginia 52, 54, 178, 204, 245n4
Western Carolina Militia 193
Western Department, Continental Army 45–46
western expansion 11–12, 205–206, 231n47
"wheel horse" 176–177, 252n7
Whigs 1, 30, 67
Whiskey Rebellion 187–188, 211
Wilkinson, James 92, 184
Williams, Edward G. 49
Williams, Ortho Holland 33
Williamsburg, Virginia 7, **8**, 99–100, 119, 126, 225n33
Wilmington, North Carolina 30, 151, 199, 209
Wilmington Minutemen 229n21
Wilson, David 23, 31, 71

Winchester, Virginia 78, 158, 176, 180, 188, 211–212
Winnsboro, South Carolina 174
Witherspoon, James 152, 248*n*33, 249*n*35
Woedtke, Frederick W. de 162
Wood, Gordon 83
Wood, James 44, 134, 137
Woodbridge, Benjamin 95
Woodford, William 14, 100, 106–108, 126, 132, 227*n*42, 241*n*18, 242*n*34, 242*n*36, 245*n*49; as a prisoner of war *4*, 103, 109–110, 156–157, 215–216; resignation of 20, 101–102, 104–106, 157
Woodstock, Virginia 134–135, 137, 145
World War I 3
World War II 227*n*49
Wright, James 42, 44

Yadkin River 195
yellow fever 110, 211
York River 7, 22–23, 144, 202
Yorktown, Virginia 7, *8*, 21–22, 61, 144–145, 202, 226*n*30
You Never Forget Your First (Coe) 9

Zambone, Andrew 23, 92, 177, 184, 187

www.ingramcontent.com/pod-product-compliance
Ingram Content Group UK Ltd.
Pitfield, Milton Keynes, MK11 3LW, UK
UKHW051850210426
5322IPUK00025B/645